A TERRIBLE BEAUTY

British Artists in the First World War

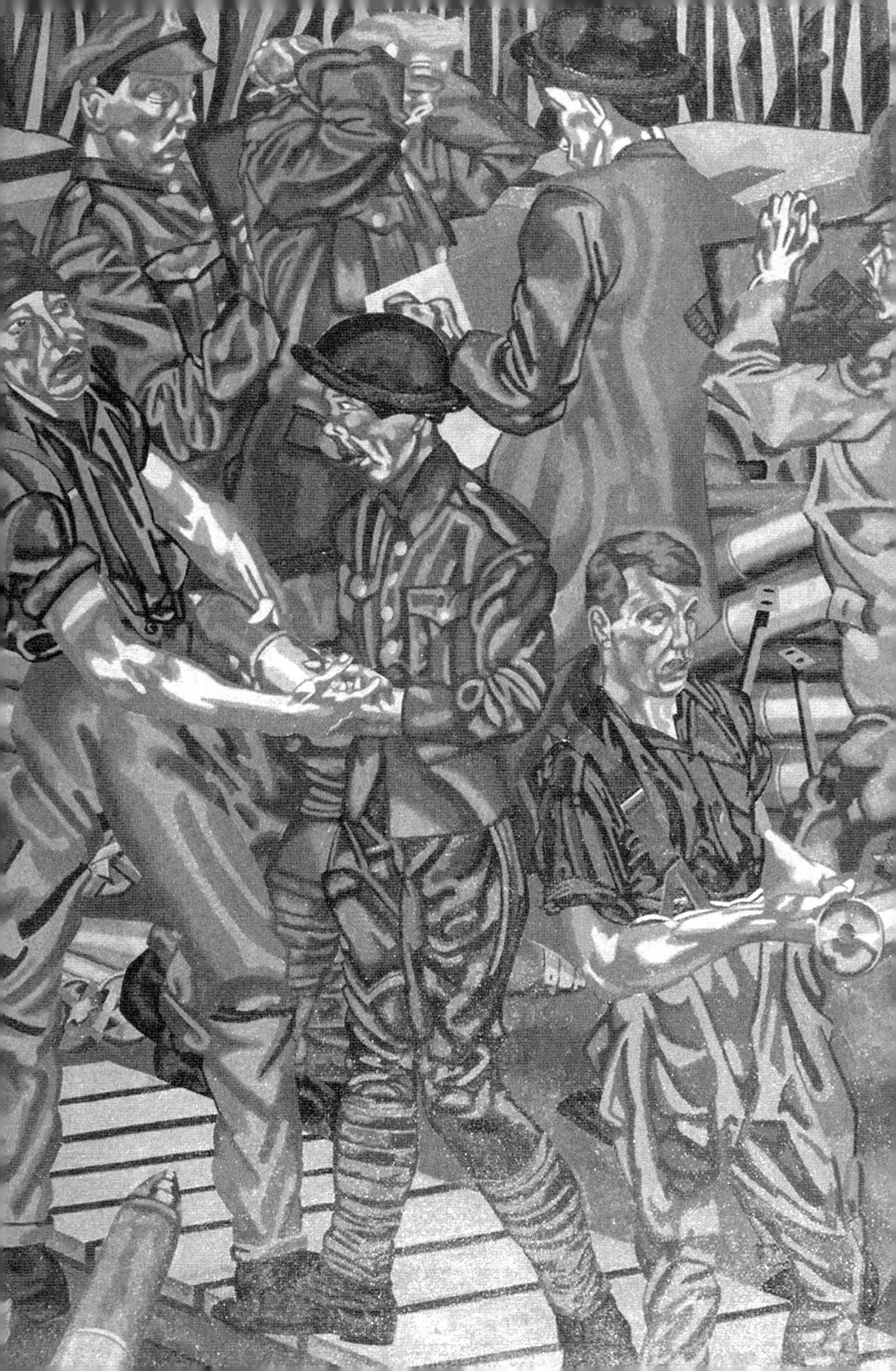

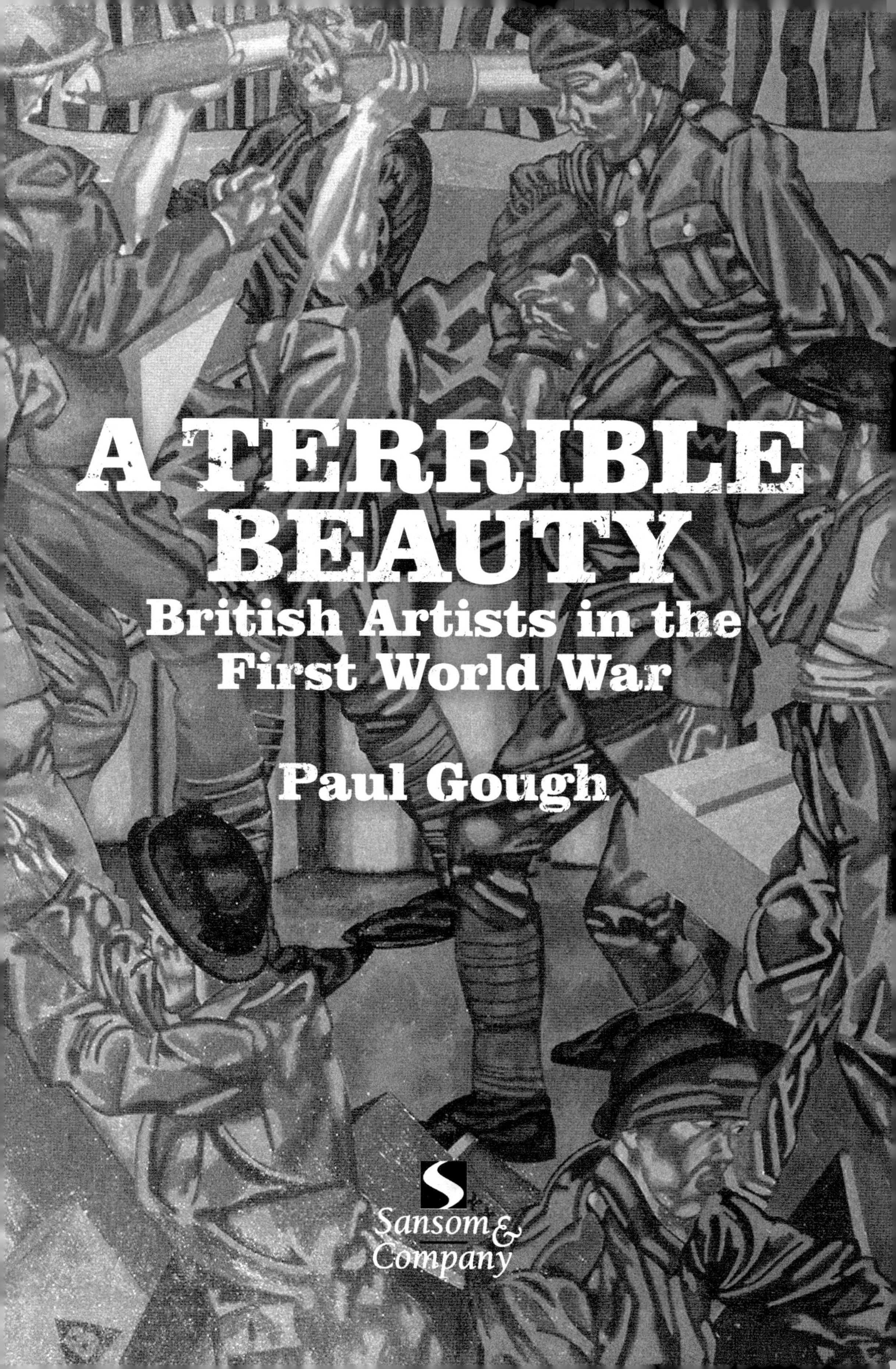

A TERRIBLE BEAUTY

British Artists in the First World War

Paul Gough

Sansom & Company

First published in 2010 by Sansom & Company Ltd.,
81G Pembroke Road, Bristol BS8 3EA
www.sansomandcompany.co.uk
info@sansomandcompany.co.uk

ISBN 978-1-906593-00-1
British Library Cataloguing-in-Publication Data
A catalogue record for this book is available from the British Library

Title page image: William Roberts, *A Shell Dump, France* (1918)

Design and typesetting by E&P Design, Bath
Printed and bound in the Czech Republic via Akcent Media

Contents

Acknowledgements

The origins of this book can be traced to long days spent in the Department of Art at the Imperial War Museum in Kennington, south-east London where, every week for four doctoral years, I pored over the rich collection of drawings, prints and paintings that constitute the most comprehensive survey of early twentieth-century art outside the Tate Collection at Millbank. So basic was the cataloguing system at that time that I supplemented my notes with thumbnail sketches of each piece of work that had once found its source in the trenches of the Western Front, the sandy gullies of the Dardanelles, or the malarial river plains of Salonika. In this pleasurable task I was aided and abetted by Angela Weight and her curatorial team, Michael Moody and Jenny Wood, as well as colleagues in other national collections of art. Parallel research in Canada, northern France, Macedonia and Turkey, and further archival work in the United Kingdom, was made possible with the support of Julian Andrews, Laura Brandon, Nigel Cave, Peter Chasseaud, David Cohen, Paul Cornish, Andrew Daniels, Dominiek Dendooven, Amanda Findlay, Adrian Glew, Jeremy Harvey, Arlene King, the late Kenneth Pople, Nicholas Saunders, Peter T. Scott, Gillian Spencer, Roger Tolson, and many others who gave generously of their time.

During the drafting of the chapters I relied on a stalwart band of critical readers to whom I extend special praise, and even sympathy, amongst them Iain Biggs, Paul Blatchford, Roger Conlon, Helen Fawkes, Verity Gough, David Haste, Verity Lewis, Rachel Miles, and Patricia Passes. As always, I thank my publisher John Sansom and editor Clara Sansom for their constant support and attention to detail.

The title of this book is borrowed from a line in W.B. Yeats's poem *Easter 1916*, and I am indebted to the estate for allowing the use of this fragment, which was also used as a part-title some thirty years ago by Heather Robinson for her astute selection of work from the Canadian war art collection in Ottawa. Although this book was composed as a set of inter-locking and unfolding narratives, each chapter can, if wished, be read as a free-standing appraisal of an artist, or in some cases a cluster of artists working on similar themes. This approach may explain why some facts or ideas are on occasion repeated from chapter to chapter, and why it has been necessary to introduce government agencies such as the 'Department (later Ministry) of Information' a number of times. It may also explain why the anecdote about Richard Nevinson tunelessly beating a bass drum during one of Marinetti's 'happenings' appears at least twice in the book, although actually it's such a nice story that it does bear repetition, unlike the English Futurist's percussion-work.

Finally, as ever, I owe a debt of gratitude to my family – Kathleen, Rachel, Harry and Isobel – who offered enthusiastic interest and encouragement during this demanding but rewarding project.

Paul Gough

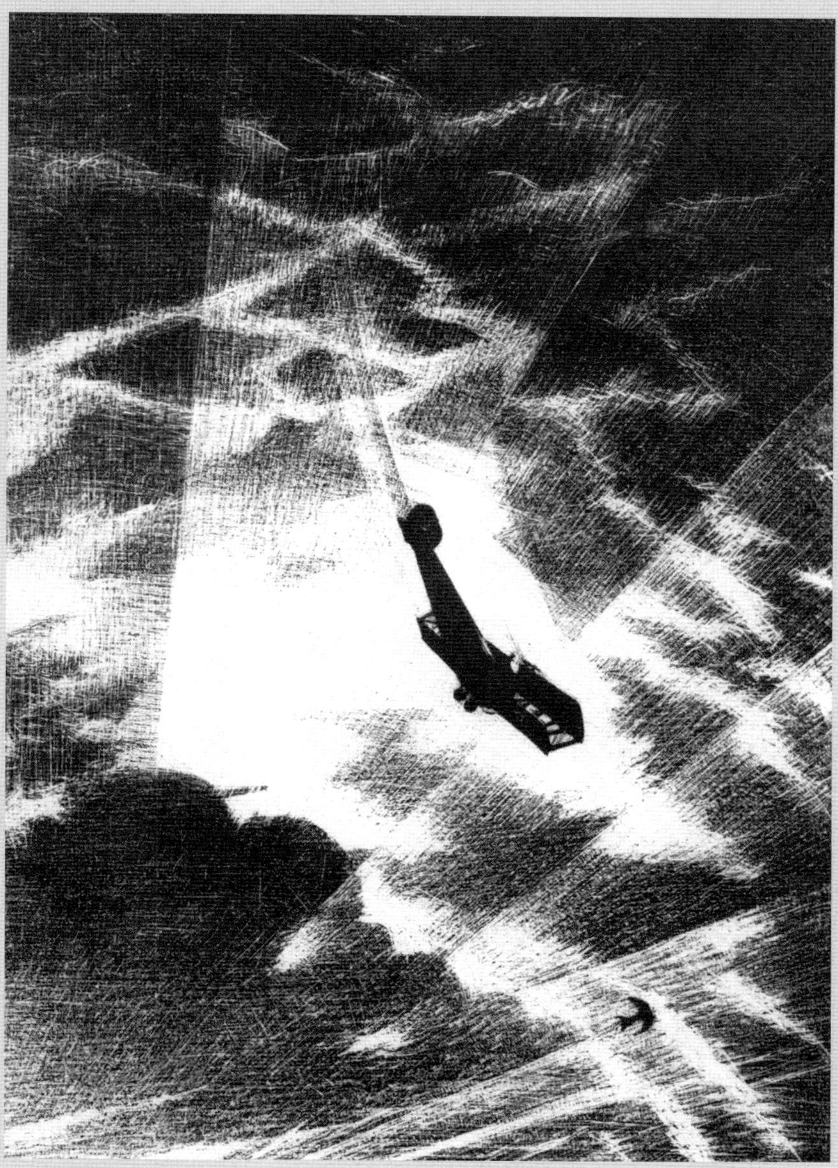

C.R.W. NEVINSON
Swooping Down on a Taube
(1917)
lithograph, 40 x 30.5 cm
IMPERIAL WAR MUSEUM, LONDON

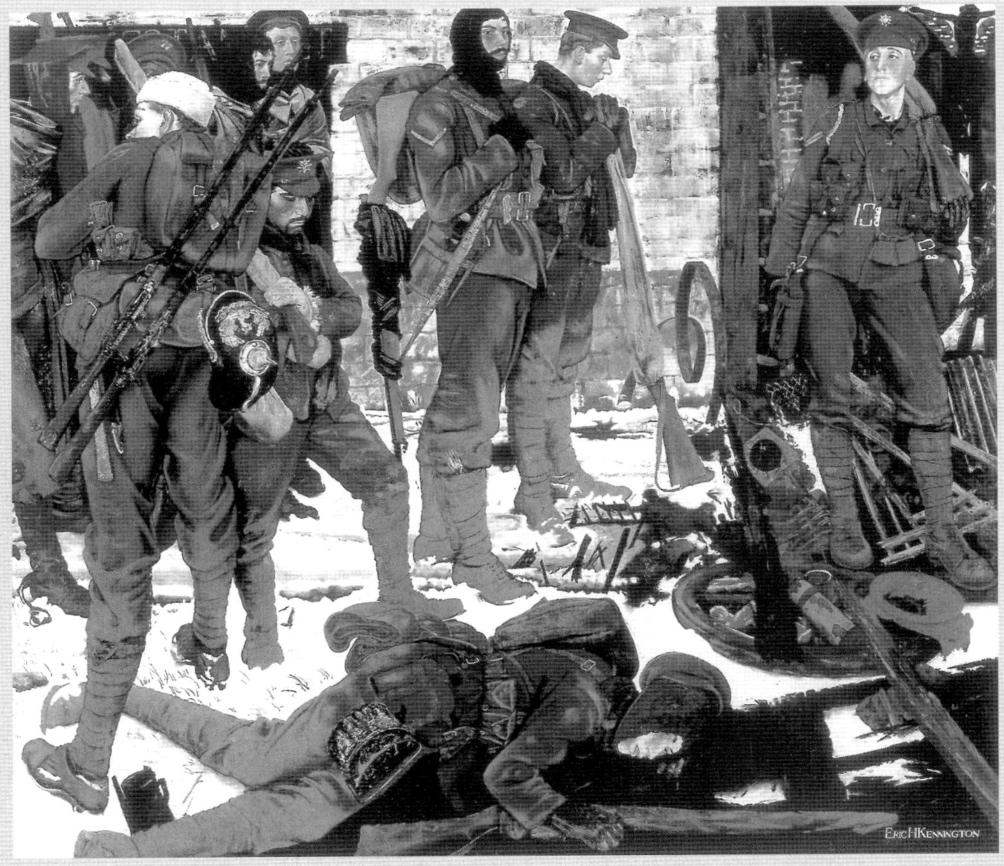

ERIC KENNINGTON
The Kensingtons at Laventie
(1915)
oil on glass, 139.7 x 152.4 cm
IMPERIAL WAR MUSEUM, LONDON

Introduction
A commission in the Army

Like many other professions caught up in the first heady months of the war, painters and sculptors – professional and amateur, famous and obscure – were called upon to enlist in the armed services. Some thirty artists joined the Royal Army Medical Corps (RAMC) *en bloc* following a single recruitment visit to the bar of the Chelsea Arts Club by the commandant of the 3rd London General Hospital.[1] *The Studio* – a popular arts and crafts magazine – ran page-long lists of those who had signed up; many joined the Artists' Rifles, an officer-training unit, which attracted painters, poets, architects, writers, and many others with artistic aspirations – if not the talent.[2] Some chose to ignore the call to arms. Many had little choice: war was bad for business. The art market shrivelled, prices tumbled, artist's materials became scarce. While emerging figures wrestled with their patriotic consciences, established artists were expected to donate items of work to patriotic causes or to offer up blank canvases for auctions organised by the Red Cross and other charities.[3]

However, not everyone in Britain thought the onset of war an unmitigated catastrophe. Many on the right of the political spectrum

1 Cited in Meirion Harries and Susie Harries, *The War Artists*, p.2.
2 See, for example, lists in *The Studio*, December 1914 and August 1915.
3 Artists of repute volunteered blank canvases for worthy patriotic causes such as the Red Cross, which hosted a number of auctions at Christie's. Those who bid the highest sum had the canvases completed to their wishes.

saw it not as the end of the golden period of Victorian and Edwardian eminence, but an opportunity to purge the nation of social maladies – amongst them feminism, industrialization, modernism, and futurism – which they felt had blighted the country in the previous decade.[4] Only war, they argued, had the power to regenerate society and purge it of 'the spectre of national decay'. Fulminating in *The Architect* magazine, W.R. Colton later gave shape to these spectres, insisting that it was 'high time' war set to work with its purifying fire:

> A wave of diseased degeneracy had submerged Philosophy, Music, Literature, and Art to such a depth that, looking forward, I venture to prophesy that future centuries will gaze back with pity upon this period of mistaken morbidness. The futurists, the cubists, the whole school of decadent novelists.[5]

In the years before the war, Futurism and the Modern movement had burst into England in a succession of noisy and bizarre interventions. Its most potent messenger had been the Italian Futurist Fillipo Marinetti, a nihilistic and bombastic artist-cum-demagogue, whose manifestos and loud proclamations galvanized and traumatized in equal measure the emerging *avant-garde* in London. Marinetti and his fellow-Futurists glorified machinery, noise, and destruction, and welcomed the prospect of war as an 'essential hygiene' that would wipe out stale value systems and structures.[6]

Not unreasonably, the protectors of those value systems reviled the posturing Italian and his radical ideas, arguing instead that a 'just' war would release sufficient positive energy to sweep away 'that vague and chaotic groping' of the last few years, heralding a positive rejuvenation of decency and culture, and bringing with it – for good measure – the extinction of cultural 'undesirables'.[7]

---

4 The conditions that prevailed in pre-war England are expertly analysed in Michael J.K. Walsh, *C.R.W. Nevinson: This Cult of Violence* (Yale: Yale University Press, 2002) pp.101–103. Equally thorough is the treatment by Samuel Hynes, *A War Imagined: the First World War and English Culture* (London: Bodley Head, 1990) and Charles Harrison, *English Art and Modernism, 1900–1939* (London and Indiana: Indiana University Press, 1981).

5 W.R. Colton, *The Architect*, 17 March 1916, p.200.

6 A good summary of the 'fanatical Marinetti' is in Denis Farr, *English Art: 1870–1940* (Oxford: Oxford University Press, 1978) p.208. Marinetti's manifesto for English art contained a rounding indictment of 'The pessimistic, skeptical and narrow views of the English public, who stupidly adore the pretty-pretty, the commonplace, the soft, sweet, and mediocre', and scorned, for good measure, Garden Cities and Morris dancers.

Of the vast literature available on the Modernist movement and its reception in Britain during the first decade of the 20th century the following might be considered especially useful: Susan Compton (ed.) *British Art in the 20th Century: the Modern Movement* (London and Munich; Royal Academy of Arts, Prestel-Verlag, 1987); David Peters Corbett, *The Modernity of English Art, 1914–1930* (Manchester: Manchester University Press, 1997); Denis Farr, *English Art: 1870–1940* (Oxford: Oxford University Press, 1978); Charles Harrison, *English Art and Modernism, 1900–1939* (London and Indiana: Indiana University Press, 1981); Lisa Tickner, *Modern Life and Modern Subjects: British Art in the Early Twentieth Century* (New Haven, Yale University Press, 2000).

7 John Ruskin, 'War', in *The Crown of Wild Olive Three Lectures on Work, Traffic, War* (London: Smith Elder, 1866) pp.143–5.

Collins-Baker, Keeper at the National Gallery, epitomized the moral stance of the British establishment by claiming in August 1914, that art would benefit in the long-term from a cleansing conflict 'great enough to engrave the world's mind deeply'[8] and he was sure it would strengthen society, make it less frivolous, and 'more serious and thoughtful in its pursuits'.[9]

Having thus shot down those social and cultural deviants who peddled their trade on the continent, the traditionalists' principal target in England was the small, but noisy, group of radicals that had raised their flag around Percy Wyndham Lewis and the Rebel Art Centre in central London. Demonised by the conservative press, lambasted by the Academy, Lewis and his gang were condemned as the 'bohemian and debauched icons' of the pre-war era.[10] In the *English Review*, one critic warned that unless these home-born *dilettanti* were purged too, 'Future historians will say that the age went dancing to its doom'.[11] Even the normally sympathetic editor of *New Age* hoped that Lewis and his fellow-Vorticists might 'all perish in the war'.[12]

For their part, few of the modernist artists targeted by such vitriol were enthusiastic about the outbreak of the conflict. Jacob Epstein typified their reluctance when he declared, 'Really I am too important to waste my days thinking of matters military,' an imperious view that rebounded badly upon him in the years to come.[13] Paul Nash was equally resistant, volunteering at first for home service only; William Roberts was similarly reticent, and, despite his outward show of martial zeal, Richard Nevinson spent much of his time trying to avoid compulsory active service. Others joined under duress, or because they could not afford otherwise.

More broadly, the moderate intelligentsia regarded the war as offering a very different set of opportunities to those on the right; some believed it could bring together the disparate factions, unifying the many conflicting artistic causes that had surfaced in the frenetic days before the war. Some asked whether it was now actually possible to rediscover a unifying visual and artistic language, to repair – even close – the chasm between art and the public? Could the vicissitudes of war, asked others, reverse the degeneration into abstraction that had mannered the arts in the years leading to 1914? Was artistic

8 C.H. Collins-Baker, 'Art and War', *Saturday Review*, 22 August 1914.

9 C.H. Collins-Baker, paraphrased by Michael J.K. Walsh, *C.R.W. Nevinson*, p.102.

10 A. Clutton-Brock, 'War and Poetry', *Times Literary Supplement*, 8 October 1914.

11 J.D. Symon, 'War and Creative Art', *English Review*, December 1915, p.520.

12 R.H.C. (A.R. Orage), 'Readers and Writers', *New Age*, 10 September 1914, p.449. Orage was focusing his contempt on Ezra Pound, asserting 'Whether he knows it or not, Vorticism is dead. It was, at best, only a big name for a little thing, that in the simmering of the pre-war period suddenly became a bubble, and is now burst. Compared with the war it is incomparably feeble.'

13 Epstein was eventually conscripted a private in the Fusiliers after what he saw as a 'deliberate conspiracy in the press', orchestrated by Augustus John. See Epstein to Quinn, quoted in Michael Holroyd, *Augustus John*, Volume Two, cited in Harries and Harries, *The War Artists*, p.89. The press 'campaign' is documented in Stephen Gardiner, *Epstein: Artist Against the Establishment* (London: Flamingo, 1993) pp.166–168.

unification possible, even desirable? Certainly, there were those, like Laurence Binyon, who argued for a doctrine of cultural and social cohesion. 'What is needed now,' he implored, 'is the fusion of one imaginative effort that shall make art again a single language expressing the whole modern man.'[14] Given the deafening cacophonies of the period, this was very unlikely; art had become 'a barometer of cultural health', it was being discussed in terms of maladies and purges, of hygiene and heroics. Art and war had become, for many of those involved, a tussle between the world of the imagination and the world of action.[15]

Of course, only a relatively small number of artists were involved in the debates generated by the threat to the avant-garde. For many others, their interests were best represented by one of the long-established academies of art that existed in London and in the regions. The students, graduates and staff of these august institutions would soon become the advocates, advisors, and artists of the official war art schemes that would be created as the war entered its second and third years. As we shall see, the government-funded schemes for commissioning official images of wartime were both a lifeline and a liability to artists. Many artists were commissioned; many who thought themselves eminently employable were to be disappointed, others had their skills redeployed into field camouflage, survey-work or cartography; many were simply overlooked or forgotten and found themselves in uniform without the advantage of rank or official status.

ERIC KENNINGTON
Soldier-artist

One of the best examples of an artist who made the difficult transformation from front-line soldier to government-sponsored artist was Eric Kennington.[16] When he was posted overseas with the 1/13th (County of London) Battalion The London Regiment – the 'Kensingtons' – in November 1914 he was no ordinary foot-soldier. At twenty-six he was a highly skilled painter, widely recognised for

14 Laurence Binyon, *The Art of Botticelli: An Essay in Pictorial Criticism* (London: 1913) p.17.

15 'Purging' was not restricted to Britain. The concept is explored by D. Peters Corbett, *The Modernity of English Art, 1914–1930* (Manchester: Manchester University Press, 1997).

16 Eric Kennington was born 12 March 1888 in Chelsea, London, son of the painter T.B. Kennington. He studied at the Lambeth School of Art and the City and Guilds School, in Kennington, south London. He exhibited from 1908 at the Royal Academy and the Leicester Galleries. Having served in France with the 1/13th (County of London) Battalion The London Regiment – the 'Kensingtons' – for some 300 days he was invalided out of the Army June 1915. After the war he visited Arabia to illustrate T.E. Lawrence's *Seven Pillars of Wisdom*. His work as a sculptor includes the war memorial to the 24th Division in Battersea Park 1924, and carvings on the Shakespeare Memorial Theatre, Stratford on Avon, 1930. He served as an Official War Artist in the Second World War, and was elected Associate Royal Academician in 1951, a full member in 1959. Kennington died in Reading on 13 April 1960. Extracted from Mary Chamot, Dennis Farr and Martin Butlin, *Modern British Paintings, Drawings and Sculpture* (London 1964).

his technical virtuosity and exceptional draughtsmanship. A frequent exhibitor at the Royal Academy annual shows, he had studied at Lambeth School of Art and at the City and Guilds School but he found little time for artistic pursuits in his time with the Kensingtons on the Western Front. Lodged in poorly-maintained trenches near the village of Laventie in the Lys Valley, Kennington experienced at first-hand the privations of front-line infantry work, a period brought ignominiously to a close after a shooting accident in which he lost a toe. Laventie was a grim and uncharitable place, evocatively remembered in a regimental memoir drawn up twenty years later:

> When the open warfare of the early autumn stagnated into the holding of trenches, little damage had been done to the villages near the line. As the enemy artillery was brought up, however, systematic shelling started, and the quiet village of Laventie was the first to suffer, situated, as it was, very close to the line. Piteous processions of refugees were to be seen carrying bundles and wheeling trucks containing some cherished possessions to less dangerous areas. The village itself was a sorry spectacle... In the village a street appeared as though a giant hand had swept all the houses on one side into ruins, while the other side was untouched.[17]

Out of this wretchedness, Kennington wrought something quite extraordinary. While convalescing in England he composed and completed perhaps the first great painting of the war – *The Kensingtons at Laventie* – a brutally beautiful composition of a platoon of British soldiers caught in the moment of forming up in a ruined street before setting off to their billets. Emotionally isolated from each other, exhausted, wan and weather-beaten, the platoon is a unit in name only. Few artists had created so uncompromising, yet so stunningly seductive, an image of contemporary war.[18]

In a detailed commentary on the painting,[19] Kennington has left a riveting account of the individual stories of Platoon No. 7. He tells the tale behind the plundered German *pickle-haube* helmet strapped to the webbing of Private McCafferty, the figure with his back to us who is also shouldering two rifles, one his own and the other previously belonging to a 'Private Perry' who had been shot by a sniper alongside McCafferty in the trenches along La Rue Tilleloy. On the right, scanning the rather dishevelled group, stands Corporal Kealey, about to give the command 'Fall in No.7 Platoon'. In the centre, Private 'Tug' Wilson remains alert, his fork and spoon tucked

17 Sergeant O.F. Bailey and Sergeant H.M. Hollier, *The Kensingtons 13th London Regiment* (London & Aylesbury: Regimental Old Comrades' Association, nd, circa 1935).

18 *The Kensingtons at Laventie, Winter 1914*, reverse painting on glass, 139.8 x 152.4 cm. painted 1915, transferred to the Imperial War Museum, 1983, Catalogue: IWM: ART: 15661.

19 Eric Kennington MS 'The Picture'. This document appears to be in the artist's own hand and is presumed to be a description of the painting as it was shown at the Goupil Gallery, London, April–May 1916.

into the top of his puttee, his rifle-sight clad in a blue scarf to keep out the mud and freezing water. To his left, the diminutive figure of Private Guy, widely respected by his fellows as one who 'never groused or slacked', looks down, without judgment, at the prone figure of the under-age Private Todd, 'exhausted' so Kennington tells us, 'by continual service, hard work, lack of sleep, long hours of "standing to" and observing'. Todd was later discharged and returned to civilian employment where, along with others in the platoon, he was tracked down and drawn by Kennington, who underscores the authenticity of the scene by including himself at the back of the group, clad in a waterproof sheet and knitted balaclava hat, nearly lost in the dense tones of the painting's left-hand strip.[20]

Exhibited at the Goupil Gallery in Regent Street, London in April and May 1916, the painting caused a sensation, not least because Kennington chose to paint in reverse on glass, an ancient and demanding technique which gives an extraordinary luminosity to the scene and accentuates the staged theatricality of the grim *tableau*.[21] Reviewers were unanimous in their praise of its technical virtuosity, its iconic colour scheme, and its 'stately presentation of human endurance, of the quiet heroism of the rank and file':

> The picture convinces us that it is real life, but it is not at all like a photograph of an actual scene. Without any sentimentality or forcing of expression Mr Kennington makes visible to us what all these men are feeling. They are ordinary men, very tired and dirty; there is none of the romance of war as it is commonly painted. No-one is enjoying the thought that he is a hero or is making history; and yet all these soldiers are at one in their common sense of duty and determined to endure; and it is this sense, made visible, that imparts beauty to the picture.[22]

Although several influential public figures objected to its harsh realism, Kennington's supporters and patrons (including several army generals) lobbied his case and he was employed (but not until August 1917) as an official war artist.[23] However, despite his cast-iron

---

20 For a full account of this painting see Angela Weight, 'The Kensingtons at Laventie: A Twentieth Century Icon', in *Imperial War Museum Review*, 1 (1986), pp.14–18.

21 The proper term for reverse oil painting in glass is hinterglasmalere. For an elaboration of this exacting technique see Wallace, K. *Examination and treatment of hinterglasmalere or reverse painting on glass* (Ottawa: National Gallery of Art, Canada, 1977). So fragile is Kennington's painting that it is installed permanently into the picture gallery of the Imperial War Museum; to allow touring and temporary exhibitions to take place in the Museum it is not moved, but covered and boxed in for the duration.

22 *The Times*, 20 May 1916.

23 Not all were convinced about Kennington's suitability: both John Buchan and Charles Masterman disliked the grubby realism of his work, and it required sustained pressure from certain committee members – Campbell Dodgson, Thomas Derrick – and the painter Sir John Lavery and etcher Muirhead Bone to have him employed. According to Weight ('The Kensingtons at Laventie', p.16) General Sir John Charteris, Head of Haig's Intelligence Staff, personally arranged for Kennington to return as an 'artist visitor' to the Western Front in December 1916, many months before his officially sponsored visit.

credentials, he did not thrive in this role: his terms of commission were strict, he had no official car, no expenses, no salary; his materials failed to arrive in France and he was constantly harassed by officials who doubted his authority and, once challenged, wearied of his notorious irascibility. To add to his problems, Kennington's preferred subject-matter – the 'fighting man' – upon which his reputation had been built, proved elusive and he was reduced to drawing 'tents and shacks and camp rubbish'. Undeterred, he eventually produced a suite of imposing pastel drawings extolling the magnificence of his revered front-line troops – raiders, bombers, 'A giant Cheshire', 'an 8th Queen's hero'.[24] Unfortunately, his subsequent one-man show in London was spoilt by a long-winded wrangle over the censoring of many titles and a graceless dispute with the war museum over the pricing of his work.[25] So, despite the critical acclaim that heralded the show – the poet Robert Graves commended his unique ability to capture 'the trench point of view' – Kennington felt artistically and financially impoverished by his experience as a war artist. The success of the 'Kensingtons' however, alerted the British authorities to the potential power of visual propaganda, and proved to be one of the tipping points in the official patronage of artists.

COMMISSIONING THE ARTISTS
Propaganda, record, and commemoration

While Kennington was being hurriedly mobilized in August 1914, the onset of war soon dispersed the Modernist group of artists and writers who had collected around Wyndham Lewis. Attacked repeatedly as they were by vitriolic tirades from the right-wing press, war had itself been declared on the *avant-garde*, indeed on the young themselves. Everything that might be regarded as new, innovative and lively was ridiculed as alien and inimical to the patriotic cause. The slightest hint of Futurism, Vorticism, or Imagism, as Samuel Hynes recounts, was derided as 'a sickness, a fraud, or a foolish triviality'.[26] Although the momentum of pre-war Modernism sustained the arts for a short while into 1915, caution prevailed.[27] Ironically, into this hesitant, at times septic, environment was introduced one of the largest and most comprehensive arts patronage schemes ever to be devised in the country. It was a scheme that is now regarded as one

24 *A Giant Cheshire*, charcoal on grey paper, 56 x 51 cm. IWM:ART 2909; *An 8th 'Queen's' hero*, pastel on tinted paper, 56 x 40.6 cm. IWM:ART 1017.

25 As Meirion and Susie Harries note, Kennington's 'bark was often worse than his bite'. He later presented seven of his works free in 1919 and 1920, and a further twenty-one between 1934 and 1938, including his oil painting *Gassed and Wounded*. (Harries and Harries, *The War Artists*, p.289, fn.23).

26 Samuel Hynes, *A War Imagined*, pp.64–65.

27 Issue no.2 of BLAST, for example, came out in June 1915, but carried a black-bordered notice announcing the death of Gaudier-Brzeska.

of the British government's 'few inspired moments' of the entire war, largely because it eventually recognised the cultural value of artistic records in addition to their initial function as propaganda.[28] It had several phases – a propaganda phase, a 'record' (or documentary) period, and a final commemorative chapter, which tried to fashion the vast body of commissioned art into meaningful shape. Few of these phases were pure; they overlapped; they repeated, they are now almost impossible to untangle. Happenchance also played a major part in the choice of artists: rivalry saw some promoted over others; prejudice denied some the opportunity to escape the tedium of active service. Those who were commissioned – and there were a great many – produced some of the most extraordinary pieces of art of the last century. Exactly how it came about is a fascinating, if slightly convoluted, tale.

The true origins of the official British war art scheme can be traced to a decision made by the Foreign Office in late August 1914 to establish a secret agency to manage and disseminate British propaganda. Headed by Liberal politician Charles F.G. Masterman, it was known simply as Wellington House, after its office address in Buckingham Gate, central London. Working in secret, it published and distributed clandestine literature aimed at neutral countries across the globe. In April 1916 a pictorial section was established and an extraordinary variety of visual propaganda was commissioned; these included war films, picture cards, calendars, bookmarks, lantern-slides as well as photographs and line drawings. An all-picture publication, the *War Pictorial,* was produced in five language editions and achieved a world-wide circulation of some 300,000 copies.[29]

It soon became apparent, however, that the limited flow of

---

28 The phrase is from Denis Farr, *English Art: 1870–1940* (Oxford: Oxford University Press, 1978) pp.226–227.

29 Born in Sussex and educated at Christ College, Cambridge, Charles Masterman (1873–1927) was a politician, writer and, from 1914, head of the British government's war propaganda bureau. He was a prolific writer, edited *Granta* at Cambridge, and published widely in the *Daily News*, *Athenaeum* and the *Nation*. His most important book *The Condition of England* (1909) explored the social condition of Britain, especially the lived experiences of the working class.

An active member of the Christian Social Union, Masterman was held by many as a future Prime Minister. His ministerial career began in 1906 with his election to Parliament as a Liberal member for West Ham North; Asquith appointed him Parliamentary Secretary of the Local Government Board in 1908, followed by posts at the Home Office (Under-Secretary of State) from 1909–12, and at the Treasury (Financial Secretary) from 1912–14. In 1914 he joined the Cabinet as Chancellor of the Duchy of Lancaster. A strong advocate of social reform, he was close to David Lloyd George, but fell out of favour having lost two Parliamentary by-elections and incurring the wrath of Lord Northcliffe, the Press Baron, over his support for the unpopular National Health Insurance bill of 1911. His descent from public position was as sudden as his ascent had been spectacular.

His tenure at the war propaganda bureau, known also as Wellington House, was his last major public appointment. Resourceful and imaginative, and supported by a coterie of well-connected advisers, he devised a comprehensive programme of clandestine publishing, issuing some 1,160 pamphlets and books during the course of the war, commissioning the first photographers and the first official war artists to work at the front. However, having been replaced by John Buchan in 1917, Masterman found himself further relegated in 1918 by the appointment of Lord Beaverbrook as Minister of Information. Masterman served both men well, and although he lost his parliamentary seat in 1918 he was re-elected to represent Rusholme, in Manchester in 1923. He died four years later.

photographs from the battlefronts could not meet the voracious needs of the department, nor could the administrative structures of a somewhat shambolic and informal secret service cope with the demands of a global propaganda campaign. By early 1916 the illustrated newspapers were also seeking authentic front-line images and were offering cash incentives to soldiers with suitable sketchbook material.[30] A chance remark made to Masterman that summer alerted him to the unremarkable news that Muirhead Bone, the well-known Scottish etcher, had been called up by the army. Might not his prodigious gift of drawing, it was suggested, be better used in the services of the government than in leading an infantry platoon? Largely ignorant of the visual arts scene Masterman had to ask his wife who Bone was. Within weeks the Scotsman had been contracted as the first Official War Artist.[31] Others contend that it was dinner-party chatter, largely promulgated by society hostess Lady Cunard, which gave birth to the war art scheme. Her motive was not merely in contriving elaborate social schemes for their own sake, but in rescuing young artists from miserable and potentially lethal duty overseas. She and her coterie were also aware that the German and French government had initiated an official scheme to recruit artists to record the war in Europe, and were already deploying dozens of official photographers at a time when the British government were vacillating over whether to send one or two. Other influential figures such as Edward Marsh, private secretary to Winston Churchill, also wielded subtle influence, openly championing younger artists such as the Nash brothers, Mark Gertler, and Stanley Spencer.[32]

At Wellington House, Masterman's intention for Bone's work was simple: he regarded it as a novel adjunct to the programme of pictorial propaganda. Accordingly, two hundred of his drawings were published for sale in ten monthly parts, starting in late 1916. The first was endorsed by an effusive foreword by Douglas Haig, Commanding General of the British Expeditionary Force in France. At a shilling each, they were affordable and each part carried an explanatory essay and helpful captions.[33] Fortuitously, the new photogravure process of large volume printing allowed images of subtle tonal complexity to be accurately reproduced even on the cheap

30 See for example *The Illustrated London News*, 24 April 1915; 4 September 1915; and *The Graphic*, 8 January 1916. The major illustrated newspapers and periodicals of the war period were: *Illustrated London News*, *Nelson's Picture Weekly*, *The War Pictorial*, *Shurey's Illustrated Great War Paper*, and *The War Illustrated*, all of which came into production only weeks after the outbreak of war.

31 Lucy Masterman, *C.F.G. Masterman* (London, 1939), p.287.

32 By comparison, the French government had established a *Section Photographique de L'Armee* by April 1915, employing fifteen photographers with eighty-six assistants and thirty laboratory technicians and mobile laboratories, producing more than 150,000 plates during the course of the war. The Germans mobilized on a similar scale, with seven mobile film units by 1916. Malvern suggests that the recruitment of artists in Britain was, in part, a remedy to the tardy response of the British authorities to create mobile picture and film bureaus. See Sue Malvern, *Modern Art, Britain and the Great War*, pp.48–49.

newsprint that resulted from restricted supplies caused by the naval blockade. Bone's graphic realism was ideally suited to this form of mass reproduction.

Had not two other factors occurred, the programme of employing artists might have ended then. First, came the rapturous reception for Kennington's painting on glass; then just months later, in September 1916, an exhibition in London of 'Paintings and Drawings of War by C.W.R. Nevinson (late Private R.A.M.C.)' aroused an extraordinary burst of critical and popular approval. It is not too great a claim to make that Nevinson's work marked the beginning of a new form of war art.[34] A brilliant reader of the public mood, Nevinson created a pictorial form that borrowed just enough of the Futurist style to flavour his rather academic compositions. His painterly style was equally unthreatening to moderate tastes, being a blend of post-impressionism textures and the grey tonality of the Camden Town Group. By an adept, indeed inspired, juggling act, Nevinson established a balance between literal representation of natural forms and the near-abstract patterns of modernist art that had been prevalent, but widely condemned in the pre-war era.[35]

The second factor was the creation in February 1917 of a new Department of Information, under the directorship of John Buchan.[36] Intended to pull together the many disconnected strands of allied publicity and propaganda, the Department was staffed mainly by civil servants, but drew on an extensive network of the most important and influential figures in the London arts scene, amongst them the novelist Arnold Bennett; gallery owner Robert Ross; Eric MacLagan, later Director of the Victoria and Albert Museum; Campbell Dodgson, Keeper of Prints and Drawings at the British Museum; Alfred Yockney, one-time editor of *Art Journal,* and Muirhead Bone himself, who proved to be an untiring champion of young artists. Individually and collectively they urged Buchan

33 Yockney later confirmed that the Western Front books, which were intended for the widest British audience, had failed in that objective: 'The Bone publications were produced at a popular price, in order that they should filter through to the homes of the workers. This effect has not been secured....' Yockney to Sanderson, 20 February 1918, IWM, M999/1, part VIII, 'The Western Front: drawings by Muirhead Bone', quoted by Malvern, p.38.

An art journalist of considerable experience, Alfred Yockney was originally employed in Wellington House as an assistant in the Eastern and Moslem Propaganda Department. Between 1917 and 1920 he was central to the administration of the British war art schemes, working closely with Masterman, Buchan, Bennett, and those associated with the British War Memorial Committee and the Ministry of Information. Upon the dissolution of the Committee, Yockney was transferred to the Imperial War Museum (effective from 1 January 1919) to carry the memorial scheme to its conclusion.

34 'Paintings and Drawings of War by C.R.W. Nevinson (late Private R.A.M.C.)', The Leicester Galleries, London, September–October 1916. Nevinson exhibited 53 paintings, drawings and etchings and one piece of sculpture.

35 Walsh argues that Nevinson was a crucial bridge between the Modernist movement and the public, bringing a much-needed respectability to Futurism. Frank Rutter supported this view in the *Sunday Times* in 1915: 'If all Futurists gave us such beauty of colour and conveyed movement with such imaginative power as Mr. Nevinson shows us in these aeroplanes rushing through space, we should have no quarrel with them.' (21 March 1915)

and Masterman to employ many of those who had enlisted or been conscripted and were by then scattered across many theatres of war. As high-minded as these individuals may have been, their aim initially was simply to create a record. Painter Thomas Derrick, another adviser, was very clear about the need for a pragmatic approach:

> I am strongly of the opinion that the conscious intention of this project should be extremely prosaic. Simply RECORD. This has been the main intention of art patronage that has produced some of the best pictures in history. The qualities that made them masterpieces were 'thrown in' by the artists. I believe that these qualities when real are always of the nature of a by-product.[37]

Masterman, however, took a more liberal attitude. Certainly, there may have been ulterior motives: after all, sponsoring the widest range of war art did allow the British government to look as if it were nurturing cultural freedom, a very different proposition to the vulgar propaganda of German *Kultur.* But by choosing to employ younger artists who had direct experience of war, Masterman recognized that he would be employing many of those who had actively been part of much-derided Modernist causes. And contrary to widespread readings of his commissioning strategy, he set no limits on what should or should not be painted. When asked directly by Nevinson if there were subjects he should avoid, he replied 'No, no... paint anything you please'.[38] Such an attitude could not hold for long. It ran foul of those in France and Belgium who had to host the artists and, as we shall see when we look at the experiences of a number of these artists, it created terrible ructions with those who had to censor work before it could be circulated for public consumption.

Masterman was aided and abetted in this role by the appointment

---

36 Born in Scotland, John Buchan (1875–1940) was a novelist, poet, statesman, and journalist. A prolific writer, by the end of his student days at Oxford he had already published five novels and numerous articles. In 1901 he became the High Commissioner's Secretary in South Africa, returning to England to head up the publishing company, Thomas Nelson & Sons. His most famous novel, *The Thirty-Nine Steps*, was published in instalments in 1914 and has remained popular for over ninety years, having twice been re-made for cinema, with a TV film in 2008.

At the outbreak of war Buchan was recruited by Charles Masterman, head of the War Propaganda Bureau, to write a serialized history of the war. *Nelson's History of the War*, in twenty-four instalments, was issued in February 1915. At the same time, he became one of just five journalists attached to the British Army, writing for *The Times* and *Daily News*. Two years later, in February 1917 he became Director of the newly formed Department of Information. His time in post was blighted by illness, by the death of his youngest brother from war wounds, and a reverse in his family fortunes, which obliged him to return to novel-writing. Lacking the political power to influence events in government, Buchan's role was diminished upon the appointment of Lord Beaverbrook as the new Minister of Information.

After the war, Buchan held many important positions, including Conservative MP for the Scottish Universities, holding the seat until he became Baron Tweedsmuir in 1935 and, that same year, he became Governor-General of Canada, a position he held until his death in Montreal on 11 February 1940.

37 Thomas Derrick was an artist and teacher at the Royal College of Art. His memorandum to Masterman is quoted by W.P. Mayes, 'The Origins of an Art Collection', an unpublished account made in 1963 of the history of the large collection held in the Imperial War Museum, London.

38 Lucy Masterman, *C.F.G. Masterman*, p.287.

of Max Aitken (recently elevated to the peerage by Lloyd George to become Lord Beaverbrook) as Director of a new Ministry of Information, which supplanted the Department of Information in March 1918.[39] Beaverbrook created a British War Memorial Committee, and bought an administrative flair and entrepreneurial zeal that had been recently honed on the ambitious Canadian War Memorials scheme, which he personally directed.[40] His methods were direct and unencumbered by layers of bureaucracy. One painter recalled his first meeting:

> About ten minutes past four up breezed a car, and in it was a slim little man with an enormous head and two remarkable eyes. I saluted and tried to make military noises with my boots. Said he: 'Are you Orpen?' Yes, sir,' said I. 'Are you willing to work for the Canadians?' said he. 'Certainly, sir,' said I. 'Well,' said he, 'that's all right. Jump in, and we'll go and have a drink.'[41]

Beaverbrook set out to replicate in England the successful Canadian scheme. He altered the direction and tone of official war art, moving it from the representation of the present (with a short-term emphasis on propaganda and documentary record) to the creation of a permanent legacy for future generations, an emblem of remembrance, a lasting memorial expressed in art. However, he reckoned without the challenge of rival factions in Whitehall, especially those in the Treasury who were suspicious of an organisation that had originally been established to create propaganda but was now acting as a patron of new artworks; nor had he anticipated the direct challenge from rival administrators at the newly formed National War Museum, who wanted both to take the initiative in gathering the existing war art and to set its own agenda for commissioning new records.[42]

Under the energetic guidance of Arnold Bennett, and with the

---

39 On 5 December 1916, Asquith resigned; on the 7th, Lloyd George became Prime Minister with Bonar Law at his side. On 9 December, Aitken (a Knight since 1911) was offered a peerage.

40 Born in Ontario, Canada, Sir William Maxwell Aitken (1879–1964), was ennobled in 1917 as Lord Beaverbrook. Initially a successful Canadian financier he retired from business in 1910 to pursue a political career, taking a seat in the House of Commons, where he represented Ashton-under-Lyne for the Conservative party. In May 1915 he was appointed as the Canadian Expeditionary Force's official records officer and, from 1916, the Canadian government's official representative in France, publishing, in 1916, *Canada in Flanders*, a three-volume account of the war from the Canadian point of view. On 10 February 1918, he was appointed to the British government, as Minister of Information.

Beaverbrook transformed the management of the British propaganda programme, commissioning posters, artists, authors and pioneering the design and use of photographic posters for recruitment purposes at home. He also introduced cinema newsreels for home audiences. He resigned from the post in October 1918. He was the owner of many popular newspapers, including the influential *Daily Express* and the London *Evening Standard*.

Beaverbrook returned to government in 1940. Under Churchill he served as Minister for Aircraft Production (1940–41), Minister of Supply (1941–42), Minister of War Production (1942) and Lord Privy Seal (1943–45).

41 William Orpen, *An Onlooker in France* (London: Williams and Norgate/Ernest Benn, 1923) p.42. As Graham Shaw notes, the original name of Beaverbrook's committee had been the 'Imperial Permanent Memorials Committee'. (See Graham Shaw, PhD thesis, 2007)

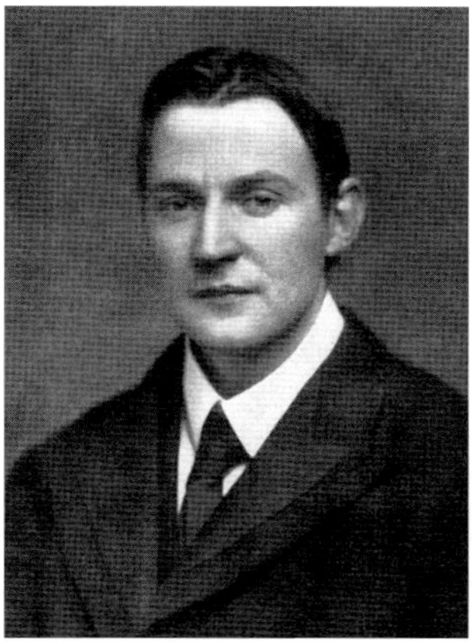

Charles Masterman

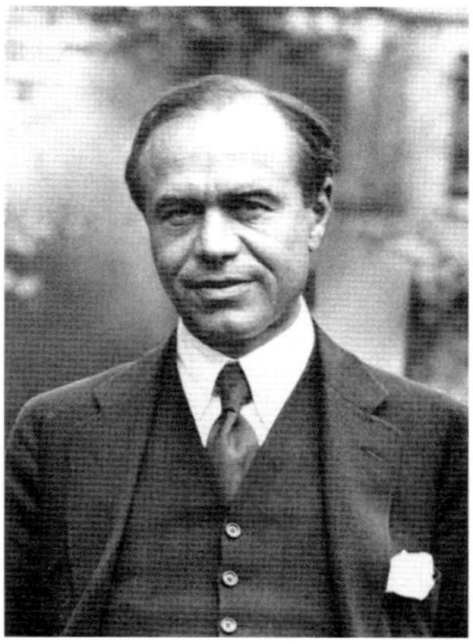

William Maxwell Aitken, 1st Baron Beaverbrook

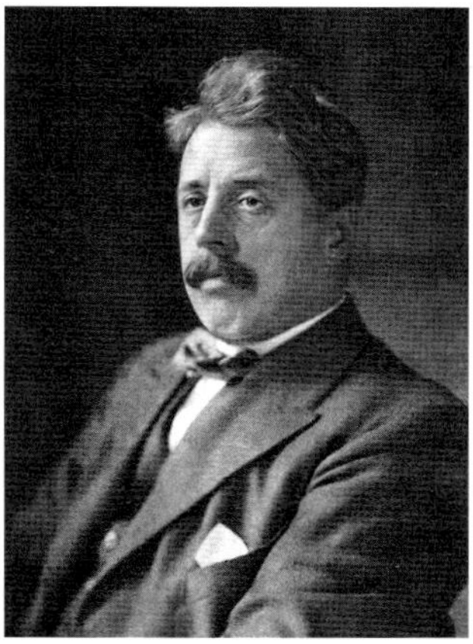

Arnold Bennett

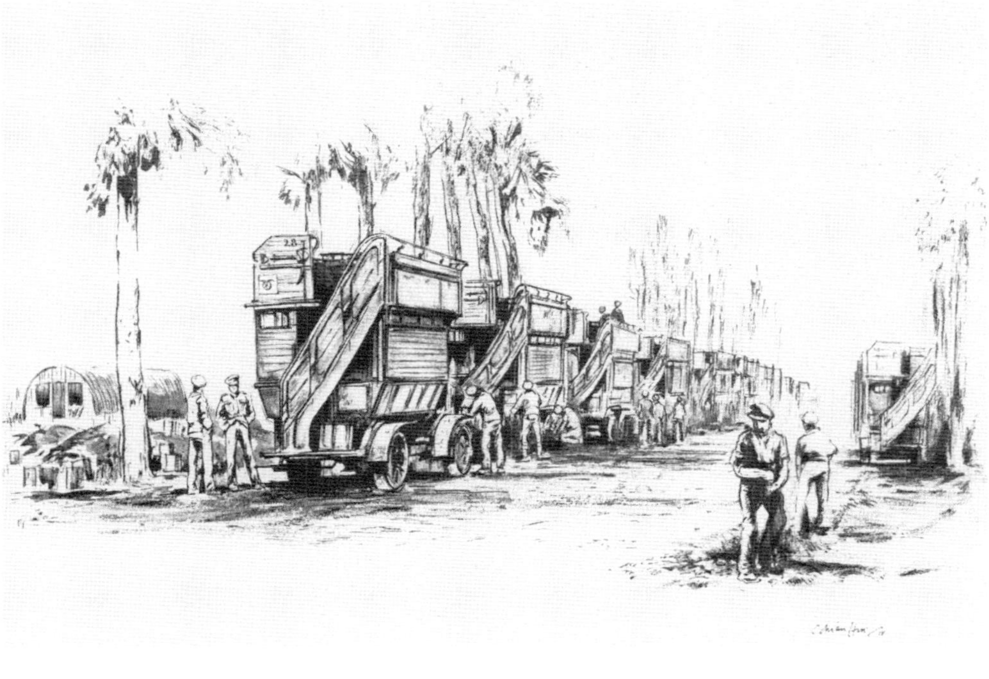

ADRIAN HILL

A Penny all the way: London Motor-Buses on the Amiens Road

(1918)

pen and ink and watercolour, 32 x 44 cm

tacit support of Beaverbrook, the British War Memorials Committee (BWMC) set itself on a very different trajectory from the War Museum. Independent and original in its thinking, even to the point of declaring open defiance, the committee did its utmost to frustrate establishment efforts to promote the old guard of British art, namely those in the Royal Academy who wanted to cream off the better commissions. Instead, Bennett and his fellow members offered work to the cadre of younger soldier-artists with the ulterior motive of assembling a significant contemporary collection that would be representative of 'the greatest artistic expression of the day'.[43]

One of the most fascinating aspects of the complex commissioning and curatorial project masterminded by the BWMC is the degree of tolerance, even at times clandestine support, afforded to modernist work. As we have seen, the right-wing and conservative factions in the press and society at large did not happily tolerate artworks that reminded them of foreign imperatives – Futurism, Cubism, Expressionism – which were regarded as alien and undesirable, and inimical to British values. Such images were relentlessly pilloried in the illustrated press, although Nevinson's work was generally endorsed as setting acceptable parameters of subject and technique.[44] Nevertheless, under the auspices of the BWMC, artists were encouraged to find their own voice and not be too swayed by cautious public opinion. Certainly, Masterman felt this way, expressing disappointment that Nevinson, having been offered an official commission, had 'abandoned his own *metier* in order to produce *official* (perhaps dull) pictures'. He, and others, urged the painter to recover the probing anger of his earlier work and 'to develop his own genius – however bitter and uncompromising'.[45]

Beaverbook intended to house these works in an imposing Hall

42 The Cabinet approved the establishment of a National War Museum on 5 March 1917, as 'a memorial and record of the effort and sacrifice of the men and women of the Empire'. From Mayes, 'The Origins of an Art Collection'. It was re-named the Imperial War Museum in the interim report drawn up by Lord Crawford and the Balcarres' Committee, dated 14 December 1917, largely, it appears, at the request of the Dominions sub-committee.

43 Arnold Bennett's article 'Officialism and War Painting', published in *New Statesman*, on 20 December 1919 (pp.347–48) recounts an insider's tale of the motivations and constraints that beset the British War Memorials Committee. As Malvern states, it was a story of obstruction and hostility by the War Office and the Treasury, but also an 'extraordinary combination of vision, talent and expertise' that succeeded in creating opportunities for artists (Sue Malvern, *Modern Art, Britain and the Great War*, p.69).

44 It was championed in particular by the Hungarian art critic Paul Konody. In Canada Paul G. Konody had been Beaverbrook's master of taste. The mid-European critic and writer had determined the list of those commanded to create art work for the Canadian War Memorial Fund, the 'Konodian Army' as it was teasingly called. Konody was an unabashed fan of Nevinson, whatever the style. He was much less tolerant of Vorticist or Futurist 'excesses', bluntly informing some of the younger artists that Cubist work was 'inadmissable' for the Canadian scheme. But, here again the true story is cloudy: in 1918 Konody ranted, raged and then rejected David Bomberg's first attempt to paint the work of a tunnelling company – describing it, it is said, as a 'Futurist abortion' – but subsequently worked closely with the painter steadying his bruised ego and nurturing him to produce further work. (In London, Konody played second fiddle to Arnold Bennett, who made the major decisions in the British War Memorials Committee.)

45 C.F.G. Masterman to Hudson, 29 October 1917, Imperial War Museum, London, Department of Art, Nevinson file.

of Remembrance; it would mirror an equally grand hall in Ottawa that one day would house the art commissioned by the Canadian War Memorial Fund. A list of artists was considered, individual negotiations took place, terms were agreed. Some artists were paid to produce a single picture for the planned Hall (£300 plus materials and studio expenses for one of the larger pictures). Younger, less established artists were offered a rather more modest deal – a salary of £300 per annum in return for their total artistic output during that period. This proposal was accepted by now familiar figures such as Paul Nash, Colin Gill, Bernard Meninsky and John Nash (all aged under thirty) but rejected by the less amenable, and somewhat contrary, Nevinson who surmised for some reason that it would 'prove a bad business proposition'.[46]

The end result was truly impressive. Not only was this the 'first twentieth-century incidence of British state patronage to commission modern history paintings', it was possibly the most ambitious, and it secured for the nation some of the best art to emerge from the conflict. Seventeen large history paintings by artists such as Henry Lamb, Wyndham Lewis, Paul Nash, John Singer Sargent and Stanley Spencer; two large sculpture reliefs by Charles S. Jagger and Gilbert Ledward, and twelve smaller canvases were produced by thirty-one artists. These formed the backbone of major exhibitions of the Nation's War Pictures that were created and toured immediately after the war.[47]

However, in some government circles the BWMC attracted little but criticism. Beaverbrook was regarded with envy and mistrust, his dual roles as both a press baron and peer of the realm were considered irreconcilable. Others on the committee were tainted by association with unpopular causes, even national scandals that made them easy pickings for hostile mandarins in Whitehall.[48] On occasion, Bennett and his fellow advisers set themselves on a collision course with the establishment; Bennett gleefully declaring in one letter that the committee had 'succeeded in 'turning down *all* of the R.A. painters, except Clausen. Some feat, believe me!'[49]

By contrast the National War Museum (which was re-named the Imperial War Museum in December 1917)[50] plotted a very different

46 Nevinson to Masterman, 10 March 1918. The painter's initial rejection of Scheme 2 was on the questionable grounds that it might restrict his artistic freedom. He made no such objection when moved to (the better paid and more secure) Scheme 1.

47 See Sue Malvern, *Modern Art, Britain and the Great War*, p.46.

48 Robert Ross, gallery owner and Trustee of the Tate was one of the key advisers to Wellington House and determined the aesthetic character and quality of the British War Memorial Committee scheme. He was also Oscar Wilde's executor and friend, and for that association – and on the dubious grounds that he was a pacifist – he became the target of public scorn and harassment. He died in October 1918 aged forty-nine.

49 Arnold Bennett, quoted by Sue Malvern, *Modern Art, Britain and the Great War*, fn.36, p.112.

50 See note 42.

course. Setting out to achieve a comprehensive visual record of the war it too began a programme of purchasing and commissioning artists. Its method was systematic and prescriptive: wartime activity was divided into eight subject groupings (Army, Navy, Air Force, Merchant Marine, Land, Munitions, Clerical and other work by Women, Public Manifestations) and artists were then found to fit these subjects. The commissioning process in this parallel 'documentary' phase could be quite draconian. Having served at the front as a signaller and scout in the Honourable Artillery Company, the young painter Adrian Hill was the first artist to be commissioned by the new museum. He was told precisely what to draw:

> Towns and localities behind the lines which are specially identified with the British Army... points of juncture between our line and the line occupied by the French, American, Belgian and Portuguese, so as to show the different nationalities side by side... labour and engineering work by Coloured Battalions which show the distinct dress of the Chinese etc., and especially some sketches of Tanks HQ showing repairing and the like.[51]

Working to these specifications Hill diligently produced an extensive portfolio of over 180 pen-and-ink drawings that documented the mundane aspects of the war in France and Belgium. Straying outside a tight brief was simply not tolerated. While his drawings were encouraged – and, it is said, highly regarded by Field Marshal Haig – Hill's oil paintings were flatly rejected. 'The committee was not favourably impressed by your oil paintings,' he was bluntly informed, 'and it was thought desirable that you should keep to drawings in future.'[52]

Tensions between the BWMC and the Museum reached a head in May 1918 when Beaverbrook unilaterally accepted (in fact, virtually commandeered) William Orpen's gift of scores of war paintings for the Ministry of Information. Orpen was largely indifferent as to which organization administered his impressive *opus*, but those in the War Museum – Alfred Mond, the First Commissioner of Works and Chairman, and Sir Martin Conway, Director-General – who felt that the work was theirs by right, began to openly plot

---

51 Ffoulkes to Hill, 14 June 1918, IWM Dept. of Art file 74/3 part II.

Home on leave, Adrian Hill had the temerity to visit the War Museum and show some of his drawings to Sir Martin Conway, the first Director-General of the museum, who admired the precise drawings as well as the young man's sense of initiative. Hill was appointed by the IWM as their first – and as it proved, their youngest – official artist in March 1918 with the rank of 2nd Lieutenant.

52 See for example the correspondence between the Director-General of National War Museum to General Haig, 1 October 1917; the letter rejecting the oils was from Yockney to Hill, 27 February 1919, IWM Dept. of Art file 74/3 part II.

See also Hill's letters of 4 October 1917 and 12 November 1917 held in the Brotherton Library, Liddle Collection, Leeds University.

against Beaverbrook, seeking to discredit him, his Ministry and the war memorial committee. The failure to progress the Hall of Remembrance may have been due to these machinations, but equally corrosive were the sheer costs of running the Ministry, and in particular Wellington House, which amounted to £1.8 million in 1918. In July of that year Beaverbrook ceded the entire operation to the Imperial War Museum, resigning as Minister of Information in October.

Inevitably, the Hall of Remembrance was not built, nor the great Canadian Memorial building intended to house Aitken's other collection of war art. However, the paintings, prints, drawings and sculpture survived and are still housed (admittedly many of them in storage) in the Imperial War Museum in London. It is probably the finest collection of British art in the country outside Tate Britain. Arguably the greatest legacy of the war's art was the scheme itself: under Beaverbrook's tutelage the Ministry of Information protected and promoted emerging artists, brought intellectual coherence to a previously haphazard programme of commissioning, and instigated what Bennett described as 'a revolution in official patronage'.[53] Twenty years later it provided the template for the War Artists' Advisory Committee headed by the respected art historian Sir Kenneth Clark, then the Surveyor of the King's Pictures at Windsor and Director of the National Gallery, London who based his structures, protocols and pricing on the programmes initiated by Masterman, Buchan, and Beaverbrook many years earlier.[54]

MANAGING ARTISTS

Managing the various war artists required logistical prowess, administrative dexterity and, perhaps most crucially, patience. Legendary (though possibly a little exaggerated) are the tales of

53 Bennett quoted by Sue Malvern, *Modern Art, Britain and the Great War*, p.75.

54 For a full account of the WAAC see: Alan Ross, *Colours of War: War Art 1939–45*, (London: Jonathan Cape, 1983). In 1942 Clark reflected on the parameters set by the committee's terms of reference:

> The War Artists collection cannot be completely representative of modern English art, because it cannot include those pure painters who are interested solely in putting down their feelings about shapes and colours, and not in facts, drama and human emotions. ('War Artists at the National Gallery', *The Studio*, CXXIII, January 1942, p.586)

He also noted, rather drily, that the Ministry of Information:

> was said to contain 999 employees... [Its] large staff had been recruited to deal with three of four different objects. The first, and most defensible, was censorship; the second the provision of news; the third a feeble attempt at propaganda through various media; and the fourth to provide a kind of wastepaper-basket into which everyone could throw their grievances and their war-winning proposals... (Kenneth Clark, *The Other Half*, London, 1977, pp.9–16)

Clark trawled far and wide for the best artists. In its first sixteen weeks the committee considered some eight hundred names, including all those employed during the Great War. Few made the grade. Nevinson was omitted. A few veterans – Paul Nash, Kennington, and Bone – were recruited. The fees offered by the WAAC were lower than those offered in the Great War; £150 to £200 was the average price of an oil painting, watercolours might be bought for as little as £10.

minor spats between artists bent on one course of (often reckless) action and those middle-ranking officials who had to corral and direct their enthusiasm. In 1917 the Department of Information had asked that a permanent 'artist's base' be set up in France to cater for greater numbers than the one-at-a-time system so far in place. This did not happen. The British Expeditionary Force (BEF) Intelligence Chief, General Sir John Charteris, argued that two artists was ample and complained of their unfortunate tendency to 'want to sit down and look at a place for a long time'.[55] And there was no shortage of artists in Britain who wanted the work. Those who administered the war artists' schemes were inundated with requests from painters who wished to sell war-related pictures, or who craved official accreditation and an opportunity to see the war at first-hand. Algernon Mayow Talmage, Royal Academician, silver medallist at the Paris Salon, bronze medallist at the Pittsburgh International exhibition, was one such artist. In May 1917 he presented his credentials to the war museum:

> No picture that I am aware of, has been really studied on the spot so as to get the real environment and atmospheric conditions and phenomenon. I have been painting in the open all my life and I feel that were it possible to give me opportunities to study this subject I could paint a picture which would be of value as a record and venture to hope as a work of art which would be something entirely different to the usual hackneyed and unconvincing picture.[56]

But, like so many others, he was turned down, rejected in a single short sentence and his letter of application filed in one of the bulging cabinets in the museum's growing archive.

MOTIVATIONS

So why did so many artists crave official recognition? Financial security may have held some attraction, though as we have seen the remuneration was rarely generous. Why were so many artists driven by a need to witness the scale of the conflict; to expose themselves to the privations of war, to test out and hone their skills in such demanding circumstances? The urge to witness, interpret and leave some form of personal testimony was a powerful incentive to those who needed to come to terms with their violent muse.[57] 'You must not miss a war, if one is going!' wrote Wyndham Lewis,

55 Charteris to Masterman, 12 March 1917, IWM file G4010/17.

56 Talmage, artist's file, IWM Department of Art.

57 For a fuller debate on this topic see Jane Howlett and Rod Mengham (eds.) *The Violent Muse* (Manchester: Manchester University Press, 1994).

with only the slightest degree of irony, 'You cannot afford to miss that experience'.[58] Others were simply astonished at what they saw on active service: 'I tell you,' wrote the soldier-artist Keith Henderson in October 1916, 'the "subjects" are endless, and in particular I long to do great big stretches of this bleak brown land'.[59] Similarly, the society portrait painter Ambrose McEvoy thought the battlefield to be 'the most thrilling sight I have ever seen'.[60]

Few of those who aspired to paint the war did so to avoid danger: in both world wars artists were exposed to discomfort and death, although only one officially-validated artist died in service in the Great War, while three lost their lives in the Second World War.[61] However, it is clear that some artists – especially those who had first-hand experience of the fighting – sought refuge and safety in the role of official war artist. Wyndham Lewis certainly did: after months in the Royal Artillery he had already lost too many close friends when he jumped at an opportunity to work for the Canadian memorial scheme. Similarly, Richard Nevinson clutched at every chance to avoid being called-up once he realised that his medical discharge for rheumatic fever no longer gave him exemption. He even considered fleeing overseas to Spain to avoid military duty.[62] Despite his disability and an honourable discharge as medically unfit, Eric Kennington became increasingly concerned that unless he was offered the post of war artist by one of the memorial committees he too might face conscription as the war dragged into a fourth year and the British male population was scoured for men.

For those artists already in the services, many found their skills in demand, though perhaps not in ways they might have expected: the Vorticist painter William Roberts – serving as a lowly gunner in the Royal Artillery – was tasked with painting his battery's name on two German field guns captured by the 51st Brigade in early 1918. The eminent Salon painter William Orpen turned his hand to sculpture, helping to model and cast a number of plaster heads for

---

58 Percy Wyndham Lewis, *Blasting and Bombardiering, Autobiography 1914–1926* (London: Eyre & Spottiswoode, 1937) p.114.
When Wyndham Lewis was seconded from the Royal Garrison Artillery and attached to the Canadian Records Office he had to present himself to the War Office in London where an indignant officer – a 'fierce little dugout Major' according to Lewis – bristled at the mention of war art: '"To paint a picture!" he exclaimed. "I've never heard of such a thing! Is that the way to win the war?" I refrained from pointing out that his own occupation was hardly calculated to put the Germans to flight.' (*Blasting and Bombardiering*, p.191)

59 Keith Henderson, *Letters to Helen*, privately published, 1917, p.66.

60 IWM Department of Art: McEvoy papers. McEvoy to Commander Walcott, undated (possibly August 1918).

61 Only one official artist died in the Great War (a naval painter, Geoffrey Allfree) whereas three died in the Second World War – Richards on the Maas, Eric Ravilious off Iceland, and Thomas Hennell in Indonesia.

62 See Michael J.K. Walsh, *C.R.W. Nevinson: This Cult of Violence* (New Haven: Yale University Press, 2002), in particular chapters 8 and 9. Nevinson's escape to neutral Spain failed when he was refused a permit to travel.

target practice. The sculptor Derwent Wood worked in the 'tin noses' room at the 3rd London General Hospital, fashioning facemasks out of flesh-coloured electroplate. Stanley Spencer's painterly duties were a little less edifying: in Macedonia he had to paint the letters designating the men's and the sergeants' toilets. As ever, Spencer brought a delicate touch to this mundane task by decorating the 'S' for Sergeants with a halo of painted dog roses.[63] In addition, professional artists – along with pre-war surveyors, architects, draughtsmen, and engineers – found themselves promptly transferred to units of the Royal Engineers. These postings were not always free from danger. While his fellow camouflage designers worked safely in workshops and paint sheds many miles behind the lines, the young painter Leon Underwood was sent on hazardous forays into No Man's Land. With his back to the enemy he was required to make detailed drawings of trees on the British trench line. These drawings were then used to construct an exact replica of a selected tree which, hollowed out and lined with bullet-deflecting metal, was installed after dark as a cunningly disguised observation post.[64] John Nash was typical of many soldier-artists who yearned for the safety of an official war art commission, but soon wearied of its demands and the constant inspections by men from the Ministry, even where these were sympathetic fellow-artists. Referring to the burden of his official work, Nash wrote that he 'had not been out much owing to the Painting, a hole in my shoes, and also I don't feel free for landscape – how I long for "my ticket"... The day I get free from the army I shall take a clean sheet of paper and go out and try and surprise myself'.[65]

It is difficult, then, to satisfactorily summarise the motivations that drove artists: many wanted merely to escape the petty tedium of service life, to be relatively free from danger and to be modestly rewarded for their talents. As we shall see when we examine the wartime experiences of a number of them, those who were naturally bellicose soon found their enthusiasms dampened; those who wanted to be officially recognized and supported were often frustrated in their aims, and nearly all of those who produced memorable art often

63 Cited in Paul Gough, *The Experiences of British Artists in the Great War*, Peter Liddle and Hugh Cecil, editors (London: Leo Cooper, 1996) p.847.

64 Underwood's large canvas 'Erecting a Camouflage Tree' was purchased (for one hundred pounds, plus twenty-five for materials) for the IWM art collection (IWM:ART 2283). There is an accompanying text: 'the construction of a steel tree by the Special Works Park R.E. – Camouflage Corps – is in progress in a line of defence. The time is early morning and the N.C.O. is seen regarding the visibility and calculating the chances of completing and hauling up the tree, or waiting for the succeeding night.' See: Christopher Neve, *Leon Underwood* (London: Thames and Hudson, 1974), pp.26–36. IWM Department of Art file 307/7 contains extensive correspondence between the museum and the painter regarding the subject-matter.

As may be evident from scrutinizing the finished canvas, all the figures were taken from the same model, the painter's brother, Horace.

65 John Nash to Dora Carrington, quoted by Ronald Blythe, *First Friends* (London: Viking, 1997) p.136.

had to do so in the face of hardship, privations, and an implacable administration which censored their work and taxed their often meagre incomes.

CHALLENGES

While we can guess at what motivated some artists to sustain their creativity during the Great War, it is simpler to list the obstacles and constraints that might have held them back. Indeed, given the conditions many had to work in one wonders how any art was produced at all. Possibly the greatest challenge was the widespread fear of spying: the suspicion that anyone wandering abroad with pencil and paper was up to no good. Even when working for the Department of Information in England, the eminent artist Sir John Lavery was not allowed anywhere near his designated subject-matter – the Fleet moored off Rosyth. His Special Joint Permit in fact disqualified him from drawing docks, harbours, munitions factories, captured ships or planes and – for good measure – 'any other place or thing guarded by His Majesty's Forces'. The permit did little to protect him from the police, Boy Scouts or over-vigilant members of the public: 'No sooner had I got to work than I was stopped by the local police,' he recalled with irritation, 'and marched off to Headquarters. They thought the permit too good to be true.'[66] Fellow painter Alfred Munnings concluded after several abortive sketching trips in England that 'there came a time when an artist dare not be seen sketching out of doors in the country'.[67]

In the war zones these irritations could escalate into major incidents. William Rothenstein was arrested on two separate occasions; once by the French when he was found sketching entrenchments in 1914; a second time by the British on the eve of the German offensive in 1918, at a time when he assumed he was protected by his status as an official artist. When an indignant Brigade Major could not decipher Rothenstein's name on his White Paper, the painter responded by pronouncing the first 'R' with an exaggerated Teutonic accent, adding for good measure: 'Now, I suppose were my name Smith, you would have me shot.'[68] One Fleet Street 'special' artist had to disguise himself as a Belgian peasant to avoid the notice of the military police. His most memorable scoop – drawings of the siege battles on the Aisne – were smuggled out of the war zone stuffed into his boots.[69]

66 John Lavery, *Life of a Painter* (London, Cassell, 1940) pp.145-146.
67 Alfred Munnings, *An Artist's Life* (London, Museum Press, 1950) p.296.
68 William Rothenstein, *Men and Memories*, pp.178–179.
69 Frederick Villiers, *Five Decades of Adventure* (London, 1921) Vol.2, pp.316–318.

On active service these problems were inevitably compounded by strict military discipline. The painter John Nash, a bomber in the Artists' Rifles, related bluntly that 'drawing wouldn't have been encouraged by a commanding officer in the Line: I might have been taken for a spy'.[70] However, another rifleman in the same unit exulted in the game of hide-and-seek necessary to produce work at all:

> I had become a keen and fairly competent sketcher in the army. It had started with military sketching as a scout, but it soon went on to filling sketchbooks with records of the towns and villages of Flanders, and of the trenches. As it was strictly illegal, the necessary care not to be detected added to the pleasure.[71]

Even with official clearance artists were something of a hindrance at the front, viewed – along with many journalists and nearly all visiting politicians – as intrusive, awkward, and inappropriately dressed. In France all visitors – press, politicians, dignitaries, and artists – came under the jurisdiction of Military Press Control, a branch of Military Intelligence, known by its acronym MI7. From mid-1917 to the spring of 1919 the officer entrusted with managing the flow of official war artists to the front was Major (late Colonel) Arthur N. Lee who acted as logistician, organiser, and censor – a powerful post that effectively dictated the movement of any British artist on the Western Front. He tended to agree with his superior, Colonel Hutton-Wilson, that artists had the habit of being troublesome, though he befriended a number of them and by the end of the war had acquired a collections of pictures they had given him.[72] Lee's differences of opinion with individual artists – especially Richard Nevinson – have become legendary in the annals of art patronage, but Lee regarded his role as a guardian of British military values and worked unstintingly to protect the army's interests while trying to facilitate each individual artist's needs. By his own admission 'not an arty man', Lee was determined that the commissioned artists should not be unduly cushioned from the actualities of the war. 'I do not believe,' he wrote, 'that those selected for other less arduous work should have any more comforts than the Line people… just because they were lionised by Society at home.'[73] However, when Nevinson absconded without permission to see for himself the build-up for

70 John Nash, 'Artists in an Age of Conflict', Imperial War Museum, Department of Sound Records, Accession No. 000323/05. Nash was interviewed by Joseph Darracott of the Imperial War Museum and David Brown of the Tate Gallery.

71 James Parkes, *Voyage of Discoveries* (London: Gollancz, 1969) p.52. See also Parkes' sketchbook 'The Red Book Volume 1, April–May 1917', in the Brotherton Library, Leeds University.

72 See Meirion Harries and Susie Harries, *The War Artists*, p.33.

73 Lee's diary entry, 6 April 1917, quoted by Meirion Harries and Susie Harries, *The War Artists*, p.32–33, which also carries a balanced account of Lee's work, character and contribution.

the Battle of Third Ypres he overstepped the mark and without hesitation Lee sent him back to England. Months later, Lee refused to pass one of Nevinson's canvases which showed a group of soldiers he had seen on the London Underground returning from leave. He objected, in effect, that they were a bad advertisement for the British Army. As we will see in the chapter on Nevinson, after some wrangling between the War Office and the Department of Information, the artist had his way. It was a different story with another painting, the ironically titled *Paths of Glory*, showing the corpses of two khaki-clad corpses. Banned from showing it or having it reproduced for publication, Nevinson upstaged the censor by pasting a strip of brown paper over the canvas inscribed with the word 'censored' in bold capitals. Again, as we shall see when we look at Nevinson's work in more detail, this was yet another show of bravado, as was the painter's reaction when he was reprimanded by the War Office: he stormed off to work for the Canadians.[74]

Lee's initials appear at the foot of many drawings that were made by artists in France and Belgium. His office was also inclined to correct what they termed factual inaccuracies. Nevinson, for instance, had to correct the direction of the traffic – from the left to the right side – in his painting *The Road from Arras to Bapaume*. All artists were warned off drawing or painting subjects that might have some obvious strategic value, or from depicting new technologies or operational procedures that might lend the enemy tactical advantage. But painters could stray unwittingly into controversy. The etcher Martin Hardie – an assiduous recorder of the French, and later the Italian, theatre of war – had several pictures removed from display because they appeared to show Britain's allies in a dim light. His rendition of *The Bathing Corner at Boulogne* was considered inappropriate because it showed French troops frolicking in an unbecoming manner; similarly, his picture of black troops landing at the same post was criticized because it 'accentuated the Kaffir features unduly'. The picture was withheld from public view.[75]

What of the dead? Nevinson had run foul of the War Office by showing dead British soldiers and he later criticized the Imperial War Museum for hiding such images from the public eye, arguing that it was an odd state of affairs 'which sheds a curious light on the

---

74 Nevinson recounts his dispute over 'Paths of Glory' in *Paint and Prejudice*, pp.110–11. There is some doubt that Nevinson ever showed the painting in its 'wrapped' form, but he certainly had photographs taken and had posters printed from it.

The title was taken from lines in Gray's 'Elegy Written in a Country Churchyard' and was the third title, preferred over 'Dead Men', and 'Shall their sacrifice be in vain'. Having been censored and forbidden from display the canvas was bought by the government in January 1918 to ensure control over its use and reproduction, but it remained in Nevinson's possession and was defiantly displayed in March 1918 with the title in the catalogue *Censored*. (See Charles E. Doherty, 'Nevinson's Elegy: "Paths of Glory"' in *Art Journal*, Vol.51, no.1, 1992, p.65.)

75 The picture is IWM: Art 939. See also Hardie File.

official mind when one remembers the grim films that have been exhibited and the books of horrible photographs that have been published'.[76] It is true that dead British soldiers were to be viewed in such films as *The Battle of the Somme*, which went on widespread British release in late summer 1916. But by late 1917 there was a ban on the depiction of corpses in official films, photographs and artworks. Token injuries such as bandaged head wounds or arms in a sling – preferably clean – were acceptable and this convention is evident in much of the work produced towards the end of the war, from the conservative figuration of Beadle's *The Breaking of the Hindenberg Line* to Henry Tonks's *An Advanced Dressing Station*, which despite its dank grimness and the whiff of fetid air is reassuring in its care for the injured. Tonks was careful to ensure that maimed limbs were well-concealed under the cover of thick blankets, and damaged flesh concealed in the gloomy chiaroscuro.[77] The formula for representing British and Allied wounded and dead did not extend to the enemy: both Nevinson and Orpen depicted German corpses, Orpen's rendition of an emaciated body in his canvas *Dead Germans in a Trench*, first shown in public in May 1918, is unflinching in its portrayal of disfigurement, the bodies contorted and bent, their flesh grey-green and ghastly. Compare the *rigor mortis* in this canvas and in Nevinson's vast Dante-esque panorama *The Harvest of Battle*, with the decorous wounds described by Gilbert Rogers in his large canvas *Stretcher Bearers after the Battle of Messines*, where the British wounded appear to suffer only minor injuries and are whole in body and limb, while the German copses are scattered fragments strewn around the edges of the painting. However, the protocols on depicting the dead were relaxed after the Armistice. John Nash's painting *Over the top: 1st Artists' Rifles at Marcoing, December 30th 1917*, painted in 1919, includes the bodies of two British soldiers lying prone in their jumping-off trench. Only acceptable after the war had been won, these British bodies serve as symbols of death, a means of indicating greater loss of life during battle, of 'individual sacrifice within the collective action'.[78] As in Nevinson's more controversial but no less brutal painting, their dignity has been reserved through the prone postures and their averted faces, which delicately preserves their anonymity.

---

76 Nevinson, *Paint and Prejudice*, p.107.

77 Further phrases were added to the Defence of the Realm Act amendment of 28 August 1914 so as '...to prevent the spread of reports likely to cause disaffection or alarm.' This was a convenient catch-all phrase which would allow the authorities a free hand in regard to censorship. In 1917 Yockney also wrote to Nevinson to remind him that 'It is stated that the War Office has prohibited the appearance of dead bodies, even German, in any official photographs or film. It is requested you should not exhibit the picture under discussion.' Nevinson was told that this was 'a formal reminder'. IWM Art-Nev files, p.116.

78 The phrase is from Graham Shaw's unpublished PhD thesis, p.119 and see also p.124.

More prosaically, artists were often confronted with rather more practical difficulties and inconveniences. In the trenches, the most pressing need was often to keep drawing paper dry. Arthur Bradbury, a subaltern in the 2nd Royal Iniskillings, recalled Somme trenches that were waist deep in mud and although he kept his sketchbook deep inside his pack the 'conditions often made sketching impossible'.[79] Lieutenant-Colonel Frank Palmer, a trainee architect before the war, carried his sketchbook 'tucked inside his tunic like a breastplate'.[80] While Orpen complained of the putrid smell of abandoned trenches in hot weather, cold snaps brought their own hazards: Paul Maze describes in his memoir, *A Frenchman in Khaki*, of a time in the appalling winter of 1916–17 when it was impossible to paint at all because his watercolour brush froze before he could apply it to the paper.[81] Painting in 1918, William Rothenstein wrote of being so cold when working outdoors that he kept a pair of fur gloves hanging from his shoulders into which he gingerly put his numbed fingers from time to time.[82]

Others took real risks. Adrian Hill – a member of a Scouting and Sniping Section before his official appointment as an artist – recalled hair-raising patrols into No Man's Land:

> I advanced in short rushes, mostly on my hands and knees with my sketching kit dangling round my neck. As I slowly approached, the wood gradually took a more definite shape, and as I crept nearer I saw that what was hidden from our own line, now revealed itself as a cunningly contrived observation post in one of the battered trees.[83]

Hill recollected making drawings as the rain poured off his paper and having to use shell-hole water to dilute his Indian-ink washes.[84] Others found the demands simply too trying. Back in Britain, the distinguished painter Philip Wilson Steer laid down exacting conditions before he even picked up his paintbrush and palette. Amongst these were: Shelter from the wind; proximity to a lavatory; shade from the sun; protection from children; and a suitable subject.[85]

And what exactly comprised a suitable subject? It would be tempting to suggest that ruins and ruination dominate the *oeuvre*, but this is patently not the case. In December 1919, one thousand of the war museum's collection of three thousand artworks went

79 Bradbury to Ernest Blaikley, Keeper of Art IWM, 14 January 1933, IWM Department of Art file 150/4 part 1.
80 Quoted in Caroline Dakers, *The Countryside at War, 1914–1918* (London: Constable, 1987) p.183.
81 Paul Maze, *A Frenchman in Khaki*, pp.205–206.
82 William Rothenstein, *Men and Memories*, p.181.
83 Adrian Hill interviewed in *The Graphic*, 15 November 1930.
84 *The Graphic*, 15 November 1930.
85 D.S. MacColl, *Life, Work and Setting of Philip Wilson Steer* (London: Faber, 1945) p.118.

on show in the plush and hallowed halls of Burlington House, the home of the Royal Academy, in London. Although ridiculed by the illustrated and popular press, and vilified in Parliament, the sheer variety of subject matter hanging on the walls was impressive.[86] The work ranged from paintings of the Home Front produced by the Women's Work Section, to the vast history paintings by Singer Sargent and Wyndham Lewis, from formal portraiture to stirring renditions of battles at sea. Not all of the great 'incidents' were represented – *The Graphic* in particular deplored the absence of familiar battle scenes, demanding to know where was the 'Battle of Mons'? – but the breadth of coverage could not be ignored. Nor has it been since.

In its comprehensive coverage of the war, and with its many outstanding large works by major twentieth-century artists, the Imperial War Museum collection of art complements, indeed rivals, the major collections of British art held across the river in what is now Tate Britain. This book tries to tell the individual stories of some of the artists who produced these extraordinary paintings and drawings. By locating them in their social, artistic and military context, I have tried to shed a little light on their motives and machinations, to understand something of what inspired them and also what frustrated them. Every one of the artists discussed in this book was changed forever by the war, not all for the good. As we shall discover, several received wounds or illnesses that blighted their later years; others never recovered from the slights they felt at the hands of those who bossed them around or who failed to give them the support they felt was their due. Yet, however sad and difficult these war years were, they were also colourful, energising and, at times, iconoclastic. Official patronage released many outstanding young artists from grindingly dull and dangerous military duty; it also gave them a level of artistic freedom that they would later regard as seminal to their careers. Few of these artists would have wholly agreed with Ruskin that 'There is no great art possible to a nation but that which is based on battle', but many of them – Nash, Nevinson, Orpen, Lewis, Lamb and Spencer – forged extraordinary and unforgettable work out of the cauldron of the Great War.

---

86 In *The Burlington Magazine*, a critic thought most of the work free from 'bombast or false sentiment', and lauded the air of 'honest observation', adding that there were 'as many examples as might reasonably be expected of real emotion appropriately expressed'. And while conceding that the general level of excellence in the principal rooms was high, concludes rather sourly that 'if there are no really great pictures there are a number of glorious failures.' ('X', 'A Monthly Chronicle: The Imperial War Museum: Exhibition of War Paintings and Other Records', *The Burlington Magazine*, Volume 36, 1920, pp.94–95). For full accounts of this exhibition see: Sue Malvern, *Modern Art, Britain and the Great War*, and Richard Cork, *A Bitter Truth*.

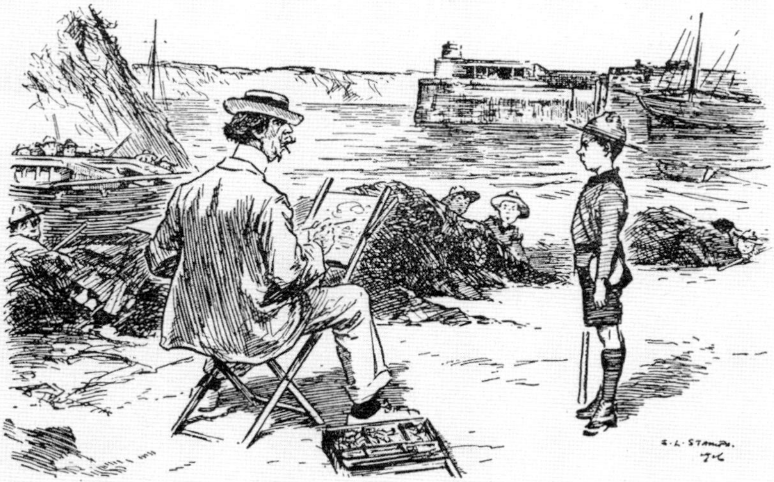

BOY SCOUT. "Sketching the harbour's not allowed."
ARTIST. "Confound you! My name's Cadmium Brown, and——"
BOY SCOUT. "Carry on, then. We've got orders to treat you as harmless."
(*November 8, 1916*)

from *Punch*, 8 November 1916

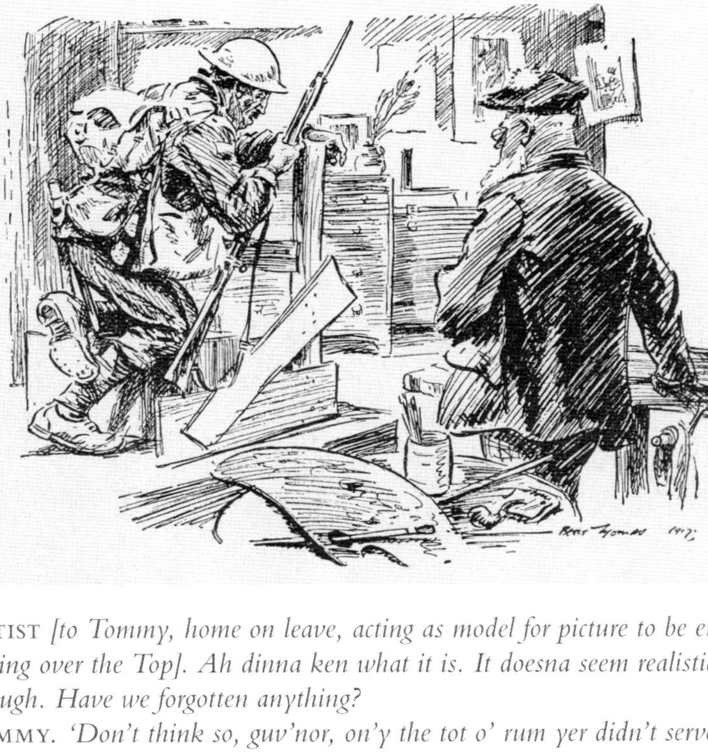

ARTIST *[to Tommy, home on leave, acting as model for picture to be entitled Going over the Top]. Ah dinna ken what it is. It doesna seem realistic enough. Have we forgotten anything?*
TOMMY. *'Don't think so, guv'nor, on'y the tot o' rum yer didn't serve aht.'*

from *Punch*, 2 January 1918

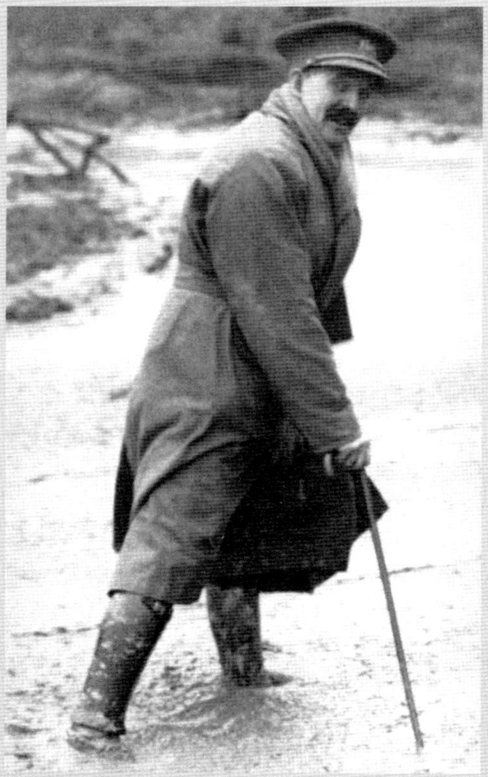

Muirhead Bone on the Somme,
sketchbook under his arm, 1916

Fact and fiction on the Western Front
Muirhead Bone on the Somme

During the Great War, studios of illustrators and desk-bound artists worked busily in Fleet Street concocting visual accounts of battles they had not seen, drawing events they had only read or heard about. Despite their best efforts, some of their work was risible. The 'special artist' Frederick Villiers, who had a previously distinguished career as a roving reporter-cum-illustrator, was reduced to depicting a patrol in No-Man's-Land carrying 'portable trenches'.[1] In another full-page sketch for the *Illustrated London News*, published on 15 May 1915, soldiers are shown finding their way across the benighted battlefield by following lines of suspended glass bottles each illuminated by small candles.[2] So distant were many of these depictions from the actualities of war that nearly all carried a cautionary note – 'Drawn by our special correspondent from information by one who was there' – so as to lend their fanciful images some semblance of authenticity.

Possibly the most eminent wartime illustrator, Fortunino Matania, was given frequent access to the war zones in France and Belgium, and he was blessed with an extraordinary visual memory. Yet, it is clear he saw little of the actual fighting and had to resort to visual aids to maintain the technical accuracy of his drawings. Indeed, he amassed so much material that some twenty years after the war he

1 *Illustrated London News*, 4 September 1915.
2 *Illustrated London News*, 15 May 1915.

was charged under the Firearm Act with the illegal possession of four rifles, a machine gun and several boxes of ammunition. In his defence he argued that he had been lent the material by the War Office to be 'used solely as models… so that the pictures should be correct in technical details'. Despite pleading guilty, the artist was exonerated and required to pay only the costs of £5 5 shillings. Dismissing the case, the magistrate Mr Griffith Jones assured the press that the case should cast no ill-light on Matania's character, recognising that the artist's pursuit of truth had even required him to dig a full-size trench in his garden in Potter's Bar.[3]

As one of the leading European illustrators of the first decades of the century Matania commanded immense authority as *the* authentic face of war. Those editors who commissioned and bought his work, valued the technical accuracy of his drawing and prized his nerveless rendition of warfare in all its guises. For them exactitude *was* truth.

Yet, one of the most contentious issues in the representation of the Great War was the matter of truthfulness, in particular the value placed on actually witnessing the conflict at first hand or at least being present at its immediate aftermath. As we have seen, Eric Kennington gained artistic credence from having been a front-line foot-soldier, authenticating his part in the war by depicting himself amongst his platoon in the snow outside Laventie. No matter that Kennington served for less than one hundred days, nor that he was invalided out with an accidental wound that some might consider a little dubious. His credentials as an artist and a combatant were beyond reproach, his service – however brief – gave a guarantee of authenticity, a special prerogative to depict the war, and his work set a standard that many wished to emulate. If we turn then, to two artists of similar age, background and experience – Muirhead Bone and Edward Handley-Read – we will see how they coped with the expectations placed upon them; expectations that focused on authenticity, visual testimony and the ability to describe war 'as it is'.[4]

---

3 Matania was born 1881, and studied under his father. At 14 he went to Milan as special artist to *Illustrazione Italiana*, at 22 worked for *Illustration Francais* and for *The Graphic*. At outbreak of war, aged 24, he joined the staff of *The Sphere* in London and became their 'official war artist' producing several hundred pictures for *The Sphere*, and for other illustrated papers and popular histories. He was awarded the Chevalier of Crown of Italy in 1918.

The incident about the court case was reported in *Daily Telegraph*, 3 December 1937. A more recent article in *The Times* (22 October 1977) focussed on his post-war work, when he became famous for his reconstructions of Biblical and Egyptian themes. The discovery of Tutankhamun's tomb bought him a rush of orders for pictures of life in dynastic Egypt. Cecil B de Mille commissioned the artist in the 1950s for images of the Biblical lands, so as to fuel his imagination while filming *The Ten Commandments*. The largest single collection of work by the artist is owned by Hollywood designer, Francis Matthews, who worked on de Mille's film. Matthews met Matania in the 1920s after a car collision.

An exhibition of Matania's work was staged by *The Illustrated London News* in 1971. A letter in the IWM file, written by Walter Mayes in November 1967, states categorically that Matania had no connection with the Official War Art scheme – 'his works are not eye-witness accounts, particularly one purporting to be behind the German lines.' Matania died in 1963. For reproductions of his work see Lucinda Gosling, *Brushes and Bayonets* (London, 2008).

MUIRHEAD BONE
'Too true to be good'

Let us start with a short aside on one of the tools of drawing. There is, perhaps, no artist's material more basic than charcoal. For centuries it has been made from willow or vine stalks that have been roasted, slowly burned in an air-tight container for over three days until the twigs are blackened and brittle, yet sufficiently strong to leave a delicate mark when drawn across white paper. Charcoal burned from vine wood produces a dark grey tone, while willow offers a deeper black. A stick – usually measuring a little over five inches (14 cm) – can be sharpened to the finest needle point, or used in broad swathes of tone that, in a practised hand, can give a pure wash of mid-tone grey.

Artists know that charcoal has many limitations: it lacks adhesion and can be blown off a piece of paper; it is fugitive and easily smudged; unless it is promptly fixed to the surface it can be accidentally brushed off by a sleeve. Without due care, a drawing can be ruined in seconds. This is perhaps why charcoal – even the fist-sized chunks preferred by scenic artists working in the theatre – has always been a preparatory medium, used to sketch out the opening strokes of a composition on canvas or as the soon-to-be hidden sub-structure of a drawing or painting. But it has the merit of speed. Unlike a pencil, a stick of charcoal stays sharp and glides easily across even the thickest of hand-made papers. It encourages confident, even adventurous drawing, and when used in combination with Indian ink or watercolour, it can assume a nobility of style that belies its humble origins as a snapped fragment of charred twig.[5]

When Muirhead Bone set out in the late summer of 1916 on his inaugural sketching trip to the Somme battlefield, he was equipped with little more than twigs of charcoal and a sketchbook of fine-quality drawing paper. He also carried with him a heavy burden of expectation. Bone's expedition from the comforts of General Headquarters was not only his personal debut on the sodden battlefields of the Somme but the first to be made by an official war artist commissioned by the British Government.

Born in Glasgow and apprenticed as an architect,[6] Bone had a solid, if unspectacular, reputation as a draughtsman and etcher.

---

4 'War as it is', is a phrase used by Charles Montague, defending Bone's work from the accusation that his drawings were too far removed from the realities of war. Sue Malvern's essay of the same title was published in *Art History*, Vol.9, No.4, December 1986, pp.487–515, and offers particular insights into the issue of authenticity and the special prerogative exercised by soldier-artists such as Eric Kennington (see also Sue Malvern, *Modern Art, Britain and the Great War*, p.14).

5 Artists have relied upon various fixatives to secure charcoal to paper; skimmed milk was apparently a favourite in the Italian Renaissance. Transparent matt varnishes are now widely used and have to be sprayed onto the paper.

6 Bone had taken up drawing at the age of twenty-two after a four-year apprenticeship as an architect, a profession for which he had little enthusiasm but which gave him a sound understanding of materials, construction and architectural scale.

His first folio of prints – published in 1904 – demonstrated a facility for capturing the complex architecture of cityscapes and earned him the enviable moniker of the 'London Piranesi'. Like the Italian master he was adept at rendering massive architectural spaces, often under construction or demolition. Where some artists might have demurred at the challenge of drawing ocean liners in a drydock or tens of thousands of shells in a munitions factory, Bone delighted in them; he was rarely intimidated by complex subjects and those who commissioned his work could always be sure that 'out of superficial chaos there [would] emerge a beautiful and ordered design'.[7] To many, Bone had the perfect credentials for his official appointment and, although thirty-eight years old at the outbreak of war, he was rescued from certain enlistment by the intervention of those in the art establishment who recognized what an asset his work might be if harnessed for pictorial propaganda for the Allied cause. Furthermore, Bone worked almost exclusively in black and white; his drawings were invariably small and their realistic intensity reproduced well in the government-funded publications of the day.[8]

Commissioned as an honorary 2nd Lieutenant, Bone arrived in northern France on 16 August 1916.[9] It was the height of the offensive on the Somme and he set to work immediately. Drawing in charcoal, pencil, pen and ink he worked out in the field, often in trying conditions, adding touches of brown or grey watercolour as he refined the drawings in his billet after a day's work. He was extraordinarily productive: between mid-August and early October he completed some 150 finished drawings, a work rate of roughly seventeen drawings a week. Despite this impressive start he was unnerved by the scale of the war and fretted about the limited range of his subject-matter, apologising for its lack of variety to his commissioners in London:

> I'm afraid that I have not done many ruins... But you must remember that on the Somme nothing is left after such fighting as we have had here – in many cases not a vestige of the village remains let alone impressive ruins![10]

So far, Bone had been touring the old front line in a chauffeur-driven car, but he began soon to set out on foot to see for himself

---

7 This phrase is from Bone's obituary in *The Times*, 23 October 1953. Bone's wife made it clear in her introduction to an exhibition catalogue at the IWM in 1967 that the contribution of the official war artist was always clear: 'that the subject should not be adapted to suit the special qualities of the artist, but rather that the artists should adapt themselves to meet the demands of the significant themes.'

8 One of Bone's blank canvases had been bought at an auction for the Red Cross by A.P. Watt, a leading London literary agent, who worked at Wellington House and learned of Bone's impending call-up. On 19 May 1916 he wrote to Masterman recommending that Bone be seconded to the propaganda department.

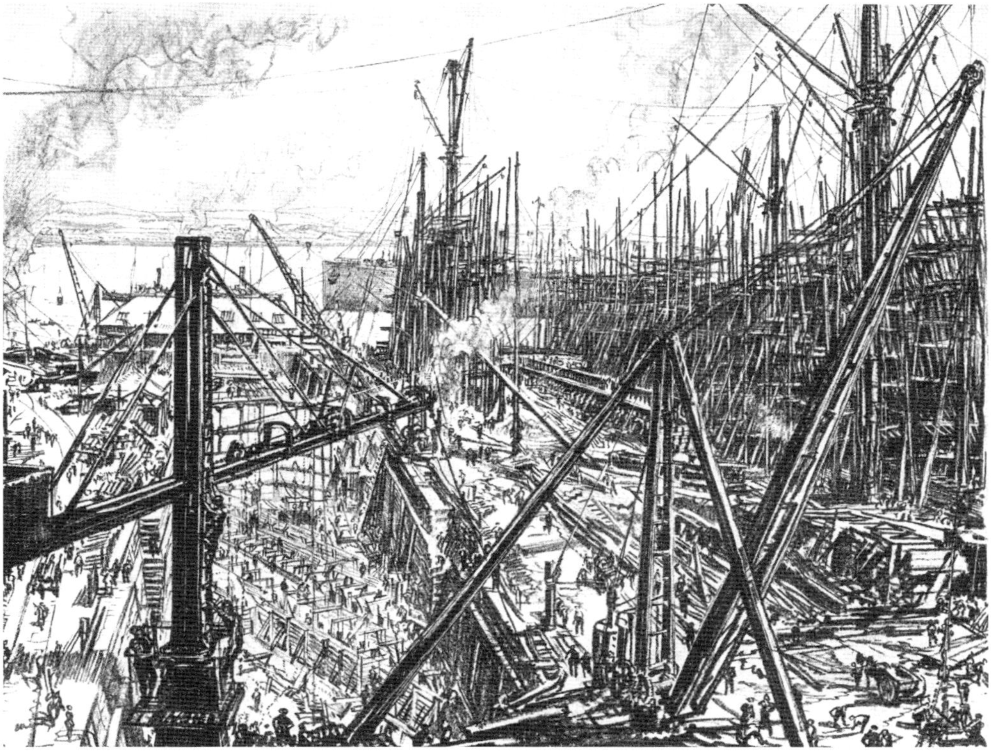

MUIRHEAD BONE
Ship in drydock

many of the infamous sites on the southern arc of the Somme battlefield – Delville Wood, Montauban, High Wood, Fricourt, Mametz Wood and Contalmaison. However, although the names remained on maps and on crudely painted signs, there was often little else to see. In fact, some of his most poignant images of the Western Front depict little more than gaps and absences. One drawing entitled *Chateau at Contalmaison* for example, depicts the remains of the fine woodland that once surrounded the residence but the centerpiece of the composition is a void; the eponymous chateau little more than a blunt stump of blasted stonework. Trained in the picturesque idiom, Bone nevertheless organised the composition so that the principal subject – the 'chateau' – is flanked in the foreground by symmetrical clumps of tree (the 'repoussoir' as they are known) which act as theatrical curtains drawing apart to reveal the missing splendours of the architectural subject. However, unlike some of the younger, more radical 'modern' artists who would soon tackle similar subjects, Bone was not being wilfully ironic. His flat, journalistic language, although ideally suited to mechanical reproduction for newspapers and posters, fell short of describing the newness of modern warfare. As one historian has noted, his drawings have the cold detachment of a 'travelogue composed by an uninvolved spectator'.[11] Bone was aware of his limitations and (to his lasting credit) later championed those younger painters who were prepared to grasp the artistic challenges that he felt were beyond him. In his own art he turned to the subjects he could do best: the teeming populations of soldiers behind the lines and those in support – the medical services, the repair and maintenance men, those who managed the complex logistics and the preparation for battle. Astonished at the resources and organisation needed to wage modern war, Bone saw how each infantryman in the front-line had to be supported by as many as ten men behind him, each one part of a system that stretched back many miles into the French and Belgian countryside where they toiled to amass provisions, supplies and ordnance to maintain the firepower of a distant trench. His best drawings reflected the industrial scale of the war effort: winding columns of men moving to the front, bulky artillery pieces taking

---

9 Wellington House exacted a good deal out of employing Bone, who could have commanded an annual salary of some £3,000–4,000. Instead he agreed to be paid £500 a year, plus travelling expenses and the right to make etchings from his drawings, in return for offering the British Museum unlimited choice of the originals and Wellington House the right of free reproduction for propaganda purposes for the duration of the war (Susie Harries and Merion Harries, *The War Artists*, p.10). Bone would have preferred a rank more befitting his seniority. He later wrote to Yockney that he was rather conscious of his 'bald head ... and my one pip!' (Bone to Yockney, 31 October 1918).

10 Bone to Ernest Gowers, 12 November 1916, File M999 pt.1, Imperial War Museum, Department of Art.

11 See Sue Malvern, *Modern Art, Britain and the Great War*, p.24. In conventional art terminology, the repoussoir is an object, motif or figure that is positioned to left and right of the foreground so as to lead the spectator's eye into the picture.

cover under avenues of trees, motorized divisions filling the *Routes Nationales*. Undaunted by this panorama of war, Bone's mastery of detail is extraordinary. His many drawings of troops resting behind the lines not only captured the individual character of the men but also their national, sometimes regional, origins. His ability to recreate the diversity of the troop population and the extent of the Empire's involvement set the agenda for later war artists – such as David Baxter and Adrian Hill – who were tasked to create an authoritative index of nationalities, groups, and occupations toiling away on the British sector of the Western Front.

Ironically, the most acclaimed drawing created by Bone on that first visit to the Front was not one of his bustling scenes in the 'rear zone', but one of his few 'action' pictures.[12] Drawn in his hallmark charcoal, *Tanks* is a little over 21 x 29 inches, and has the distinction of being the first drawing of this innovative war-machine after its inaugural combat on 15 September 1916. Bone's vision of this lumbering weapon shows the true versatility of his draughtsmanship. Seen from below, a leading tank dominates the horizon and appears ready to charge across the clear space ahead of it. This triangular part of the drawing is clean of charcoal marks so as to exaggerate the tonal difference between the metallic mass of the machine and the space it commands. In this single drawing we realise just how versatile Bone was in varying the ways that charcoal could be applied. Often messy and unstable, in the hands of an expert it can be used to produce a tight and exact line as well as fluid washes of tone. *Tanks* shows how Bone used the full range of charcoal from broad and calligraphic gestures in the lower foreground, to highly detailed notation on the tank's tracks and its armour. By using an eraser Bone also creates subtle tonal effects that suggest the directional energy of the machine, creating a spray of lighter marks immediately behind the tank, marks that suggest momentum and speed, and belie the tank's slowness, its notorious unreliability and jerking momentum.

When he used charcoal in broad swathes of tone, Bone was able to suggest something of the proximity to the front-line and the dangers of the Western Front without ever really showing soldiers fighting or artillery shells finding their mark. In a sketch of *Mametz Wood* he does not attempt to capture much detail. Instead, using the broadest gestures on a coarse paper he loosely renders the broken earth of a trench parados and the heaped sandbags of the parapet to give us what one commentator, rather playfully, describes as 'a rousing glimpse of trench life at a moment of action'.[13] The distant and

12 *Tanks*, charcoal on paper, 53.4 x 73.6 cm. IWM: ART 2121.
13 'Trench Scenery', *The Western Front*, Vol.III, March 1917.
14 Sue Malvern, *Modern Art, Britain and the Great War*, p.26.
15 *Manchester Guardian*, 30 August 1917.

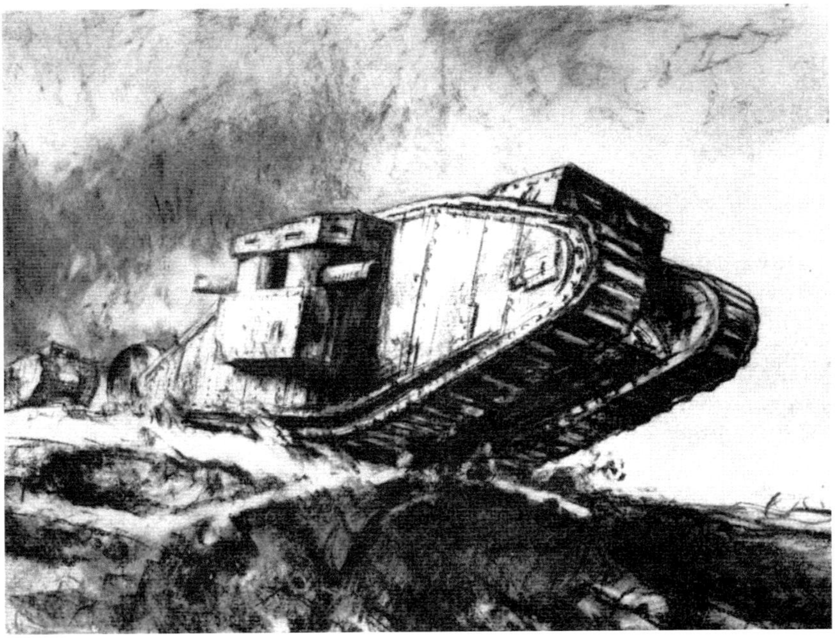

MUIRHEAD BONE
Tanks
(c.1916)
charcoal, 54.6 x 75 cm

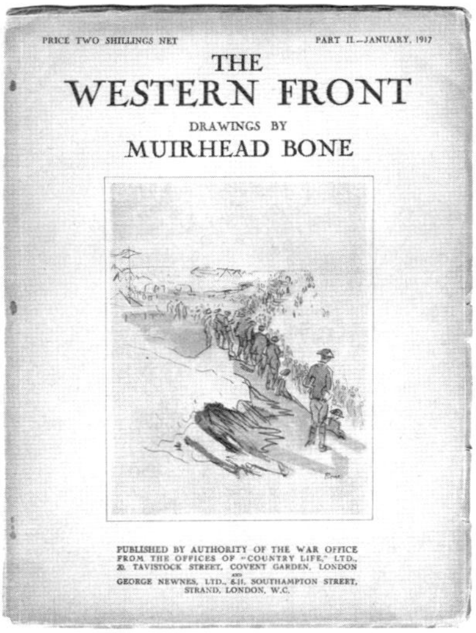

The Western Front
(January 1917)

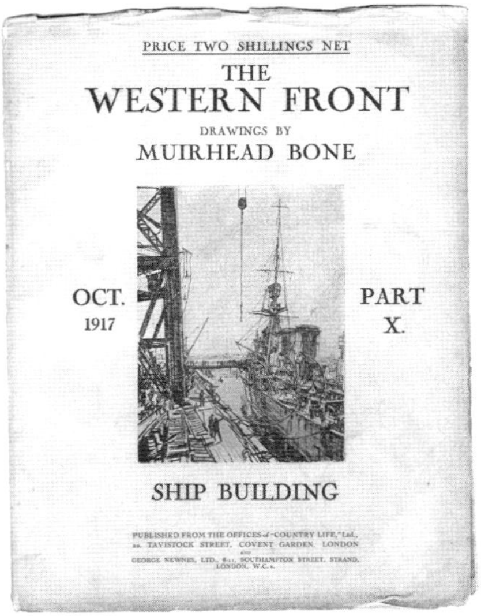

The Western Front
(October 1917)

dangerous copse of shattered trees is suggested by abbreviated – but always accurate – patterns of upright strokes, and the densest concentration of charcoal is restricted to the trench itself where a band of deepest black is twice punctuated by concisely drawn figures safely huddled beneath the top edge of the sandbags. Despite its painterly flourishes this is a tense image; a front-line snapshot apparently seized in a few minutes of focused concentration. Another of his Somme drawings – a panorama of an artillery barrage – was equally welcomed by those in charge of pictorial propaganda, even though it drew on rather hackneyed conventions of topographical art. The lack of finish in these drawings from 1916 lent an air of unquestionable authenticity which delighted those at Wellington House who had sent him to the Front. The broad handling of the charcoal evoked immediacy and honesty, emphasising that the work was 'unpretentious, genuine and personally observed, not fabricated'.[14]

All in all, the drawings from his first visit had met their expectations: they had the thrill of authenticity underpinned by a commanding draughtsmanship; the work was factual as well as moderate in its portrayal of a brutal war. However, back home not everyone agreed that this was how war should be recorded. Even after his second visit to the Western Front in 1917, there were many who felt that his representation of the conflict was too distant – even remote – and although Bone was deemed to have successfully caught the awesome scale of events, his battlefield drawings were held to be shorn of the actualities of front-line life, and death. One reviewer wrote cleverly they were 'too true to be good'. Another said they were 'like a peep at the war through the wrong end of the telescope'.[15] It may well have been Bone's work that earned the ridicule of the young Wilfred Owen when, on home leave, he scorned those 'Somme pictures'.[16]

Those at Wellington House who had championed Bone went to pains to stress their front-line credentials. To this end, his drawings were packaged during 1916–17 as a series of part-works called *The Western Front,* under the imprint of *Country Life* magazine so as to mask its official funding. Each of the 16 issues of *The Western Front* was printed in an edition of some 30,000 copies – 12,000 for sale in Britain, 6,000 for distribution in USA; the remainder for myriad uses as pictorial propaganda. Bone's reproductions proved popular and exhibitions of the originals attracted sizeable attendances: over 25,000 visitors went in one week to see an exhibition of drawings in Sheffield. The master stroke, though, lay not in the cloak-and-dagger

16 Letter written by Wilfred Owen, 19 January 1917, quoted by Edmund Blunden, *Memoir*, 1931. Others would not have agreed: the young painter John Nash wrote from the trenches in 1917 to ask his girlfriend 'Have you seen Muirhead Bone's drawings out here. I think they are good, how I wish I could be allowed to do the same.' Letter XIV, *Love letters from the Front: John Nash to Christine Kuhlenthal, France 1916–1917* (eds. Allen Freer and Peter Widdowson), Gloucester: Cyder Press, 2007, p.37.

antics of Wellington House, but the recruitment of the journalist and leader writer for the *Manchester Guardian*, Charles E. Montague, an intelligence officer now responsible for conducting visitors around the trenches of the British lines. Forty-seven years old at the outbreak of war, married with seven children, a man described by H.G. Wells as 'a real gentleman… with a most adventurous intelligence', and with brief service as a soldier in the front-line to his credit, indeed Montague merits a biography of his own, rather than being seen merely as an adjunct to Bone.[17] Although he had been a consistent advocate of his newspaper's anti-war line, in December 1914 he dyed his grey hair and joined the London-based 24th (Sportsmen's) Battalion, Royal Fusiliers inspiring the memorable words of a fellow correspondent: 'We had often heard of men whose dark hair had gone white through fear but Montague was the only man whose white hair had turned dark through courage.'[18] Injured in a bomb-training accident, Montague returned to France in July 1916 to join the Intelligence Department at GHQ as a liaison (or conducting) officer for British war correspondents. Although his primary role was to censor press reports and collate military information, he became notorious for his guided tours of the front-lines where he subjected his guests to what he (rather modestly) termed 'several graduated degrees of exposure'.[19] By every account these were hair-raising escapades. Bone recalled one visit to an advanced dressing station in the cellars of the wrecked chateau of Contalmaison where, on a slight slope in the land, they ate their lunch while surveying a British attack unfolding before them:

> Below us was the battle and despite the mesmerism of Montague's calm elation at the scene, my sandwiches and my teeth didn't seem to keep proper time together. The day was brilliantly hot, and close to us some soldiers had taken the fancy to bathe in the rusty pools, and my dazed head was full of the impression that their naked figures made an odd sort of foreground to a modern battle.[20]

In October 1916, a day after he had returned from a round trip to England to collect a troupe of visiting Japanese generals around the

17 As a Grenadier-Sergeant Montague claimed to have 'liked the trench life', although he found the 'scenery beastly'. Letter to Oliver Elton, 8 May 1916, written whilst on leave.

18 Henry W. Nevinson, quoted in Oliver Elton, *C.E. Montague – A Memoir* (London: Chatto and Windus, 1929). An obituary notice in the *Manchester City News* later noted, 'No greater and richer event came to this scholar and peace lover than the War, which found him a willing combatant, then an onlooker and historian, in the end a brooding moralist.' *Manchester City News*, 2 January 1928.

19 Montague to his wife 19 October 1916, quoted by Oliver Elton, p.148. Keith Grieves suggest that Montague gained a diverse – perhaps even unique – range of experiences during the war, which included trench life in 1915, propagandist in 1916, expert observer and interpreter of artillery battles in 1917. See Keith Grieves, 'C.E. Montague, Manchester and the Remembrance of War, 1918–1925', *Bulletin of the John Rylands University Library of Manchester*, Vol.77, No.2, summer 1995, pp.85–104.

front-lines – 'all bespangled and twinkling with orders and medals', he explained his motives to his wife:

> I feel a kind of grudge against the mere sightseer who comes out to see the war as a sort of show, accompanied by all sorts of luxury and petting. It seems they were rather scared at the place I had brought them to on Sunday, where the shells were falling all about, and I have been rebuked, not very gravely, for imperiling the army's guests – not very gravely, because I think we all feel in our hearts that the sightseer's only chance of saving his soul alive is that he should get a taste, if only for a few minutes, of the kind of thing that our soldiers are bearing all day.[21]

Few of his distinguished guests shared his 'craze for being under fire' nor his taste for 'warm corners' (to borrow Bernard Shaw's phrase).[22] Bone, however, was especially fond of him, valuing his brief friendship as 'a prize to be cherished, something to boast of'. In a short but astute memoir of the writer, the artist saw something of a mirror image in age, rank, and background, but most crucially in their shared role as 'incomparable spectators'. Indeed, in this passage Bone could almost be writing about himself:

> Yet who could equal his zest, those days on the Somme, when his duty – a duty too good to be true – took him along the front as a spectator? He was an incomparable spectator, watching everything with a keen exaltation of all his senses. Sympathetic visitors must sometimes have suspected that their conductor would have been a still happier man if they had tactfully faded out of existence and left him to his uninterrupted observation... His salute as a brother-at-arms was a joy – he had the artist's passion for getting the thing just right. I suppose we must have looked a singular pair of elderly second lieutenants.[23]

A familiar figure at General Headquarters (in fact, Bone once heard Haig allude to Montague as our 'white haired lieutenant') and revered as 'perhaps the best journalist in England', he was tasked with drafting short texts to accompany Bone's drawings. Although he later dismissed them as 'drivelettes of letterpress'[24] his captions

---

20 Bone recalls a story of Montague earnestly taking H.G. Wells around the trenches under the illusion that 'such a guest could not but want to see everything'. Wells may have been less than earnest, for Bone recalls the distinguished writer returning 'up to his eyes in mud, and. I think, missing his boat.' (Quoted by Elton, p.138)

21 Somewhat self-mockingly, Montague considered himself to be 'one of the best equipped guides to the battlefield in existence after the war, and could make quite a decent subsistence by taking millionaire Americans round it for the rest of our lives'. Letter to his wife 25 September 1916.

22 Quoted in Elton, p.162. Bone revered Montague's calm steadfastness: 'To us of the weaker knees it seemed to breathe the very words, 'Keep calm, and it won't hurt you. He had the complete calm of a man whose courage of mind and heart liberated him from all anxieties.' (Quoted in Elton pp.138–9)

23 Quoted in Elton, p.139.

24 Letter to Oliver Elton, 10 May 1919, quoted in Elton, p.236.

are models of their type, informative without being laboured, precise as well as elegant:

> At most parts of the line a man in the front trench is cut off from landscape. To look at a tree behind the enemy's lines may be to give a mark to a sniper hidden in its boughs. By day you see the upper half of the dome of the sky, and through loopholes, a few yards of rough earth or chalk, then the nebulous wire, and through its thin places, perhaps a few uniforms, blue, grey or brown, lying beyond, among the coarse grass and weeds. At night you see all the stars well, and on moonlight nights, if you walk the trench softly, you can watch strange friezes sharply silhouetted on the sky line of the parapet, the wars and loves of capering rats 'flouting the ivory moon'.[25]

Written in the style of a travel writer, Montague's carefully chosen words re-present Bone's drawing as illustrations for a guidebook to the Western Front. This is largely because Montague knew they were intended for a home audience – 'armchair tourists' – who had no wish, nor the means, to see these 'non-places' for themselves, but who were familiar with the names and had a sort of dread fascination for the dystopia of the Western Front. Montague took Bone's vast *oeuvre* and reshaped it into familiar, even comforting, narratives. Take for example, the text to accompany Bone's loose charcoal and watercolour wash of the shattered Mouquet Farm near Thiepval – a drawing he entitled *A Via Dolorosa*. In Montague's imaginative hand it becomes a road marked with 'improvised memorials… tragic and noble finger-posts', which took on the mantle of the 'Stations of the Cross of soldierly self-sacrifice'.[26] His knack of describing complicated scenes exactly matched the dexterity of Bone's draughtsmanship. Here, for example are two captions that accompanied drawings made by Bone at Boulogne; writing that is detailed and realistic, but above all reassuring; in fact they are paradigms of the essential English qualities of stoicism and decency:

> *Taking the wounded on board*
> Wounded men from the Somme ordered to England by the Medical Officer commanding the General or Stationary Hospital in which each man has been a patient, are being put on board a hospital ship at the base. In the centre of the foreground is seen the timber framework of the ship's large red cross of electric lights. With this, and the tier of some sixty green lights running from stem to stern, a hospital ship at night is a beautiful as well as an unmistakable object at sea.

25 *Trench Scenery*, February 1917.
26 *The Western Front*, Volume Two, July 1917, notes to plate XLVII.

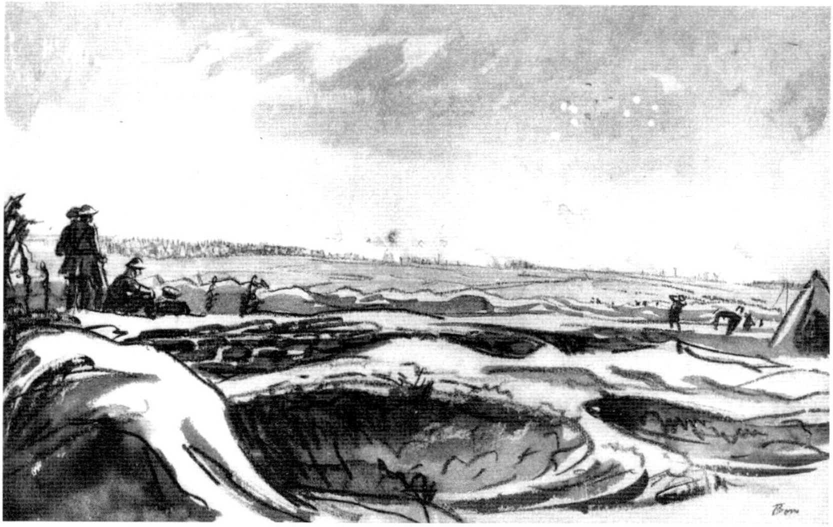

MUIRHEAD BONE
The Battle of the Somme
(1916)
pencil and wash, 33 x 51 cm

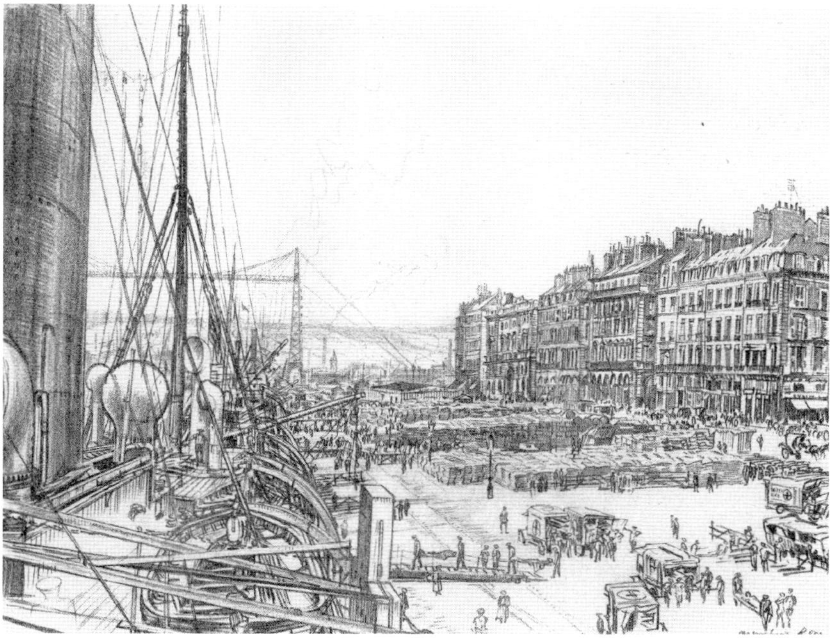

MUIRHEAD BONE
Taking the Wounded on Board
(1916)
pencil and wash, 33 x 51 cm

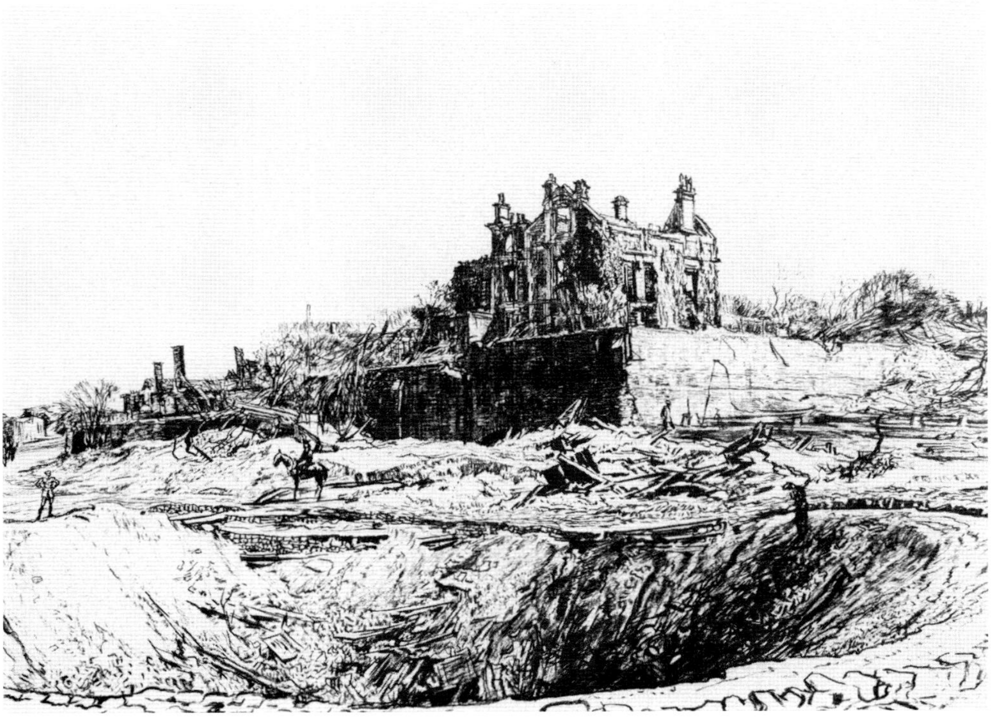

MUIRHEAD BONE
The Great Crater, Athies, May 1917
(1917)
conté crayon charcoal on paper, 56.2 x 76.2 cm

> *A British Red Cross depot at Boulogne*
> Dead low water at Boulogne Harbour, and a slack time for the motor ambulances parked on the quay above. The work of the R.A.M.C. inevitably comes in rushes, with lulls in between. The great thing is, when a rush comes, to treat every case with a rapidity exactly proportioned to its urgency, removing instantly to the base hospitals or to England every serious case which will be the better, or none the worse, for a slight delay in operation. To work this system perfectly there must always be in readiness, at every point where wounded are entrained or transhipped, a supply of ambulances equal to the maximum call.

In the late autumn of 1916, as the weather deteriorated, Bone wanted to switch to drawing the munitions factories in Britain where, on more familiar ground, he knew he would revel in their cavernous interiors and complicated apparatus.[27] Aware that other artists were already at work in these demanding settings, he was keen to pit his artistic wits on the intricate fretwork of aeroplane construction and the epic scale of gun manufacture. And true to form, his drawings of this period are majestic in their understanding of the industrial sublime.[28] Several months later, in March 1917, he worked for three weeks with the Grand Fleet at Rosyth recording every aspect of life at sea, from the warlike – practice firing, stretcher drill, gun laying – to the less martial, such as his sketch of *A Cinema on Board a Battleship, HMS Repulse.*

Bone returned to Flanders in mid-April 1917. He was discouraged from returning to the old Somme battlefield – now dismissed by GHQ as 'a little stale'[29] – and was instead directed to the land reclaimed after the Germans withdrew to the Hindenburg Line. Having failed to find any grand ruins during his first visit he was almost overcome by the thoroughness and the extent of the chaos wrought by the retreating enemy. He was quite overwhelmed by subject-matter. Over the next six weeks he roamed the area, recording the systematic despoliation of the countryside – statues neatly decapitated, entire orchards painstakingly sawn down, stained glass windows blown out of churches, cottages and farmsteads expertly ransacked, vast tracts of land methodically spoilt. To meet these

27 Bone's anxiety to turn to these demanding subjects is partly explained by his ambition to match others who had taken on similar subjects. He wrote to Masterman: 'To tell truth I feel that these scenes of great works are particularly my own and I would much like to have a 'go' at them and to prove that I could do better than Pennell!' (Bone to Masterman, 12 November 1916, M999 part 1). American lithographer Joseph Pennell (1861–1926) had taken it upon himself to visit munitions factories and in return for arranging these visits, Wellington House had use of the prints as reproductions in its propaganda publications.

28 Returning to England in December 1916, Bone spent two months working in munitions factories in Coventry and Middlesbrough, and at Chilwell, Nottinghamshire, National Filling Factory No.6, the site of a terrible explosion on 1 July 1918.

29 Quoted in Meirion Harries and Susie Harries, p.11.

challenges he modified his drawing style: gone were the broad sweeps of charcoal and the washes of watercolour that summarised the Somme mud-scapes. Instead he employed finer-tipped drawing tools – sharpened charcoal, pen and ink – to lend a neat delineation to his images, as if he were more conscious of making a neutral log or inventory of the wanton damage. In fact, the fractured ruins of shattered chateaux, collapsed church towers, and the sawn branches of orangerie and orchard were better suited to his precise draughtsmanship, and gave full vent to his artful organization of dereliction. His rendition of *The Great Crater*, at Athies, drawn in May 1917, offers a pictorial truthfulness that could rarely be matched by contemporary photographers.[30] With his usual zealous attention to detail, Bone catalogued the chaos of the scene; his mastery of texture and tonality proof of someone at the height of his form, both fascinated by the bizarre subjects around him but also repelled. Given the painterliness of his first portfolio of Somme charcoal drawings, one can barely believe it possible that the same medium could be stretched to make so many different marks and evoke so many different surfaces, from the clutter in the crater, to the fine brickwork supporting the damaged house with the ivy creeper still clinging to its gable ends.

Twenty-five years later Bone would again serve as an official war artist – one of the few to achieve this distinction – and he was continually hurried to scenes of devastation in Britain's bombed cities before the clearance and salvage workers had a chance to 'spoil' the aesthetic effect. 'Damage by bombing' asserted a member of the war artists' committee, 'is most spectacular when seen soon after the event'.[31] And, as in the Great War, Bone's accomplished, almost nerveless, observational skills produced microscopically detailed drawings that were unflinching in their exactitude: 'The kind of document,' noted Kenneth Clark, 'one would produce as evidence before a commission on bomb damage.'[32]

If Bone's second set of front-line drawings substituted a general sense of place with increasing detail and particularity it was not achieved without considerable effort. In fact, Bone's reserve of energy was slowly being wasted by long, exhausting days in the field. In May 1917 he shared a car with the somewhat irascible John Masefield, author of *The Old Front Line* and later Poet Laureate, who grumpily recalled a long wait for the 'Scotch etcher' who had wandered off to complete even more drawings:

---

30 *The Great Crater, Athies*, May 1917, charcoal on paper, 55.8 x 76.2 cm. IWM: ART 2164.

31 E.M. O'Rourke Dickey to Randolph Schwabe, 17 November 1940. Both men were members of the War Artists' Advisory Committee; Dickey was the secretary; Professor Schwabe was Henry Tonks's successor at the Slade School of Art. Kenneth Clark considered Bone to be 'one of the most honest, warm-hearted and unselfish men I have ever known'. Kenneth Clark, *Another Part of the Wood: a Self-portrait* (London: John Murray, 1974) p.59.

32 Kenneth Clark to Duncan Grant, 7 July 194, quoted by Susie and Meirion Harries, p.186.

> When he [Bone] had drawn Mouquet [Farm], & he only drew the cellar or tank laid bare by a shell, not the ghastly & heroic heaps which killed our men, he wanted to do Thiepval, so I took him there & left him on the castle ruins (a heap of earth). It was now 1, & time for lunch. He had left his lunch in the car 2 or 3 miles away. There was nothing for it but to give him half mine, which I did. We agreed to meet at 3.30 at a dump in the valley... I went up to see the Stuff Redoubt, which wasn't much of a place, & the Hohenzollern redoubt, which was the devil of a place, all sunken concrete machine gun emplacements as wicked as hell... Then at 3.15 I went down to the dump & waited. The d___d Scotch etcher never turned up till 5.15, so I lost half my lunch, all my tea, & nearly all my time for writing, so you may guess the mood I was in... Never again, if I can help it, does a Scotch etcher make me wait 2 hours on a dump.[33]

Masefield's cutting remark that Bone avoided the unpalatable brutality of the war became a common theme amongst many who felt that his front-line trench drawings, with their flower pots and their sentimental name boards – 'Ye Rat Hole', 'The Ritz' – failed to reflect the suffering of the soldiers. Certainly, Bone saw death and misery: it occasionally creeps into the captions for some of his drawings – 'perforated helmets, fragments of shell... broken stretchers, boots not quite empty' – but Bone lacked the creative nerve to summarily include the obscenities of war, a dilemma that faced many official artists both then and as recently as the Falklands Conflict.[34] Linda Kitson, the artist travelling with the Task Force in 1982, had to decide which aspects of war to record. At the site of the Battle of Goose Green she reminded herself:

> My brief was to record the sights that might be recognised as common experiences. I decided then that the horrifying sight of parts of human bodies, a helmet with a head still in it – pictorially sensational and relevant though they were – were not part of my brief; neither were the war graves, which were recorded on news film and in photographs.[35]

Similarly, in Bosnia in 1994 the official war artist Peter Howson recognized the limitations of mere reportage. 'My job,' he argued, 'is to do the things you don't see, that the army doesn't even get to see.' Refusing to be a mere 'illustrator' he flinched from sketching

33 John Masefield to his wife, 1 May 1917, in Constance B. Smith, *John Masefield: A Life* (New York, 1978).

34 The description of 'perforated helmets, fragments of shell...' is in the caption text for *Ruined Trenches in Mametz Wood*, in the introduction to the second volume of *The Western Front* (1918) – 'War as it is'.

35 In her book on the Falklands War Kitson pondered her attitude at the time: 'I still question that decision. Would it have been a stronger, cautionary record if I had used such shock tactics?' (Linda Kitson, *The Falklands War: A Visual Diary*, London: Mitchell Beazley in association with the Imperial War Museum, 1982, p.65).

the bloodied residue of a roadside atrocity, preferring to absorb such dreadful scenes and later re-create them into strong and memorable paintings and drawings.[36] Like Bone, he recognized that the sketchbook was simply inadequate to the task: yet unlike Bone, Howson was never constrained by his own literal-ness; rarely tempted to be seduced by outward appearances. Montague, of course, was well accustomed to the charge that Bone was a slave to superficiality, a mere illustrator ignoring the realities of war. As a writer who understood how 'one's standard of horribleness changes with circumstances',[37] he tussled with these questions of principle in the midst of censoring reports and interviewing generals. In late 1917, irritated by a scathing review of Bone's *Western Front* exhibition, he challenged the view, which was then in vogue, that 'everybody writing out here keeps back all sorts of untold horrors of physical suffering from people at home', arguing (not altogether convincingly) that:

> ... just as in ordinary life one does not go out of the way to describe details of a friend's death by cancer or locomotor ataxy. So one does not keep harping on details of incised, contused, and lacerated wounds and of the special agonies one has seen in some few cases. But why should one?[38]

'To see carnage,' he wrote in a subsequent letter to his wife, 'isn't a revelation at all – it's only verification,' and he asserted that his previous detestation of war would be just as firmly held at the end of the fighting.[39] Despite this steadfastness Montague entertained personal doubts, and these surfaced in some of his picture captions. In the *Introduction* to the Second Volume of Bone's drawings he hinted that were the public to be told and shown the ghastly realities of war – 'as it is' – the consequences would be cataclysmic, indeed, 'if leaked out, would make the world lay down its arms on the spot'.

Equally professional and resolute, Bone continued to churn out dozens of drawings in all weather, but by later summer 1917, just over one year after taking on the mantle of *the* British Official War Artist, he was more or less burnt-out.[40] 'I watched him the other day,'

36 'I'm not aiming to be controversial. But I wanted to cut out all the reportage. It's not my job to do that. My job is to do the things you don't see, that the army doesn't even get to see, not be an illustrator, not to tell stories, but to produce strong images of things.' Peter Howson quoted in Robert Crampton, 'Facing Fear: Peter Howson in Bosnia', essay in the catalogue *Peter Howson: Bosnia* (Imperial War Museum, London, 1994).

37 Montague to his wife, 1 August 1917, quoted in Elton, p.142.

38 Montague to his wife, 5 September 1917, in Elton pp.193–4.

39 Montague to his wife, 3 October 1917, in Elton, p.194.

40 There is one large drawing in the Imperial War Museum dated as 'Passed by the censor 6 11 17' on which Bone has written 'Drawn on Lithographic paper, pouring rain' and the image – of a dreary road at the front – is now badly cracked.

wrote his wife, 'looking at a pencil as though he didn't know what to do with it... Isn't it possible for the Authorities to consider that 500 drawings in a year ought to be counted for an artist's righteousness and to let him have space to breathe?'[41]

Looking back at Bone's appointment we now realise that it was a watershed in the history of government patronage of artists. The success of his work lay in its apparent veracity and the seemingly unambiguous reportage of places and events. Montague's skilful texts both interpreted and endorsed the authenticity of the drawings, underpinning Bone's integrity as a neutral recorder, even though his drawings are, in fact, selective interpretations of carefully chosen subjects.[42] While the art press was less enthusiastic, the public flocked to see his work. Bone had proved that artists could cope (indeed prosper) in the adverse conditions of the front and produce newsworthy images. Much of his best work on the Western Front had a freshness and spontaneity which benefited from being started and finished *en plein air* and this principle of witnessing an event or a place soon became enshrined in the commissioning policy of the Department of Information and its successors. By comparison, reconstructions, fabrications and second-hand interpretations were held in deep mistrust and consigned to those with over-fertile imaginations ungrounded in the actualities of war, namely the Fleet Street 'studio' artists.[43]

'BY ONE WHO WAS THERE'?

There can be absolutely no doubt that Muirhead Bone saw for himself the sites and stations of the Western Front. On one occasion he was photographed ankle-deep in a vast pool of glutinous mud on the Somme, half-turned to the camera and leaning heavily on a walking stick to steady himself. There were in fact many, many others who wanted to be there too, no matter how thick the mud or how grim the surroundings. A file in a cabinet at the Imperial War Museum contains sheathes of letters from artists pleading to be permitted to visit the Front, to witness the devastation before (as one of them wrote rather tactlessly) 'it is all mended and tidied up...'[44]

Edward Harry Handley-Read was 46 at the outbreak of war; eight years older than Bone, two years younger than Montague.

41 Gertude Bone to Yockney, 18 August 1917: Bone file, IWM, Dept. of Art.

42 Especially insightful in this respect is Sue Malvern, *Modern Art, Britain and the Great War*, pp.24–29.

43 The most thorough analysis of the Fleet Street 'special' artists-reporter is Peter Johnson, *Front Line Artists* (London: Cassell, 1978).

44 These are the words of painter Rowland Henry Hill who was equally desperate to visit the front 'to make some record of our true battlegrounds and of all the immensely picturesque material.' (IWM Dept. of Art file 156/5 part II). For a short appraisal of Hill's adventure see: Paul Gough, 'The Landscape at War' *The Independent*, 1 July 1991.

His name can be found in a long list of British artists 'Serving with the Forces' that was included in *The Studio* magazine in April 1915, although it was mis-spelt as 'Handley-Reed, E. Rifleman 8th Batt. Isle of Wight Rifles'. He served subsequently with the Artists' Rifles and exhibited with them at the Leicester Galleries, London in March 1916, and later transferred to the Machine-Gun Corps where he reached the rank of Captain. For much of the war he was based at the Machine Gun Training Camp, at Harrowby, near Grantham where as Quarter-Master Sergeant Instructor he ran his own studio producing instructional leaflets that helped explain the workings of the many machine-guns in use in the British Army. Possibly his most valuable contribution to the war effort were his 'cutaway' illustrations that displayed and explained the function of the Vickers Machine Gun. They were used for training purposes until the gun was withdrawn from service in the 1960s. He also drew and manufactured landscape targets – some as large as five feet by three – which were used for target indication and machine-gun training. His clear diagrammatic style and his ability to communicate clearly, without jargon, earned him a notable reputation, and many thousands of his leaflets and coloured diagrams were produced and circulated to all corners of the Empire. For this work he was later awarded the MBE.[45]

Like Bone, Handley-Read was endowed with prodigious energy: in addition to his training duties at Grantham, he produced many hundreds of charcoal and wash drawings of the Flanders battlefields. In 1916 he entered the history books as the first artist to exhibit war pictures of the British front. Staged at the Leicester Galleries in London, his exhibition – the first of three one-man shows of his war work – was entitled 'The British Firing Line' and featured seventy watercolour and charcoal drawings of the Western Front. Many of them were evocations of the battered landscape and included familiar landmarks – *The Crater at Hooge, The Ruins of Ypres, The Leaning Madonna at Twilight, Festubert Church in Ruins* – that Bone had also drawn.[46]

---

45 Handley-Read had studied at the Westminster School of Art and the Royal Academy Schools winning the RA Creswick Prize for Landscape Painting. He practised as a commercial artist, his work was published in *The Graphic* and *The Illustrated London News*, and he exhibited regularly at the Royal Academy and the Royal Institute. In the IWM Dept of Art, the file 'Handley-Read' contains biographical details from Yockney's notebook and an obituary from the *Sussex Daily News* (11 December 1955).

Handley-Read's artistic contribution to machine-gun training is largely unattributable. It is not possible to identify any of his art work in *Machine Gun Notes* (the MGC officer's 'bible'), or the *Machine Gunner's Pocket Book*. All, or almost all, of the sketches in both come from the Machine Gun Training Centre Studio. This may, or may not, be the 'Army Studio' which he is credited as having organized and was presumably one of the reasons for his being awarded the MBE. As the historian Peter T. Scott explains: 'I cannot but think that his most valuable contribution to "war art" were his cutaway and "exploded" drawings that displayed and explained the function of the Vickers Machine Gun. They went on being used for training purposes until the gun was withdrawn from service in the 1960s, although the later versions were modified and lacked his name or initials that appeared on the early examples.' Correspondence with author, April 2008.

There were also some powerful images of battle: *Killing Germans: the Machine Gun at Work,* an aeroplane under fire, a barrage on the Somme. The drawings have a strong sense of graphic realism, their colouring is muted but evocative, the sense of place and occasion is finely tuned. The shows were popular: a well-illustrated review in *The Graphic*, on 27 May 1916, praised his renditions of 'a country sullen, desolate and untenanted' and some time later *The Graphic* reproduced two studies of tanks under the banner headline 'the weirdest aspect of the war'[47] and urged its readers to 'see this remarkable collection of pictures which, both by reason of their artistic qualities and the subjects illustrated make a unique appeal'. Despite such praise, there is, however, a nagging doubt that Handley-Read ever experienced the front-line at first-hand.

The suspicion is first aroused by a short review in *The Times* (5 May 1916) which reported that: 'The artist has been helped by minute descriptions and material supplied to him by officers in different sections of the front.' The reviewer may have also noted the photographic verisimilitude of the work, a strong sense that there is something too perfect about the images, everything is too precise, too cleanly articulated and a little too polished. The titles and the words scribbled onto the drawings seem to suggest that they originated from first-hand observation and may have been re-worked in his studio in Grantham, but there is little evidence that they were manhandled around dirty trenches. Many artists, it is true, have strong visual recall or the ability to work up fully finished pictures from scrappy and cursory thumbnail notes, but other suspicions continue to undermine Handley-Read's front-line credentials.

In early 1916 at an exhibition staged in London by the Artists' Rifles, Handley-Read displayed an evocative image of a countryside ravaged by war. Reproduced in *The Studio*, praised by Hilaire Belloc as 'dealing faithfully with the greatest conflict in history', and reviewed in the *Observer* by no less a figure than Paul Konody, his large watercolour was described as a 'picture of a rutty, muddy road bordered by tattered trees [where] fighting has presumably taken place, and has left desolation in its wake'.[48] The word 'presumably' is telling, for we might well ask whether this is in fact an image of

---

46 His first exhibition, 'The British Firing Line' (catalogue no.229) held at the Leicester Galleries in May 1916, was hailed as the first show of war pictures of the British Front. A portfolio of facsimile prints selected from the 70 pictures in this show was published and widely advertised in the press. A second series of drawings – the 'Advance on the Somme' – were shown in May 1917 (catalogue no.241) and a third series of watercolour drawings 'The British Firing-Line in France and Flanders' (catalogue no.259) was held at the Alpine Club Gallery, Conduit Street, under the direction of Ernest Brown and Phillips (of the Leicester Galleries) in June and July 1918.

See Ernest Brown & Phillips Ltd., *The Leicester Galleries. An index of 1422 catalogues of exhibitions of European Modern Art and 20th Century British Art, held between 1902 and 1977*, available at: www.ernestbrownandphillips.ltd.uk

47 *The Graphic*, 14 April 1917.

48 *The Observer*, 16 January 1916; *The Studio*, March 1916.

military conflict at all. The fallen bough, the rutted track, and the plume of smoke might just as well suggest high winds, agricultural normality and prosperous village-life, as much as they imply the after-effects of an artillery barrage, troop movements, and civilian casualties. Handley-Read's choice of title – 'Somewhere in France' – has been carefully chosen to locate the image firmly in a war setting, but in this one example, it is easy to see how an innocuous landscape could be rendered more menacing by a wisp of smoke, a charred tree, and a lowering sky dotted with shell-bursts. Indeed, many of his first batch of drawings were militarized versions of landscapes drawn on sketching tours in Flanders before the war.[49]

Other doubts linger as to Handley-Read's authority as an eye-witness. In a file in the Imperial War Museum's Department of Art one of the artist's catalogues has been annotated by Alfred Yockney. Scribbled across one of the advertisements for Handley-Read's exhibition in 1916 are the cryptic words: 'Mond (?) says these not done on the spot.' (Sir Alfred Mond was Chairman of the Imperial War Museum; Yockney one of its key administrators.) In another file, there is a rather intense exchange of letters between the artist and a Colonel Marsh who had purchased one of Handley-Read's works. The officer suggested that the date and place of the drawing – Irish Farm, St Jean – were wrong, the artist was at least six months adrift and there was no action at this particular spot when it was being drawn, and furthermore the artist's unit was not even in France by the date of the action. Handley-Read defended the alleged error, citing the hurried arrangements for his show in London, but Marsh remained unconvinced and left a pointed note in the file.[50]

In a letter to the museum, written in December 1918, Handley-Read claimed to have been at the front on three separate occasions during hostilities. He was eager to see more: 'The subjects appeal to me immensely,' he wrote, 'I am very keen to get sketches of the areas I have not seen… to get as much pictorial record before the landscape alters.'[51] Inundated with similar requests the museum could not grant permission, especially for an unofficial artist with three London shows already to his credit. Like many painters, Handley-Read was clearly working under intense commercial pressures: his shows at the Leicester and Alpine Galleries had been successful, he had produced dozens of limited edition prints. His work had even been packaged as 'an interesting presentation gift, containing twelve selected

49 For a fuller examination of this habit see: Paul Gough, 'Drawing on the Devastation: Edward Handley-Read on the Western Front', *Journal of Western Front Association*, January 1998.

50 In the note appended to the artist's explanation Marsh argues that 'the date should apparently be April 1915 as there was no battle in Oct. *1915*, though the first battle of Ypres was in Oct. 1914 but the Artist's unit, a Hon. Artillery Column had not gone out then.' IWM Dept of Art, Handley-Read file; the artist responded to Colonel Marsh on 19 December 1920.

51 Handley-Read to Ffoulkes, 28 December 1919, file no.1019.

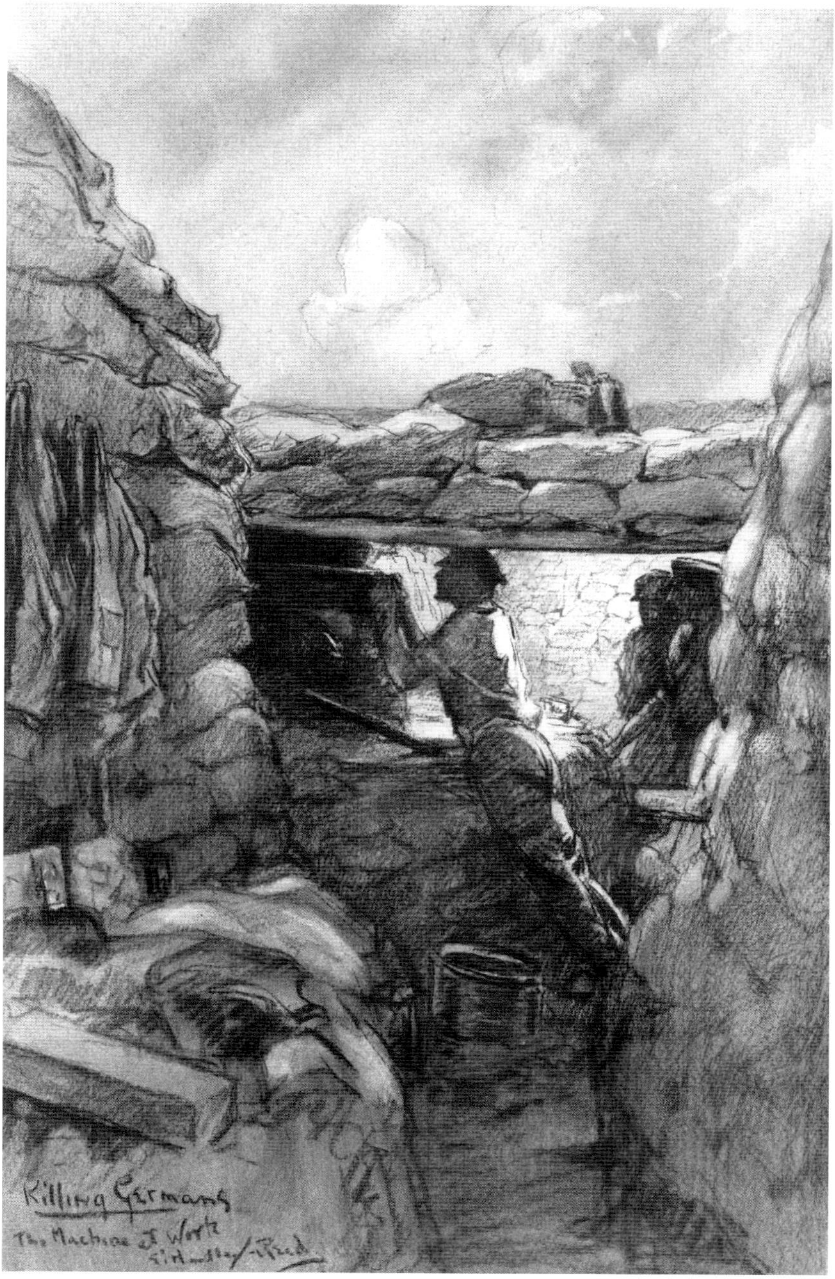

E HANDLEY-READ
Killing Germans: The Machine at Work
(1917)
charcoal watercolour on paper, 45.7 x 30.4 cm

IMPERIAL WAR MUSEUM

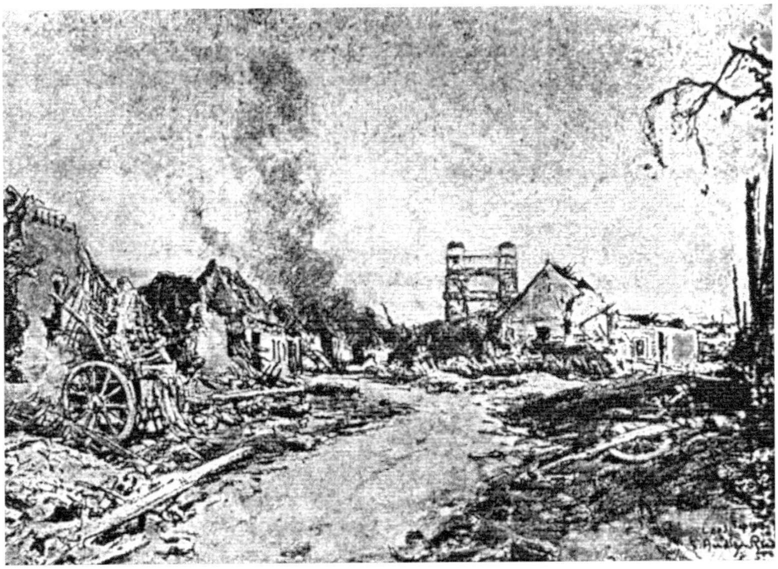

E HANDLEY-READ
Loos and Tower Bridge
(1915)

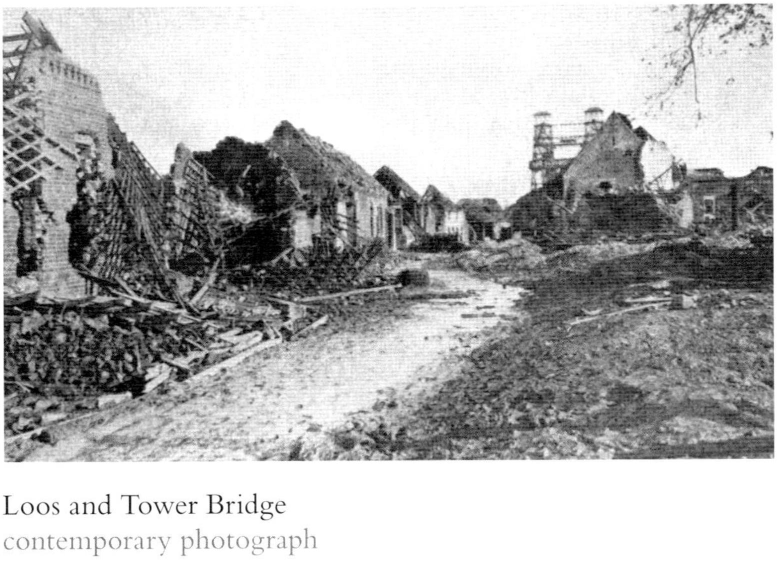

Loos and Tower Bridge
contemporary photograph

subjects reproduced in colour from the originals, with a foreword by Hilaire Belloc and photogravure of the artist' made available in a limited edition of 500 signed copies for five guineas.[52] The pressure to remain topical was intense and it is more than likely that Handley-Read supplemented his necessarily brisk visits to France and Belgium, by 'borrowing' liberally from photographic reproductions in the illustrated press.

His drawing *The Road to Loos* (exhibited in 1916) is identical in its design to a photograph that was widely reproduced in contemporary histories, such as *The Times History of the War* and the *Illustrated London News*,[53] even down to the inclusion of a large staff car in the middle distance. Even more striking is the resemblance between the artist's drawing of the landmark *Tower Bridge at Loos*[54] and an official photograph reproduced during the course of the war in such popular publications as Mumby's *The Great World War*.[55] To add a martial flavour, Handley-Read has added a plume of smoke in the buildings to the left of the winching tower (known as 'The Crystal Place' or 'Tower Bridge') and a bedraggled tree on the right. There are other examples – compare the artist's *Hill 60 and a German Barricade*,[56] with an identical photograph of *A German Barricade: The Enemy's Defence across Railway Cutting near Hill 60* which was published in the *Illustrated London News* in May 1915.[57] These are just a few of the many Handley-Read compositions that show the hallmarks of having been copied or collaged from a number of photographic sources. Others were complete fabrications: an encounter between a British Mark v tank and one of the few gigantic German ironclad machines would have been a rare sight indeed, but Handley-Read drew it, thus undermining his authority as a privileged 'eye-witness'.

There is, however, no deep shame in having done so. Clearly, Handley-Read was an indefatigable worker and was under considerable pressure from his gallery to produce ever more 'war'

---

52 Belloc's colourful introduction to *The British Firing Line* emphasized the apparent emptiness of the battle landscape and Handley-Read's suitability to describe such strange scenes:

> There has never been such a secretive war. A man may travel miles to his fire trench, and never appear above ground. He may be in the same neighbourhood for weeks and see nothing of it beyond the glimpse that his loophole or periscope affords... so it is these sketches, dealing faithfully with the greatest conflict in history, show nothing of exciting action, little indeed of the human element at all... Ruin, emptiness, heart breaking dreariness are their keynotes, and it is for this reason that there never was a war which, in the main, so lends itself to the art of the landscape painter.

53 See for example, *The Times History of the War*, Volume 6, Chapter CVI, p.373 and *The Illustrated London News*, 16 October 1915, double-page photograph, pp.484–5).

54 *Tower Bridge at Loos*, exhibited in 1917, and also reproduced in *The Graphic*, 27 May 1917.

55 Mumby, *The Great World War*, Volume 4, p.256.

56 *Hill 60 and a German Barricade*, IWM Dept. of Art 1352.

57 *Illustrated London News*, 8 May 1915 (56) pp.584–5. One of Handley-Read's drawings of a metal spiral staircase standing proud of the ruins in an Arras square is similar to a photograph that appeared in *The Graphic*, 28 April 1917 (the drawing is reproduced in the *Artists' Rifles Roll of Honour*, 3rd edition, 1922). However, other artists were also drawn to this 'freak of bombardment', see Walter Starmer's drawing of that title (IWM: ART 5195).

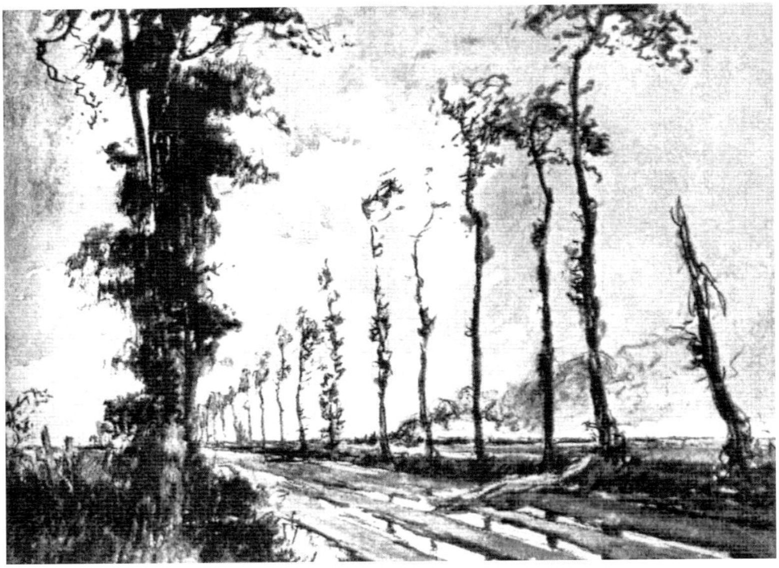

E HANDLEY-READ
Somewhere in France

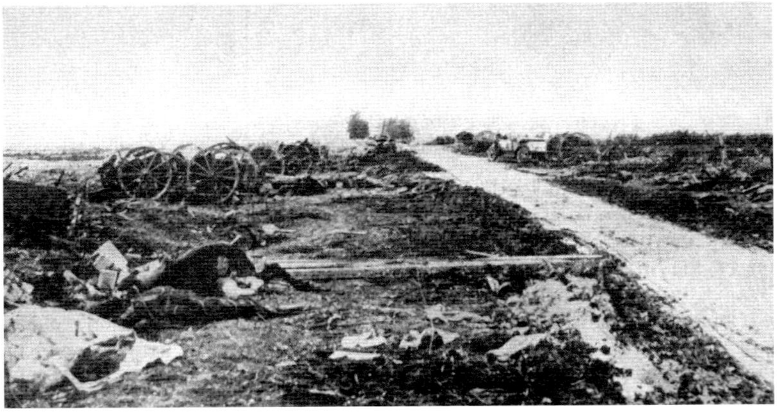

Loos battlefield

pictures to keep up his annual average of 70 new pieces per year, a rate he had maintained for three consecutive years. This was in addition to his considerable duties as an instructor. His service record and Medal Card in the Public Record Office show that he was entitled to the British War Medal, which would indicate that he did see overseas service, but there is no way of proving whether he went anywhere near the fighting line.[58] A similar charge could be levelled at several of the official war artists whose work still carries the stamp of authentic witness. That aside, Handley-Read's work was recognized by art critics and fellow painters, and he lent his support to other artists. Richard Nevinson, for example, on a fruitless trip to Grantham to seek out vacancies in the Machine Guns Corps as a modeller, map drawer or a draughtsman, wrote of his meeting with a 'Captain Reid [sic] who had also done some war paintings, [he] did his utmost for me, but the doctors did not like my physical condition and I was turned down'.[59]

By comparing the visual testimony of Muirhead Bone with the more polished drawings made by Edward Handley-Read, we have raised some important questions about the nature of war art. Questions, indeed, that were being asked during the conflict: what actually constituted an authentic image? How might a painting or drawing be modified or transformed by an accompanying text, or for that matter, by a misleading title? How much front-line experience did an artist need – if any at all – to create convincing representations of modern war? This last question is especially pertinent when we examine the work of the soldier-artists Richard Nevinson, Wyndham Lewis and Paul Nash. Their value as young Modernist painters was further validated and given special authority by their front-line experience, even if – like Nevinson – they may have rarely seen a shot fired in anger, or like Nash, they experienced only quiet trenches and spent a relatively short time on the Front.

It is easy to criticize Bone and Handley-Read for being safe, distant or even phoney. But they both produced extensive portfolios of impressive work and perhaps for this alone they should be commended and remembered; the acclaim that greeted their work and their support for younger artists paved the way for successive deployment of painters who otherwise might have perished in the war or watched their talents fritter away.

58 Handley-Read's service record in the NA/PRO is WO 339/67615. His Medal Card shows that he was entitled to the British War Medal, which would indicate that he did see overseas service. It does not indicate on the card that he was entitled to or indeed received the Victory Medal. It is also possible that his Victory Medal was issued on a separate card due to his service with the Artists' Rifles, especially if he appeared as, say, Read, Edward H. (I am grateful to Peter T. Scott for this information.)

59 C.W.R. Nevinson, *Paint and Prejudice*, p.93.

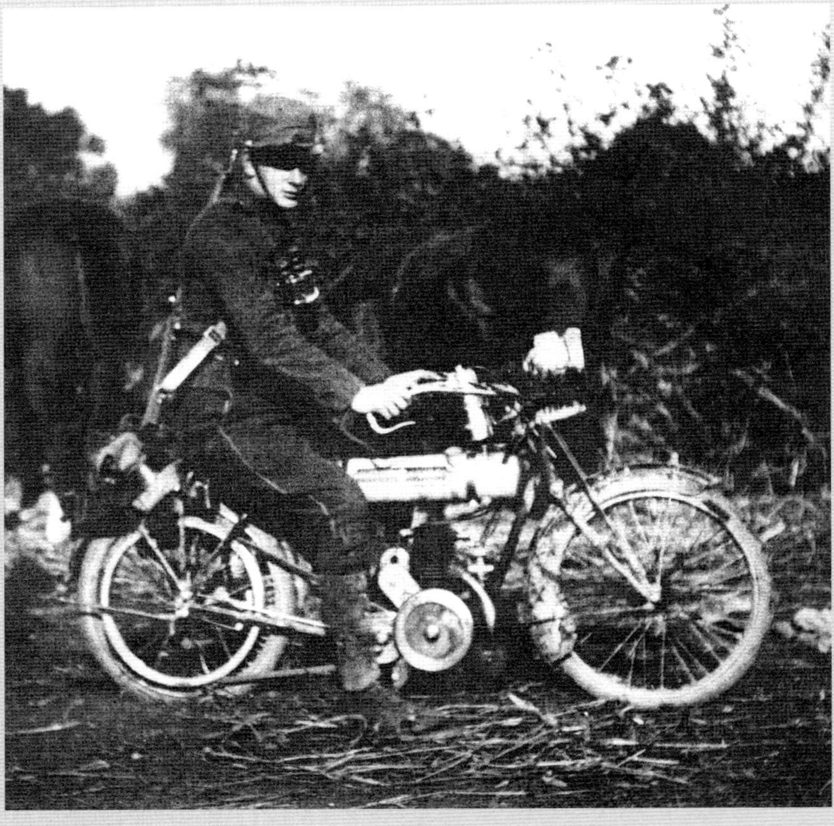

Paul Maze

Drawing as a means of calibrating the battlefield

Paul Maze, Adrian Hill and Sydney Jones

In autumn 2008, as the 90th anniversary of the Armistice approached, British newspapers, internet sites and news channels were saturated with the story of a commercial artist who had performed daring feats of courage in no-man's-land, armed with little more than 'a sniper's rifle in one hand and an artist's brush in the other'. Sapper Len Smith's front-line diary and the pictures he made from lonely and exposed positions were celebrated as a significant and novel find, not least for his delicate studies of a decapitated tree some twenty yards from the German line. These had to be highly detailed drawings, so detailed that an identical hollow steel tree could be fabricated by the camouflage department and installed in the place of the original at the dead of night. The replica tree – one of forty-five devised during the war – was then used as an elevated observation post.

Yet possibly more extraordinary was the panoramic drawing that Smith made of a section of the pulverized contours of Vimy Ridge. Two metres long and highly finished in every detail, Smith wrote of it in his diary:

> This was a far easier job to command than to do. It was quite too utterly fierce to attempt to draw up there at this period, the Huns' shelling was almost incessant. So I had to scramble over the top, making rough pencil notes over a period of four days.[1]

Although the popular press appeared to be taken aback by this strange fusion of artistry with audacious courage, others who knew the stories of the Western Front were less surprised. The value of artists as snipers, observers and scouts is widely known to many historians, but pretty much ignored by the art world, for whom such work was regarded as little better than jobbing reportage, admittedly a little more hazardous than was customary for commercial artists.

Many of the soldier-artists who volunteered or who were picked upon to carry out such work had only the rudiments of art school training. Some had seen their studies interrupted by the outbreak of war and resented the work; others took to it with a relish, setting aside their pre-war styles and developing a graphic language that might directly aid the military effort. Often undertaking hazardous forays into no-man's-land, their ability to look closely and scrutinise natural forms gave them a method of translating the chaotic appearance of the battlefield into easily legible and useful visual texts. Their panoramic sketches were used to augment aerial photographs and eye-witness accounts, so as to provide the fullest record of the battleground beyond the parapet. This practice of military sketching involved many more artists and soldiers than is commonly thought. It was a skill that could be learnt by anyone, and resulted in the need for instructors who could teach disciplined observation, basic line drawing, and the production of intelligible landscapes. It also brought to the fore a breed of artist-adventurers who liked to hone their craft in the most hazardous circumstances. One such character was the French-born painter Paul Maze.

PAUL MAZE
'A Frenchman in Khaki'

Maze was born in Normandy in 1887. His Anglo-French parents were friends with many of the major artists of the period – Renoir, Monet, Dufy and Pissarro – and the young Maze learnt the rudiments of painting from seeing their work, but in the 1890s he left France for schooling in Southampton. Something of an adventurer he turned his back on a possible career in commerce to travel the world, working as a lumberjack and a mariner before returning to France intent on taking part in the Great War. However, despite his age (he was then only twenty-seven) he was declared unfit for active service in the French Army. Undeterred, he set out on foot from Paris to Le Havre in August 1914 and 'attached' himself as an interpreter to

1 Sapper Leonard Smith's remarkable story was retold in the weeks leading up to Remembrance Sunday, November 2008, on the BBC Radio 4 *Today* Programme, Trevor MacDonald's *News at Ten* on ITV, in the *Daily Mail, Guardian, Independent, The Times, Daily Telegraph, Daily Express, The Mirror, The Sun* and numerous websites including www.greatwarartist.com/index.html which offered the illustrated diary as an e-book. Smith had originally enlisted in the 'Shiny Seventh', 7th battalion the London Regiment.

the Royal Scots Greys. His unofficial status led to some harrowing escapades. During the retreat from Mons he was separated from his host regiment and narrowly escaped capture by the enemy, only to be mistaken for a German spy by British officers from another unit. Because he was wearing odd items of British uniform and lacked any official papers he was summarily condemned to execution by the Provost-Marshal. Fortunately, as he was being marched to face the firing squad he was recognised and rescued by a cavalry officer who was leading a squadron of the Greys through the village. Such close scrapes were to prove rather characteristic of Maze's war.[2]

After proper enlistment, Maze came to the notice of General Hubert de la Poer Gough, then commanding officer of the 7th Division. Quickly sensing his courage and usefulness, Gough appointed Maze as a liaison officer with extensive duties as interpreter, guide and (once his drawing abilities were recognized) the role of scout and front-line draughtsman. Maze took to his new duties with a zeal that often bordered on the reckless: in the following four years he was wounded on three occasions and decorated four times for bravery, earning a Distinguished Conduct Medal, the Military Medal and Bar, the Croix de Guerre and the *Legion d'Honneur.* For the duration of the war he worked closely with Gough, whose meteoric rise saw him become a lieutenant-general at the age of just forty-six, and eventually commander of the 5th Army in 1916.[3]

In May 1915 Maze was working for Gough's headquarters, which was then situated behind the Aubers Ridge in northern France. On 9 May, in one of the first set-piece battles of the war, four divisions of British troops and two Indian divisions attacked but failed to take their objectives on the ridge. Maze had watched in frustration as the badly beaten troops fell back from the unbroken German line.[4] Chaos ensued in the British trenches and on the roads leading to the narrow front; Gough himself undertook a personal reconnaissance only to recognize that further forward movement that day was impossible. Maze was tasked to make sketches of various objectives to augment the intelligence material being gathered by divisional staff. Under the scrutiny of German spotters suspended overhead from sausage

2 For a full account of this traumatic episode see Chapter One in Paul Maze's war memoir, *A Frenchman in Khaki* (London: Heinemann, 1934).

3 General Sir Hubert de la Poer Gough, GCB, GCMG, KCVO (1870–1963) commanded the British Fifth Army, 1916 to 1918. His meteoric rise through the ranks followed his command of a relief column during the siege of Ladysmith in the Second Boer War, command of a Brigade in 1914, leadership of 7th Division, then a Corps, at the start of the Battle of the Somme in mid-1916. His reserve army was renamed the 5th Army in October 1916, and deployed at Third Ypres (where it suffered very high casualties) and was effectively broken during the German Spring Offensive of March 1918. A controversial figure, Gough came in for much criticism during and after the war.

4 Paul Maze, *A Frenchman in Khaki*, pp.111–115. Maze described how the approach to the trenches always gave him an unusual sensation: 'In a quiet part it felt like entering a sanctuary where one was inclined to walk about on tip-toes. It seemed like any other trench at first; but then you realised that the enemy was a few yards beyond, squatting in the same way between two narrow walls of sandbags…' (p.113).

balloons, he had first to make his way along the Bethune to Laventie road via the notorious village of Richebourg L'Avoue. Taking up position in a front-line trench parallel with the main street of the village, his view was at first obscured by a camouflage screen erected by the Germans to conceal motor traffic on a distant road. The practicalities of his task were daunting. 'To find places from which to make my drawings,' he later wrote, 'was at times difficult. I had to use a periscope and crane my neck over the sandbags quickly and peep, but the parapet was very high and I kept slipping off'.[5] He had also to hold a drawing board, to maintain his balance in the busy trench, and avoid unnecessary movement that might attract the enemy's attention. To further complicate his task, Maze preferred to draw rapidly with charcoal, which may be good for making schematic notes but is a messy and unstable medium. Many of his drawings are very long – some nearly 6 feet – they are sometimes drawn on a single sheet of paper, but more often on two or three pieces later joined together. By all accounts the drawings that resulted were highly valued by staff officers. The official war artist William Rothenstein, when working with the 5th Army, glimpsed the results of Maze's front-line work in a headquarters briefing room. He recalled seeing a long panoramic view of the battlefield, assembled from Maze's drawings and augmented by aerial photographs, to make a considerable view of the German front. Rothenstein wrote admiringly of Maze's bravery in 'creeping, day after day, beyond our front lines [in] an act of rare courage and devotion'.[6]

Indeed, by autumn 1915, during the Battle of Loos, he had become an invaluable 'pair of eyes' for Gough.[7] Taking cover from heavy shell-fire in a trench full of German corpses he drew the Guards Division's belated attack on Hill 70, his panoramic drawing marked with dozens of little dots to represent the lines of guardsmen advancing in parade-ground order.[8]

Maze must have presented an odd sight. Wearing a mixture of British and French uniform he traversed the battlegrounds on a battered Triumph motorbike, roaming the trench lines at will, carrying with him the authority of a Brigadier-General and wearing the insignia of a sergeant-major. His fearlessness became legendary.

---

5 Paul Maze, *A Frenchman in Khaki*, p.114.

6 Rothenstein, W. (1932) *Men and Memories: Recollections of William Rothenstein 1900–1922* (London: Faber and Faber, 1934) Volume 2, p.334.

7 Maze came under fire while watching the Guards Division attack on Hill 70, their columns moving in perfect alignment across the shell-swept ground. As he watched and drew, 'a piece of ragged shell thumped into the earth about a yard from where I lay; the unburied part of it like the raw edge of a saw and as hot as a red-hot poker.' (*A Frenchman in Khaki*, p.123)

8 It was during these desperate attacks to shore up the line near Hill 70 that Lieutenant John Kipling of the Irish Guards and only son of the writer Rudyard Kipling went missing. For a thorough account of the battle see Lyn Macdonald, *1915: The Death of Innocence* (London: Penguin, 1997) pp.532–552. John Kipling's death is covered on pp.556–557.

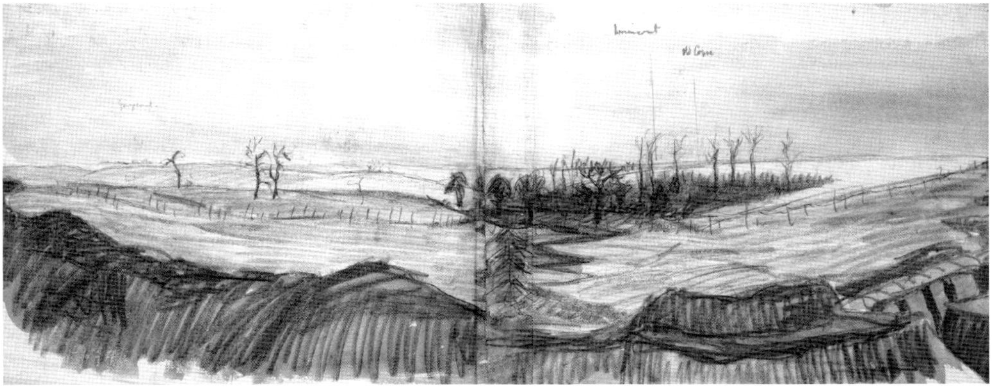

PAUL MAZE

Panorama Indicating Gouzecourt and Honnecourt

(c.1916)

charcoal watercolour on paper, 46.9 x 120 cm

IMPERIAL WAR MUSEUM, LONDON

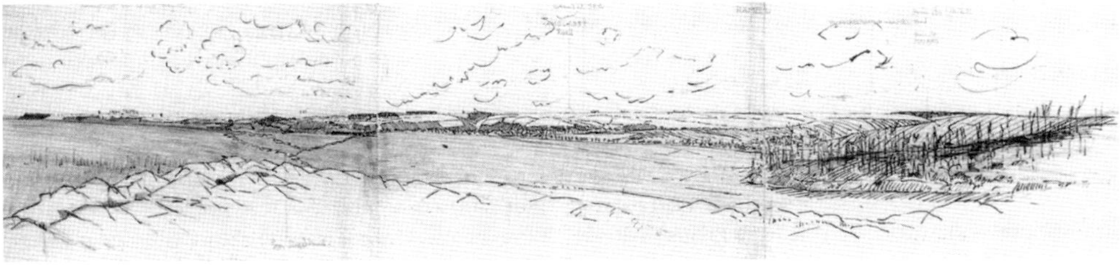

PAUL MAZE

Panorama Including Corbie, Sailly le Sec, Hamel, Bois de Vaire and Detailing Military Positions

(1916)

charcoal, 39.3 x 172 cm

IMPERIAL WAR MUSEUM, LONDON

To the French in particular he became something of a phenomenon and, by the end of the war, he was known simply as 'l'institution Maze'. Indeed, senior officers took advantage of his close relationship with Army Command and often dropped heavy hints for resources, materials and provisions in the hope that he would pass them on to the relevant commander. Such favours earned him tremendous authority. As for the men, Maze seems to have mixed with them equally as well. His drawing abilities clearly amused and puzzled the infantry whom he worked alongside, one soldier remarking perceptively that Maze seemed to draw in shorthand. On one notable occasion he was making his way up a busy trench in the Thiepval Salient to make a drawing of the line around the notorious Mouquet Farm. Carrying a roll of paper tied with a red band, he was with difficulty elbowing his way through the crowded trench when he overheard a soldier shout out playfully, 'For God's sake let him pass, it's a bloke with the Peace Treaty'.[9]

In mid-1916 Maze was sent out time and time again by Gough, now in command of the Reserve Army, to reconnoitre the front-line of the Somme battle. On 2 July 1916, during the confused fighting around La Boiselle, Maze was ordered to report on the state of the fighting. His hazardous voyage into the maelstrom must surely stand as one of the great narratives of that terrible battle. At a point beyond Usna Hill he watched a group of soldiers preparing to go over the top:

> Amongst much older men a younger Tommy was waiting his turn. He seemed weighed down by his kit and the loose belts of extra ammunition hanging from his shoulder; his small head was buried beneath his tin helmet. In a long nervous hand he held a rifle with fixed bayonet, and looked anything but anxious to use it. Heavy thoughts seemed to be in that boy's mind, and the lack of enthusiasm displayed by the rest filled me with misgivings as to the ultimate success of the attack. Vitality is low at that hour...[10]

It was on the Somme sector that Maze produced some of his most interesting drawings. One watercolour sketch of no-man's-land[11] shows little but a deserted landscape. In the centre sits a battered copse and a zig-zagging communication trench; the foreground is strewn with heaps of soil that mark the edge of the British parapet. It is clear that Maze was drawing from a very exposed position

9 Paul Maze, *A Frenchman in Khaki*, p.183.

10 Paul Maze, *A Frenchman in Khaki*, p.140. Maze left many equally observant anecdotes, such as the time he had just started sketching when he saw the bald head of a German framed against a shirt laid out to dry on the parapet of an adjacent trench. In a hushed voice Maze called for the sentry, only to be told: "I know, he's been there all the morning doing nothing but picking fleas off his body. Lousy, that's what he is." 'Evidently', stated Maze, 'in his opinion being lousy was trouble enough for one man.' (p.322)

11 Paul Maze, *Western Front Panorama*, charcoal and wash on paper, 1916, IWM: ART 6070.

– in the right hand side of the long drawing he is actually looking down on his own trench – and he was working with some haste. But there is no loss of detail: his broad sweeps of charcoal indicate the foreground shapes while also defining the individual character of the trees and the lie of the land in the middle distance. In a finer hand Maze has picked out the spires and larger buildings of a distant village. Maze revelled in the task:

> Bit by bit we dissected the ground with our field-glasses, and I made drawings from every possible angle, marking every possible obstacle which could hinder the advance of our troops.[12]

Working alone, or occasionally with local scouting officers (of whom many had been stalkers in civilian life), he continued to take extraordinary risks, sneaking quick glances above the parapet to fully gather the information he sought. In one of his few front-line drawings that have survived, he attempted to draw the enemy line near Hamel on the Somme, but even he knew when to give up. Scrawled across the foot of the right-hand page on one drawing are the words 'Could not go through heavy shelling'.[13] It was also uncomfortable work: on one occasion during the winter he noted in his diary that he had not been able to make any sketches that day as his watercolour brush froze each time he tried to mix the paint and lay it on the paper.[14]

For the duration of the war Maze worked for the 5th Army on the Somme Front. It was rarely without hazard or discomfort, especially in the spring of 1918 when Gough's depleted army faced the onslaught of the German offensive. Occasionally, however, Maze allowed himself to take small pleasures in the act of observing and recording:

> I worked from a ridge and looked right down into this sunny valley, having observation on the enemy line running along the next spur. The report of the guns coming from the distant high ground or ours fired behind me could not disturb my contact with the radiant landscape. I would forget that I was drawing for military purposes, and become engrossed in form and colour, letting myself go completely. The spurts of water from shells falling into the river didn't disturb me either.[15]

---

12 Paul Maze, *A Frenchman in Khaki*, p.130.

13 *Panoramic sketch*, charcoal and watercolour on paper, IWM: ART 6072. In March 1916 Maze worked with 2nd Army at Bailleul on the battle ground around Messines and Wytschaete. There he worked with a Captain Nelson, of the Lothian and Border Horse, who had control of all observation: his team of trained observers were posted along the line and were ideally suited to the task, many having been stalkers in civilian life.

14 Paul Maze, *A Frenchman in Khaki*, p.205.

Such moments of repose were few and far between. Although his memoir teems with colourful, richly observed vignettes he was kept too busy by the British Command to draw much more than his daily panoramas. Every night, he recalled, the general would look at the day's work, asking him to explain the lie of the land, which he then followed on a map and compared with piles of charts and diagrams. A few hurried sketches of the Cloth Hall at Ypres, one or two of ruins on the Somme and that is all Maze had time to do in the few periods between his front-line sketching and mapping the face of war. In fact, precious few of his reconnaissance drawings survived. After all, they were not intended for posterity, they were made on poor paper and discarded as soon as their immediate usefulness was over. Indeed, despite their portrayal of a land rarely seen by daylight, they are not that typical of the type of panoramic military sketching that was taught and approved by the British army. For that story we have to cast back to the eighteenth century, to the origins of the formal training of gentlemen officers in the leafy Home Counties of southern England.

'BREAKING GROUND'
The military academies

Ever since the establishment of the training academies in the eighteenth century the military have taught drawing as a navigation and exploratory tool. At Woolwich and Dartmouth, gentlemen cadets and sailors were trained to analyse and record landscape and coastline as a method of neutralizing, codifying and controlling enemy-held terrain. With the establishment of a military academy at Woolwich in 1741, drawing became a core element of the curriculum. The Rules and Orders required the Drawing Master to 'teach the method of Sketching Ground, the taking of Views, the drawing of Civil Architecture and the Practice of Perspective.'[16] Its most famous instructor was none other than Paul Sandby who served as Drawing Master from 1768 until 1796. One of the originators of the Royal Academy of Art in London, Sandby was then at the height of his fame as a water-colourist, and his appointment at the Military Academy reflects the importance of drawing in the training of the artillery and engineer cadets. Under his guidance the quality of observation and draughtsmanship was consistently high, and

15 Paul Maze, *A Frenchman in Khaki*, p.321. By this time Maze was in the fourth summer of the war, on this occasion drawing the valley of the river Somme 'which had retained a picturesque aspect, in spite of the heavy shelling to which it had been exposed. The river bent in graceful loops along the foot of thickly covered slopes, where the mellow ruins of villages stood outlined against the green…' (p.320).

16 Lt.Col. H.D. Buchanan, *Records of the Royal Military Academy, 1741–1892*. (Woolwich: Cattermole, 1892) p.33.

a number of his pupils went on to prove themselves expert draughtsmen, most notably during the Napoleonic Wars, often making crucially important reconnaissance drawings and finely illustrated reports of previously unmapped terrain.[17] With the establishment of new staff and junior military colleges in 1801, drawing became further established as essential to the training of infantry and cavalry officers. An accurate drawing, however hastily made, was often more useful than a verbal or written description, and the officer-draughtsman cadre played a significant part in Wellington's Peninsular campaign.

Instructors were paid well, but many artists were wary of what they considered to be jobbing work. John Constable was one who resisted the temptation of becoming a teacher, arguing that had he accepted 'it would have been a death blow to all my prospects of perfection in the Art I love'.[18] Many others felt little but disdain for mere topographic art. Whether for artillery or infantry use, military drawing puts a premium on producing an accurate report shorn of artistic and aesthetic trappings. For all its remunerative attraction, military sketching was regarded as little better than a process of 'tame delineation', of reducing the aesthetics of nature to something ordinary or (to borrow Thomas Gainsborough's dismissive phrase) something 'mappy'. He wrote of the opprobrium cast upon artists who regarded themselves as 'topographers', rather than 'interpreters' of the landscape. Naturally, the military requires a factual, accurate drawing, however clumsy, rather than an idealized landscape picture.

Drawing for such purposes can be separated into two distinct fields of vision, requiring two different sets of skills. These correspond approximately to the different arms of the military: on the one hand are those drawings made during mobile reconnaissance – usually by light cavalry patrols or units of advanced infantry, or indeed individuals such as Paul Maze 'peering over the parapet' – that are used to record intelligence about enemy positions and key terrain. On the other, are drawings known as panoramas that are made from a static position, usually an elevated vantage point that commands an uninterrupted view of the enemy front. These are normally drawn by specially trained artillery or engineer officers and are vital for indicating targets and determining range and arc of fire.

The principle of panoramic drawing, when used in an artillery sense, was developed from the role of the Forward Observation Officer (F.O.O.). He occupies an advanced post on the very edge of known and secure ground and is responsible for directing the fire of guns located much further back. Through close observation

17 Martin Hardie, *Watercolour Painting in Britain*, Vol. 1, *The Eighteenth Century*. (London: Batsford, 1966) p.216.

18 John Constable to John Dunthorne, 29 May 1802.

the F.O.O. was able to engage targets very rapidly across the whole arc of view. If a number of targets had already been pre-registered, and engaged to an exact point on the ground, that point could be marked on a drawn panorama. This drawing would also be copied to the gunners in the rear who would then be able to engage the same target number with greater speed and efficiency. In effect, the panorama became a surrogate view for the distant artillery blinded by dead ground or topographic barriers.[19] This was the main duty – and an extremely hazardous one at that – required of the painter Wyndham Lewis during his many months as an artillery officer on the Ypres Salient in 1917.

As we have seen with the work of Paul Maze, the patrol sketch is often a collage of hasty impressions later re-arranged to form a tactical narrative. By contrast, the panorama is primarily concerned with scopic control and spatial dominance. Whereas the sketch made on patrol deals with local detail, the panorama is not concerned with the foreground but focuses on the distance, on a calculable future that may lie miles to the front. However, both practices have the same overall aim, namely that detailed surveillance and graphic recording will help neutralize a dangerous terrain and eventually assure mastery over it.[20] On the septic terrain of the First World War battlefield the panoramic drawing was an integral part in segmenting and immobilizing perceived space; when used in conjunction with a panoply of other surveillance devices it allowed systematic observation of the distance, making certain that the slightest movements were noticed, and all activity recorded.[21]

'...AVOID ARTISTIC EFFECT'
The Drawing Manuals

Throughout the war artistically talented soldiers of all ranks found themselves sought out to work in the Camouflage Corps or for the Field Survey. Not all went willingly. Harry Bateman, having volunteered for service with the Royal Field Artillery, ignored a sergeant's request at his first parade for any artist present to make himself known, remaining silent as he wanted to 'go and fight'.[22] Others advertised their skills quite freely. Adrian Hill combined

19 This is essentially a twentieth-century development. Indirect fire was only developed from the turn of the century onward, having been made practicable by the advent of quick-firing artillery. In British terms, serious developments of the techniques took place only after the outbreak of the First World War. See S. Bidwell and D. Graham, *Fire-Power, British Army Weapons & Theories of War 1904–1945* (London: George Allen & Unwin, 1982).

20 For a fuller exposition see Nicholas Alfrey and Stephen Daniels, (eds) *Mapping the Landscape: Essays on Art and Cartography* (Nottingham: Nottingham Castle Museum, 1990).

21 Michel Foucault, *Discipline and Punish: the Birth of the Prison* (London: Allen Lane, 1977) p.197.

22 Quoted in Malcolm Brown, *Tommy Goes to War* (London: J.M. Dent, 1978) p.185. Bateman's drawings are held in the Imperial War Museum, Department of Art nos. 6319–6338.

his drawing abilities with his work in a Scouting and Sniping Section of the Honourable Artillery Company. He recalled a typical patrol into No Man's Land:

> I advanced in short rushes, mostly on my hands and knees with my sketching kit dangling round my neck. As I slowly approached, the wood gradually took a more definite shape, and as I crept nearer I saw that what was hidden from our own line, now revealed itself as a cunningly contrived observation post in one of the battered trees.[23]

The illustrator Sydney Jones, who was serving on the Western Front as a Lieutenant in a Field Survey Company of the Royal Engineers, also found it a simple task to produce highly detailed line drawings of enemy positions. Indeed, John Buchan, Director of the Department of Information enthused over his work, praising his unique ability to produce an 'extraordinarily good record, not only of the buildings but of the contours of the battlefields'.[24] Equally, another graphic artist, Warwick Lendon, an officer with the 'Maps' section of the First Army in France was happy to subordinate his extensive design skills to produce factual panoramas of the Loos battlefield.[25]

Others found their previous education was poorly suited. Painter and poet David Jones, serving with the 15th (London Welsh) Battalion, Royal Welch Fusiliers, had five years' art school training to his credit when he was recommended to the 2nd Field Survey Company based at Second Army Headquarters at Cassel. Jones,

---

23 Adrian Hill interviewed in the *Graphic*, 15 November 1930. Born in 1895 Hill was the youngest soldier-artist to work for the official government war art schemes when he was commissioned by the War Trophies Section of the Imperial War Museum between December 1917 and March 1919. He recalled how he 'used to sit and observe, and make little drawings rather than shoot at the enemy, so that I was well versed in drawing in very odd positions in a very unique environment.' Transcript of interview, IWM Department of Sound Recordings.

24 Born in 1881, Sydney Robert Fleming Jones studied architecture at Birmingham School of Art and exhibited etchings regularly in the 1920s (ten times at R.A.), receiving an Honourable Mention at Paris Salon, 1922. He was particularly prolific as an author and illustrator of books on English rustic traditions, vernacular architecture and poster design.

A full list of the 27 articles and special publications written and illustrated by Jones for *The Studio* is available in *The Studio: A Bibliography of the First Fifty Years 1893–1943* (London: Sims and Reed, 1978). Amongst this sizeable collection are the 163-page *The Village Homes of England* (*The Studio* Special, 1912) with text and illustrations by Jones, and *Thames Triumphant* (*The Studio* Special, 1943). Other post-war articles in *The Studio* appeared in Vol. 84, 1922, pp.99–103 (four etchings of London) and Vol. 82, 1921, pp.58–61 ('Jottings from the Sketch-Book of Sydney R. Jones').

He served on the Western Front as a Lieutenant in a Field Survey Company of the Royal Engineers with the 59th Division. The IWM has four fine watercolours by the artist (5273: the country between Amiens and Abbeville painted in July 1917, and 5274: a chimney stack standing in the wilderness of the Somme countryside in Spring 1917, and two others, 5222, 5221). His work is best seen in Charles Vince's fine history of the 59th Division, *England in France* (Constable, 1920) which is illustrated throughout with ink-drawings of the battlefield by Jones. One reviewer thought them 'the best the artist has given us... a high standard or artistic excellence' (*The Studio*, no.322, January 1920).

IWM Dept of Art file 158/5 contains an interesting letter of 17 January 1918 written by John Buchan enthusing about Jones's work. Buchan praised the artist's ability to produce an 'extraordinarily good record, not only of the buildings but of the contours of the battlefields.' The IWM felt less enthusiastic, replying that they already had 'large numbers of similar drawings of destroyed buildings, etc'. Jones died in 1966.

however, appears to have lacked the requisite technical skills needed for map drawing, and was instead sent to one of the Company's four observation groups as a Survey Post observer. Having already been promoted sideways from 'Maps', Jones did not last very long as an observer – 'Got the sack from that job because of my inefficiency in getting the right degrees of enemy gunflashes'.[26] Further up the line, yet another artist struggled in the seemingly simple task of 'breaking ground':

> From the OP (Observation Post) I saw a completely featureless landscape, save here and there a few broken sticks of trees. I made a pencil drawing of this barren piece of ground, but what use my superiors would be able to make of this sketch I could not imagine.[27]

Thus ended the Vorticist painter William Roberts's first and only foray into reconnaissance drawing. In fact, surprisingly few of the other young 'modern' artists serving in the armed forces during the Great War could channel their talents in the pursuit of technical objectivity.

One officer who felt that it was not enough to entrust military drawing to adventurers or bemused avant-garde painters was William Newton of the Artists' Rifles. A trainee architect, Newton proposed that it was possible to teach a novice how to draw a battle landscape after just one lecture and two days drawing in the field. This was an ambitious programme; after all, front-line infantry scouts usually took up to six weeks to train.[28] Newton laid out his ideas in *Military Landscape Sketching and Target Indication* – a manual published commercially in 1916. In the introduction, Lieutenant Colonel H.A.R. May, commanding officer of the Artists' Rifles, applauded Newton's method:

---

25 Having served in the Boer War, Warwick William Lendon applied in early 1914 for a commission in the London Regiment and was gazetted as 2nd Lieutenant in its 22nd Battalion (The Queen's). Following the outbreak of war he was promoted to Lieutenant and served in the 47th (London) Division, a Territorial formation, which fought at Aubers Ridge and Festubert in May 1915. He left his battalion with a groin injury, was invalided home and was found fit for light duty in mid-1915. He was asked to return to France to carry out duties in the Map Section at Headquarters, leaving for France just four weeks before the Loos battle opened. He was attached to 'Maps, First Army' and although this had been intended as a temporary appointment, he remained with 1st Topographical Section and its successor, 1st Field Survey Company, until September 1916 (when he transferred to the Royal Flying Corps). By 21 October 1916 he had transferred to No.2 Squadron, First Wing, RFC, as a records officer. When demobilised on 8 March 1918 he was a substantive captain.

Lendon's drawing of the Loos Battlefield made on 10 June 1915 is an early example of a panorama sketch. As Peter Chausseaud comments (in an extended note to the author) 'these panoramas, both photographic and drawn, emphasised the difficulty of this variegated agricultural, coal-mining and industrial landscape.' The drawing is in the IWM Department of Art collection.

26 R. Hague (ed.) *David Jones, Dai Greatcoat* (London: Faber and Faber, 1980) p.241; see also Peter Chasseaud, (1993) 'David Jones and The Survey', *Stand To! The Journal of the Western Front Association*, no.39, pp.18–22.

27 William Roberts, *Memories of the War to End all Wars: 4.5 Howitzer Gunner R.F.A. 1916–1918* (London: Canada Press, 1974) pp.27–28.

28 Lt L.C.R.D.J. Cameron, *Infantry Scouting: a Practical Manual for the use of Scouts in Training at Home and at the Front* (London: John Murray, 1916).

> The test of each solution is whether a stranger can with ease and rapidity identify the exact place intended; and tested in this manner the results of his teaching have been most successful and many officers in the trenches have benefited by the care and devotion he has given to his work.[29]

In his opening pages Newton took issue with the leaden instruction of most drawing manuals published by the military. Instead, he proposed that the military sketch should be regarded as simply 'a form of report, without the ambiguity of language. It is graphic information. For information, clearness is essential, and clearness is attained by two avenues: a) thought, b) draughtsmanship'.[30] In taking this approach Newton distances himself from previous military manuals that prescribed heavily annotated sketches, and the use of a pictorial language rooted in the conventions of maps. The real challenge, argued Newton, was how to simplify the visual chaos of a landscape, especially a landscape damaged by battle. To do so:

> It is... necessary to analyse, to bring order out of chaos. For this purpose there are three main methods of analysis – separation of planes, encircling or framing in, division of a whole into parts.[31]

Possibly the most novel of these three methods is the first – the separation of planes. Newton suggests that the trainee soldier-draughtsman should try to imagine a landscape as a series of horizontal (but not straight) bands that stretch from one side of the paper to the other. It might help, he suggested, to imagine the country as something like the scenery of an outdoor exhibition with each ridge, hill, wood cut out of sheets of wood and laid one behind the other. Having done this, a point can clearly be marked on the drawing, and its approximate distance from the viewer indicated by the number and density of horizontal lines representing fields, meadows, and tree lines in between the draughtsman and a chosen point.

Newton's manual abounds with similar pragmatic advice. He emphasized the draughtsman's duty in guiding the eye to salient

---

29 William G.Newton, *Military Landscape Sketching and Target Indication* (London: Hugh Rees, 1916), p.6.

30 William G.Newton, *Military Landscape Sketching and Target Indication,* p.8.

31 Newton, p.9. For a fuller examination of the limited quality of official manuals in map-making, sketching and panorama drawing see Paul Gough, 'Tales from the Bushy-Topped Tree: A Brief Survey of Military Sketching', *Imperial War Museum Review* no.10, November 1995, pp.62–73; and Paul Gough, 'Calculating the future – panoramic sketching, reconnaissance drawing and the material trace of war', in Saunders, N and Cornish, P. (eds.) *Contested objects: material memories of the Great War,* UCL Press, London, in press.

During the period before the Great War, proficiency in drawing was widely acknowledged as offering an advantage to boys competing for places at the military academies. Yet the varying qualities in the teaching of drawing across the 'public' and middle-class schools constantly undermined the calibre of cadet applications to the military colleges. Both the Clarendon Commission of 1864 and the Taunton Commission four years later remarked on the erratic, often poor, quality of art teaching in schools, and the impact this might have on the quality of draughtsmanship in the professions and in the military. See G. Sutton, *Artist or Artisan?* (London: Pergamon Press, 1967).

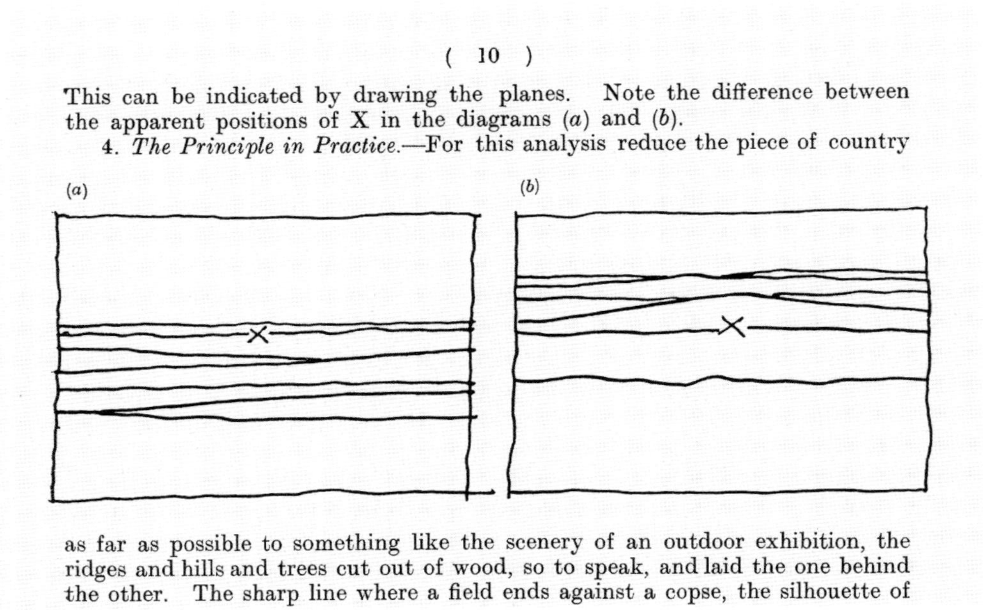

(10)

This can be indicated by drawing the planes. Note the difference between the apparent positions of X in the diagrams (*a*) and (*b*).

4. *The Principle in Practice.*—For this analysis reduce the piece of country

as far as possible to something like the scenery of an outdoor exhibition, the ridges and hills and trees cut out of wood, so to speak, and laid the one behind the other. The sharp line where a field ends against a copse, the silhouette of

WILLIAM NEWTON
from *Military Landscape Sketching and Target Indication*
(1916)

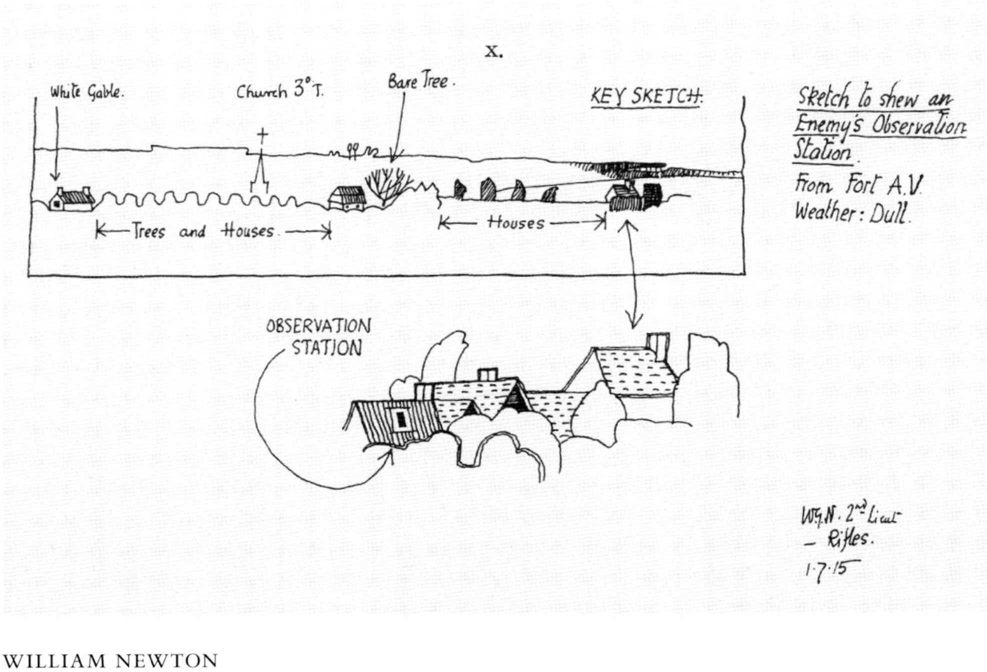

WILLIAM NEWTON
Sketch to show an Enemy's observation station
(1915)

points in the landscape by using key devices in the terrain – an isolated chimney, a single red roof amongst black roofs, three silhouetted bushes on a crest line – as so many 'labels' that indicate particular targets or tactically vital features. He avoids the tendency of other instructors to construct complex drawing frames, or string and protractor gizmos.[32] Instead, he argues for clarity of purpose at all times, and insists on using a sharp pencil and throwing the India rubber away – 'the aim should rather be to do a clear sketch from the first, because in the field opportunities of subsequent polish are limited'. His didactic style is peerless:

> A line should be as sharp and precise as a word of command. A wavering line which dies away carries no conviction or information because it is the product of a wavering mind. Every line should be put in to express something. Start sharply and finish sharply. Press on the paper.[33]

Such instruction may sound a little uncompromising, but it was born of a belief in the superiority of careful observational drawing as a method of study and analysis. Without the rigorous discipline advocated by Newton, military drawing can (and did) descend into a parody of itself – dull, repetitive diagrams in which trees have been reduced to a formula, resulting in a rather contrived landscape drawing that resembles 'nursery wall paper'.[34] This was due in part to the consequence of drawing trees in outline, which tends to make them resemble cartographic symbols – usually bushy-topped deciduous trees or 'Christmas tree' firs. It is also the consequence of drawing in outline alone and so accentuating the top line of trees and

32 A.F.U. Green, *Landscape Sketching for Military Purposes* (London: Hugh Rees, 1908) p.25. In *The Active Service Pocket Book* by 2nd Lt. Bertrand Stewart (1907) the author dedicates eight pages to freehand sketching, offering step-by-step advice on drawing in outline, using the pencil as a measuring instrument and mastering the challenging problem of perspective. The manual is clearly aimed at the novice. Stewart, for instance, recommends the construction of an oblong drawing frame attached to a stick with a pointed end. The frame is to be divided at regular six-inch intervals by stretched wire, thus forming a drawing grid which will help simplify any landscape seen through it. Drawing on squared paper, the soldier is encouraged to make an exact outline copy of the view through the frame, though conveniently the author skips over the difficult matter of situating the frame, piercing hard ground, and avoiding enemy detection.

In summer 1994 a replica of this drawing frame was built according to the specifications laid out in a 1907 drawing manual. It was used during the making of a television documentary *Drawing Fire* to help train artillery officers in the rudiments of freehand sketching. Although useful as a drawing device it proved a large, rather unwieldy piece of equipment, difficult to camouflage and even more difficult to drive into the ground.

33 Newton, p.27.

34 The unimaginative style of most military manuals of the late nineteenth century reflects the low status of drawing in the army's thinking. Invariably, freehand sketching was relegated to an item of 'special interest', and regarded as little more than an adjunct to map work. Manual writers leaned heavily on the conventional language and symbols of military cartography, transforming a single lesson in landscape drawing into little more than a matter of contours and geometric symbols. See for example *Rapid Field Sketching and Reconnaissance* (1889, reprinted 1903) which laid heavy emphasis on map and compass work, with only a cursory description of the merits of freehand drawing. Commercial manuals such as Major R.F. Legge's *Military Sketching and Map Reading* (1906) ignored observational work completely, concentrating instead on map co-ordinates, measurement of slopes, magnetic bearings, and using the service compass.

buildings with a minimum of shading and colour. The end results, however, have a certain aesthetic appeal with many military drawings appearing to resemble the arts-and-crafts-style woodcut illustrations that were popular in the first decades of the century. *The Studio* magazine was quick to note the similarity. In February 1916 an illustrated article applauded the army's work in broadening the education of the common soldier, noting with pleasure that 'instruction has been extended to the rank and file because the authorities recognize the immense value on active service of men who can use a pencil in making topographical sketches'.[35] The writer marvelled at the short period of instruction, proof that 'one can just as easily be taught to draw the formation of objects in nature as to trace the design of the letters of the alphabet' but was most impressed by the unsophisticated appeal of the drawings:

> These sketches are, of course, not intended to be artistic in their handling, but at the same time there is a certain charm in their simplicity, and the conventional method does not detract from their interest.[36]

The accompanying line drawings show a verdant landscape of rolling pastures and tidy villages – in truth, not that dissimilar from the images regularly reproduced in the magazine each month. Similar pastoral scenery was widely used by the army for target practice. One subaltern wryly noted the popularity of the rural idyll:

> 'Two fingers right, four o'clock from the haystack, at five hundred yards at the bushy-topped tree – fire!' I don't think that a tree that was not bushy-topped existed in the picture, which at least saved any strain on the School of Musketry's vocabulary or inventiveness.[37]

To the military mind, though, such aestheticism was anathema. Although 'Major Pearson's Drawing Manual' of 1906 proffered a wider range of tree types – pine, poplar, Scots fir, the banana – that was intended to wean his students from the tyranny of the 'bushy topped' formula, every drawing instructor warned his pupil to guard against 'artistic effect'. 'Indeed,' argued the author of the 1912 manual, 'it is almost better that the artistic sense should be absent, and that instead of idealising a landscape it should be looked at with a cold matter-of-fact military eye.'[38] A soldier-sketcher had to concentrate on the potential of the countryside for military purposes and not be distracted by 'its beauties of colouring or the artistic effects of light and shade'.

35 'R.F.C.' (1916) 'Topographical Sketching in the Army'. *The Studio*, February 1916, pp.44–45.
36 'R.F.C.', *The Studio*, p.45.
37 H.E.L. Mellersh, *Schoolboy into War* (London: William Kimber, 1978) p.52.

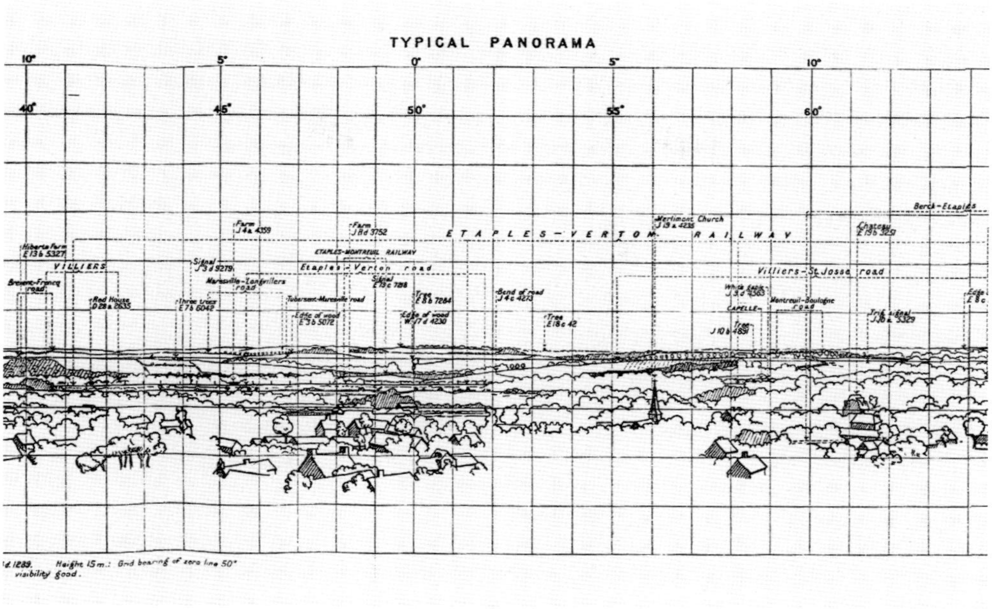

LIEUTENANT J. SMITH, ROYAL ARTILLERY
Typical Panorama
(1918)

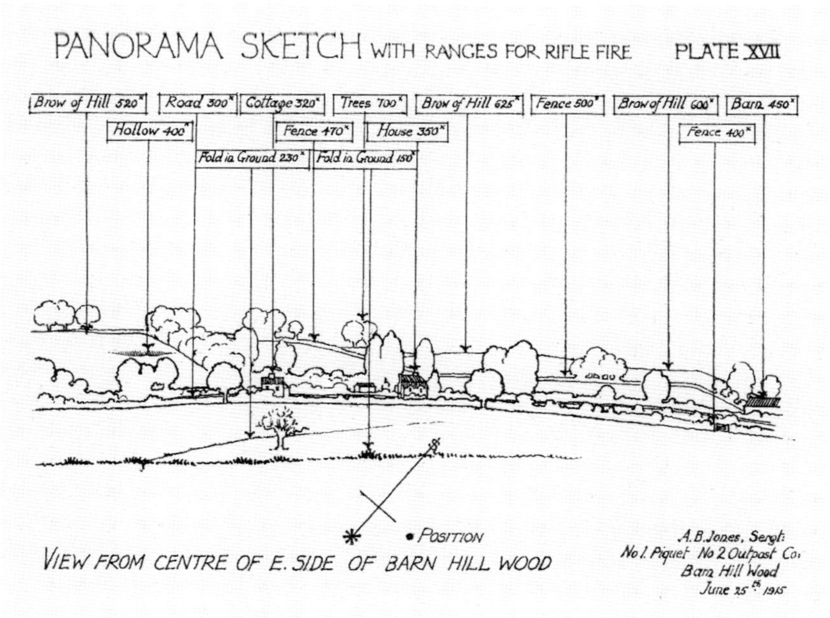

SERGEANT A.B. JONES
Panorama sketch
(1915)

To certain military artists, though, the call of landscape art would always overwhelm purely tactical considerations. Perhaps the least exacting type of military sketch is the conventional landscape painting that has been simply ruled off with vertical pencil lines to mark out the degrees of artillery fire. Wilfrid de Glehn chose this method.[39] A professional artist and painting companion of John Singer Sargent, de Glehn served with the Royal Garrison Artillery on the Italian theatre of operations in 1917. From observation posts on the hills above the Isonzo Valley he painted a number of striking watercolour landscapes of the battlefield and the distant Austrian lines. Exquisitely painted and beautifully luminous, they are, however, rather limited in their description of tactical information – important contour lines are lost in the refined brushwork, keypoints in the enemy line are sacrificed to the principles of aerial perspective, vaporous watercolour technique obscures hard military fact. Only the unwavering vertical lines marking out the arc of artillery fire remind us that this is a dangerous killing zone. Similarly, the sculptor Gilbert Ledward, who was stationed with the Royal Garrison Artillery on the Italian Front during 1917–1918, made a panorama from a high vantage point above the village of Camporovere. His elegant watercolour captures something of the charm of the wide valley, but its military value is limited, relying almost entirely on dotted lines and numerical code to indicate the 'approximate location of hostile batteries'.[40]

LEGACY

Few of the graphic innovations in battlefield drawing advocated by Newton survived the Great War. A sample panorama provided with the 1921 *Manual of Map Reading* shows a wide tract of country either side of the Etaples-Verton railway in northern France. Drawn on 3 July 1918 at 0900 hours by a 'Lieutenant J Smith, Royal Artillery' from an observation post some 15 metres high, it is an archetypal panorama – an endless vista of verdant land described in neutral outline. It uses none of Newton's graphic innovations. Instead, it relies almost entirely on annotations and graphic indicators – arrows, icons, conventional symbols. It premises literal description at the expense of pictorial invention.

38 War Office, *Manual of Map Reading and Sketching* (London: HMSO, 1912) p.75. Many such official and private manuals were available, for example: Major R.F. Legge, *Military Sketching and Map Reading* (Aldershot: Gale and Polden, 1906) and B. Stewart, *Active Service Pocket Book* (London: William Clowes, 1907). For a full account see: Paul Gough, 'Tales from the Bushy-topped Tree: a brief survey of military sketching', *Imperial War Museum Review*, no.10, 1995, pp.62–74.

39 Wilfrid Gabriel de Glehn RA, *The Valley of the Isonzo*, 1917, watercolour 25.4 x 53.3 cm, IWM:ART 278.

40 Ledward's only surviving panorama was made on 27 April 1918 from 94th Brigade Observation Post, at square H20. It is now housed in the Ledward Archive at the Henry Moore Institute, Leeds. I am grateful to Dr. Catherine Moriarty for bringing this work to my attention.

In artillery and infantry training manuals between the wars, freehand sketching took a poor second place to the technical demands of map work and field survey. Panoramic work was regarded as an adjunct to map drawing and was afforded modest coverage in training texts. This trend continued after the Second World War. It seemed that the era of the panoramic sketch as the hand-drawn material trace of war was gone forever.

In today's era of photographic surveillance and computerized simulation, we appear to have achieved powers of total and ultimate surveillance. Retinal observation has been wholly supplanted by digital scrutiny. Global Positioning System satellites and digital technology can triangulate geographical locations to within centimetres, allowing a degree of space and time accuracy that would have been unthinkable to the armed forces of even thirty years ago.[41] However, it may come as some surprise that freehand drawing is still practised in the British armed forces today (as indeed it is in the US Marine Corps).[42]

For much of the time, light forward units of the British Army's Royal Artillery rely on powerful binoculars, night sights and thermal imaging devices, but the skill of field sketching is still a part of their work, requiring little more than a pencil, paper or sheet of transparent acetate and a keen eye. In concealed positions far ahead of their guns, operating from a known grid, Forward Observation Officers, normally with the rank of Captain, observe the ground to the front of their battery, determine targets and order fire. The value of drawing is simply explained:

> Drawing is very important to the artillery, and to the observers particularly. We produce a panorama on a flat piece of paper, so that if we have to hand the position onto another party they have to be able to instantly pick up and identify features to the front. When we're drawing we look for key reference points – a prominent contour line, lone trees, buildings and so on. Although we have the latest technologies to spot an enemy, we never forget that kit can break down. That's why we learn to draw.[43]

---

41 S. Graham, 'Geographies of surveillance', in M. Crang, P. Crang, and J. May, (eds.) *Virtual Geographies: bodies, space and relations* (London: Routledge, 1999) pp.131–148.

42 Anthony Swofford's narrative of his work in a US Marine Surveillance and Target Acquisition Platoon in Iraq contains this account of a two-man team's work:

> There is a moment when the target disappears, when the shooter sees only the clear, lovely intersection of the recticle, as if a bucket of sun had been poured into his scope, and the light means it's time to pull the trigger. For the best shooting teams this is the exact moment that the spotter begins his soft, religious chant: *Fire, fire, fire.*
>
> Well before the shot is taken, the spotter will have drawn a field sketch, so that distance is easily estimated and the target rapidly acquired. The spotter might say to the shooter, 'Officer without insignia, directing troop movement. Three o'clock from the stand of trees.' Of course, in the Desert we anticipate exactly zero trees in our field sketches. We assume our point of origin will be the burnt hulks of personnel carriers and tanks and the occasional gentle rise of the desert.

From Anthony Swofford, *Jarhead: A Soldier's Story of Modern War* (London: Scribner, 2003) p.135.

Carefully avoiding 'artistic effect', one of the observation party will use a felt-tipped pen to make a diagrammatic picture of the enemy terrain. But, unlike those drawings made by Adrian Hill or Paul Maze, none of these images will be preserved for history. As the Observation Post prepares to move to a new position, the soldier takes a damp cloth and wipes the drawing cleanly off the sheet of acetate. Material trace is rendered immaterial.

And what of those artists who undertook such hazardous tasks to make their invaluable sketches? Newton went on to become the Professor of Architecture at the Royal College of Art in London, whose Principal was none other than the same William Rothenstein who had glimpsed Paul Maze's drawings on the wall of 5th Army headquarters in March 1918. Maze went on to a distinguished career as a painter, and became a regular painting companion (but, as he insisted, definitely not the tutor) of none other than Winston Churchill who wrote the introduction to Maze's war memoir, praised Maze's abilities to record 'the battle scenes of Armageddon', and described him as one 'who not only loved the fighting troops and shared their perils, but perceived the beauties of light and shade, of form and colour of which even the horrors of war cannot rob the progress of the sun'. Maze exhibited often in London, and a large show was held at Wildenstein's, New Bond Street on the occasion of his ninetieth birthday in 1977. Another leading soldier of his day, Lieutenant-General Anthony Farrar-Hockney wrote an introduction to the catalogue.[44]

Sapper Len Smith had a fulfilling career as a commercial artist. Warwick Lendon worked as an illustrator for *Punch*, *The Sketch* and *The Tatler*, though some of his most evocative drawings were used to illustrate *Fifty Amazing Stories of the Great War*, published by Odhams in 1936. Equally prolific was Sydney Jones, who had already published *The Village Homes of England* before the Great War, and enjoyed a busy career as an illustrator of English building types. Perhaps his most impressive work was done for *The Studio*, including 'Thames Triumphant', a *Studio Special* of 1943. Even more prolific was the painter, draughtsman, and television presenter Adrian Hill who became renowned for his weekly articles in numerous newspapers, which advised budding artists on how to improve and hone their skills. He produced dozens of books on art and the mastery of technique, and was elected to many of the country's arts organisations and societies, becoming the President of the Royal Institute of Oil

---

43 Author's interview with Captain Tim Henry, Forward Observation Officer with 266 (GVA) Battery, 7th Royal Horse Artillery, a converted parachute light gun battery. Henry described this method [to the author] as 'fag packet gunnery', impromptu, rudimentary, but effective.

44 Currently, the only monograph on the artist is Anne Singer's *The Lost Impressionist* (Aurum Press, 1983) which gives a full account of his work. Obituaries appeared in *The Times* and *The Daily Telegraph* (19 September 1979).

Painters in 1968. Until shortly before his death, eleven years later, he was still able to espouse the pleasures of painting and had a singular ability to teach simple techniques of observation, graphic outline, and the tame delineation of a landscape, usually on these occasions with 'artistic effect'.[45]

---

45 For some of the information gathered during the early construction of this chapter, I would like to thank John Baker and Ray Evans RI (formerly 8th Survey Regiment), Lt. Col. Charles H.T. MacFetridge RA (Retd), WO ii BSM Douglas Gough RA (Retd), Major J.D. Braisby RA (Retd), Major A.S.Hill RA (Retd), Lt.Col. P.N. Mason RE (Retd), Col. G.S. Hatch CBE RA (Retd), Brigadier K.A. Timbers RA (Retd) Historical Secretary The Royal Artillery Historical Trust. The field research would not have been possible without the enthusiastic support of Brigadier Bruce Jackman OBE MC; Major Mark Walton MC 7 RHA; Capt. Tim Henry 7 266 (GVA) Battery 7 RHA, and Bombardier Steve McNally 266 Battery (GVA) Battery 7 RHA.

Thanks are due also to Suzanne Bardgett and Janet Mihell, Dr Peter Chasseaud, David Cohen, military art dealer, Ken Atherton curator at the Hydrographic Office, Taunton, the late Bob Headley-Lewis, drawing master at Britannia Royal Naval College and to the support team at HTV Bristol: Abigail Davies, director, Stephen Matthews and Jeremy Payne, executive producers, and Mike Hastie, cameraman, all of whom worked with the author on the television documentary, 'Drawing Fire', ITV June 1994.

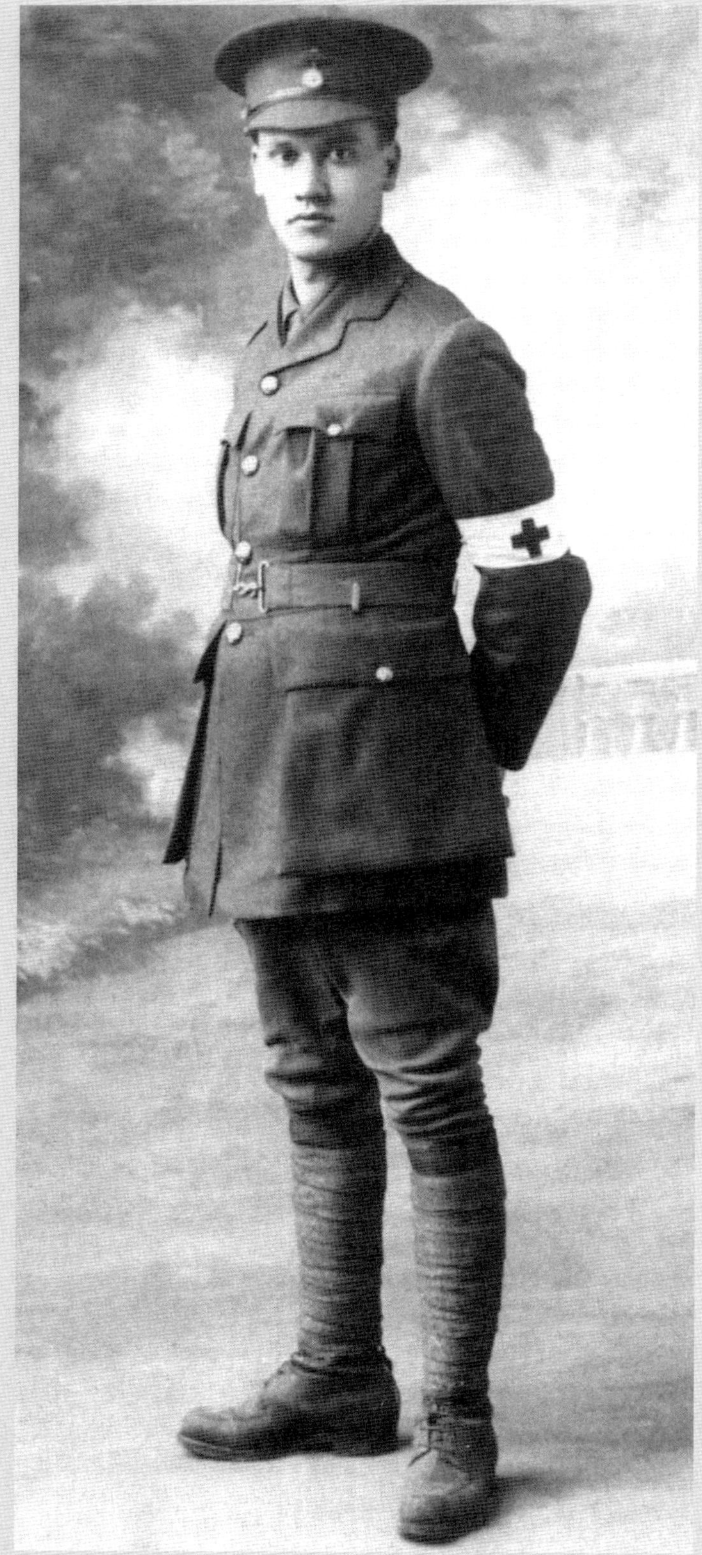

C.R.W. Nevinson

C.R.W. Nevinson
A painter with prejudice

While I was painting for my one-man show [in 1919], the Canadian War Memorials hired Burlington House for the exhibition of the paintings of their Official artists; and it was here that I first encountered the hostility of the intellectuals, who ferociously attacked my work. It is interesting to note that nowadays the same breed cannot speak too well of my war paintings, and wisely shake their heads over my deterioration. They forget that twenty years ago they were doing the same thing over the work they now praise. When I was twenty-one I painted my self-portrait which is now in the Tate Gallery, and when it was exhibited at the New English Claude Phillips remarked in his criticism that he had been much struck for some years by the deterioration of my work... One grows a little tired of the same note. My aeroplane pictures particularly annoyed the critics, and one of them headed his column 'Exit Nevinson'.[1]

A painter, printmaker, polemicist and self-publicist without parallel, Nevinson left a memorable impression on all who encountered him. He is 'a desperate fellow,' wrote one admirer in 1917, 'without fear... only anxious to crawl into the front line and draw things full of violence and terror'.[2] To others he was a self-indulgent poseur,

---

1 From Nevinson's war memoir *Paint and Prejudice* (London: Methuen, 1937) pp.117–118. This account must be treated with some caution. In parts it is inaccurate, inconsistent, and misleading, and has even been described as 'one of the least trustworthy documents in 20th Century British art history'. J.Beechey, 'C.R.W. Nevinson: A Controversial Modernist', *Lancet*, 15 January 2001, p.241.

a shameless attention-seeker and an irritant to his rival *avant-garde* artists who were suspicious of his motives and his artistic integrity. Amongst the public at large, however, he was lauded as the archetypal 'Modern Artist' – loud and colourful, ebullient and charismatic, but above all, the creator of novel images that were capable of being easily understood.[3]

Although Christopher Richard Wynne Nevinson – to give him his full name – has emerged as one of the most recognisable war artists of the last century his reputation has long been in abeyance. Perhaps it has never fully recovered from the drubbing given it by parts of the art establishment during and after the Great War, an influential faction that regarded much of his work as facile and banal, offering little more than a veneer of modernism and riddled by inconsistencies of style. Regardless of the popular acclaim, his work was condemned by the *cognoscenti* because – as one critic sourly stated – it had for its 'subject something that everyone was under an almost irresistible compulsion to expel from their memory'.[4] Despite his best efforts to assure an artistic legacy, Nevinson's profile has paled by comparison with Paul Nash, Wyndham Lewis, or John Singer Sargent – whose grand manner of picture-making Nevinson publicly loathed. Worse than that, a large part of his war paintings have been dismissed altogether. One art historian recently condemned Nevinson's later work as little better than a 'boudoir vision of war, irreproachably tasteful but almost disgracefully irrelevant'.[5] Another described him as little more than a 'pontificating poseur'.[6] What could have fuelled such vitriol? And why should this opprobrium have been aimed at an artist whose first rendition of the Great War, *La Mitrailleuse*, was proclaimed by none other than Walter Sickert to be the 'most authoritative and concentrated utterance on war in the history of painting'.[7]

PRE-WAR PAINTER

C.R.W. Nevinson – as he is more commonly known, though he preferred the forename 'Richard' – was born in 1889, the only son of two well-known figures in journalism and politics. His father was a renowned writer for *The Times* who had built a formidable reputation during the Boer War; his mother a radical left-wing

---

2 C.F.G. Masterman to John Buchan, 18 May 1917, Masterman files, Department of Art. Imperial War Museum, London.
3 Denis Farr, *English Art: 1870–1940* (Oxford: Oxford University Press, 1978) p.226.
4 John Rothenstein, *Modern English Painters*, Volume Two (London: Eyre and Spottiswoode, 1956) p.120.
5 Richard Cork, *Vorticism and Abstract Art in the First Machine Age*, two volumes, (London: Gordon Fraser, 1975 and 1976) Volume Two, p.510.
6 John Ferguson *The Arts in Britain in World War One* (London: Stainer and Bell, 1980) p.74.
7 *Burlington Magazine*, September/October 1916.

pamphleteer and advocate of women's suffrage. Their contacts within the spheres of journalism, government and the arts would greatly assist the young Nevinson in his rise to prominence, and his father, in particular, spared no effort to protect and promote him during the war years. After a miserable schoolhood, characterised by illnesses and fighting, he was encouraged to attend St John's Wood School of Art, then considered the nursery ground for the Royal Academy Schools in London. Instead (and in keeping with his contrary disposition) Nevinson chose to attend the Slade School of Art. In 1908 he arrived at Gower Street to take his place in one of the most outstanding student classes ever to emerge from a British art school. Amongst his colleagues were David Bomberg, Mark Gertler, Paul Nash, Ben Nicholson, William Roberts, Stanley Spencer and Edward Wadsworth.[8] One of the lesser talents of that remarkable cohort, Nevinson never secured the approval of Henry Tonks and in 1910 he left the Slade condemned by the Professor as a failure. Paul Nash remembered the young Nevinson as 'the school bully, in a playful sort of way, on a mental, rather than a physical, plane'[9] who was renowned for his withering sarcasm and unbounded self-confidence. But others – in particular, Stanley Spencer – regarded him as a fearsome adversary and shared some notable escapades which invariably resulted in cuts and bruises. Unusually, Nevinson does not appear to have held much of a grudge against the Slade; after all it had turned him towards serious painting, whilst giving him licence for what he liked to call 'high-spirited and exhausting diversion' such as his twenty-first birthday party:

> Everybody came; all the Slade gang, the Academy students, men such as [William] Strang and [Augustus] John, and a crowd of professionals, singers mostly, men, women, and girls. We had a whole dancing troupe to keep the party going, and one of the girls danced naked. No doubt we all felt very Harry Thaw-ish and tried to look like decadent geniuses with a strong tinge of the anti-bourgeois. At that time such a thing was as unusual as it is now commonplace, the only difference being that when I say naked I mean naked.[10]

Nevinson's last days at the Slade were marred by a complex love

8 See essay by Richard Carline, in *Stanley Spencer RA*, catalogue of Royal Academy exhibition, London, 1980, pp.9–18; Richard Ingleby, 'Utterly tired of chaos', essay in *C.R.W. Nevinson: The Twentieth Century* (London: Merrell Holberton, 2000) pp.9–25; The Slade period is fully covered in Michael J.K. Walsh, *C.R.W. Nevinson: This Cult of Violence* (Yale: Yale University Press, 2002).

9 Paul Nash, *Outline: An Autobiography and Other Writings* (London: Faber and Faber, 1948) p.90. According to William Roberts' biographer, Nevinson was the self-possessed and self-proclaimed wag of the life room, forever coining nicknames for fellow students and the life models. His 'unabashed wit and cocky bravado' won as many admirers as it did detractors. (see Andrew Gibbon Williams, *William Roberts: An English Cubist*, London: Lund Humphries, 2004, p.15).

10 *Paint and Prejudice*, pp.28–29.

tangle between two of his closest friends, Mark Gertler and Dora Carrington, which ended with Nevinson losing both of them as intimate allies. So, rejected by the Slade, cut loose from his peer group, Nevinson sent himself into 'exile' in Paris for the next two years. Although his account was fabulously embellished in his extremely unreliable, but no less colourful, autobiography (aptly named *Paint and Prejudice*) he certainly had an eventful time. He met many artists and writers, including Severini and Boccioni, mixed at the Saturday salons with Gertrude Stein, shared a studio with Modigliani, copied at the Louvre (allegedly alongside Matisse and Picasso), met Lenin, and liked to be known in Montmartre as 'Nevinski'. In between the soirées he assimilated the newness of Futurism, Cubism and the colour theories of Kandinsky, and was exposed to a language of visual form that had not yet been seen in London. On his return to England he began mixing again with the 'advanced guard' of Percy Wyndham Lewis, Jacob Epstein and Henri Gaudier-Brzeska, although he was equally at home with the Camden Town painters Charles Ginner and Robert Bevan, whose subdued impressionistic style his work still resembled. His paintings were selected for such landmark shows as the *Post Impressionist and Futurist Exhibition* organised by the influential critic and curator Frank Rutter.[11]

Much has been written about Nevinson's clash with and eventual defeat at the hands of the Canadian-born Wyndham Lewis, the emerging leader of the younger English Modernists.[12] Lewis, clever and overbearing: Nevinson, not unintelligent, but manipulative and histrionic. Each man ambitious in different ways and wary of being caught in the other's shadow. For a short while they worked in tandem, co-hosting in November 1913 a visit to London by the Italian Futurist Filippo Tommaso Emilio Marinetti – 'the intellectual Cromwell of our time' – but Lewis shared little of Nevinson's adulation for the Italian, and gradually distanced himself from his noisy bombast and strident manifestos. Nevinson, on the other hand, was enraptured by the Futurist creed, their condemnation of the past, their celebration of machines, speed, electricity, their commitment to a life of 'steel, fever, pride and headlong speed'.[13] During one memorable dinner at the Florence Restaurant in Rupert Street, Lewis and fellow artists watched in

11 The period in Paris is covered in detail in Michael J. Walsh, *C.R.W. Nevinson: This Cult of Violence* (New Haven and London: Yale University Press, 2002). The exhibition was held at the Dore Galleries, London in October 1913.

Of the three most powerful figures in history – Lenin, Mussolini and Chaplin – that Nevinson met, he thought Lenin the greatest, although he thought him 'the worst actor'. (*Paint and Prejudice*, p.67)

12 Nevinson regarded Lewis as the 'most brilliant theorist' but little knew that he 'was to become my enemy' (*Paint and Prejudice*, p.56). On Wyndham Lewis see Paul Edwards, *Wyndham Lewis: Art and War* (London: Wyndham Lewis Memorial Trust and Lund Humphries, London, 1992).

bemusement as the Italian theatrically denounced English art, condemned British customs, ridiculed middle-class tastes and slated much else besides, whilst Nevinson stood behind a curtain banging a drum ceaselessly and (it is alleged) rather unmusically. The Futurist duet was accompanied by the band downstairs playing *You made me love you, I didn't want to do it...* over and over again. 'It was grand,' wrote an intoxicated Nevinson, 'if incoherent'.

However, in his eagerness to embrace the Futurist cause Nevinson committed a terrible blunder. Completely ignoring Lewis' own ambitions to create his Rebel Art Centre and draw up his own Vorticist manifesto, Nevinson joined forces with Marinetti in making unilateral calls for 'an English Art that is strong, virile and anti-sentimental'.[14] The proclamation that was published in several British newspapers was typically uncompromising:

> I am an Italian Futurist poet, and a passionate admirer of England. I wish, however, to cure English art of that most grave of maladies – passé-ism. I have the right to speak plainly and without compromise, and together with my friend Nevinson, an English Futurist painter, to give the signal for battle.[15]

Unfortunately for Nevinson, the announcement displayed the address of Lewis's new centre and listed, without consent, eight fellow artists. Suspecting a putsch, Lewis and his nascent Vorticists promptly distanced themselves from this outburst of continental Futurism, demanding to be disassociated from Signor Marinetti 'and his followers'.

Relegated to a mere 'follower', ridiculed in public as 'an interloper and a heretic',[16] Nevinson had at a single stroke succeeded in alienating himself from his contemporaries: 'once again he had become the outsider'.[17]

---

13 These phrases are taken from declarations in Marinetti's 'Initial Manifesto of Futurism' published in *Le Figaro*, 29 February 1909.

To many art historians, it is almost impossible to under-estimate the influence of Marinetti on modern conceptions of art in Britain. He radically challenged and overturned conventional ideas of literature, he invented the idea of the artistic manifesto, and originated the idea of an 'avant garde' in art.

14 The Manifesto was published in *The Observer*, Sunday 7 June 1914, as 'Vital English Art: A Futurist Manifesto.' Lewis's comments about Marinetti as the 'Cromwell of our time' are from his article in 'Man of the Week: Marinetti', *New Weekly*, 30 May 1914, p.29.

Nevinson was later acutely embarrassed – 'a black thought for me...' – by his association with Futurism, 'which ended in Fascism... Mussolini seized on it and worked his thug will. What a fate for an intellectual idea!' (*Paint and Prejudice*, p.66). Despite his stylistic borrowings he was equally disparaging of 'the Cubist movement which promised so much has ended in sterility, a dehumanized geometrical formula, producing little except incomprehensible articles by Herbert Read, Grigson, Sevier, Clive Bell, Marriott...' (*Paint and Prejudice*, p.67).

15 Nevinson claims it was published in *The Times*, the *Observer*, and the *Daily Mail*. Although not satisfied with that course of action, he threatened to visit galleries and theatres and toss the manifestos from the circle onto their unsuspecting heads (*Paint and Prejudice*, p.60).

16 Percy Wyndham Lewis, *Blasting and Bombardiering, Autobiography 1914–1926* (London: Eyre & Spottiswoode, 1937) p.35.

WAR
'The unrestrained savage self'[18]

At the outbreak of war in August 1914 Nevinson was twenty-five years old. Chronic rheumatism prevented him from joining the army, but nevertheless, prompted by his father, he took a course in motor engineering and joined a Friends' Ambulance Unit. Within hours of donning his 'uniform' he found himself in Dunkirk working in a shed nicknamed 'The Shambles' which was teeming 'full of dead, wounded and dying'.[19] The French medical service had collapsed, the railways were disorganized, hordes of casualties had been abandoned in cattle trucks, they spilt out into a filthy shed. There were just six medical assistants to care for three thousand wounded and dying French soldiers. 'In five minutes,' wrote the stunned painter, 'I was nurse, water-carrier, stretcher-bearer, driver, and interpreter'. After a week at The Shambles his former life seemed to be years away:

> ... When a month had passed I felt I had been born in the nightmare. I had seen sights so revolting that man seldom conceives them in his mind and there was no shrinking even among the more sensitive of us. We could only help, and ignore the shrieks, pus, gangrene, and the disembowelled.[20]

As the front-line solidified and the trenches were dug deep into the earth, greater organisation was brought to the rear zones, and the French authorities began to take on the burden of care from the Red Cross. It was during this period that Nevinson, now working as a driver, had a shell go clean through the back of his ambulance. 'To say I was impressed,' he wrote somewhat nonchalantly, 'does not meet the case. I was amazed, and a trifle indignant.'[21] The truth, as so often, was less dramatic. Blighted by his rheumatism Nevinson managed only one week as a driver, proving unable to steer the

---

17 Richard Ingleby 'Utterly tired of chaos: the life of C.R.W. Nevinson', in *C.R.W. Nevinson: the Twentieth Century* (London : Merrell Holberton, in association with the Imperial War Museum, 1999) p.16.

18 There was a significant level of manipulation at Wellington House in considering how they might manage Nevinson. When Derrick first saw this latest batch of realistic paintings he shared his disappointment with Masterman, suggesting ways of unshackling the painter's more difficult side:

> I will tell him that I have reason to believe that his own unrestrained savage self can appear in subsequent work, without giving offence in official quarters. I believe that this is so. And that his restrained, decorous, official self is valued rather less highly...' Derrick to Masterman, 16 November 1917, Nevinson file, IWM.

19 *Paint and Prejudice*, p.71.

20 *Paint and Prejudice*, p.72–74. See also Meaburn Tatham and James E. Miles (eds.), *Friends' Ambulance Unit 1914–1919. A Record* (London: Swarthmore, 1920) p.7.

21 For further elaboration of the ambulance story see: Michael J.K. Walsh, *C.R.W. Nevinson: This Cult of Violence* (Yale: Yale University Press, 2002) pp.96–97. Nevinson's father's record of his son's driving is contained in the Henry Nevinson journals, Bodleian Library, Oxford University e.618/3, 14 November 1914, cited in Walsh, pp.95–96.

unwieldy vehicles and manage the gearing. A shell did indeed hit one of the ambulances but it is likely that it had been parked in the Transport Pool at the time.

However, such incidents wore at his nerves and in early 1915 he returned to England. Undeterred by this grim induction to modern war Nevinson renewed his relationship with the press, cultivating an impression that the work of an ambulance driver was not only hazardous, but also 'exciting, dynamic and mobile' as befitted the sole English Futurist. Crafting his artistic image as carefully as ever, Nevinson made sure his name always guaranteed colourful copy:

> Mr C.R.W. Nevinson, the Futurist artist and painter of smells [sic], has just returned from the front, where he has been engaged in Red Cross work. The above paintings, photographed exclusively for The Daily Express, record his impressions of modern warfare. They have not been passed by the Censor.[22]

Four of Nevinson's war pictures were exhibited at the Second London Group Exhibition in March 1915. Crowds flocked to the show in record numbers; reviewers focused on two works in particular – Epstein's sculpture *The Rock Drill* and Nevinson's canvas *Returning to the Trenches*. Both were real achievements that encapsulated the industrial vitality and the human frailty of modern warfare.[23] In the painting he combined impressionistic painterliness with a simple geometric design, and used overlapping wedges of red, blue, copper and silver steel to suggest both the unstoppable momentum of a column on the march as well as the 'hurried and harassed melancholy' of military service.[24] It was an object lesson in how to make modernism palatable, which impressed some and disappointed others. Lifelong supporter Paul Konody in the *Observer* described the painting as 'the most logical, the most convincing practical demonstration of Futurist principles that I have so far seen'.[25] Typically, Nevinson chose to pick a fight with those who

---

22 Caption to an image of *My Arrival at Dunkirk, 1914* with a photographic portrait of the artist inset, *The Daily Express*, 25 February 1915. Nevinson worked hard to carefully nurture his image as an artistic adventurer, distributing photographs of himself in military garb, correcting in letters to the press any impression that he had been traumatized by his sights of war. 'It was', as Peters Corbett has observed 'a gift to the journalists, who could present himself as a basically sound fellow, brought back to his senses by a dose of real life at the Front, and willing to talk about it.' D. Peters Corbett, *The Modernity of English Art 1914–30* (Manchester: Manchester University Press, 1997) p.50.

23 *Marching Men*, 1916. Pastel on paper, 13.9 x 20.3 cm. IWM:ART 5218; *Returning to the Trenches*, 1914, oil on canvas, 50.8 x 76.2 cm. National Gallery of Canada, Ottawa. A woodcut version of the latter was reproduced in the 'War Number' of *Blast*, published in July 1915.

24 Wyndham Lewis, 'The London Group, 1915', (March) *Blast* No.2, p.77. Nevinson's moderate brand of post-Cubist modernism has been described by Charles Harrison as essentially 'a matter of rendering rounded surfaces by means of facets', and establishing crystalline pattern in place of graduation, flat linear rhythms in place of modulation in depth. (Charles Harrison, *English Art and Modernism*, pp.122–123).

25 P.G. Konody, *Observer*, 14 March 1915.

demurred at such a view. 'The intellectuals made violent attacks on them,' he recalled, 'and I remember Harold Munro saying "What on earth are you doing journalistic clippings for?"' He summarily dismissed the Bloomsbury crowd for their judgment of his work as being 'merely melodramatic', and was untroubled by *The Times* report that the pictures were 'not a bit like cricket'.[26] Ignoring what he regarded as an establishment conspiracy, Nevinson claimed that his singular viewpoint was unparalleled in western painting:

> To me the soldier was going to be dominated by the machine. Nobody thinks otherwise today, but because I was the first man to express this feeling on canvas I was treated as though I had committed a crime.[27]

However, his progress as a painter of modern war was held in check for seven months during a period of excruciating tedium as a volunteer hospital orderly at the 3rd London General Hospital in South London.[28] Like Stanley Spencer, trapped in a military hospital in Bristol, Nevinson hated its 'dullness and squalor', and regarded the matrons as the 'most repulsive bosses' imaginable. At the Third LGH his work was little more than repetitive hard labour and he felt press-ganged into having to 'make roads, to equip huge new wards, and to cook'. For variety, he also had to meet and unload hospital trains, and on occasion help in the operating theatre. Not robust enough for this sort of physical work he was invalided out of the medical corps by January 1916.

An eager public had not long to wait before Nevinson burst back into view with his painting *La Mitrailleuse,* which went on show in March that year.[29] Painted over two days during his honeymoon in Ramsgate, this surprisingly small picture made a huge impression when it was first exhibited. It depicts a French machine gun team bent over their fearsome weapon. Everything is locked into place,

---

26 *Paint and Prejudice*, p.107.

27 *Paint and Prejudice*, p.107. In fact, the critical press was divided on Nevinson's work. Hardened anti-modernists welcomed Nevinson's semi-realist style seeing in such canvases as *Returning to the Trenches* a 'return from the barren wilderness of abstractions.' (Clutton-Brock, 'Junkerism in Art: The London Group at the Goupil Gallery', *The Times*, 14 March 1915). For his part, Konody regarded such work as evidence of Futurist experiments now built on a 'lucid basis of realism' (P.G. Konody, 'Art and Artists: The London Group', *Observer*, 14 March 1915).

28 Nevinson's period at the 3rd London General is covered briefly in *Paint and Prejudice*, which he summarized as 'I helped to make roads, to equip huge new wards, and to cook; I met hospital trains, and I helped in the operating theatre', p.78–79. He eventually was moved to look after the 'balmy' ones in the observation ward. His father had been present at his signing in, and sought reassurances that Nevinson would not be detailed for foreign service. The father did much to support his son during this period, shielding him from some of its grimmer aspects (see H.W. Nevinson's journals, Bodleian Library, Oxford University, e.619/1, 1 June 1915, p.2).

29 *La Mitrailleuse*, 1915. Oil on canvas, 61 x 50.8 cm. Tate Gallery, London. no.3177.
La Mitrailleuse was painted during Nevinson's leave and while he was on honeymoon, part of it spent in Ramsgate. In *Paint and Prejudice* Nevinson recounts that the canvas and *The Deserted Trench on the Yser* (also known as *Flooded Trench on the Yser*) were painted on their return to London. (p.82). The latter painting is an oil on canvas, 50 x 61 cm. Private Collection.

the three living figures hemmed in by a stockade of wooden beams, the jagged sky barred by an interlocking web of barbed wire. A fourth figure lies sprawled in the shallow foreground, pale and wasted, sinking into the deep mire of the trench while the remorseless noise of the gun fills the composition. For sheer intensity of purpose few painters could rival Nevinson; he was a master of economy, able to design deceptively simple but strikingly bold compositions by relying on a limited repertoire of colour and an unfussy painted surface that might be considered bland were it not for the clarity of his central idea. Critical and popular acclaim was unanimous. 'The best and the most ruthless illustration of the menace of this deadly machine war... produced to date,' wrote Charles Lewis Hind as he saluted the 'self-sacrificing automata' captured by Nevinson.[30] Crowds thronged to see it. Gallery attendants were posted to protect it. As we have seen, Sickert wrote in glowing terms about it.[31]

Nevinson's success is often attributed to his energetic self-publicity campaigns, his bombastic personality and an innate (and, at times, entertaining) truculence. It was, though, a carefully considered act and for the duration he adopted a calculated air of steely aloofness that he thought suited the 'role' of the artist at war. But his qualities as a painter should not be underestimated. Although he had limitations as a draughtsman and was not a natural colourist, he was able to simplify and summarise form like few other painters of that time, excising unnecessary clutter and avoiding distracting decoration in pursuit of a singular image. Above all, he grasped the essential dilemma of the war, the appalling truth of 'a world of men enslaved to a terrific machine of their own making'[32] and he was singularly able to capture its dreadful nihilism in uncomplicated pictorial form. But perhaps his real genius lay not merely in articulating the dehumanization of the modern condition but 'making palpable the soldier's sufferings, and of communicating to others the feelings of pity and horror that have driven him to paint'.[33] Many poets and painters recognized his achievements, if somewhat begrudgingly, and amongst his peer group his imagery helped shape the very way they saw the war. From the Ypres Salient in March 1917, Paul Nash asked his wife to buy Nevinson's small etching of a front-line bombardment as it seemed to encapsulate a world in which he was now becoming immersed.[34] Of all Nevinson's impressive portfolio of war paintings, *La Mitrailleuse* is the single most successful synthesis of these talents,

30 Charles Lewis Hind, *The Evening News*, 16 March 1916 (Tate Gallery Archive, 7311.2A-145).

31 Sickert, *Burlington Magazine*, September/October 1916.

32 Laurence Binyon, *New Statesman*, 12 May 1917. Binyon adds that the work 'has absorbed into itself the youth of this country.'

33 *L'Europe Nouvel*, 20 July 1918 in Richard Cork, *A Bitter Truth: Avant-Garde Art and the Great War*. (New Haven: Yale University Press, 1994) p.74.

34 Paul Nash, *Outline*, p.192.

combining cold metallic colour, a taut geometric framework and bold design to proclaim a powerful and singular vision of man and machine.[35]

EMPLOYMENT
'The restrained, decorous, official self'

Success and acclaim were guaranteed. In his first one-man show held at the Leicester Galleries in London in autumn 1916, there were no fewer than thirty-five paintings, eighteen drawings and etchings, and one sculpture, all of which drew on the terrible scenes he had witnessed at St Pierre Hospital and on the roads behind the front line. Applauding his versatility and insight, Frank Rutter named him as the first British artist to have given 'really profound and pictorial expression to the emotions aroused by the War'.[36] Outwardly his work could not have seemed more different from other war artists such as the Scottish etcher Muirhead Bone or the portraitist John Lavery, but for all its radical modernism the work remained 'intelligible and unintimidating'[37] especially to soldiers home on leave. It was also powerfully memorable. In *The Daily Telegraph*, one writer admitted to being both repelled and fascinated by Nevinson's trademark 'curious cold intensity' and identified it as the ingredient that made his work linger in the memory.[38] By the close of 1916 Nevinson stood unchallenged as the one British artist capable of describing modern war: he had the support of influential critics; important collectors bought his war paintings; his sell-out shows made him (as he proudly attested) 'the talk of London'. His show was even lauded by the military; General Sir Ian Hamilton providing a rather rhetorical preface for the catalogue, which began:

---

35 For a probing analysis of Nevinson's significance at this time see Charles Doherty, 'The War Art of CRW Nevinson', *Imperial War Museum Review* (London: Imperial War Museum and Leo Cooper, 1993) pp.48–62. There is no way of verifying whether Nevinson saw these machine-gunners for himself, indeed there is little evidence that he ever reached the front-line during this time. Instead, we have an imagined re-construction of war, an abstracted idea garnered from diverse sources.

36 Frank Rutter, *Sunday Times*, 28 September 1916. As well as his influential role at the *Sunday Times* Rutter was also the curator of the Leeds City Art Gallery and was building a reputation as a forward-looking collector of contemporary art.

Nevinson lists the major figures who attended his show as Ramsay MacDonald, Philip Snowden, Balfour, Winston Churchill, Lady Diana Manners, Mrs. Asquith, Bernard Shaw, Joseph Conrad, Sir Michael Sadler, Arnold Bennett, and of course the critics who supported his work: Frank Rutter, Lewis Hind, P.G. Konody (see *Paint and Prejudice*, pp.85–86). A little later he met Siegfried Sassoon, Robert Ross, Robert Nichols, John Masefield – a rather '*recherche* set' as he described them in his memoir. (p.90) See note 17 for source of the phrase 'restrained, decorous, official self'.

37 Meirion Harries and Susie Harries, *The War Artists*, p.39. Still fearful of Futurist excesses, critics described his work at this time as 'a compromise between clear illustration and Futurist abstraction, which is absolutely intelligible without being… literal representation.' P.G. Konody, 'Art and Artists: the Friday Club', *Observer*, 26 March 1916.

38 Sir Claude Phillips, *The Daily Telegraph*, 19 March 1918, Tate Gallery Archive, 226-AG-469), cited in Jonathan Black, 'A curious cold intensity', Imperial War Museum, catalogue, p.28.

> The appeal made to a soldier by these works lies in their quality of truth. They bring him closer to the heart of his experiences than his own eyes could have carried him.
>
> In France, that flesh and blood column marching into the grey dawn deemed simply – a column of march. Seen on this canvas it becomes the symbol of a world tragedy – a glimpse given to us of Destiny crossing the bloodiest page in History.[39]

Promoted as both a hero and a patriot, Nevinson was also seen as an artist who could capture the poignancies of war. One of the drypoint-etchings exhibited at the Leicester Galleries, for example, depicted a soldier carrying a wounded comrade on his back; another shows the death of a child after an aerial bombardment, the prostrate figure lying awkwardly across bloodstained paving stones.[40] 'There,' wrote Nevinson, 'the small body lay before me, a symbol of all that was to come.'

Given the tide of interest in the exhibition, it was inevitable that he would be commissioned by the Department (later Ministry) of Information as an official war artist. Amongst his advocates was Muirhead Bone (an artist whom Nevinson later chose to publicly deride) and Sir Alfred Mond (later Director of the Imperial War Museum)[41] but the real driving force behind the appointment was his father, who lobbied tirelessly to have his son removed once and for all from the prospect of military service as a combatant.

BACK TO THE FRONT

For a while Nevinson appeared to revel in the role of the front-line war artist. Arriving in France in July 1917 for a four-week tour he was enthralled by the scale and complexity of the static war machine, but became increasingly irritated by the odd company of dignitaries and visitors he was forced to keep while ensconced in the Chateau d'Harcourt, south of Caen, where he returned each day after long motoring trips around the front. He soon transferred to join the

---

39 Nevinson senior's pursuit and cultivation of Sir Ian Hamilton is retold in Michael J.K. Walsh, *C.R.W. Nevinson*, pp.137–139. Indeed, the very title of the show – *'...by C.R.W. Nevinson (Late Private R.A.M.C.)'* may have been chosen to further cultivate an idea that the artist had died during active service; his work – like Brooke's poetry – martyred to the noble cause.

40 Nevinson, *A Taube*, 1915. Oil on canvas, 63.5 x 76.2 cm. IWM:ART 200.
Nevinson later claimed that he had seen this sight at Dunkirk after one of the first aerial bombardments, and that he was 'one of the first men to see a child who had been killed by it.' (*Paint and Prejudice*, p.76).

41 So extraordinarily successful had Nevinson's exhibition been that a full study of his paintings was undertaken by P.G. Konody and published by Grant Richards in January 1917. *Modern War Paintings by C.R.W. Nevinson*, placed the painter in the great tradition of battle art.
Twenty years later, as another world war threatened, both artists again offered their services. Bone, with an embellished reputation as *the* artist of the industrial sublime, and knighted for his services to the art world, again became the first official British artist to see action in the Second World War.

4th Division at St Nicholas, between the old Hindenberg Line and Arras, where he toured the battle zones, flew over the enemy line on a reconnaissance flight, visited artillery batteries, took a somewhat hazardous balloon ascent, and on one memorable occasion gave the slip to his military minder to make an unauthorised visit to Ypres on the eve of the Passchendaele offensive. This venture brought his time in France to a rather abrupt end and added to his self-embroidered reputation for wanton recklessness. He did however recall, with characteristic tetchiness, one occasion when drawing close to the British front line:

> I nearly got done in a few days ago at the observation post with some Lovat Scouts. We were spotted and got shelled, had to stick glued against a bank for an hour wondering when Fritz would leave off. I wondered why on earth I had not devoted myself to painting 'nice nudes' in a warm studio, instead of risking so much for a picture which will probably not sell, be accused of being faked and certainly be abused by the inevitable armchair journalist.[42]

Returning from France in early August 1917, Nevinson spent some seven months in the studio on Robert Street (off the Hampstead Road) working up his front-line and aerial sketches in preparation for a major show in London in the following spring.[43] Simply entitled 'War Pictures by Nevinson. Official Artist on the Western Front' the exhibition marked another shift in the artist's style: gone were the diagonal geometrics and fragmented surfaces of the earlier war work. Instead the painter had shed his modernist veneer and turned to a more realistic style, one intended to evoke suffering, endurance and the stark realities of static warfare. However, apart from the memorable design of the striking exhibition poster, much of this new work was considered profoundly dull, both in its lack of apparent spectacle and the absence of colour. In a word, Nevinson's work had lost the advantage of novelty.[44] Taken aback by what they saw as a uniform 'dullness', officials in the Department of Information complained that this body of work lacked the 'violence and terror' that had been so keenly anticipated.[45] One of the Department's publishers offered the view (without wishing to appear 'rude') that the new work even had a touch of the 'pavement artist 'about it.[46]

---

42 Nevinson to C.F.G. Masterman, 30 July 1917, Nevinson file, Imperial War Museum, London.

43 Nevinson intended to stay three weeks but remained for one month: 5 July to 4 August 1917; following his return to London he produced some seventy-five paintings and prints during the following seven months.

44 The work no longer had 'a novel attitude to war, a novel style, and the novelty of modern technology.' Meirion Harries and Susie Harries, *The War Artists*, p.44.

45 Derrick to C.F.G. Masterman, 16 October 1917, Imperial War Museum, London, Department of Art, 226-A6-192.

46 Hudson to Masterman, October 1917, Department of Art, Imperial War Museum, London.

In truth, too much had been expected – and promised – of Nevinson. He was clearly exhausted, close to a nervous breakdown and had now realised that the era of modern warfare brought little else but banality, boredom and 'brutishness'. Now indifferent to the technologies of killing, Nevinson had become interested in the human subjects and wanted to tell their stories of self-sacrifice, to celebrate the ordinary Tommie's unsung heroics to an audience at home that had been denied the 'real truth'. This drastic shift of emphasis is perhaps most evident in the brutally frank canvas *The Doctor*, which is unstinting in its depiction of terrible pain.[47] Nevinson was fully aware of the paradigm shift he was making: 'I regard this picture,' he wrote to Robert Ross, 'quite apart from how it is painted [as expressing] an absolutely NEW outlook on the so-called "sacrifice" of war'. It is, he contested, 'the last word on the "horror of war" for the generations to come'.

Not surprisingly, such graphic realism brought him into conflict with the War Office censors. In a series of vitriolic exchanges with Major A.N. Lee, the GHQ officer in charge of all British war artists in France, Nevinson defended his right to portray the brutal realities of the fighting. In late autumn 1917 Lee refused to pass one of Nevinson's canvases which showed a group of soldiers he had seen on the London Underground returning from leave.[48] His case was simple: 'the type of man represented is not worthy of the British Army'. Suffering increasingly with nervous stress bordering on paranoia, Nevinson responded first with sarcasm, asking Lee to 'let me know what you consider a pretty man' and then with measured indignation:

> I will not paint 'castrated lancelots' though I know this is how Tommies are usually represented in illustrated papers etc. – high souled eunuchs looking mild-eyed, unable to melt butter on their tongues and mentally and physically incapable of killing a German. I refuse to insult the British army with such sentimental bilge.[49]

In fact Nevinson never sent the letter. Regardless, Lee was not to be moved. As official censor he was adamant, firmly believing that 'if [the painting] ever gets into German hands I will lay a shade of odds that the Germans use it against us'.[50] However, after some wrangling between the War Office and the Department of Information, Nevinson had his way. Not so with another painting, the ironically

---

47 Nevinson, *The Doctor*, 1916. Oil on canvas, 57.1 x 41 cm. IWM:ART 725. Nevinson to Ross, 11 June 1918, quoted in Margery Ross, *Robert Ross – Friend of Friends* (London: Cape, 1952).

48 Nevinson, *A Group of Soldiers*, 1917. Oil on canvas, IWM:ART 520.

49 Nevinson to Lee, undated and unsent; see *Paint and Prejudice*, pp.148–151. The letter was eventually given to Masterman.

50 Lee to Yockney, 13 December 1917, Nevinson file, Imperial War Museum, cited in Harries and Harries, *The War Artists*, p.45.

titled *Paths of Glory*, which depicted a tract of battlefield with the corpses of two khaki-clad soldiers. Nevinson's simmering relationship with Lee boiled over. Justifying his stance, Lee cited a directive from MI7(A) which stated that 'representations of the dead have an ill effect at home ... photographs of this kind are now rigidly suppressed'.[51] In reply Nevinson argued that dead Germans (and indeed dead Scottish troops) had already been seen in the official film of the Somme battle (released in August 1916) and also in the Royal Academy's show of Canadian photographs in July 1917. Flouting the regulations, he chose to exhibit the piece in his March 1918 show. He wrote later: 'Under the belief that the censors would pass it [*Paths of Glory*] at the last moment I had it hung [and] when permission was finally refused I pasted brown paper over it... and wrote "Censored" across it'.[52] This provocative gesture, he noted with relish, 'caused a GREAT sensation!'[53] But it earned him a stinging reprimand from MI7(A) and proved to be his last significant act as an official war artist. Worn out by nervous exhaustion and critical antipathy towards his recent batch of war paintings, Nevinson bowed out as a government-funded painter, preferring to nurture his self-proclaimed role as 'the soul of indiscretion'.[54] Long suspecting an establishment plot to ruin him, he insisted that his motivation in these recent works had been solely 'to make a fine record [to] give the civilian public some insight as to the marvellous endurance of our soldiers and the real meaning of hardships they are called upon to face'.[55]

ISSUES OF STYLE

During his time as an Official War Artist – August 1917 until February 1918 – Nevinson produced over seventy oil paintings,

---

51 MI7(A) informed the Press Bureau at GHQ in France, on 5 December 1917 that press photographers were to be prohibited from taking pictures of Allied dead and wounded soldiers. However, there is no record of this ruling being extended to cover official war artists (Public Record Office, Kew, London, HO-139-42). Alfred Yockney, at the National War Museum in London wrote to C.F.G. Masterman that 'representations of the dead have an ill-effect at home, photographs of this kind are now rigidly suppressed.' Imperial War Museum, London, Department of Art files 226-A6-129.

Ironically, panoramic colour photographs of the war, containing dead soldiers, were on display at the Grafton Galleries, and frequently reviewed alongside Nevinson's exhibition. See for example a review (with photographs of dead bodies) in 'British Battles in Photography: the Camera as War Correspondent', in *The Graphic*, 9 March 1918, p.293.

52 *Paths of Glory*, 1917. Oil on canvas, 45.7 x 61 cm. IWM:ART 518. The image of the painting with 'Censored' taped across it appeared in the *Daily Mail*, 2 March 1918. The painting was bought by the Imperial War Museum, presumably to control its future exhibition and reproduction, and was actually removed from display before the end of the show to be replaced with *A Tank*.

53 *New York Evening Post*, 31 May 1919. (TGA7311.4-789) in Jonathan Black, 'A curious cold intensity', p.35. For further discussion of the censorship issue see Charles E Doherty, 'Nevinson's Elegy: "Paths of Glory"', *Art Journal*, spring 1992, Vol.51, no.1, pp.64–71.

54 Nevinson to Masterman, 4 January 1918, Nevinson file, Imperial War Museum, London, Department of Art. Although he bowed out of the British scheme, Nevinson was still employed by the Canadians.

55 Nevinson to Masterman, 30 June 1917, p.224.

pastels, watercolours and prints related to the war. Before then, his output had been equally impressive. It is tempting to divide his war work into two distinct phases – early work that is characterised by modernist angularity, diagonal lines and an occasional use of intense colour, most notably the vermilion and cobalt blue of *Marching Men* and *Returning to the Trenches*.[56] And a second phase characterized by pictures such as *Paths of Glory* and *Reliefs at Dawn*[57] which is more obviously factual, lacks the pictorial dynamics and fractured surfaces of the earlier work. In this second body of work a dull khaki-brown coloration predominates, the implied movement is lethargic and deep pictorial space is created by traditional use of tonal recession. Compare the bold and simplified treatment of *Flooded Trench on the Yser* (painted in 1915) with *After a Push*, made two years later. Although they depict similar tracts of the battered Flemish landscape they could not be more different in their pictorial treatment.

However, if we simply divide Nevinson's war work into two styles – one radical, one not – we ignore the fact that overtly 'realistic' and non-modernist works like *A Taube* were painted in his first phase of unofficial employment.[58] Similarly, a number of his most ambitious and pictorially daring images (such as *Swooping Down*, *In the Air* and *The Bomber*) were made much later in the war, when Nevinson was employed by the British and Canadian government schemes as an official artist.[59]

Nevinson himself did not see his work as an irreversible progression of modernist styles. In a very important comment on his working practices he asserted, in October 1916, to fellow artist William Rothenstein that he wished 'always to work within the limits of some self-imposed convention and a different one in relation to each new subject'.[60] This is an important statement for any artist. It alerted his artistic friends to a possible change of direction, but it also announced his decision to adopt whichever visual language was best suited to meet the demands of a given subject. Elsewhere, he celebrated his eclecticism, arguing that the individuality and personality of the artist should take precedence over intellectual mannerisms. 'I do not believe,' he argued, 'the same technique can be used to express a quiet static moonlight, the dynamic force

56 *Marching Men*, 1916. Pastel on paper, 13.9 x 20.3 cm. IWM: ART 5218; *Returning to the Trenches*, 1914, oil on canvas, 51.2 x 77 cm. National Gallery of Canada, Ottawa.

57 *Paths of Glory*, 1917. Oil on canvas, 45.7 x 60.9 cm. IWM: ART 518; *Reliefs at dawn*, 1917. Oil on canvas, 71.1 x 91.4 cm. IWM: ART 513.

58 *A Taube*, 1915. Oil on canvas, 63.5 x 76.2 cm. IWM: ART 200.

59 *Swooping down on a Taube*, from the series 'Britain's Efforts and Ideals' 1917, lithograph, 40 x 30.4 cm. IWM: ART 696. Nevinson's period of employment through the Canadian War Memorial Fund is related in Maria Tippett, *Art at the Service of War – Canada, Art and the Great War* (Toronto: University of Toronto Press, 1984).

60 Nevinson to William Rothenstein, 22 October 1916, Houghton Library, Harvard Univ. BMS Eng.1148-1080-2, cited in Black, 'A curious cold intensity', p.33.

of a bomber, and the restless rhythm of mechanical transport.'[61] To many observers, this chameleon-like approach to art, with its ready abdication of a presiding pictorial language was regarded as fickle and opportunistic, a wilful abandonment of the Modernist project. To Nevinson, it made absolute sense, as he firmly believed that his stylistic shifts were responses to external stimuli and shifting pressures. One such stimulation may have been the burgeoning film industry which offered new approaches to arranging time and space, and laid down a direct challenge to photographers, writers and artists.

NEVINSON AND DOCUMENTARY FILM

One of the most significant cultural events during the course of the war was the public issue in England of the first ever full-length documentary film *The Battle of the Somme*.[62] Released in August 1916 just weeks after it had been shot by two official cameramen, Geoffrey Malims and J.B. McDowell, the film purported to be a 'short history' of a battle that in fact lasted for some five months. So as to make sense of this vast and sprawling battle, the film was structured into a number of sections – preparation, assembly of troops, bombardment of the enemy line, the advance, medical treatment of the wounded, escorting prisoners, collection of enemy guns, and finally, occupying captured ground. Indeed, the film pivots on the memorable sequence (since proved to be inauthentic) of British troops climbing out of a 'trench' and advancing into no-man's-land.[63] The film aroused extraordinary critical and public acclaim. It brought new narrative possibilities to the art form, introduced dramatic editing and other filmic treatments to the subject of war and (as Nevinson was quick to note) it offered the painter new ways of visualizing the world.

The popular press was also aware of the threat posed by documentary film. In response, serial images of the fighting on the Western Front began to appear in the illustrated newspapers. During 1916 *The Graphic* ran several sequences of photographs connected by a simple storyline. *Cause and Effect at Verdun* was a sequence of three photographs in which the first showed a battery of 75-mm guns in action, the next a row of ruined houses, a third, an image of the ruins of Fort Douamont.[64] A later sequence attempted

61 Nevinson, *Paint and Prejudice*, p.109. Nevinson's pursuit of 'truth to subject' and his autonomy from theory or doctrine, is explored in detail by Michael J.K. Walsh, *C.R.W. Nevinson*, pp.164–168.

62 For a historiography of the film see Roger Smither, *Viewing Guide: the Battle of the Somme*, Department of Film and Information Retrieval, Imperial War Museum, London, 1987.

63 See Geoffrey H. Malins, *How I Filmed the War* (London: Herbert Jenkins, 1920). For a close reading of film and film-making on the Western Front see Nicholas Reeves, 'Through the eyes of the camera: contemporary cinema audiences and their experience of war in the film "Battle of the Somme"' in *Facing Armageddon: the First World War Experienced* (London: Leo Cooper, 1996) pp.780–798.

64 Reproduced in *The Graphic*, 18 March 1916.

to manipulate both space and time as only film could do, by showing three stages of the underground war: *the miner, the moment, the mischief.* The first image showed a soldier-miner in a tunnel, the second 'the moment' of the explosion, and the third, the vast crater caused by the explosion, somewhat disingenuously described as 'the mischief'.[65]

Nevinson experimented with the three-part image. In fact, *La Mitrailleuse* was first shown as one of three, flanked by two less figurative works, the group hung as:

Violence, An abstraction
Mitrailleuse, An illustration
Night: Light: Crowd, An Interpretation

One critic noted the didactic intention, reviewing the paintings as a 'representational essay' that was both hierarchical – like a triptych – but also episodic like a film. Recognising his skill at rendering dynamic movement using geometrical simplification and 'lines of force' *Lloyds Magazine* featured a caricature of the artist as 'The Man who Paints Motion'.[66]

Nevinson returned to the idea of sequential images later in the war. In 1917, under the auspices of the National War Aims Committee, a folio of prints was commissioned by the British government. Eighteen artists were invited to make lithographs on the theme of 'Britain's Efforts and Ideals'. While the 'Ideals' largely took the form of individual allegorical images (such as *The Triumph of Democracy* by William Rothenstein, and Charles Shannon's *The Rebirth of the Arts*) the 'Efforts' were commissioned as sets of six lithographs, each set depicting an aspect of the war effort – munitions factories, naval training, aircraft production, the medical services, and so on.[67] A number of the artists commissioned to produce work for the 'Efforts' series recognised that the six-part format would allow an episodic or sequential approach to their allotted subject. Claude Shepperson, a former illustrator for *Punch*, recorded the separate stages in the evacuation and rehabilitation of a wounded soldier from a Regimental Aid Post just behind the front-line to convalescence in a mansion-cum-hospital deep in the leafy Home Counties. He mimics the dramatic structure of British propaganda films: the narrative is reassuring and optimistic, each stage in the evacuation process is

65 Reproduced in *The Graphic*, 16 June 1917.

66 In the exhibition at the Allied Artists Exhibition, Grafton Galleries, London in March 1916 the triptych was shown as catalogue numbers 100, 101, and 102. The critical review appeared in *The Nottingham Guardian*, on 8 March 1916. The caricature illustrates an article by Louis J. McQuilland, Tate Gallery Archive, London.

67 Little is known about the background to the *Efforts and Ideals* series. A fire in the HMSO in the 1980s destroyed most of the relevant records. It is known that the series was executed under the auspices of the Department of Information and was probably commissioned by the National War Aims Committee that had been established in 1917 to combat 'war weariness'.

separated into discrete pockets of time. In Eric Kennington's portfolio the narrative unfolds in three pairs of prints, each showing the stages of training, preparation and action. In the first two prints, troops are depicted at *Bayonet Work* and at *Gas Practice*; in the third and fourth, soldiers are shown preparing to enter the trenches. The fifth shows the moment of attack; the sixth its fruitful consequences – *Bringing in the Prisoners*. By using this episodic structure Kennington's portfolio almost repeats the narrative shape of the *Battle of the Somme* film, and like the film it presents an idealised sequence of events shaped for the home audience.[68]

For his series of six prints Nevinson had been asked to depict the British aircraft industry, then set almost entirely to military production. He decided to make three images that described aircraft construction and three of the vehicle in combat.[69] The latter are decidedly cinematic: in print four the aeroplane is shown on patrol, in print five it banks into the attack; in print six it swoops down on its unsuspecting victim. Though their pictorial language is conservative the organisation of the narrative is quite innovative, it conveys the 'whole newness of vision'[70] that Nevinson experienced when flying but which he – like many other artists – could not portray in a single image. Konody enthused over such 'dynamic experiments' and he celebrated the artist's 'cinematographic method of introducing successive stages of movement [to] produce as near a sensation of rapid flight as can be obtained on a painted canvas'.[71] Others, however, regretted the painter's lapse into what they regarded as bland figuration. At Wellington House Charles Masterman expressed sadness that Nevinson had 'abandoned his own *metier* in order to produce *official* (perhaps dull) pictures'. He, and others, urged Nevinson to recover the probing anger of his earlier work and 'to develop his own genius – however bitter and uncompromising'.[72]

These differing responses to the artist's work reveal the polarisation between those who remembered the pictorial daring of works such as *La Mitrailleuse* and *Returning to the Trenches* and those, like Konody, who recognised that Nevinson was trying to comprehend the battlescape as a more complex spatial and temporal

---

68 Claude Shepperson (1867–1921) six lithographs, IWM:ART 703–708; Eric Kennington (1888–1960) six lithographs, IWM:ART 667–672.

69 IWM:ART 691–696.

70 Nevinson, *Paint and Prejudice*, p.96.

71 P.G. Konody, *The Observer*, 26 March 1916, in a review of the *Friday Club* at the Alpine Gallery, Nevinson cuttings book, Tate Gallery, Volume 2A January 1914–April 1916, 7311.2. Charles Marriott, in the *Evening Standard* similarly recognized Nevinson's use of Futurist language to depict 'a very convincing impression of a stern chase' in the air. Referring to his canvas *A Taube Pursued by Commander Samson*, Marriott realised that Nevinson was one of few painters who could capture the essence of movement 'which no realistic snapshot could equal'. 'C.M.', *Evening Standard and St. James Gazette*, 16 March 1915, quoted by Walsh, *C.R.W. Nevinson*, p.117.

72 C.F.G.Masterman to Hudson, 29 October 1917, Imperial War Museum, London, Department of Art, Nevinson file.

domain, one that required more than superficial fragmentation of the painted surface. In order to refine this understanding, Nevinson had to move away from Cubo-Futurist artifice to a more graphic realism that allowed him to play with the movement of a motif through both space and time. We can see how this was developed in two large paintings, *The Roads of France* and *The Harvest of Battle*.

THE ROADS OF FRANCE

As we have seen, Nevinson's second one-man show, held in the Leicester Galleries in March 1918, was markedly different in character from his *debut* show two years earlier. He felt that his first show 'dealt largely with the horrors of War as a motive' while his second 'attempted to synthesize all the human activity and to record the prodigious organization of our Army'.[73] Gone was the visual fervour and pictorial energy of works such as *Returning to the Trenches*, to be replaced by an unusually discursive, more panoramic vista of total war. As an official war artist Nevinson had been deeply impressed by the vast scale of the industrialised military occupation of northern France. He had witnessed every stage in the life of the war 'machine' from its production in Britain, conveyance to the war zone, and deployment over enemy lines. In the new work Nevinson revealed one of the new truths about the nature of total war; namely, modern warfare had become 'rationalised, routinised, standardised'; it had now become its own normality, rather than an interruption to peacetime.[74] Nevinson saw how siege warfare created its own complex social system and elaborate supply chains. By the middle of the war, for example, it required up to nine servicemen in the rear of each sector to equip, feed, and support just one combatant on the front-line. An illustration in one of the weekly newspapers showed the huge stock of foodstuffs needed each day to sustain an infantry division in the field: 140,000 lbs of beef carried in six ten-ton wagons, 84,000 loaves of bread, and 35,000 lbs of flour. It is perhaps little wonder that Nevinson's work took on an outwardly dry, documentary appearance, an art of exacting reportage that was needed to record and illustrate the layers of organization that lay behind the front-line.

As we have seen, one of Nevinson's most enthusiastic supporters was the Hungarian-born Paul Konody, widely rated as the leading critic of the day, who articulated his opinions on conttemporary art

73 Cited in Richard Cork, *Vorticism and Abstract Art in the First Machine Age*, p.509.

74 Donald Horne, *The Great Museum, the re-presentation of history* (London: Pluto Press, 1984) p.228. 'Colossal rather than dramatic', was W.D. Griffith's impression of the Western Front at this stage of the war. The illustration showing 'The Daily Requirements of an Infantry Division' appeared in *The Graphic*, 25 March 1916.

in the columns of the *Daily Mail* and the *Observer*. His tastes were rather narrow, and he could not fully embrace Vorticism, condemning much of the work by Bomberg and Wyndham Lewis as little better than 'geometrical obfuscations', but he was a fan of Nevinson. Wanting to be impressed by line, order, harmony, and 'the poetry and rhythm behind [the] subject' he valued Nevinson's compromise of 'clear illustration and futurist abstraction', because it was 'absolutely intelligible without being in any sense of the word literal representation'.[75]

Nevinson remembered a visit by Konody, then acting on behalf of the Canadian War Memorials Fund, and recalled that 'the first thing he did was to come along to my Exhibition and buy four pictures of the "Roads of France"'.[76] His second act was to commission Nevinson for the Canadian scheme. *The Roads of France* was one of the largest pieces in the 1918 exhibition and it was a return to an image of soldiers on the march, a familiar theme in his war work and one of the *leitmotifs* of the Great War on the Western Front. It took the form of four panels, each measuring 25 inches high by 67 inches long (64 cm x 170 cm), an elongated format that was unusual for Nevinson but one designed to emphasise the length of the column of marching men, animals and vehicles as they move from right to left.

The first panel in the sequence – *Roads of France 'A'* – shows ten motor vehicles and several figures moving in column along a dusty road bordered at regular intervals by tall pollarded trees. Panel 'B' shows the artillery in the column, with two large howitzers, one drawn by a horse team and the other by a caterpillar tractor. There are more walking figures than in Panel 'A', but fewer trees. The foreground is littered with lumber, ladders and construction materials, as distinct from the agricultural setting of panel 'A'. There is a more abrupt shift in Panel 'C' which shows the column, formed now of a mass of marching soldiers and the horse team of an artillery battery. The terrain is damaged and war-torn, the avenue of trees now denuded to stripped poles. Panel 'D' completes the frieze; the column consists now of small groups of soldiers marching towards a smoke-filled firing line through great piles of rubble and waste.

---

75 Konody, in 'Art and Artists', *Observer*, London, 8 March 1915, and Konody, 'Art and Artists', *Observer*, 26 March 1916, which is a review of the *Friday Club* at the Alpine Gallery. These can be most readily accessed in Nevinson's cuttings book Vol. 2A January 1914–April 1916, 7311.2 Tate Gallery Archive.
See also *Globe*, Toronto, 2 September 1920, cited in Maria Tippett, *Art at the Service of War*, p.32. Konody's appreciation of Nevinson is best expressed in the introductory essay in Paul Konody, *Modern War: Paintings by C.R.W. Nevinson* (London: Grant Richards, 1917).

76 *The Roads of France, A, B, C, D.*, oil on panel, 64 x 170 cm. Canadian War Museum, Ottawa, nos. 8652–8655 (the catalogue numbers are not listed in hanging order: 'A' is CWM 8654, 'B' is CWM 8655, 'C' is CWM 8652, 'D' is CWM 8653).
For a full exploration of the imagery of roads on the Great War battlefields see Paul Gough (1996), 'The Avenue at War', *Landscape Research*, Vol.18, no.2, 1993, pp.78–90.

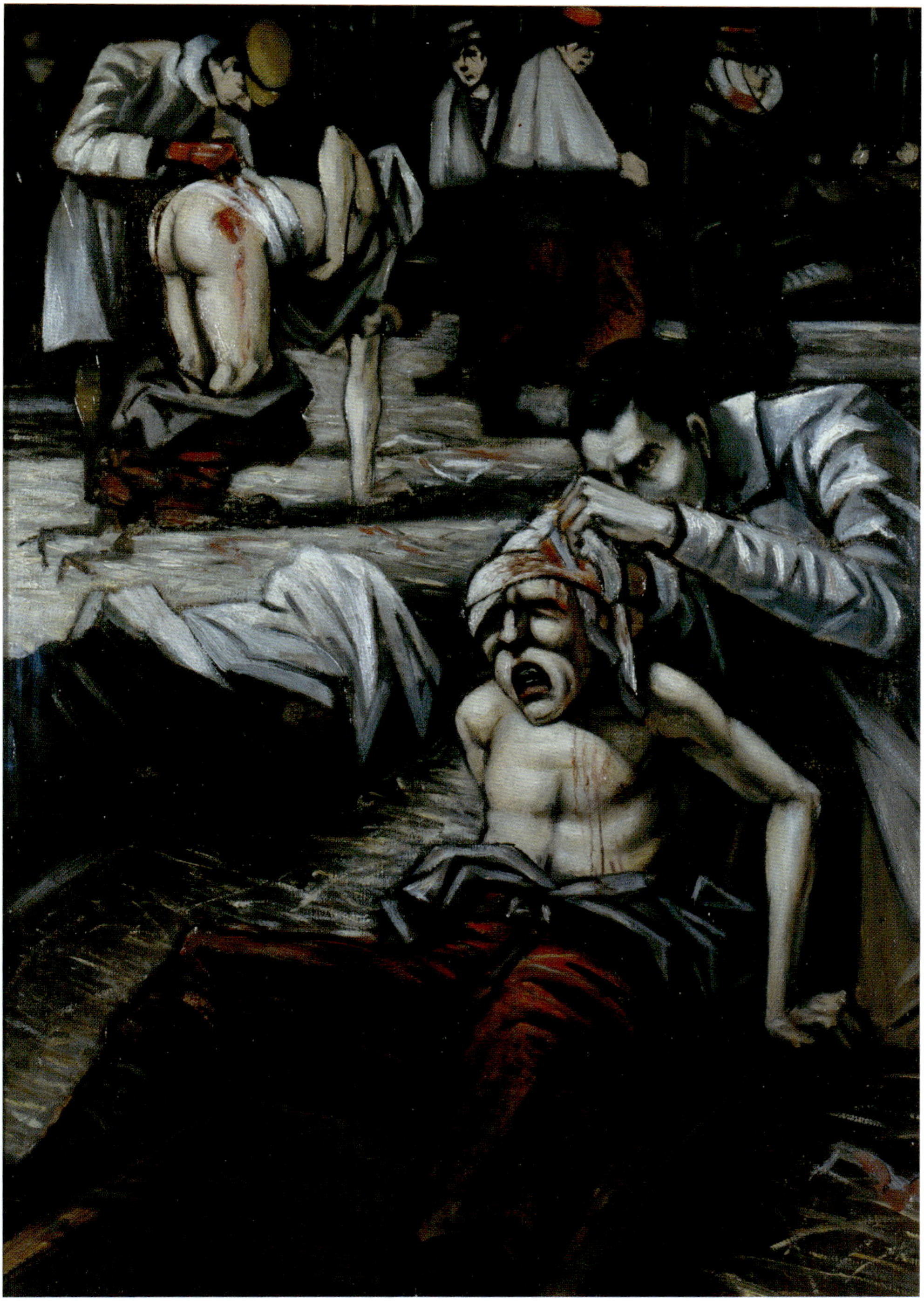

C.R.W. NEVINSON
The Doctor
(1916)
oil on canvas, 57.1 x 41.2 cm
IMPERIAL WAR MUSEUM, LONDON

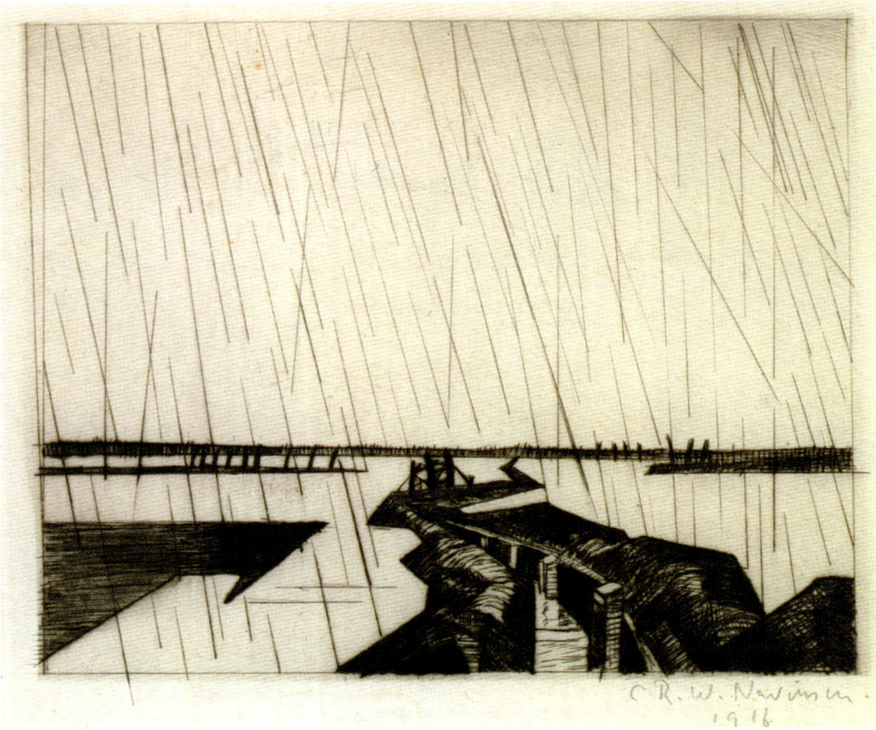

C.R.W. NEVINSON

A Flooded Trench on the Yser

(1916)

drypoint etching on paper, 29.3 x 45 cm

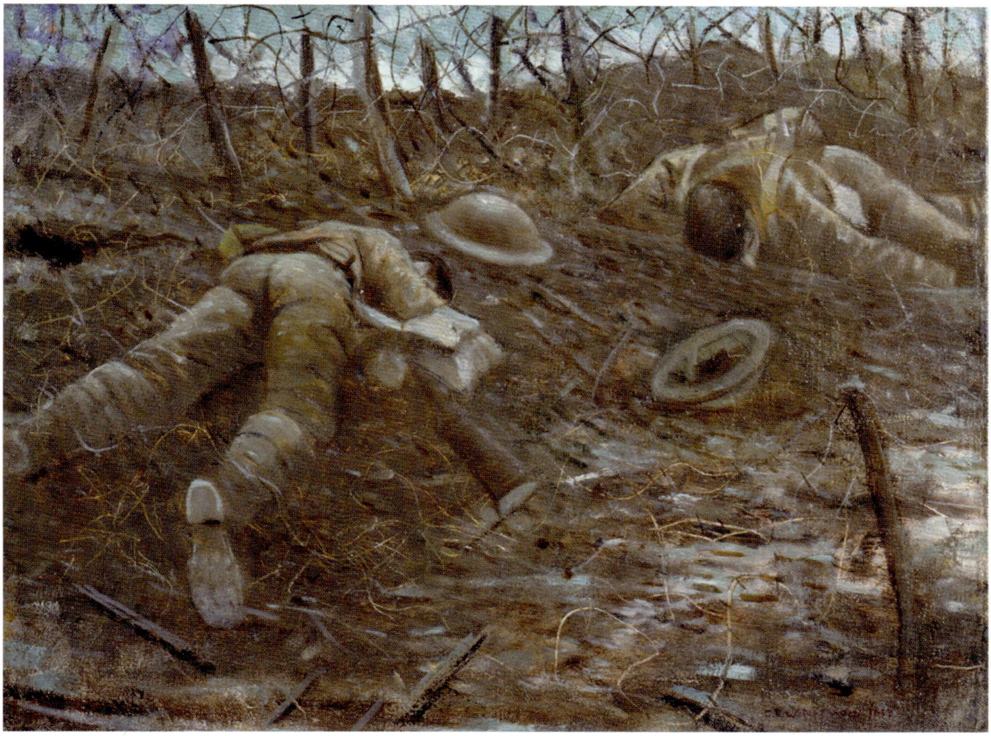

C.R.W. NEVINSON
Paths Of Glory
(1917)
oil on canvas, 45.7 x 60.9 cm
IMPERIAL WAR MUSEUM, LONDON

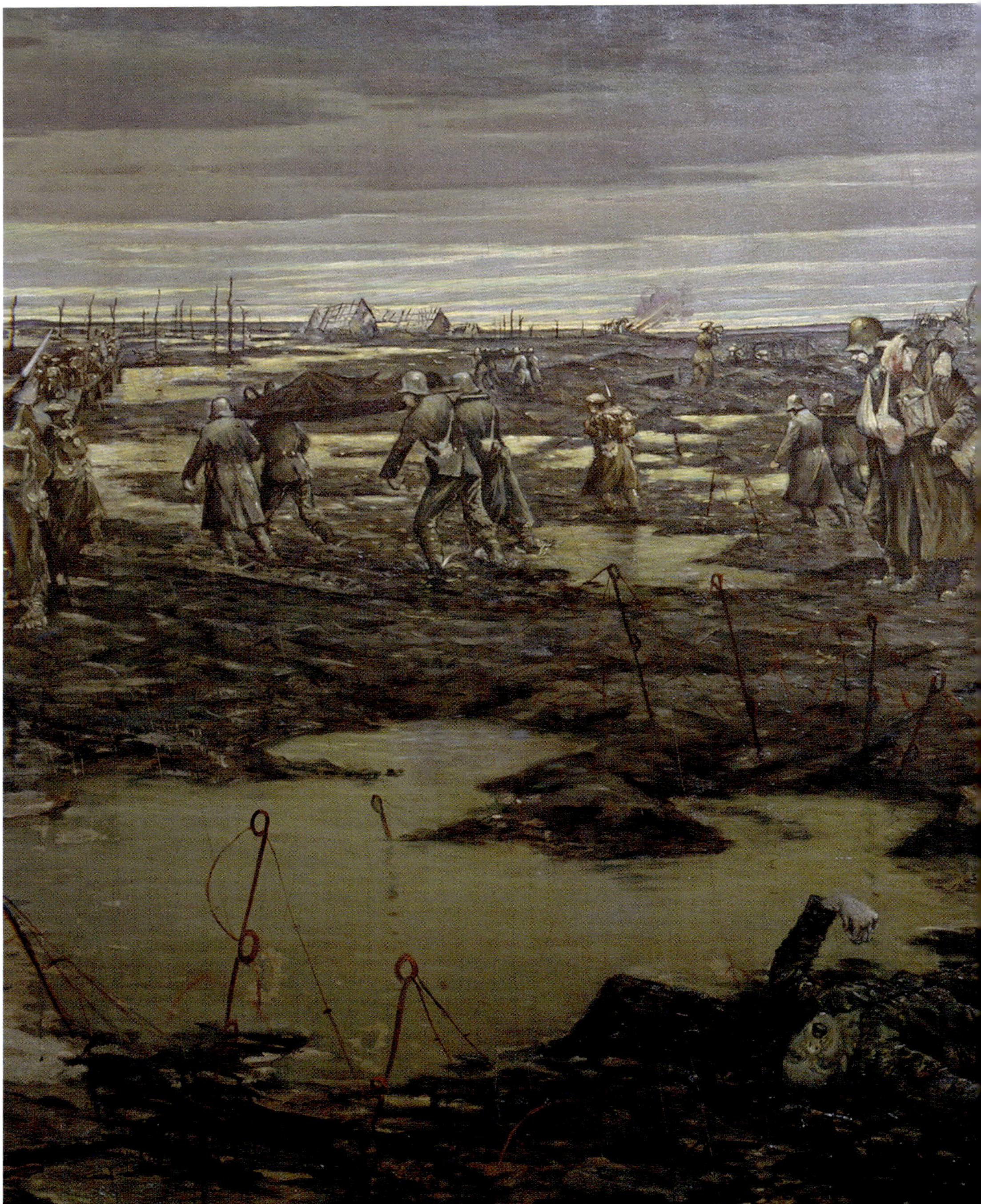

C.R.W. NEVINSON
The Harvest of Battle
(1919)
oil on canvas, 182.8 x 317.5 cm
IMPERIAL WAR MUSEUM, LONDON

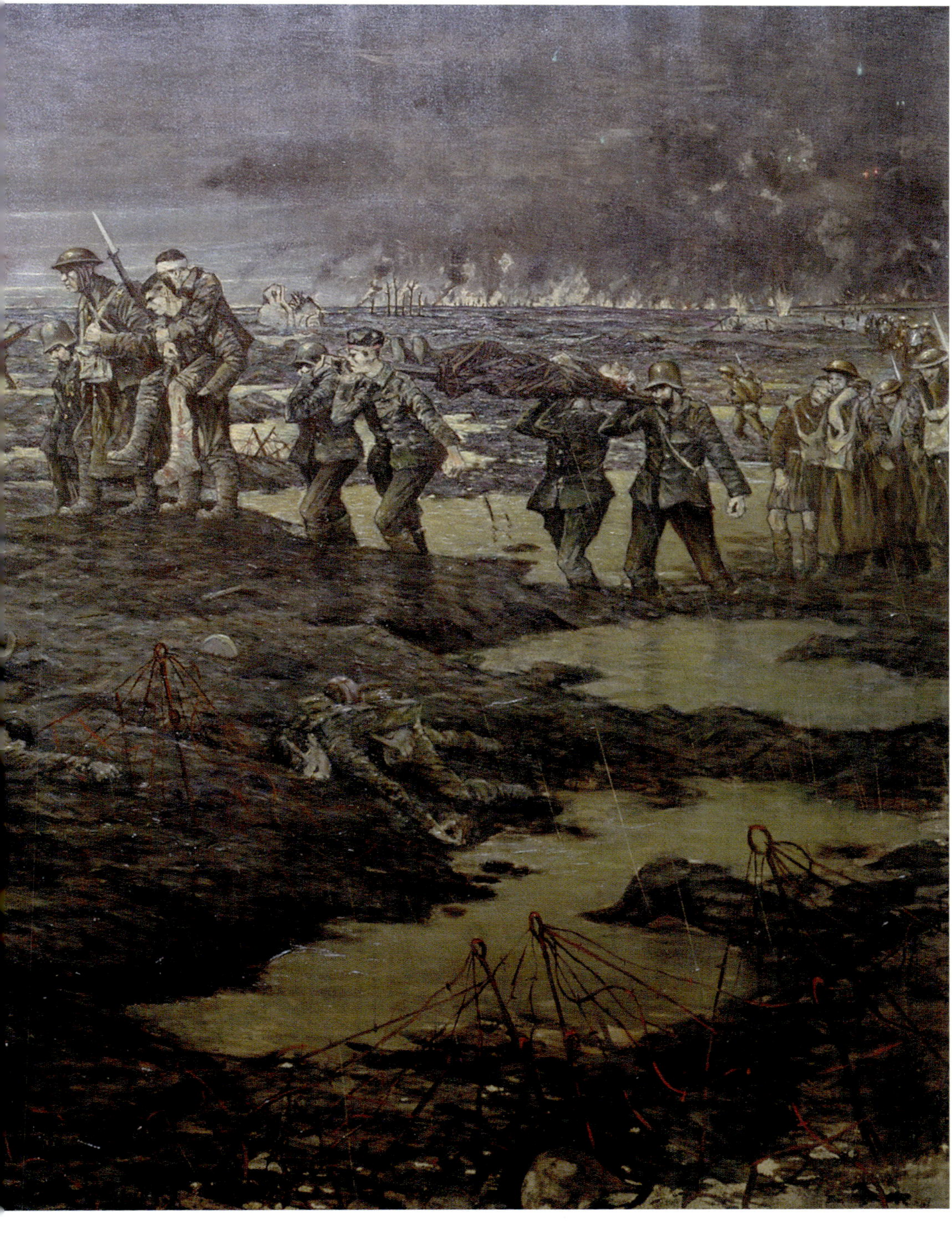

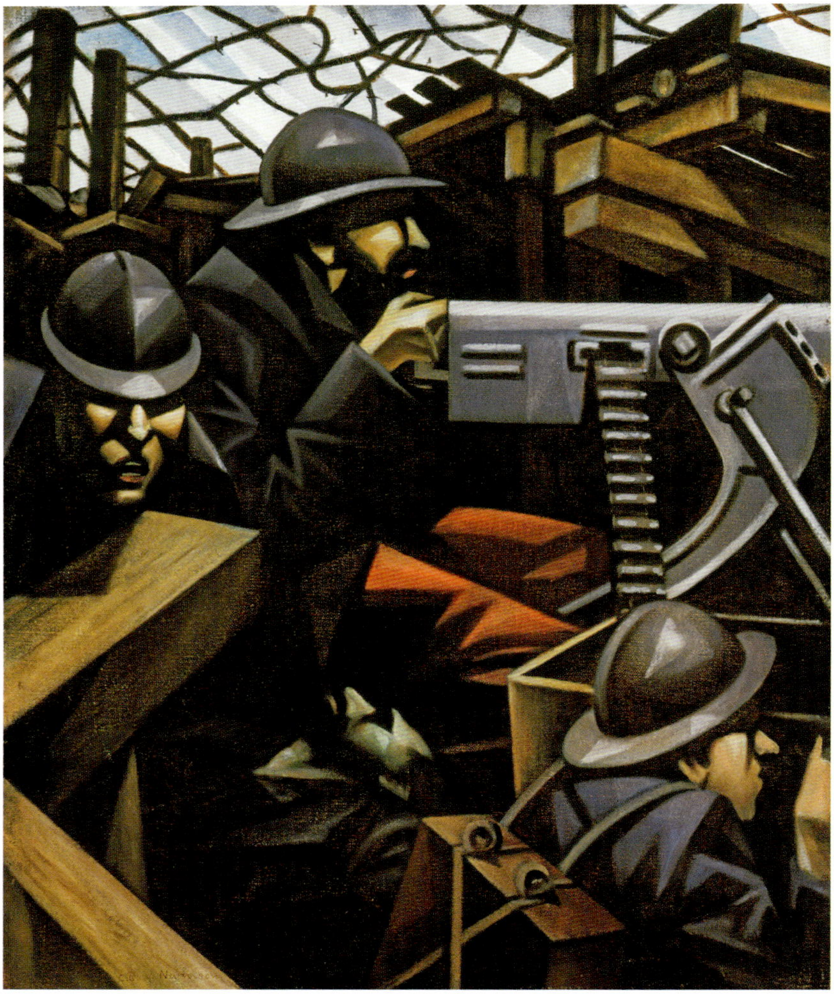

C.R.W. NEVINSON
La Mitrailleuse
(1915)
oil on canvas, 61 x 50.8 cm

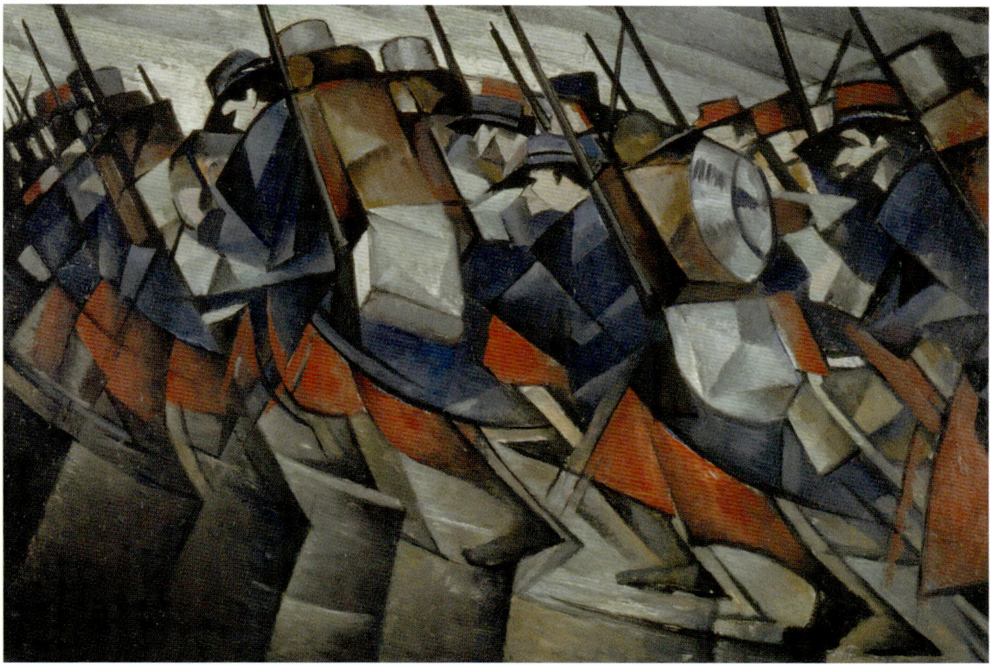

C.R.W. NEVINSON
Returning to the Trenches
(1914)
oil on canvas, 51.2 x 76.8 cm

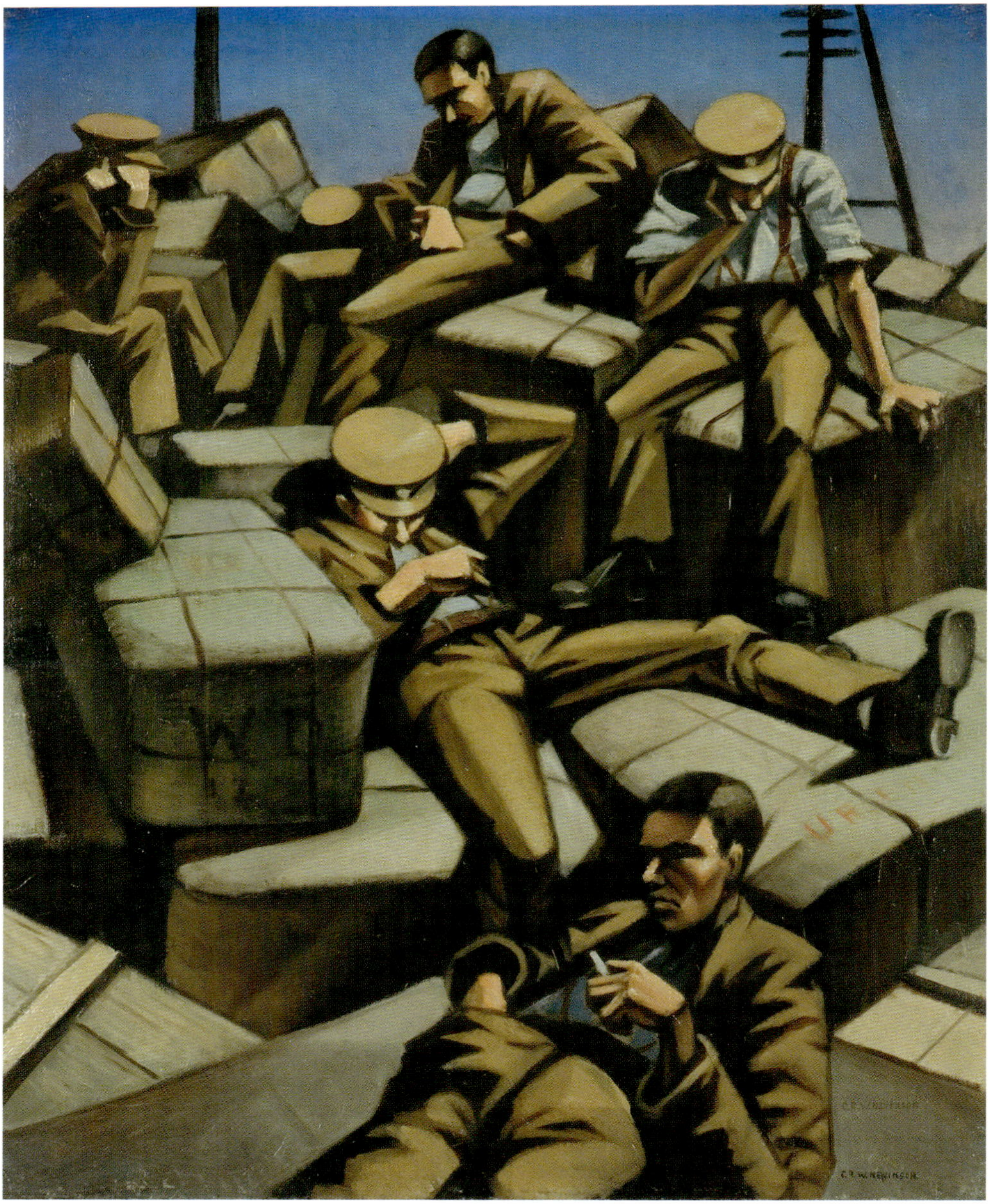

C.R.W. NEVINSON
Dog-tired
(1916)
oil on canvas, 76 x 64.7 cm

In the first three panels the light is luminous, the horizon hazy and diffuse; by contrast, in the fourth panel the sky is dark and threatening.

The Roads of France might be regarded as further evidence of Nevinson's deterioration as an artist. The work has been denounced as an irreversible demise towards '[a] boudoir vision of war, irreproachably tasteful but almost disgracefully irrelevant'.[77] However, as we have seen in his sequence of 'Efforts' prints Nevinson was trying to devise innovative spatial schemes whilst employing an outwardly conservative pictorial language. If each of the panels in *The Roads of France* were hung side by side, the primary elements of the column would join in one seamless strip of movement: the rear of the wagon in Panel 'A' connects with the front portion in Panel 'B'; the gun barrel at the left-hand edge of Panel 'B' is part of the gun team in Panel 'C'. The head of the marching column in Panel 'C' intersects with the groups of marching men in Panel 'D'. The cusp between panels 'C' and 'D' is the least satisfactory from this point of view. Indeed, in its tonality, overall colour and spatial arrangement, panel 'D' might be considered an image in its own right, relating little to the 'previous' three panels. Perhaps Nevinson was using this structural point to underline the extreme differences between the front-line areas and the rear zones.

But the most innovative device in the four panels is the artist's interpretation of the landscape. Unlike the column, which remains consistent in form, the land is represented by four shifts in appearance, changing abruptly panel by panel from rural and agricultural in the first panel through to abject ruination in the last. In this way, whereas the column of men is represented as a single idea on one spatial plane, the physical location occupies different fragments of time. Previously Nevinson had rarely used the battle landscape in this way. It was, however, a pictorial 'tactic' that was well attuned to the actualities of the war. Combatants recalled how the landscape would change over time and through space:

> Along the voluminous velvety roads one rolls under plumy avenues of trees. And then the road becomes less velvety, and the avenues by degrees less plumy, till at once they are only stark skeletons, gap-toothed and shell-shattered in their rows.[78]

In other places, and at other times, the transition was more abrupt. A Royal Scots Guard officer, Major Anderson, recalled a much more dramatic change in the landscape while marching along a poplar-lined road west of St Eloi. Although it appeared to stretch ahead

77 Richard Cork, *Vorticism and Abstract Art in the first Machine Age,* p.510.

78 Reginald Farrer, *Void of War : Letters from Three Fronts* (London: Constable, 1918) p.131.

'as straight as an arrow for miles' the marching column emerged from a small wood into a very different environment:

> ...we find ourselves back again on the Anzin Road and are immediately struck by the sudden changes in the landscape, the village of St Aubin is in ruins and only stumps of trees line the road.[79]

Transitions between avenue, road, track and trench became a popular motif for British and Canadian artists working on the Western Front. We can see it in the work of artists as diverse as William Rothenstein, Harold Sandys Williamson and Paul Nash[80] but few artists used the device in such a radical manner as Nevinson.

THE HARVEST OF BATTLE

Nevinson would develop this dialogue between time and space in one of his largest war paintings: *The Harvest of Battle*.[81] It was commissioned in the spring of 1918 by the British War Memorials Committee as one of the so-called 'super pictures' intended for permanent exhibition in a Hall of Remembrance whose centre piece was to be John Singer Sargent's vast frieze *Gassed*. Initially, Nevinson expressed an interest in the subject of a casualty clearing station, indicating that he felt 'most competent to do this side of war as I became familiar with it in the Ranks and it is the side that interests and moves me the most'.[82] To refresh his memory he was granted permission to return to the Western Front over a long-weekend to tour casualty stations.[83] The visit did not quite go to plan and he chose instead a desolate battlefield in which a weary column of wounded soldiers, German prisoners, and stretcher-bearers make their way from right to left. A distant conflagration fills the horizon to the right; emaciated bodies lie in pools of stagnant water, their limbs bent and mis-shapen. When it was finished and exhibited in 1919, this dystopian vision was described in one British newspaper as 'a combination of the Deluge, the Last Day, Dante's Inferno, and

79 Department of Documents, Imperial War Museum, London, 85/23/1. Anderson, Major A. MS account of his service with 9th Battalion Royal Scots in training and guard duty in Scotland, in France at Vimy Ridge (April–July 1916), at Beaumont Hamel and High Wood (8–25 July 1916) and with 1/9 Battalion, 51st Division.

80 See for example: William Rothenstein, *The Avenue at Chaulnes*, 1918, IWM:ART 1193; Harold Sandys Williamson, *The Route Nationale*, IWM:ART 1470; Paul Nash, *Men Marching at Night*, lithograph, 51 x 41.2 cm, Victoria and Albert Museum, London.

81 *The Harvest of Battle*, 1919. Oil on canvas, 182.8 x 317.8 cm. IWM:ART 1921.

82 Nevinson to Ross, 21 April 1918, pp.56–59.

83 Nevinson to Yockney, 21 December 1918, pp.2–4. For this brief visit Nevinson made the error of refusing an honorary commission as a Second Lieutenant. Relegated to the status of visitor his freedom of movement was restricted and he suffered from 'the maddening distraction of constant conversation' by his conducting officer, who, he claimed, kept him away from dressing-stations. (Cited in Harries and Harries, *The War Artists*, p.104)

"The Sea Giving up its Dead"'.[84] Nevinson later offered a more deadpan description:

> A typical scene after an offensive at dawn. Walking wounded, prisoners, and stretcher cases are making their way to the rear through the water-logged country of Flanders. By now, the infantry have advanced behind the creeping barrage on the right, only leaving the dead, mud, and wire; but their former positions are now occupied by Artillery. The enemy is sending up SOS signals and once more these shattered men will be subject to counter-battery fire.

Hoping perhaps for another fierce indictment of war, the war records committee were lukewarm about *The Harvest of Battle* which Nevinson took as further proof of a prolonged establishment conspiracy against the work, complaining that it had been deliberately left out of the Royal Academy summer show in 1919, and hung in 'badly-lit and obscure corners' in the huge exhibition of British war art staged at Burlington House later that year.[85] Some of this resentment may be put down to Nevinson's acerbic relationship with certain elements within the art establishment, and to his innate irascibility and habit of creating intrigue where there was none. The painting however left a memorable impression on those who saw it. Following its subsequent showing in the galleries of the Science Museum, South Kensington, one regional newspaper referred to the painting as 'striking the reviewer silent'.[86] Later generations of art critics have been less impressed. Like the four-panel frieze *The Roads of France*, *The Harvest of Battle* is regarded as further evidence of Nevinson's demise as an artist. 'It looks melodramatic,' writes one art historian, 'rather than genuinely moving... the work of a man who, having lost his most potent style, struggles hard to compensate by manipulating the viewer's response with a bludgeoning lack of subtlety.'[87] Much of Nevinson's post-1916 work is regarded in this light: having rejected the Cubo-Futurist idiom of 1914–1915, he was seen as no longer in command of a pictorial language that was 'forceful enough to convey his bitterness'.[88]

Of course, this tells only half the tale. The case against Nevinson rests largely on the accusation that he lost his nerve, consciously rejecting the innovative use of broken pictorial surfaces, frenetic movement and spatial dislocation that mannered his early works and were the hallmark of the Modern movement. However, as we

---

84 *The Express*, 28 March 1919.
85 Nevinson, *Paint and Prejudice*, p.164.
86 *Bristol Times and Mirror*, 14 November 1924.
87 Richard Cork, *A Bitter Truth*, p.223.
88 Cork, *A Bitter Truth*, p.223.
89 Nevinson to William Rothenstein, 22 October 1916.

have seen, Nevinson did not regard his less angular style as an abandonment of artistic daring. Rather, he deliberately set out to explore other approaches to picture-making which did not have to rely on the shattered facet-work of Cubism, but which were in themselves equally innovative.[89]

In *The Harvest of Battle* Nevinson returned to one of his favoured motifs, the column of marching men. However, unlike the striding, purposeful and abstracted soldiers in his 1914–15 work, and the disciplined momentum of *The Roads of France,* Nevinson's final painting on this theme shows the column now replaced by a shambolic queue of the wounded, the weak and the lost, caught under a sky as tall as the mud is far. Even those armed soldiers acting as guards appear caught in this dreadful malaise. However, where the pictorial dynamics of the earlier work tends to be linear in composition, invariably arranged in a right-to-left dynamic dashing from one side of the picture frame to the other, *The Harvest of Battle* contains more complex sets of movement within a multi-tiered narrative field. By adopting (as he did in *The Roads of France*) a high viewpoint, and a deep foreground that occupies over a half of the total painted surface, Nevinson compresses the principal elements of the narrative flow into a narrow band in the centre of the canvas. But unlike the column of figures in those other paintings, here the figures do not move easily across the picture surface from one side to the other. Instead they are caught up in a bold elliptical movement running clockwise from the right-hand side of the painting in a broad arc to the far left. Easy to overlook at first sight, this immense arc forever locks the figures into the maelstrom of the battle.

The circular movement begins on the top right of the canvas where the column emerges from the epicentre of the fighting, and continues down the right-hand side of the painting, into the foreground towards (but does not spill into) the spectator's space. Two important formal elements occur here: first, a compact group of three figures break the taut edge of the horizon line, secondly, a possible exit out of the maelstrom is 'blocked' by several prone bodies laid across a narrow mud-bridge between pools of water. (A similar pictorial 'barrier' is used by Paul Nash in his comparable 'super-picture' *The Menin Road.*)[90] As a result the straggling column is further compressed between earth and sky into the middle of the canvas, where it is pushed to the left-hand side and turns back into the picture space towards a copse of burnt-out trees. Far from being a motley crew of survivors leaving the maelstrom of war, the elliptical trajectory of the ragged column suggests that they are in fact being turned back into the fighting. They appear to have lost any means of self-

90 Paul Nash, *The Menin Road,* 1919. Oil on canvas. 182.9 x 317 cm. IWM:ART 2242.

determination and are subject only to external and arbitrary controlling authority.[91] To further accentuate this spiralling effect, Nevinson pivots their rotational movement on the gun barrel in the very centre of the painting. He must have recognized that this clever pictorial device would also act as a visual metaphor, with the shambling column of destitute combatants 'turning aimlessly about the controlling axis of the randomly firing guns'.[92] Comparing this nihilistic vision of war with the positive stridency of *Returning to the Trenches*, or with the simplistic dogma of *Paths of Glory* it is clear that *Harvest of Battle* struck a convincing balance between drama and documentation.[93] It does so by a set of rather sophisticated ideas that incorporate an innovative understanding of symbolic space within a wider framework of the discourses of power.

Nevinson gained an immense authority through his war work. He had, as Konody wrote, 'become famous overnight and was discussed by people who had never seen any of his work. Interviews and reporters kept the ball rolling'.[94] His fame and reputation were truly international; the several volumes of his press clippings in the national archives attest to his ability to generate publicity. Could it outlast the war years? Sadly not. While other artists flourished, Nevinson floundered. After the Great War his work lost its dynamic energy and polemic intensity; like so much English painting in the 1920s it lacked a distinctive flavour and a guiding principle. It is true that popular acclaim lay ahead in the 1920s and 1930s but the artist invariably performed better than the art, largely because – as Frank Rutter astutely noted – Nevinson was only 'at his best when he is painting something he greatly hates'.[95] In 1940 his application to become an official war artist was turned down and the pictures he submitted were rejected. Although he gained an independent commission from the Royal Air Force, he was deeply upset by the official rebuff and later suffered a severe stroke. Typically, he continued to argue his case even applying for a menial clerical post as assistant to the War Artists' Advisory Committee. 'Though an eye is lost,' he wrote in late 1942, 'my hand is not and there is every hope of getting it right back.'[96] Four years later Nevinson died, aged fifty-seven, having learned to paint with his left hand.

---

91 Jon Bird, 'Representing the Great War', *Block* (3) 1980.

92 Jon Bird, p.51.

93 The observation here is by Charles Harrison (*English Art and Modernism, 1900–1939*) who is more sympathetic to Nevinson's more naturalistic style, and his synthesis of melodrama, memory and personal feeling. (see pp.123–125)

94 P.G. Konody, 'The Art of C.R.W. Nevinson', *Art in Australia*, 15 February 1931, p.21.

95 Quoted in Pontus Hulten, *Futurism and Futurisms* (New York: Abbeville Press, 1986) p.529. So traumatised by the long war, and so unsettled by the peace, Nevinson considered suicide in 1919, but as Walsh tells, he 'came out fighting, as angrily and as vociferously as one would have expected from the ex-rebel, Futurist and soldier.' Michael J.K. Walsh, *C.R.W. Nevinson: This Cult of Violence* (2002) p.206.

96 Nevinson to Bracken, 31 December 1942, Imperial War Museum, Department of Art, Nevinson file.

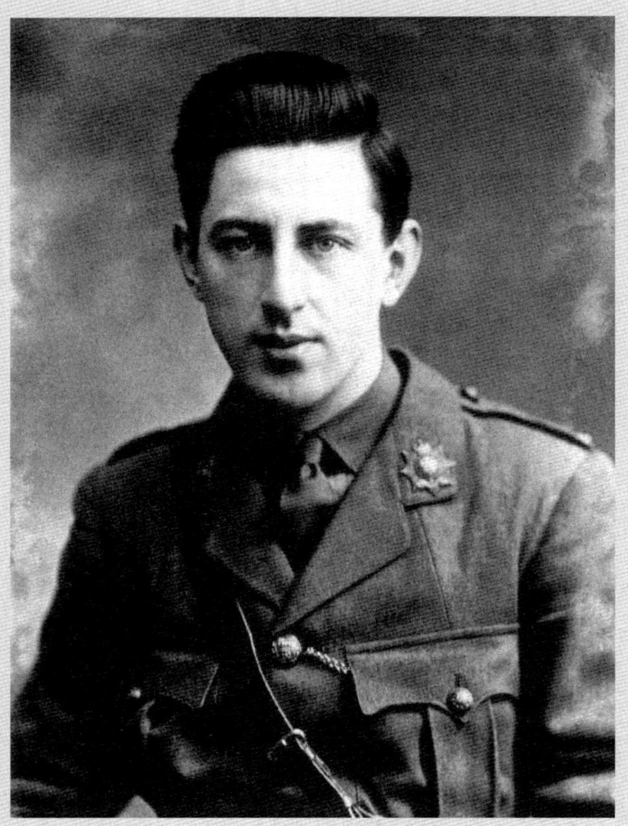

Paul Nash

'Barren, silent, godless'[1] The anti-landscape visions of Paul Nash

Of all British artists of the last century, Paul Nash is perhaps the one most readily associated with the sanctity and loveliness of trees. Absorbing the 'pathetic fallacy' into his very being Nash always regarded them as an extension of his own body.[2] Enthusing about their properties in 1912, he wrote:

> I have tried... to paint trees as tho' they were human beings... because I sincerely love & worship trees & know they *are* people & wonderfully beautiful people – much more lovely than the majority of people one meets.[3]

As a visionary painter, Nash also understood their metaphysical potential, sensing how trees linked the underworld, the earth's surface and the skies.[4] All this would change when warfare overwhelmed the natural order in northern France and Belgium.

---

1 The phrase 'Barren, silent, godless' is taken from Cormac McCarthy's novel, *The Road* (London: Picador, 2007). McCarthy's grim and spare tale about a father and his young son walking in fear through a post-apocalyptic land offers a number of striking parallels with Nash's war imagery and some of the novelist's phrasing has been used throughout this chapter.

2 Richard Cork, *A Bitter Truth: Avant-Garde Art and the Great War.* (New Haven: Yale University Press, 1994) p.201.

3 Nash to Gordon Bottomley, c.1 August 1912, in C.C. Abbot, and Anthony Bertram (eds.), *Poet and Painter: Being the Correspondence between Gordon Bottomley and Paul Nash*, 1910–1946 (London: Oxford University Press, 1955) p.42. Republished with a new introduction by Andrew Causey (Bristol: Redcliffe Press, 1990).

Across the verdant plains of Flanders, Artois and Picardy, trees offered vantage and protection, they provided raw materials and nourishment, they lay in thick forests as well as neat copses. Their destruction was remembered by all who witnessed it:

> I never lost this tree sense: to me half the war is a memory of trees; fallen and tortured trees; trees untouched in summer moonlight, torn and shattered winter trees, trees green and brown, grey and white, living and dead. They gave their names to roads and trenches, strong points and areas. Beneath their branches I found the best and the worst of war.[5]

Amidst the devastation, human relationships with Nature, and with trees especially, were forced to change. 'Wood, leaves, roots and branches took on new symbolic meanings and sensorial qualities.'[6] Camouflage mimicked their elegant patterns, fake trees concealed snipers and observers, copses hid batteries of artillery, subterranean dugouts were filled with the smell of freshly-hewn wood, and ancient willows were bent into shape as revetments for front-line trenches. Woodlands were transformed into strongholds that were fiercely fought over by both sides. Single, isolated trees became a registration point for enemy artillery. Soldiers soon learned to avoid such places:

> The 'Lone Tree' was the assembly point for the wounded, and all around on the grass there were dozens of wounded on stretchers waiting to be taken down by the ambulance column. This tree was a favourite for the German artillery and I could never understand why the wounded, transport, cookers and ambulances were allowed to congregate in this area. Apparently, somebody later recognised the danger and the tree was felled.[7]

Surely this was one of the cruellest ironies of that terrible war? A once attractive, free-standing tree has now to be feared, regarded as a point of maximum danger. What was once an icon of nature to be cherished as a place of refuge and shade had become horribly inverted by the chaos of war. During the course of the fighting, trees, and especially small woods, were to become notorious death traps. Mansel Copse, Inverness Wood, Thiepval Forest, and dozen of others, some no larger than a hockey pitch, were to become

4 Bottomley believed that Nash had the 'most interesting and personal landscape vision of our time, while in technique, texture and accomplishment your landscapes are whole ages ahead of your early figure pictures.' Though he always spurred Nash on to include the human figure in his work. (See *Correspondence*, 8 September 1917, p.90)

5 Richard Talbot Kelly, *A Subaltern's Odyssey: A Memoir of the Great War, 1915–1917* (London: William Kimber, 1980) p.5.

6 Nicholas Saunders, correspondence with author. See also: Nicholas Saunders, (2001), 'Matter and memory in the landscapes of conflict: the Western Front 1914–1919', in Barbara Bender and Margot Winer (eds.) *Contested landscapes: movement, exile and place* (Oxford: Berg, 2001).

7 A. Stuart Dolden, *Cannon Fodder* (Blandford: Blandford Press, 1980) p.39.

infamous killing grounds, sites of extraordinary mayhem fought over for months.[8] On trench maps, the very words – 'copse', 'wood', even 'forest' – soon became irrelevant as trees were felled by artillery shells, reduced to splinters, charred by fire, and felled for military use. So systematic was the destruction and so ruthless the cutting it was estimated that it would take half a century for many areas to be able to produce decent timber again. Indeed, French horticulturalists coined the term 'forest trauma'.[9] Today a few ancient trees remain: a hornbeam that miraculously survived the utter devastation in Delville Wood, its trunk still speckled with fragments of metal; another rooted in a barrel of cement marks the point in No-Man's-Land where hundreds of inexperienced soldiers from the Newfoundland Regiment gathered in search of a gathering-point, only to meet a sudden, bloody and unnecessary end in the first forty minutes of the first day of the Battle of the Somme. It stands today, an ashen stalk once promising succour, but delivering only pain and death.

Nash saw all this. In the Ypres Salient he was aghast at the sight of splintered copses and dismembered trees, seeing in their shattered limbs an equivalent for the human carnage that lay all around or even hung in shreds from the eviscerated treetops. In so many of his war pictures, the trees remain inert and gaunt, failing to respond to the shafts of sunlight; their branches dangle lifelessly 'like melancholy tresses of hair', mourning the death of the world and its values that Nash held so dear.[10]

Was Nash aware that a century earlier, another young British painter had devised an extraordinary image of an equally poisoned and murderous landscape? At its centre was the notorious 'Upas Tree'.

> This fabulous tree was said to grow on the island of Java, in the midst of a desert formed by its own pestiferous exhalations. These destroyed all vegetable life in the immediate neighbourhood of the tree, and all animal life that approached it. Its poison was considered precious, and was to be obtained by piercing the bark, when it flowed forth from the wound. So hopeless, however, and so perilous was the endeavour to obtain it, that only criminals sentenced to death could be induced to make the attempt, and as numbers of them perished, the place became a valley of the shadow of death, a charnel-field of bones.[11]

The fable of the dreaded *Upas Tree* is based on the tale of the poisonous anchar tree, first revealed by the eighteenth-century

---

8 See Paul Gough (2004) 'Sites in the imagination: the Beaumont Hamel Newfoundland Memorial on the Somme', *Cultural Geographies*, 11: 3 pp.235–258.

9 See Hugh Clout, *'After the Ruins': Restoring the Countryside of Northern France after the Great War* (Exeter: Exeter University Press, 1996) Chapter Two: 'The Intensity of the Devastation', in particular pp.30–34.

10 Richard Cork, *A Bitter Truth*, p.202.

11 Richard and Samuel Redgrave, *A Century of Painters*, 1866, pp.483–9.

botanist Erasmus Darwin. During the Romantic era it became a familiar and potent image adopted by such poets as Samuel Taylor Coleridge, occurring in Lord Byron's *Childe Harold's Pilgrimage* and in Robert Southey's epic poem *Thalaba*. But probably the most significant evocation of this bizarre plant is in the vast canvas painted by the Bristol-based painter Francis Danby.[12] He painted *The Upas, or Poison Tree, in the Island of Java* in 1819, when he was just 26; a year later it heralded his triumphal arrival on the London art scene. By the standards of its time it is not a huge painting – some 5 feet by 7 – but its sense of scale is striking. A cowering figure is dwarfed by the landscape, the tree – little but a vertical stalk – dominates the surrounding terrain; and the rocky valley – said to have been modelled on the Avon Gorge – is a hazardous, leafless place of crags and fissures, surrounded by the wasted corpses of fated men.[13]

The painting was equally doomed. After mixed reviews it sold for £150, but the fee went straight to a host of creditors, Danby having worked up an impressive debt during his stay in Bristol. Within years the picture had declined in quality: sloppy technique and thick varnish had rendered the image almost unreadable. By 1857 the picture was barely visible: it was as if the poisonous exhalations of the motif had spread to the very paint surface. Extensive cleaning and removal of layers of dark varnish have since revived the painting, but even after laborious conservation it still catches the light and is difficult to see. Like the eponymous tree itself one approaches the vast canvas with squinting eyes and a cautious tread.

Ninety-nine years after Danby finished his painting, Paul Nash – also in his late twenties – was struggling with his own *magnum opus*, the huge canvas now known as *The Menin Road*, the painter's first foray into oil paint, an act – as he put it – of 'great audacity'. Like Danby's image it describes a blighted land – the dystopian wilderness of the Western Front, a pestilent waste of shattered trees, toxic soils and scattered bones. Perhaps here, for the first time since Danby depicted the corrupted 'poison anchar of Java', might be found the *Upas* in its modern incarnation.

ENCHANTED VISION

Bitter truths, 1914–1917

> I have just returned, last night, from a visit to Brigade Headquarters up the line and I shall not forget it as long as I live. I have seen the most frightful nightmare of a country more conceived by Dante or Poe than

12 Francis Danby's painting was most recently exhibited in a large retrospective show held at Bristol Museum and Art Gallery, November 1988–April 1989.

13 Francis Greenacre, *Francis Danby: 1793–1861* (London: Tate Gallery 1988) pp.89–91.

> by nature, unspeakable, utterly indescribable… It is unspeakable, godless, hopeless. I am no longer an artist interested and curious, I am a messenger who will bring back word from the men who are fighting to those who want the war to go on for ever. Feeble, inarticulate, will be my message, but it will have a bitter truth, and may it burn their lousy souls.[14]

Paul Nash was twenty-five at the outbreak of war. He had studied a few years earlier at the Slade School of Art amongst a cohort of remarkable students – amongst them Christopher Nevinson, Stanley Spencer, Mark Gertler, William Roberts, Ben Nicholson and Edward Wadsworth – who would dominate the British art scene for decades. Unlike many of his contemporaries Nash was no child prodigy. Born in Kensington into a middle-class family, his childhood had been blighted by the erratic illness of his mother who spent many of his formative years in rest homes and mental institutions. Her illness cast a long shadow over his youth. Already a nervous, imaginative boy, prone to daydreaming at school, he took refuge in dark hiding places in the gardens near his home or in remote corners of his grandfather's large house in Hampshire, and his nights were haunted by vivid abstract dreams which, in retrospect, seem to be harbingers of his mature paintings. One particularly horrid one 'consisted in being hemmed in by vast perpendiculars of changing dimensions'. In another he found himself 'in a tunnel which was either closing in or had narrowed imperceptibly [in which he] was trapped, horribly, unable to squeeze through or to back out'.[15] Outwardly a model child with impeccable manners and a quiet bearing, Nash developed a strong, if rather formal, relationship with his father, but after the uncertain mood swings of his mother Nash found little warmth or tenderness in his immediate family, and suffered cruel bullying at St Paul's where he showed aptitude for little but soccer. His parents' wish for him to become an architect were thwarted by his abysmal grades in mathematics and one of his few happy memories was a chance encounter with fellow-pupil Eric Kennington effortlessly 'knocking off likenesses of the plaster casts' in the corridors of the school. The seed of an artistic career may have been planted, but it took many uneasy years to germinate and he left St Paul's 'impaired in body and spirit, more or less ignorant and equipped for nothing'.[16] Nash arrived at the Slade, via Chelsea Polytechnic and a course for

---

14 *Outline* was compiled largely by Margaret Nash soon after the painter's death in 1946.

15 Both dreams are recounted in *Outline*, p.26. Nash wrote of the profound impact of seeking refuge in the gardens of the Kensington Parks, where he 'listened to a new kind of silence.' (In Bertram, 1955, p.128)

16 Nash's experiences at school are retold in some detail in *Outline*, p.72, and also in Anthony Bertram, *Paul Nash, the Portrait of an Artist* (London: Faber and Faber, 1955); Margot Eates, *The Master of the Image 1889–1946* (London: John Murray, 1973) and James King, *Interior Landscapes: a Life of Paul Nash* (London: Weidenfeld and Nicholson, 1987).

commercial artists in Fleet Street, where his drawings displayed a strong attachment to the Pre-Raphaelites, especially to Dante Gabriel Rossetti and his fresh-faced visions of romantic death. Faces soon vanished from his work (though an often-invisible human presence never did) to be replaced with strange moon-lit landscapes, which fused ancient landmarks with anthropomorphized natural forms.[17]

As a mature painter Nash would live much of his life in his imagination, composing poetry, and 'envisioning passionate dramas in the night sky'.[18] However, beneath this quiet lyrical pastoralism, lurked a darker side, which germinated during his time at the Slade. Nash, like all students who studied there, had to withstand the withering tuition of the venerable Henry Tonks. Few students would forget their first encounter:

> Tonks cared nothing for other authorities and he disliked self-satisfied young men... His surgical eye raked my immature designs. With hooded stare and sardonic mouth, he hung in the air above me, like a tall question mark, moreover... of a derisive, rather than an inquisitive order. In cold discouraging tones he welcomed me to the Slade. It was evident he considered that neither the Slade, nor I was likely to derive much benefit.[19]

Yet, like many of his contemporaries Nash grew to revere Tonks and flourished under his tutelage, although there were moments when he thought him 'beautifully mad'.[20] Even as a student Nash cut a dashing, if slightly aloof, figure, his imposing physical presence augmented by an exacting attention to his bearing and a fastidious dress sense. At his first private view in 1912 he appeared in 'silk hat, snuff-coloured trousers, a black jacket and white spats' sporting a silver-headed Malacca cane. On one memorable day he made such an impressively measured appearance in the Slade studios that Nevinson – as barbed as ever – asked loudly if he were 'an engineer', a jibe that caused great hilarity, but one that misjudged Nash's own sense of irony and self-deprecation.[21] His appearance, like his fine sense of poise, may have been an act but he performed it with great aplomb. Friends recalled his impeccable manners, his cool objectivity and a studied carefulness. In every act, whether it be knotting a coloured scarf, spreading a sheet of drawing paper, drinking a glass of wine, or expressing an opinion, Nash was precise and measured, although as his friend Bertram notes there were occasional bouts of

---

17 For fuller analyses of such early works see Andrew Causey, *Paul Nash* (Oxford: Oxford University Press, 1970).

18 Andrew Causey, Introduction to *Poet and Painter*, Redcliffe edition, p.xiv.

19 Quoted in Bertram (1955) p.39. Nash is one of many artists mentioned in Tonks' biography: Joseph Hone, *The Life of Henry Tonks* (London: Heinemann, 1939). See pages 145 and 258.

20 Nash to Nell Bethell, 20 October 1910, cited in Bertram (1955), p.39.

intense wit and fun. Everyone who met him became immediately aware of the penetrating power of his blue eyes which seemed to epitomise a sense of conviction, unerring clarity of vision and integrity of purpose.[22]

Sadly, only black and white photographs survive; in each of them Nash is frozen in a pose of calculated formality that betrays little other than a striking profile, a thick wave of swept-back hair and an averted gaze, locked in the mid-distance as if pondering something vaguely mystical.[23]

Having finished at the Slade he was gaining a modest reputation as a painter of neo-Romantic nocturnes and visionary landscapes, and was nurturing a network of patrons, supporters and buyers when war broke out. A reluctant volunteer, Nash did not much relish the prospect of overseas service.[24] On 10 September 1914 he joined the 28th Battalion London Regiment (Artists' Rifles) for home service only, believing that he had first to learn his job as a soldier in the ranks before assuming the responsibilities of other men's lives. Not aggressive by nature, Nash could however see the lighter side of uniformed life. He described to his lifelong friend and confidant Gordon Bottomley that he was 'now an Artist in a wider sense!'

> ...having joined the 'Artists' London Regiment of Territorials the old Corps which started with Rossetti [,] Leighton & Millais as members in 1860. Every man must do his bit in this horrible business so I have given up painting and bid it adieux for – who knows how long, to take up the queer business of soldiering... and I enjoy the burst of exercise – marching, drilling all day in the open air about the pleasant parts of Regents Park and Hampstead Heath.[25]

---

21 These observations on Nash's particular and precise mannerisms are from Bertram (1955) p.47–49 who knew Nash, and is particularly revealing on this aspect of Nash's personality. In less discreet moments he was known to parade in a brown tweed cloak and red silk scarf, smoking a cherry-wood pipe and carry an ebony shepherd's crook. Bertram noted that his fastidiousness was based on a deep integrity, 'the power of a whole personality ceaselessly occupied with choosing the best, even in the most trivial matters'.

Lance Sieveking, a fellow soldier in the Artists' Rifles relates in *The Eye of the Beholder* (p.56) an occasion when, fitting for a new uniform jacket in Holborn, Nash became infuriated that the tailor had 'absolutely ballsed it up'. Neither Margaret Nash nor Sieveking could detect any fault in the cut. Nash, however, was extraordinarily finicky, exclaiming: 'Why, damn it all! Just look at the left shoulder.' Sieveking, relates James King, failed to see how the uniform fell short of perfection (in King, 1987, p.75, and Lance Sieveking, *The Eye of the Beholder*, London: Hulton, 1957).

22 These observations are taken from Nash's obituary by Archibald Russell in *The Times*, 23 July 1946.

23 See for example the carefully posed photographs of Nash in *Outline*. In the first of these, Nash is as erect, posed and unyielding as the measuring instrument he holds in his hand.

24 This is not quite how Margaret Nash later saw it. 'He had a very clear and simple conception of his duty towards his country, which he passionately loved, and although he was the last human being in the world to tolerate the horror and cruelty of war, he had an immediate and firm conviction that he must fight for England.' Margaret Nash, *Memoir* – typescript now on deposit in the Victoria and Albert Museum, London, p.8.

Margaret and Paul were married on 17 December 1914 at St Martin-in-the Fields, London.

25 Nash to Gordon Bottomley, c.27 September 1914, in *Poet and Painter*, p.74.

After officer training – preceded by a stint as a map-reading instructor at Romford, Essex – Nash eventually signed for overseas service, he was gazetted second lieutenant and assigned to the Third Battalion of the Hampshire Regiment, and then posted to the 15th (Service) Battalion of the Hampshires in early 1917. Much of his induction period was inevitably dull, although he became adept at working things to his advantage, wangling his fair share of sleeping-out passes, and learning how to make himself comfortable. With an air of wry amusement, he described his company as a mixture of 'old crusted B.E.F. warriors with wound stripes... and the rest, boys'. His job, he wrote to his wife, is 'generally to superintend, criticize and make suggestions – rather in my line'.[26] After the customary cycle of unexplained delays, mis-information, and a bout of measles, Nash eventually embarked for France in late February 1917, having narrowly missed being sent to Salonika with an earlier draft. Wandering around the crowded troopship he noted:

> The men are odd creatures. They are very ill-housed here, huddled like beasts at night in hard angular places below decks, in an atmosphere foetid and sickly – they must be terribly bored, yet doing nothing is better to them than doing anything. They cheered when we sailed at last, they cheered louder when we stopped.[27]

This rather detached, even cynical, view of his charges was complemented in his letters by rich visions of the benighted world he was now entering. Sensitive to the unusual and the unnatural and always able to detect the 'sinister beneath the innocent',[28] Nash's writing at this time is flavoured by darkness and mystery, albeit laced with a still youthful, chivalric idealism:

> The ship, blacker than anything, surged along, the bell clanging from time to time, the hooter uttering all kinds of different noises of warning, occasionally an electric bell would ring and be answered below by another. On the bridge strode the Captain peering into the fog. Stark against the night. Seeming to strain upwards but having an extraordinarily proud steady look, was the foremast bearing the light at its heads. The thing fascinated me and I gazed and gazed up at it. To me it seemed a kind of guide and spirit of the ship, piercing the dark, greeting the unknown ahead.[29]

---

26 These tales of his joining up are in *Outline*, p.179–181. Paul Nash is mentioned in the 'Second List' of British artists serving with the forces published in *The Studio* a few months later (April 1915) as Nash, P., 28th Batt; London Regt. (Artists' Rifles).

27 *Outline*, p.181.

28 From John Ferguson, *The Arts in Britain in World War One* (London: Stainer and Bell, 1980) p.104.

29 *Outline*, p.182.

Disembarking at Le Havre, Nash reached the Ypres Sector a short while later. The Salient was unusually subdued. 'There is not much danger,' he wrote to his wife, 'Raids are not very feasible and the line is seldom badly shelled.'[30] His wife was not easily assured and throughout his short sojourn at the front she prayed that Paul would be protected by a 'merciful providence'.[31] Nash was much taken by the enchanted scenery of the French landscape and he revelled in its novel charm. His letters brim with picturesque detail and local colour, summarized in his report of a small cemetery that he liked to visit:

> It was a wonderful sight, little wooden shrines over each grave filled inside with some sort of wire wreaths and small flowering trees, a little bower pale blue and green in colour and always there was a little cherub doll upon a thread. Wind and weather had washed white shrines to a moist delicate grey – had faded the bowers to a mysterious pale blue. The wind passing through the place set the cherubs flying gently over the wire trees and the flowers... Never have I seen such curious beauty connected with graves and burials...[32]

Nash's happiness changed to astonishment as he left behind such bucolic pleasures for the battle zone. Although war had wreaked its havoc, nature was proving extraordinarily resilient. Nash wrote of walking through a wood, or at least what remained of it after the shelling, when it was just 'a place with an evil name, pitted and pocked with shells, the trees torn to shreds, often reeking with poison gas'. Two months later, to his great surprise, this 'most desolate ruinous place' was drastically changed. It was now 'a vivid green':

> the most broken trees even had sprouted somewhere and in the midst, from the depth of the wood's bruised heart poured out the throbbing song of a nightingale. Ridiculous mad incongruity! One can't think which is the more absurd, the War or Nature...[33]

Nash was both bemused and maddened by the strange absurdities all around him, unsure whether to aim his eloquent anger at the war, at nature, or at 'we poor beings [who] are double enthralled'. And how eloquent Nash had become. Gone were the rather sentimental and derivative ideas borrowed from his Pre-Raphaelite phase, sidelined was the chivalric idealism of his late youth, to be replaced by a tougher language that matched the novel and grim

---

30 This letter is dated 4 April 1917, in *Outline*.

31 Margaret Nash, *Memoir* p.32.

32 *Outline*, p.186.

33 *Outline*, p.187.

conditions facing him. Never before had he been subject to circumstances and places that were so 'pitiless, cruel and malignant'. For possibly the first time Nash was seeing for *himself*, not applying the tired conventions of an art-practice or imposing the vision of others. As Bertram so vividly remarks: 'He saw it'.[34] He had now to internalize the experience, and capture what he saw on paper, and above all, he had to do this in the most debilitating of conditions.

Nash's wife, Margaret had noted that it was the very 'irksomeness' of his duties as an officer that seemed to deepen his integrity as an artist. Indeed, she claims it was during his service at the front that 'he developed that astonishing industry which afterwards enabled him to work under almost any circumstances, however ugly, noisy or inhibiting'.[35] And by early March 1917, despite the strictures of military duty, Nash had produced his first batch of drawings, which he dispatched to his dealer in England, accompanied by a note from his commanding officer which confirmed (rather fortunately) that they were of 'no military importance'. The drawings captured his fascination with the rejuvenated Flanders landscape, often cruelly juxtaposed with scarred hills and 'stick-like trees'. Nash is probably best known for the nocturnal sensibility which later haunted his visions of the war, but these early drawings – like many of his letters – are often saturated with light and colour:

> Here in the back garden of the trenches it is amazingly beautiful – the mud is dried to a pinky colour and upon the parapet, and through sandbags even, the green grass pushes up and waves in the breeze, while clots of bright dandelions, clover, thistles and twenty other plants flourish luxuriantly, brilliant growths of bright green against the pink earth. Nearly all the better trees have come out, and the birds sing all day in spite of shells and shrapnel. I have made three more drawings of all these wonderful ruinous forms which excite me so much here.[36]

As Paul Fussell has so brilliantly observed of the 'English' passion for the rural and the bucolic: 'if the opposite of war is peace, the opposite of experiencing moments of war is proposing moments of pastoral'.[37] But to Nash this was more than nature as an antidote to the brutalization of war. He appears to have been genuinely revitalized by his duties at the front-line: 'I feel very happy these days,' he wrote in March, 'in fact, I believe I am happier in the

34 As always Bertram is at his most insightful here; Nash's accelerated transition from poetic to pragmatic is well recounted in Bertram (1995) p.91.

35 Margaret Nash writes about her husband's working habits in the Introduction to the war correspondence in *Outline*, p.177.

36 *Outline*, p.188.

37 Paul Fussell, *The Great War and Modern Memory* (London and Oxford: Oxford University Press, 1975), p.231.

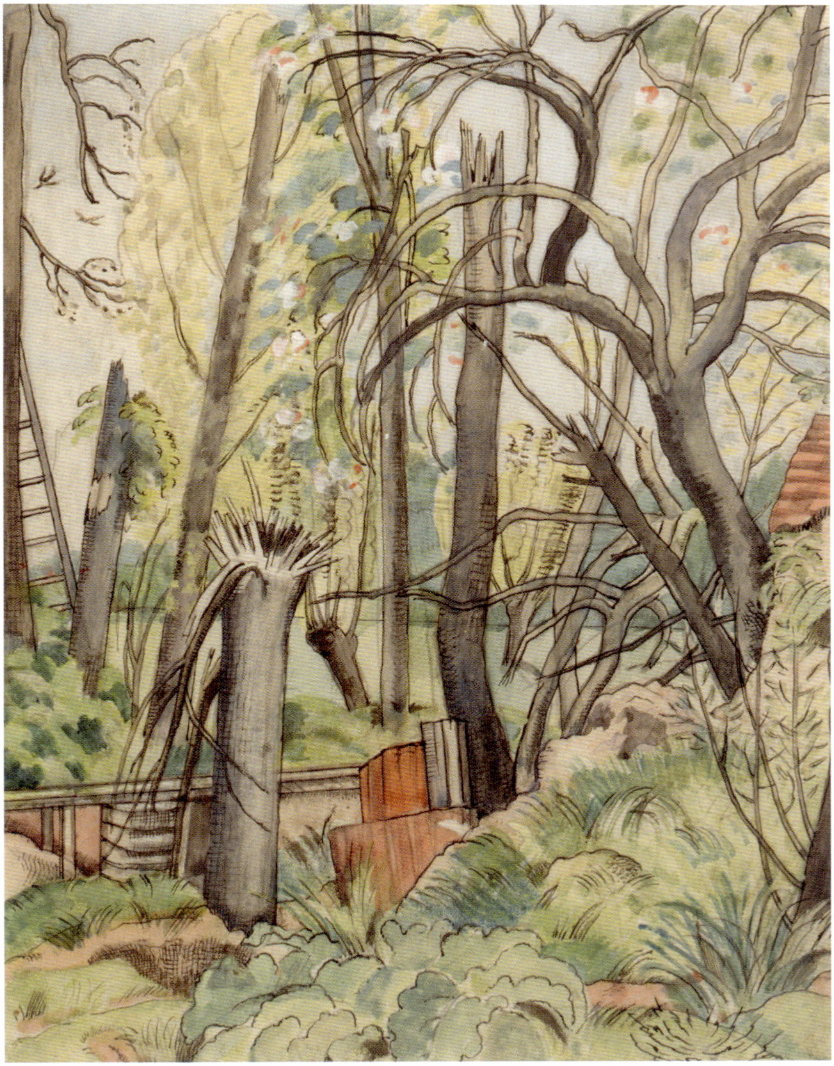

PAUL NASH
Chaos Decoratif
(1917)
pen and black ink, pencil and watercolour with body colour,
25.6 x 20.2 cm

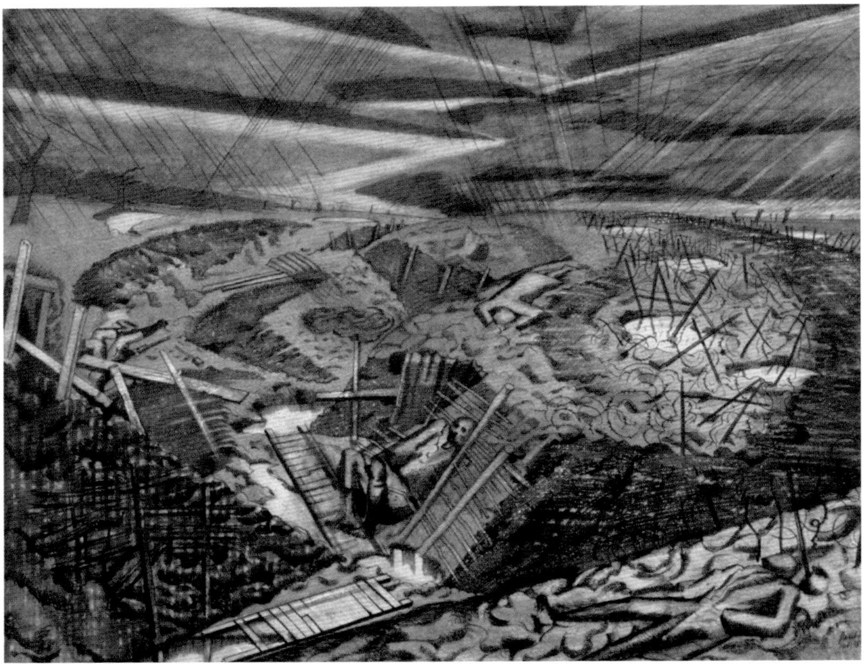

PAUL NASH
After the Battle
(1918)
ink watercolour on paper, 59.8 x 73.3 cm
IMPERIAL WAR MUSEUM, LONDON

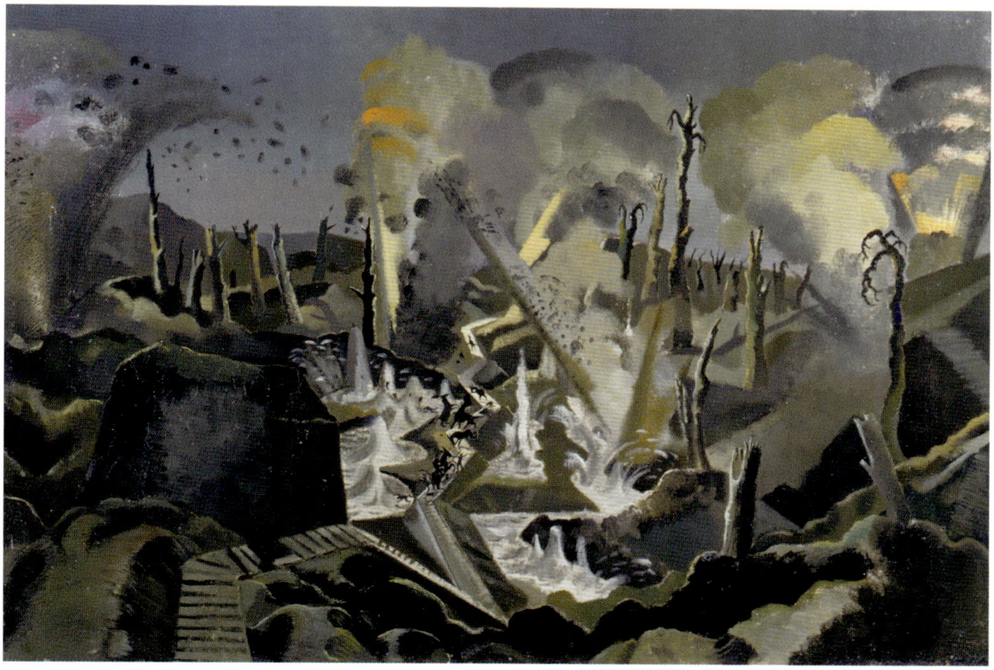

PAUL NASH
The Mule Track
(1918)
oil on canvas, 60.9 x 91.4 cm
IMPERIAL WAR MUSEUM, LONDON

PAUL NASH
Wire
(1918–19)
ink chalk
watercolour on paper,
48.6 x 63.5 cm
IMPERIAL WAR MUSEUM,
LONDON

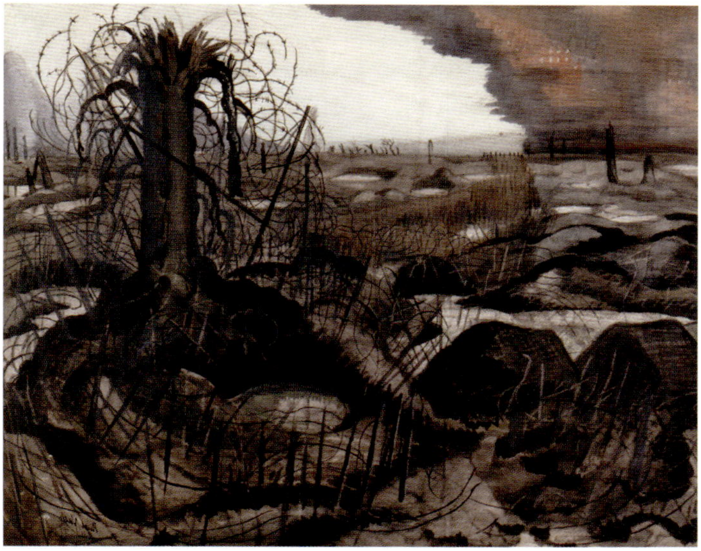

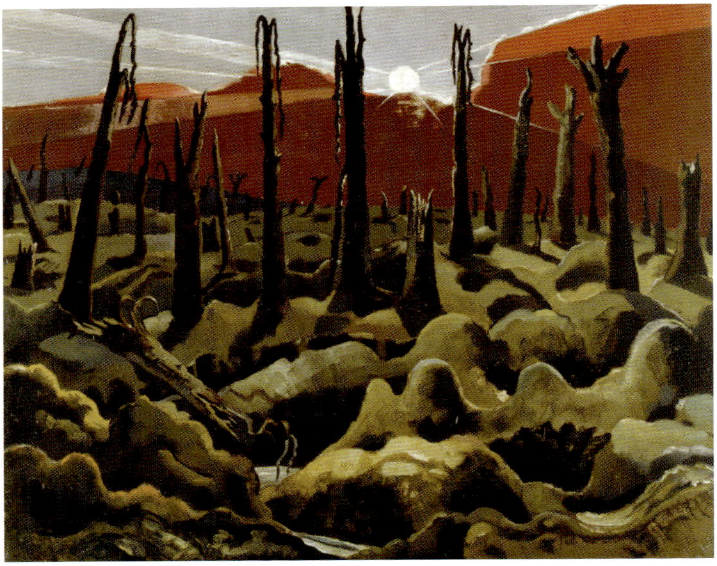

PAUL NASH
We are Making a New World
(1918)
oil on canvas, 71.1 x 91.4 cm
IMPERIAL WAR MUSEUM, LONDON

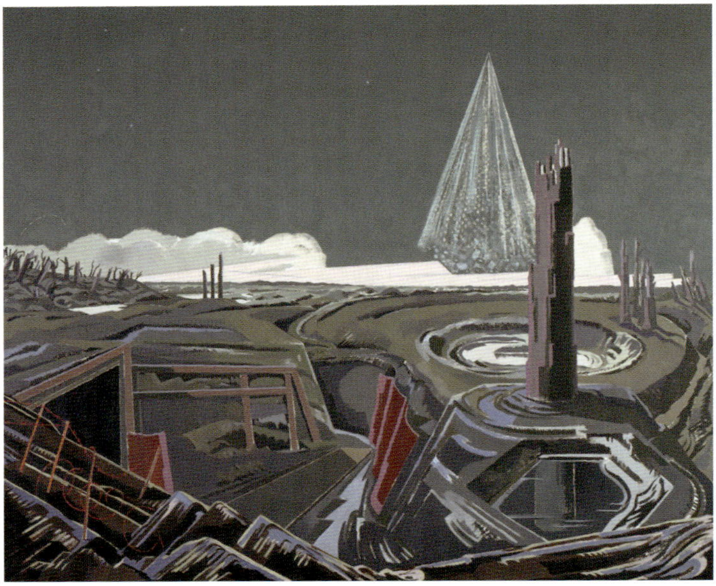

PAUL NASH
Void
(1918)
oil on canvas, 71.4 x 91.7 cm
NATIONAL GALLERY OF CANADA, OTTAWA. PHOTOGRAPH © NATIONAL GALLERY OF CANADA
TRANSFER FROM THE CANADIAN WAR MEMORIALS, 1921

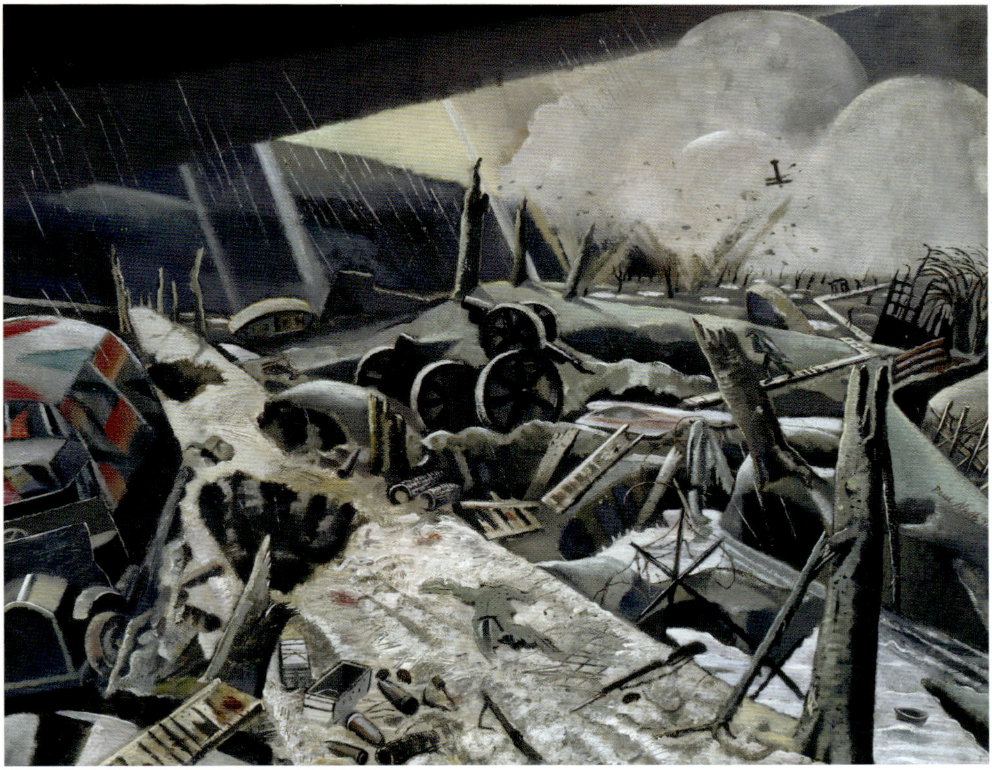

PAUL NASH
A Night Bombardment
(1919–20)
oil on canvas, 182.9 x 214.4 cm

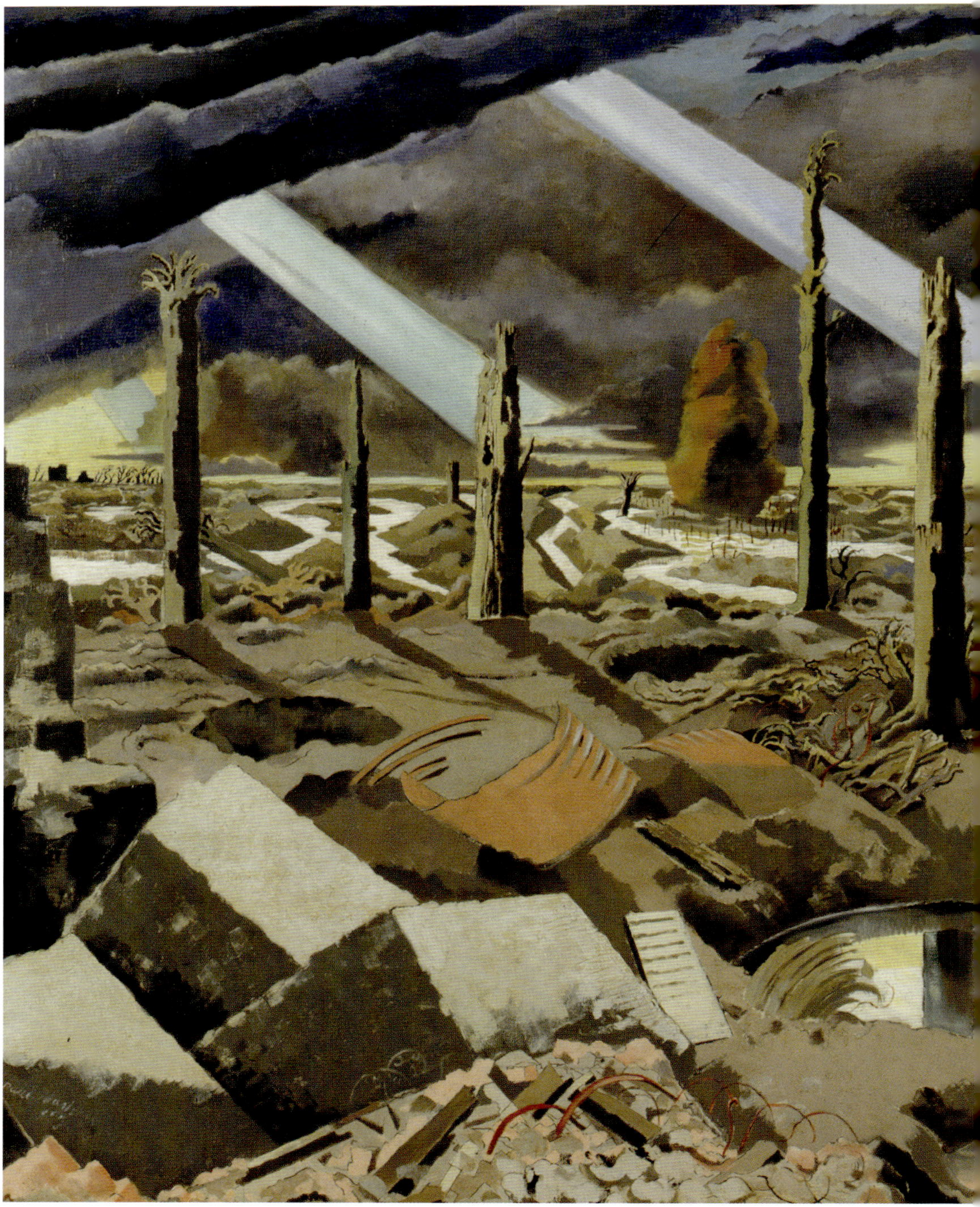

PAUL NASH
The Menin Road
(1919)
oil on canvas, 182.8 x 317.5 cm
IMPERIAL WAR MUSEUM, LONDON

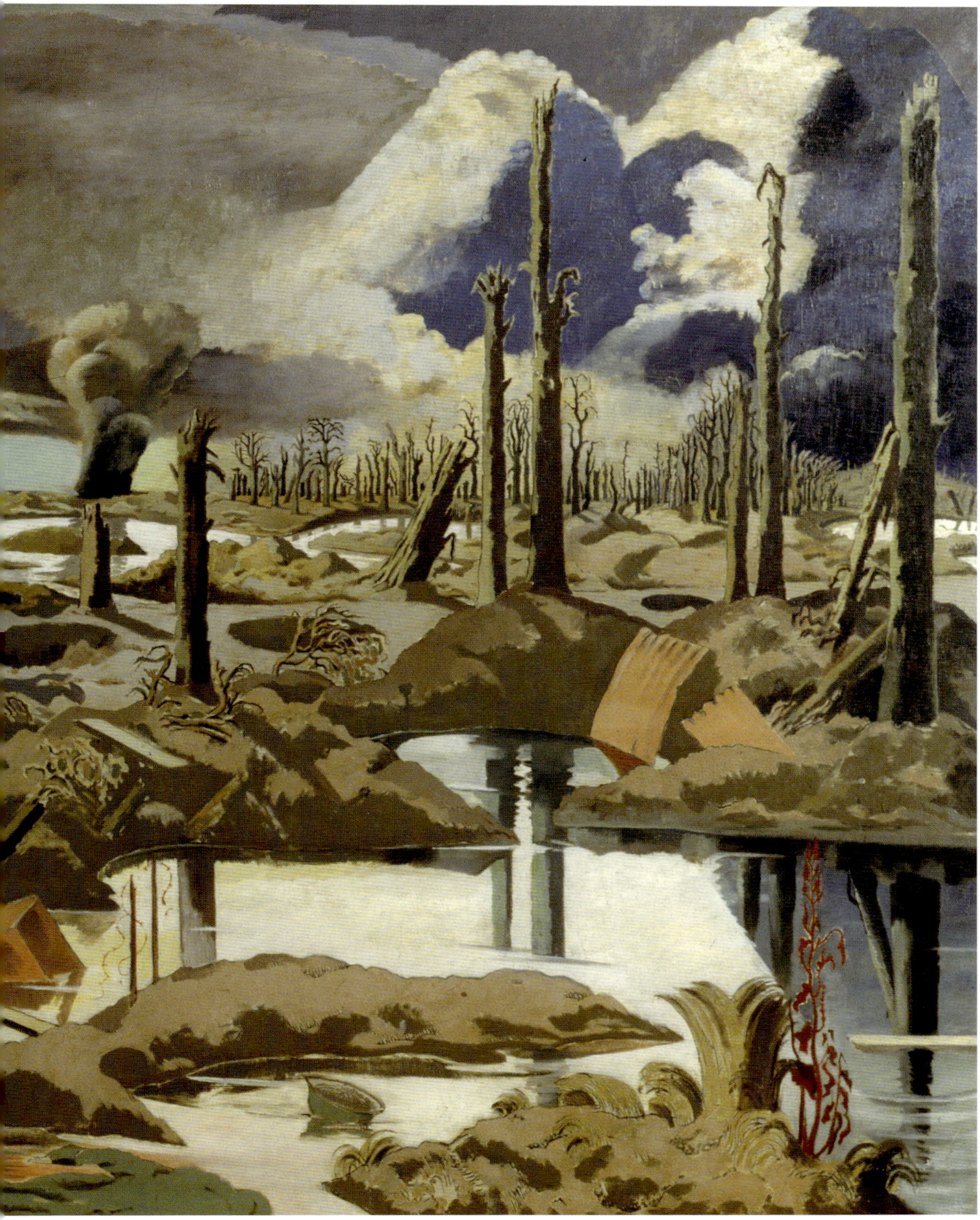

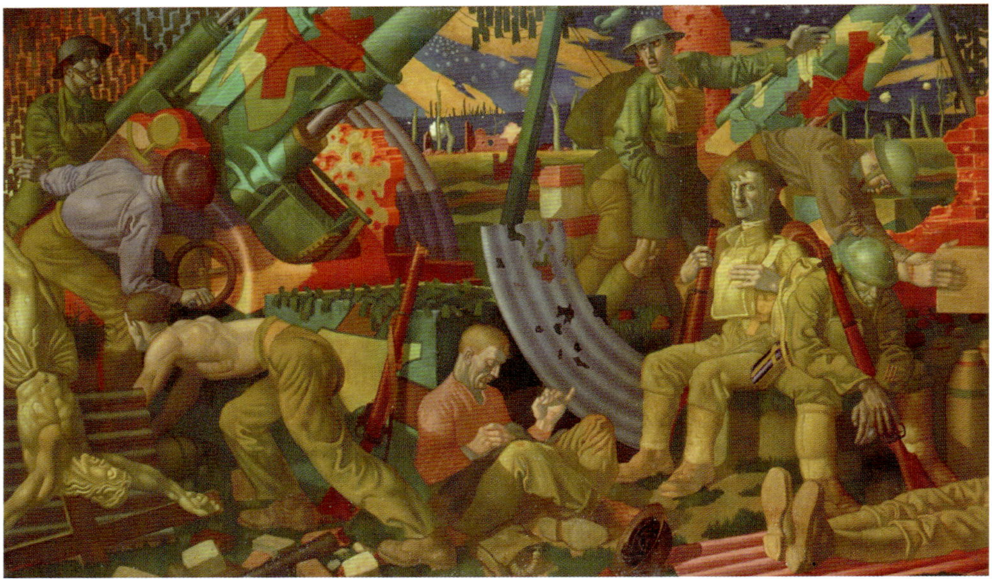

COLIN GILL
Heavy Artillery
(1919)
oil on canvas, 182.8 x 317.5 cm
IMPERIAL WAR MUSEUM, LONDON

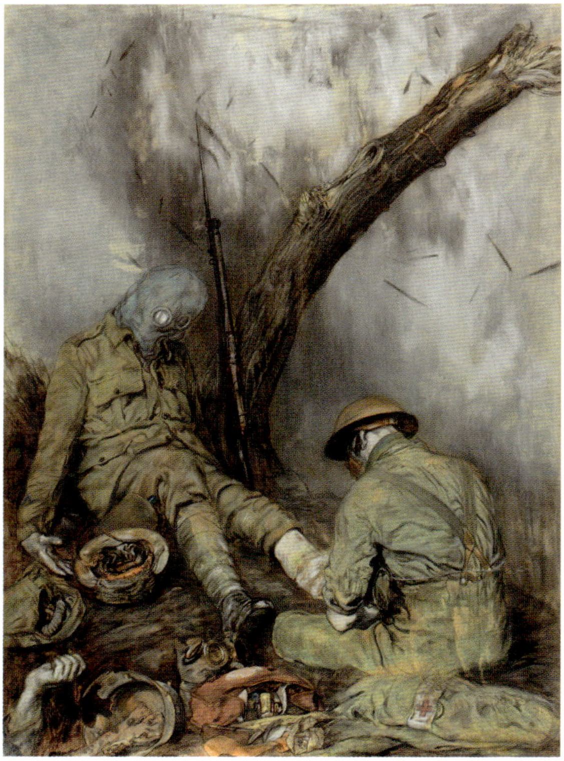

AUSTIN SPARE
Dressing the Wounded During a Gas Attack
(1918)
pastel on paper,
101.2 x 75.9 cm
IMPERIAL WAR MUSEUM, LONDON.
GIFT OF THE BRITISH RED CROSS SOCIETY
AND ORDER OF ST JOHN OF JERUSALEM, 1920.

trenches than anywhere out here. It sounds absurd, but life has a greater meaning here and a new zest, and beauty is more poignant.'[38] Here, perhaps is the tipping-point in Nash's slow purging of all that he once held true as a painter.

Of course, Nash was serving at an unusually quiet time on the Salient but he was constantly exposed to the daily rigours of trench life. Nowhere could be considered safe or 'quiet'. Sensing this, he repeatedly reassured his wife and friends that raids were few and the shelling sporadic, though he confessed to disliking machine gun-fire 'especially when I go the lavatory; I don't mind being shot during my duty, but not that sort of duty!' Like every other subaltern in a line regiment, his work was repetitive and unrelenting. After dark he would patrol the benighted trenches, treading cautiously along slimy duckboards with his sergeant, 'inciting a listless sniper to fire or the Lewis gunners to play a burst, just to show the Huns we are really awake'. Yet all the time he was alert to the 'weird beauty' of the St Eloi front:

> Twilight quivers above, shrinking into night, and a perfect crescent moon sits uncannily below pale stars. As the dark gathers, the horizon brightens and again vanishes as the Very lights rise and fall, shedding their weird greenish glare over the land... So night falls gradually... At intervals we send up Very lights, and the ghastly face of No Man's Land leaps up in the garish light, then, as the rocket falls, the great shadows flow back shutting it into darkness again... Maybe you can feel something of the weird beauty from this little letter.[39]

As his time at the front dragged into weeks so he began to question the motives behind the war and to worry about the slump in morale that was beginning to infect the Home Front. He aimed his ire at the profiteers and 'the damned almighty Press' for peddling 'humbug and drivel' and grew intensely angry at intolerable greed and inequities. 'We need,' he wrote on 18 April 1917, 'a spirit to stamp out cant and lies from England, a race of men and women in England to supersede a brood of efts and leeches'. While Nash's negative anger was compensated by a 'positive pride and passion'[40] in his work and in the men he was leading, we can detect in these intense tirades the seeds of his subsequent outcries against the prolonged madness of the war, an invective that would pour out of his work in less than a year. Yet, all the while, Nash – like so many artists, writers and poets on the Western Front – wrestled with the

---

38 *Outline*, p.189.

39 This and the other extracts are taken from *Outline*, pp.193–197.

40 From Bertram (1955) p.92.

cruel irony that the destruction and depravity all around him was actually feeding his imagination. It was a conundrum brilliantly caught in one letter:

> We are all sent out here to glean – painter, poet, musician, sculptor – 'He that hath eyes to see let him see, he that hath ears to hear, let him hear' – no one will return empty-handed but bringing his sheaves with him.[41]

By this time he had a further twenty drawings, most of them made in the precious moments between routine jobs, parades, lectures and the other duties that 'imprisoned' him. There were, of course, lighter moments. During a training course Nash dimly remembered a midnight obstacle race over poles, wires, ditches, and sandbags that had been convened by the Commanding Officer, umpired by the sergeant-major, and performed by some twenty 'entirely blotto' officers; a race which remarkably, given his inebriated condition, Nash appears to have won 'by a foot, and found myself hugging one part of the sergeant-major, while an East Surrey man hugged the other, each yelling out we had won'. As Nash triumphantly noted, the verdict went the way of the Hampshires. 'I remember clearly,' he reminisced, 'the C.O. dancing a waltz with me, and of dancing a sort of typhoon tango with a boy in the Queen's'.[42]

Nash found camaraderie not only with his fellow mess-mates. He had developed a profound appreciation for his men. Watching them on a three-day march in May 1917 he admired their 'quiet confident strength, an easy carriage and rough beauty'. At times, their magnificent vulnerability almost reduced him to tears. This sense of belonging is apparent in his later lithograph of a column of troops marching at night: the powerful momentum of the troops echoed in the plunging perspective of the endless avenue. Although he would not serve long at the Front, Nash knew death and was aware that his colleagues and contemporaries were dying elsewhere. Contemplating the loss of his friend, the poet Edward Thomas, he tried hard not to become morbid, but it is clear from his letters that he was brooding on it 'dully'. The prevailing air of war-weariness cannot have helped. Those rambling Edwardian nature walks and the long shadows of a balmy English summer must have seemed so very remote. By mid-May, although the work was not difficult, the weather temperate, and the surroundings pleasant enough to make him 'dreamy and satisfied', he was 'sick with longing for the end of this awful unending madness'. His prolonged reflections, however,

41 *Outline*, p.198.
42 *Outline*, p.201.

had the effect of making him realise how much he had changed as an individual, whilst also confirming his passion for nature and for the sights of his cherished Hampshire. When all other emotions seemed to have turned bitter and dead, and the cause of war to be futile and mean, Nash realised that the effects on him would be profound and huge. 'No terrors will ever frighten me into regret,' he wrote, and asked, 'What are the closing lines of Tennyson's "Maud"? – "I have felt I am one with my native land."'[43]

In fact, Nash was to find himself back in his native land sooner than he could have ever predicted. On the night of Friday 25 May, only eight weeks after he first set foot in France, he was beckoned from his dug-out to witness a short bombardment over the enemy line. For someone so familiar with the night sky and the powers of the stars and moon, Nash failed to register the intensity of the dark and stumbled:

> The earth opened suddenly and I disappeared amid a roar of laughter. I suppose all very sudden disappearances are funny, but from my point of view it was not humorous at all, because I was jammed in a narrow trench and had a sharp pain in my side... I limped back into the dug-out feeling rather as if I had broken in the middle like a doll.[44]

Nash had fractured a rib and was sent down the line to the dressing station and thence onto the No.14 General Hospital, 'the last place before England'. Convalescing back home Nash later learned the terrible news that most of his fellow-officers had been killed in an attack on Hill 60 that presaged the offensive on the Messines Ridge.[45]

Recovering in England gave Nash the opportunity to work up some of the sketches he had made at the Front. From being a

---

43 Hill 60 was formed in the 1860s as a consequence of the building of the railway between Ypres and Comines. A cutting was dug to ease the gradient at the northern end of the Messines Ridge and the resulting spoil was dumped in three piles at the top of the climb, forming three small mounds. The biggest of these was marked on the British maps as 'Hill' – its height above sea level indicated in metres – so that it appeared as 'Hill 60' and this became its name on military maps.

Hill 60 is today owned by the CWGC and is little changed since 1918. A plaque at the site records that it was taken from the French by the German forces on 10 December 1914, recaptured by the British on 17 April 1915, retaken by the Germans on 5 May 1916, ceded back to the British on 7 June 1917 (the first day of the Messines offensive), taken once again by the Germans in April 1918 (during the great spring push) until its final capture by the British on 28 September 1918. The actions on and around the 7 June 1917 would have involved Nash's unit. Nash's reflections on Tennyson are in *Outline*, p.203.

44 The War Office records give the date of the incident as 30 May, but Nash's letter in *Outline* (to Margaret p.205) suggests it occurred on the night of the 25 May 1917. By this date the artillery barrage on the Wyschaete Ridge was building in intensity. Nash probably owed his prompt return to England to the need to clear beds in France and Belgium in readiness for the anticipated casualties from the coming offensive. He remained at the Swedish Hospital in London until 21 June.

According to Margaret Nash he suffered a broken, floating rib and not as the Base Hospital Report stated a misplaced cartilage. In *Memoir*, p.43. Ronald Blythe states that Nash fell while making a drawing (Blythe. *First Friends*, p.107) but this is not mentioned in any other account.

45 For a full study of this battle see Ian Passingham, *Pillars of Fire: the Battle of Messines Ridge, June 1917* (Gloucester: Sutton, 1998).

draughtsman of rather fey, dreamy landscapes his work took the first of several radical turns. Before the war, he had been worried by his limitations as an artist: 'My method of expression,' he wrote, 'was still very limited and consisted almost entirely of drawings made in pencil and tinted with washes of bistre and blue, which were reinforced by over-drawing in diluted ink with a steel pen, sometimes with the addition of a little hard chalk'.[46] He feared, too, that his subject-matter was equally confined:

> Groups of trees in an 'upright' view seemed to be my sole interest. I very seldom worked on a horizontal plan or attempted landscapes involving receding planes or scenes wherein the forms were not those of trees with some surrounding undergrowth. In short I had got into my first rut.[47]

His brief service in the front-line trenches blasted him out of any rut. In July 1917 he mounted a show of eighteen small drawings at the Goupil Gallery in London which marked a distinct shift in his style. Gone were the fluffy elms, to be replaced by splintered woods and panoramic views of the hollowed Salient. Although he knew of the Vorticists, and had recently asked his wife to purchase a copy of one of Nevinson's drypoints of Ypres, his drawing did not yet display the technical advancement of his contemporaries, nor did it display the scream of tragedy that would fill his later works, but it was instantly memorable. As one observer noted with admiration, the work had 'an actuality, an immediacy, that brought to life everything about the front which people had read and heard, but had found themselves quite unable to visualize'.[48] One rather sensitive drawing, tellingly entitled *Chaos Decoratif*, suggests in its very title that Nash was still enamoured of the graceful curves and decorative arcs produced by the fallen boughs of once-elegant trees.

---

46 See *Outline*, p.139. After his discharge from hospital in August 1917, Nash was attached to the 3rd (Reserve) Battalion of the Hampshire Regiment at Gosport.

47 *Outline*, p.139.

48 Quoted in Margot Eates, p.22. The exhibition held at Goupil Gallery in July 1917 was entitled *Drawings made in the Ypres Salient by Paul Nash*. Much to Nash's delight, the exhibition was given a supportive review by John Cournos in *Land and Water*, 28 July 1917. The painter was much taken with Cournos's evocation of 'accurate mystery' that he divined in the work, 'not thro' vanity', explained Nash, 'but because he seems to have explained things so well, & to be intelligently explained is a pleasure to any artist.' (See Nash to Gordon Bottomley, c.23 August 1917, letter no.104 in *Poet and Painter*, p.85–86.) The painter was aggrieved, however, that in spite of enthusiastic reviews and good sales he was in pocket by only five pounds. (See Ronald Blythe, *First Friends*, p.115)

Nash most valued perhaps his brother's pencilled letter: 'We have always liked or not liked each other's work and it has always appeared quite simply either good or bad. They are good and I like them.' In Bertram (1955) p.93.

In regard to Nevinson: in March 1917 Nash had asked his wife to obtain a copy of Nevinson's 1916 drypoint, *Ypres after the First Bombardment*, as it was now 'a part of the world I'm interested in' (*Outline*, p.192). Although temperamentally the two artists had little in common (except perhaps a mutual dislike for Roger Fry) Nevinson had helped Nash learn lithography (in July 1917) and later purchased Nash's drawing *Obstacle* from his Leicester Galleries show in May 1918. It is perhaps the most Futurist of the work in that show. For a full exposition of Nash's interest in Nevinson's work see the lengthy footnote in Andrew Causey, *Paul Nash* (Oxford: Clarendon Press, 1980) p.73.

Warfare is implied rather than impressed upon the viewer; the sombre tones, scored surfaces and dramatic diagonals that would manner his later war work have yet to emerge and Nash is clearly searching for a graphic language that mirrored his experiences as a soldier. His search took him in unusual directions: one particularly tense drawing made on leave in Gloucestershire depicts the serried ranks of bald orchard trees, separated from the viewer by ditches, sturdy fence posts and barbed wire, while overhead two birds appear to collide in a dispute over territorial dominance. Nash had rarely been attracted to sites of such strict land management and may have sought refuge in its reassuring symmetry. However, the war does not seem very far away from his thoughts, and in these first war pictures Nash had proved to himself, and to a growing crowd of admirers, that he could extend his earlier experiments with the southern English landscape into new locations and be equal to its peculiar demands.[49]

The show was popular, half the work was sold and it attracted favourable critical and popular attention, not least from Edward Marsh – patron of so many young artists at that time – and, as Churchill's Private Secretary at the Ministry of Munitions, in a position to influence the selection of front-line artists for government-funded work. Nash cultivated their relationship, and began to canvas support from a coterie of friends and buyers. As always, he was clear about what he would and would not do, telling Marsh:

> Let me say at once that I don't want one of those HQ jobs – driving about in a car and all that – merely a permit or special licence to draw in the line and facility for seeing all the different [sectors].

Ending with a frequent plea: 'as ever I turn to you'.[50] Marsh did not disappoint. He firmly believed that Nash was one of a small group of artists – 'les jeunes' as he called them – who were a force 'to be reckoned with', and he orchestrated the influence of William Rothenstein, Laurence Binyon, Frank Rutter, John Drinkwater, Henry Tonks, and Charles Holmes (amongst others) to support Nash's ambitions.[51] At the Department of Information, John Buchan eventually and rather grudgingly gave his backing: 'I think we will

---

49 *The Cherry Orchard* was made at John Drinkwater's home, Winston's Cottage, Far Oakridge, Gloucestershire, where Nash went to convalesce after his fall in France and to prepare for his one-man show at the Birmingham Repertory Theatre. King (p.82) writes well about Nash's ability to extend his painting domain beyond southern England. See also: Andrew Causey and Margot Eates, *Paul Nash: Paintings and Watercolours*, catalogue for the Tate Gallery, London, 1975.

50 Marsh to John Buchan, 17 August 1917 (Paul Nash file, Imperial War Museum). Marsh also added that he considered Nash 'a man of brains, humour and character which will support his specific gift – I mean, not one of the promising wasters whose little talents so often run to seed.' An appreciation of the part played by Eddie Marsh in the Nash brothers' lives at this time is told in Ronald Blythe's *First Friends* (London: Viking, 1997), pp.91–92).

have to send Paul Nash as one of our artists to the Front,' he confided to Charles Masterman, 'There is a tremendous consensus of opinion about his work, with which MacLagan [another advocate in the Nash camp] agrees. I DO NOT, but he is a good fellow and understands the front line'.[52] So, Nash was seconded from the army and became an Official War Artist on 12 October 1917.

THE SALIENT

A 'blackness without depth or dimension' 1917–1918[53]

Nash had begun 1917 in reflective mood. On New Year's Eve he speculated about the year ahead and what might await him overseas:

> It is strange to stand on the edge of the year and look across and think of the extraordinary things that may happen during this new year – what does it hold for me I am wondering. A more crowded life than I have ever lived before, more anxiety, more pain, more excitement, more vivid impressions that I have ever felt before. Or just death. I feel most interested for I cannot say I have premonition of this or that, only I realise a rather dramatic moment, this, at the end of the other years, before the one that really matters, dawns. I wish things didn't matter so much, that I was answerable to none but myself.[54]

Ten months later he embarked on his campaign to paint the war. Although the fighting around the pulverised village of Passchendaele was in its last agonising phase, Nash did not find it easy to see it for himself. He complained to Masterman that he was struggling to 'set the machinery of a somewhat reluctant headquarters to working on getting me put at least within gunshot. The truth is that it takes

---

51 Amongst Nash's advocates were: Rothenstein, Eric MacLagan (at the V&A), Laurence Binyon, Claude Phillips, Frank Rutter, A. Clutton Brock, John Drinkwater, Roger Fry, Henry Tonks, Michael Sadler, Charles Holmes. Nash was delighted with the backing he received from supporters such as Gordon Bottomley, thanking him in September 1917 for the commendation sent to John Buchan 'I think he cannot but be impressed' (Nash to Bottomley, in *Poet and Painter*, p.88).

52 Buchan to Charles Masterman, 14 December 1917, Nash file, Imperial War Museum. Another of Nash's advocates, Francis Stopford, wrote to Buchan in August 1917 stressing the propaganda to be gained, arguing that Nash's images of the Ypres Salient provided 'a much better understanding of German brutality and of the needless havoc and destruction which German armies are committing under orders in occupied territories' (Francis Stopford to John Buchan, 16 August 1917, Nash file, Imperial War Museum).

Paul Nash also lobbied to have his brother, then serving as lead bomber in a bombing squad in France, become an official artist; he wrote to Marsh at least twice about Jack (John Nash) 'All my own success and happiness turns bitter while I think of Jack in the trenches' (Nash to Marsh, 8 January 1918; quoted in Bertram (1955) p.95).

Nash was almost bound for Egypt with the Hampshires but was released when 'at the same hour a wire arrived from the War Office cancelling my name from the list... It was damned lucky I woke Buchan up last week he has been just in time to save me' (Nash to Bottomley, *Poet and Painter*, 10 October 1917, pp.95–96).

53 Cormac McCarthy, *The Road*, p.70.

54 Nash to Bottomley, *Poet and Painter*, 1 January 1917.

hours getting backwards and forwards through the traffic, which is very heavy and complicated about here.'[55] Luckily, he was in the hands of a plucky Irish driver who drove him and his small entourage fearlessly across the exposed battlefield. His outings were rarely without incident. On one occasion his 'chef' was 'precipitated into the windscreen and messed up his mouth. With true spirit and the nice feeling of a faithful servant he said, "How fortunate it wasn't you, sir!"' (Earning Nash's praise that he 'was most touched'.) Despite nagging irritations over his accommodation, his meals and having to pay for his chauffeur's food, Nash did not dawdle. His work reached a new peak of intensity. Producing some twelve to twenty sketches in a single day, he had by 16 November made sufficient 'good ones' to realise that these were the core of new work. They had, however, been hard-won. Nash has been close enough to the fighting to be 'damned near killed – the bosche seems to have got wind of my coming & shelled me most rudely every time I opened my book'.[56] Indeed, he probably exposed himself to greater danger as an official artist than he ever had as an infantry officer. Nash's notes record the intensity of his work at this time:

> I realise no one in England knows what the scene of the war is like. They cannot imagine the daily and nightly background of the fighter. If I can, I will show them. ...Visit to Brigade H.Q. Zillebeke. The chance I have been waiting for. Sanctuary Wood at dawn. Gheluvelt. The German pill-box. I escape from the Brigadier. Adventures in Passchendaele. I draw the German Front line. The mule track. Sunrise at Inverness Copse. About noon I get back to H.Q. I have made fourteen drawings. I fall asleep for hours.[57]

The snappy, staccato style of Nash's notes began to find its parallel in his drawings; his graphic language mirrors the vivid intensity of his prose. Out of the infinite horror, he began to distill a new poetry.[58] Compared to the benign and enchanted scenery of St Eloi, his observations are now raw, even brutal:

> See the beauty of these camps by the roadside, all the tents are painted in savage patterns of green, red, orange and black. The bright red rusted corrugated iron roofs have been skillfully mottled with a huge design of black tree shapes spreading over the scarlet rust... How interesting

55 Nash to Masterman, 4 November 1917; Nash file, Imperial War Museum. Nash summarized his frustrations thus: 'I was expected to operate from G.H.Q. I am determined to operate around the Front Line trenches. I begin my campaign. Difficulties of an infantry subaltern behaving like a Staff Captain. I evolve a technique. Eventually I get where I want to be' (in *Outline*, p.216).

56 Nash to Masterman, 16 November 1917; Nash file, Imperial War Museum.

57 *Outline*, p.216.

58 John Rothenstein, quoted in Ferguson, *The Arts in Britain*, p.106.

in form these once stiff houses look, a rhythmic ruin of tumbling forms. What wonderful things are ruins, I begin to believe in the Vorticist doctrine of destruction almost.[59]

Having been witness to camouflage and chaos, dereliction and danger Nash translated the trauma that he had experienced around Passchendaele into austere drawings and biting prose. He now had something to say. His message was unsparing and uncompromising; his writing amongst the most vivid to come out of the entire war:

I have just returned, last night, from a visit to Brigade Headquarters up the line [he wrote to his wife in late 1917] and I shall not forget it as long as I live. I have seen the most frightful nightmare of a country more conceived by Dante or Poe than by nature, unspeakable, utterly indescribable. In the fifteen drawings I have made I may give you some idea of its horror, but only being in it and of it can ever make you sensible of its dreadful nature and of what our men in France have to face. We all have a vague notion of the terrors of a battle, and can conjure up with the aid of some of the more inspired war correspondents and the pictures in the *Daily Mirror* some vision of battlefield; but no pen or drawing can convey this country – the normal setting of the battles taking place, day and night, month after month. Evil and the incarnate fiend alone can be master of this war, no glimmer of God's hand is seen anywhere. Sunset and sunrise are blasphemous, they are mockeries to man, only the black rain out of the bruised and swollen clouds all through the bitter black of night is fit atmosphere in such a land. The rain drives on, the stinking mud becomes more evilly yellow, the shell holes fill up with green-white water, the roads and tracks are covered in inches of slime, the black dying trees ooze and sweat and the shells never cease. They alone plunge overhead, tearing away the rotting tree stumps, breaking the plank roads, striking down horses and mules, annihilating, maiming, maddening, they plunge into the grave that is this land; one huge grave, and cast up on it the poor dead. It is unspeakable, godless, hopeless. I am no longer an artist interested and curious, I am a messenger who will bring back word from the men who are fighting to those who want the war to go on for ever. Feeble, inarticulate, will be my message, but it will have a bitter truth, and may it burn their lousy souls.[60]

Nash's anger was converted into a suite of taut drawings, each one scooped out of the muddy places, barren ridge lines, and filthy puddles of the Salient. In such works as *Rain: Lake Zillebeke* or *After*

59 Nash to Margaret Nash, 21 March 1917.
60 Letter, 13 November 1917, to Margaret, *Outline*, pp.210–11.

the Battle (both 1918) Nash created a new calligraphy of war; his drawings are scored and scratched with uncompromising diagonals, the incessant rain is engraved in stabbing lines across the surface, the ashen wastes of the battlefield are dense with impenetrable strokes of his pen. Nothing daunted him: neither the weird sight of a tree-trunk adorned with barbed wire nor a close-up of driving raindrops falling heavily into the convulsed earth. Even where the textures are sensuous, the line is invariably stiff, with a caustic edginess that is entirely right.[61] Nash's interpretations of this toxic world, wrote Arnold Bennett, were without parallel or precedent:

> Lieutenant Nash has seen the Front simply and largely. He has found the essentials of it – that is to say, disfigurement, danger, desolation, ruin, chaos – the little figures of men creeping devotedly and tragically over the waste. The convention he uses is ruthlessly selective. The wave-like formations of shell-holes, the curve of shell-bursts, the straight lines and sharply defined angles of wooden causeways, decapitated trees, the fangs of obdurate masonry, the weight of heavy skies, the human pawns of battle.[62]

Fifty-six new pieces of work – five of these in oil, five lithographs, a significant portfolio of original drawings on brown paper – were exhibited in what was clearly an extraordinarily powerful show at the Leicester Galleries in May 1918. Nash had created a distinctive vision of war, one that brought new insights into the way that artists could depict the absences, the emptinesses, the abraded surfaces, and the defiled hollows that were the essence of the Western Front. To understand exactly how innovative this approach was, we must peer, with him, into that crowded emptiness.

VOIDS OF WAR
Nash and the idea of emptiness

Not far from where Nash was hunched in concentration over his drawing board amidst the shell-torn terrain of Ypres, the official Australian photographer Frank Hurley was adjusting the cumbersome paraphernalia of his plate-glass camera and tripod. A veteran of Ernest Shackleton's ill-fated second expedition to the Antarctic in 1914–16, he was also struggling with the near-impossibility of fixing the sprawling mess of the battlefield in a single frame:

61 Paul Nash, *Rain: Lake Zillebeke*, 1918. Lithograph, 25.5 x 36.2 cm. IWM:ART 1603.
Paul Nash, *After the Battle*, 1918. Pen and water-colour, 59.8 x 73.3 cm. IWM:ART 2706.
Paul Nash, *Wire*, 1918. Ink, pastel and water-colour, 48.5 x 63.4 cm. IWM:ART 2705.

62 Arnold Bennett, Foreword, *Void of War*, Leicester Galleries, May 1918.

> Everything is on such a wide scale. Figures scattered, atmosphere dense with haze and smoke – shells that would simply not burst when required. All the elements of a picture were there, could they but be brought together and condensed.[63]

Having endured the barren wastes of the southern ice-fields Hurley was deeply frustrated by the diffuse character of the war in Flanders – the lack of focal points, its vastness and sprawling anonymity. Other equally perplexed photographers – such as the Canadian Ivor Castle – fabricated their own battle compositions in the darkroom, combining negatives one on top of another to create a composite version of trench warfare. With a little judicious cropping an innocent image could be transformed into something more aggressive, and, like Hurley, he superimposed shrapnel clouds and bomb-bursts into the clear skies. Being flat for long distances, the Flanders landscape was a convenient and uncomplicated setting for these staged multi-layered 'combats'.[64]

But photography could not visualise emptiness; it could only allude to absences. Even words failed to convey the intensity of its emptiness. Faced with the phantasmagoric, lunar spaces of the Western Front, the imagination froze:

> It seemed quite unthinkable that there was another trench over there a few yards away just like our own... Not even the shells made that brooding watchfulness more easy to grasp; they only made it more grotesque. For everything was so paralysed in calm, so unnaturally innocent and bland and balmy. You simply could not take it in.[65]

One writer who visited the Western Front in 1916 – Reginald Farrer – suggested that it was in fact wrong to regard the 'huge, haunted solitude' of the modern battlefield as empty. 'It is more,' he argued, 'full of emptiness... an emptiness that is not really empty at all.'[66] Paul Nash visualised this idea – borrowing Farrer's phrase the 'Void of War' and populating its emptinesses with latent violence. The very concept of space as an undifferentiated, homogeneous void which surrounded solid objects had already been challenged by contemporary artists; cinema was revolutionizing the organization of time; the act of film editing fractured continuous events, reshaping

---

63 Hurley's diary, quoted in Lennard Bickel, *In Search of Frank Hurley* (Australia: Macmillan, 1980) p.61.

64 See Jane Carmichael, *First World War Photographers* (London: Routledge, 1989).

65 Reginald Farrer, *The Void of War: Letters from Three Fronts* (London: Constable, 1918) p.113.

66 Reginald Farrer, *Void of War*, p.55.

Paul Nash wrote to Gordon Bottomley from the Western Front over Easter, 1917: 'In the midst of the monstrous event stands Man; the thousands and the hundreds of thousands, the combatants and the non-combatants; who all have one wish and one goal; to cast aside the war; to render its effect invisible so far as they can be understood; to let a well-earned Peace grow its grass over the victims and to carry on as before.' In *Poet and Painter*, Easter 1917.

and compressing story-lines into new patterns of broken narrative. Scientific research pioneered by Albert Einstein argued for a number of distinct spaces equal to the number of unstable reference systems. Braque and Picasso smashed forever the belief in a neat pictorial system based on the single static eye of one-point perspective. It was a period of extraordinary innovation, it was as though 'an earthquake had struck the precisely reticulated sidewalks of a Renaissance street scene'.[67] War accelerated these changes: when Picasso saw trucks heading out of Paris towards the Front he is said to have pointed at their camouflage and exclaimed 'yes, it is we who made that, that is cubism' and to a degree he was right. Deceptive and disruptive camouflage is the perfect exposition of the new way that the world's spaces had to be seen, or to be more exact, not seen.[68]

Adapting the pictorial conventions of Cubism and Futurism – with their geometric shapes, staccato movement, and fractured planes – Nash created a tense and busied surface which did away with the normal hierarchies between motif and background, presenting both negative and positive forms as equal, implying that objects in a landscape are not standing free but are locked in place by overwhelming invisible forces – sound waves, noxious gases, pervasive dangers, and, overhead, reconnaissance planes and sausage balloons – the ever-present 'eye in the air'. He had long been aware of these inversions in the reading of spaces. On one occasion, trudging along a road leading to the Front he had become more and more aware of 'a humming in the air', a sound rising and falling:

> You look up and after a second's search you can see a gleaming shaft in the blue like a burnished silver dart, another then another. Then comes a new noise, two or three cracks from somewhere in the near farms, a second, and as you gaze the blue sky is charmingly speckled by little shining clouds of white.[69]

Like every other front-line combatant Nash knew that danger was omni-directional, threat lay in every conceivable direction not merely from the fixed enemy line to one's front but from underneath, overhead, and from the rear. All along the Western Front tunnelling companies dug deep into the earth, burying huge piles of explosives underneath the enemy's line; overhead the skies were patrolled and fought over by squadrons of flimsy aeroplanes. Furthermore, the war stretched further afield than ever before; for the first time in history the Home Front was becoming as vulnerable as the fighting line: Zeppelin raids occurred in London; artillery fire in Flanders could

67 Stephen Kern, *The Culture of Time and Place (1880–1918)*, (Massachusetts: Harvard University Press, 1983).
68 Gertrude Stein, *Picasso* (1938, reprinted New York: 1959) p.11.
69 *Outline*, 21 March 1917.

be heard from the Home Counties. The gap between fear and safety was narrowing.[70]

Painters tried to respond to these new conditions. If we look across the range of work produced during and immediately after the war, we can detect a shift in the way that artists arrange their compositions. Increasingly, we can see that the components of many of the larger paintings have been assembled without heed of normal pictorial hierarchies; their arrangements lack dominant and sub-dominant groupings, the foreground has become as vital as background, the relative values of 'negative' and 'positive' forms are inverted, there are numerous vanishing points, and previously superior motifs have become confused and dispersed across the design. In Colin Gill's huge painting of a battery of heavy artillery, for example, the elements are spread almost evenly across the picture surface.[71] Identity seems to have been stripped from each individual. The figures are difficult to distinguish from the machines; confusion reigns, the supposed 'key' parts are subordinated to a diffuse design. In William Roberts's painting of the first German gas attack at Ypres it is almost impossible to separate out the individual soldiers from the hectic movement because each part of the picture surface vies for our attention as we struggle to make sense of the narrative.[72] In the hands of some artists this radicalisation of time and space led towards non-figurative abstraction, but painters and printmakers did not have to adopt extreme postures to convey this concept of a fragmented and impenetrable nothingness. Certainly Paul Nash was not yet ready to abandon representation, and even a rather more conservative artist like Austin Spare understood likewise. In his masterly large drawing *Dressing the Wounded during a Gas Attack* Spare created a sense of crowded pervasiveness by filling the 'negative' space around the two figures in a web-like matrix of random marks and scribbled graffito. The busy picture surface becomes a pictorial equivalent to the impenetrable and lethal space above the parapet that could be so casually swept by machine-gun fire.[73]

This heightened sense of spatial awareness helps explain the complex narratives of Nash's paintings that he showed at the Leicester Galleries. In *The Mule Track*[74] the sense of confusion and dislocation could not be more acute; it is as if we are watching a film with

---

70 At the height of the great artillery barrages on the Western Front the firing could be clearly heard on Beachy Head; the huge mine explosions on the Messines Ridge in 1917 were heard by the Prime Minister in Downing Street, and were said to have been audible as far as Dublin. It is argued that the combined sound of the simultaneous mine explosions comprised the loudest man-made explosion ever made.

71 Colin Gill, *Heavy Artillery*, 1919. Oil on canvas, 182.9 x 317 cm. IWM:ART 2274.

72 William Roberts, *The First German Gas Attack at Ypres*, 1918. Oil on canvas, 304.8 x 365.8 cm. National Gallery of Canada, Ottawa. Transfer from Canadian War Memorials, 1921.

73 Austin Spare, *Dressing the Wounded during a Gas Attack*. Pastel, 101.5 x 73.6 cm. IWM:ART 3635.

74 Paul Nash, *The Mule Track*, 1918. Oil on canvas, 61 x 91.4 cm. IWM:ART 1153.

numerous incidents occurring simultaneously in every corner, explosions are rendered as strange animations; artillery barrages are represented as force-fields; sharp diagonal edges sit uncomfortably next to diffuse patches of paint; the pictorial impact is 'eccentric, fantastic and unreal'[75] but at the same time immediately convincing. In these key drawings and paintings Nash was beginning to clarify the mysteries of the battle landscape in concrete terms. Through exposure to the irradiated landscape of the Front, his use of colour had also become more ambitious and he no longer feared it as an expressive medium. 'Huge spouts of black, brown and orange mould burst into the air amid a volume of white smoke, flinging wide incredible debris, while the crack and roar of the explosion reverberates in the valley.'[76] In one of his most powerful renditions of the savage inferno, *Void*,[77] these acidic colours are used sparingly but to great effect; specks of orange are trickled across the canvas like a trail of blood that links the abandoned lorry, a flattened corpse, the shattered duckboards, and a tank pitched headlong into the mire of the middle-distance. 'Barren, sightless, godless', this is pitiless tragedy on an epic scale.[78]

'THE ALIEN SUN COMMENCING ITS COLD TRANSIT'[79]

'We are Making a New World' and 'The Menin Road', 1918–1919

The deadpan titles of Nash's work in his second exhibition of war paintings might have been lifted straight from a gazetteer of the Western Front; comprising as they did a litany of ominous place names – Ridge Wood, Hill 60, Gheluvelt, Lake Zillebeke, Vimy Ridge – that would become revered sites of memory after the war. Yet, possibly the most acclaimed of his work in the Leicester Galleries was the heavily ironic *We Are Making a New World*, a brazenly symbolic canvas developed from a drawing of a sunrise at Inverness Copse, a derelict woodland deep in the Ypres Salient.[80] In dispensing with any reference to a particular place Nash is signalling that this bold, rather economic, design summarised his feelings about the war. In both drawing and painting the sun is white against a pale

75 Bertram explores the eccentric, fantastic and unreal battlescapes in Bertram (1955) p.98; as does Herbert Read in his examination of the 'phantasmagoric' in Herbert Read, *Paul Nash* (London: Penguin, 1944) p.8.
76 Nash to Margaret Nash, 6 June 1916.
77 Paul Nash, *Void*, 1918. Oil on canvas, 71.4 x 91.7 cm. National Gallery of Canada, Ottawa. Transfer from the Canadian War Memorials, 1926.
78 Cormac McCarthy, *The Road*, p.2.
79 Cormac McCarthy, *The Road*, p.189.
80 Paul Nash, *We are Making a New World*, 1918. Oil on canvas, 71.2 x 91.4 cm. IWM:ART 1146.

blue sky, and the undulating earth a porridge of ochre, but Nash chose in the canvas to render the mass of cloud as a dull but potentially virulent red, not unlike the colour of dried blood. Precisely why he did this is difficult to gauge. Could he have been suggesting that the very 'source of life has spilt its blood' or that it may yet regenerate the waste which is so brilliantly illuminated by the rising sun?[81] Sunrise and sunset, of course, were moments of heightened tension in the trenches of the Western Front, associated with the anxious minutes of 'stand to' when combatants peered into the greyness of No Man's Land in readiness for a twilight assault on their lines. Any lingering Romantic or poetic allusions associated with the rising or the setting of the sun were soon dashed in the actualities of the trenches. However, the emotions embedded in this canvas can seem a little forced; the heavily ironic title unnecessary; the quality of observation has given way to rather easy lines and uncharacteristically casual arabesques that are prophetic of Nash's dream-landscapes of the decades ahead.[82]

We must not forget, however, that Nash was taking radical steps in attempting to paint at all. 'Oils for me,' he wrote from his studio in the Chilterns, 'were a complete experiment you know – a piece of towering audacity as I had never painted before'.[83] His audacity paid off. Indeed, his first three oil paintings were purchased by the British government, and the fourth for the Canadian War Memorial Scheme. Given his previously conservative approach to methods and materials it is something of a surprise that Nash described his new ventures in large-scale oil painting as 'a real adventure & I did enjoy it'.[84] In fact, he had little choice: the Hall of Remembrance scheme required large iconic paintings, and Nash knew that to be reckoned as an artist alongside the other commissioned *grandees* – William Orpen, John Singer Sargent, D.Y. Cameron, Charles Sims – as well as his younger rivals, he had to produce a 'signature' painting. It cannot have been easy, not least as by June 1919 he was ensconced with his brother in a temporary studio – a herb-drying shed at Chalfont St Giles – many miles and months from the front-lines.

81 Alternatively, the pale disc might be taken for the moon, its pale whitish light more suited to Nash's preference for nocturnes. Given the title of the canvas this is unlikely, but the ambiguity remains and an ominous sense permeates the image. After all, he knew (as did all front-line soldiers) that it was not the sun that had to be feared on the front, but a clear moonlit night that illuminated No Man's Land and made patrols stand out in sharp relief – an easy target for the enemy.

82 Paul Fussell writes about this in *The Great War and Modern Memory*, in Section VII 'Arcadian Recourses' and John Ferguson, in *The Arts in Britain*, draws comparisons between this canvas and the painter's later works (Ferguson, p.106).

83 Nash to Gordon Bottomley, *Poet and Painter*, 16 July 1918, p.98.

84 In 1912 Nash confessed to Bottomley that he was rather slovenly in regard to his understanding of artist's materials: 'I have an unhappy thirst for bad paper I always do my best drawings on bad paper, I'm positively superstitious about it... As soon as I begin a design of pure white Whatman sheet I feel uneasy and invariably shave it and bathroom tap it to a state of emaciated collapse... But with regard to my mixed methods and muddled mediums I know I am rather a crawler... I feel tho' it all points to beginning oils I *want* to and I *ought* to, so I shall.' (Nash to Bottomley, *Poet and Painter*, 21 August 1912)

'How difficult it is,' he wrote to Bottomley, 'folded as we are in the luxuriant green country, to put it aside and brood on those wastes in Flanders, the torments, the cruelty & terror of this war. Well it is on *these* I brood for it seems the only justification of what I do now – if I can help to rob war of the last shred of glory the last shine of glamour.'[85]

Nash chose as his subject the main arterial road between Ypres and Menin, a road in name only as it had been torn up and severely damaged by accurate shellfire and was usually deserted by daylight. Considered to be one of the most dangerous parts of the entire Western Front, many notorious sites of battle were strung out along the road as it headed east – Sanctuary Wood, Hooge Crater, Inverness Copse and the infamous Hellfire Corner, formed at the junction of two strategically important roads. Nash knew the place well. On one memorable sketching expedition along the Menin Road his Irish chauffeur had 'piloted the car so skilfully that he timed the constant shell bursts on the road, any of which might immediately have killed' both of them.[86]

At first sight, the painting appears to be the customary *leitmotif* of the Western Front – scattered shell-holes, tree stumps, an infinite vista of mud and mire – a wasteland inimical to human life.[87] But Nash knew that he had to design an image that was much more than an eleven-feet panorama of unco-ordinated chaos and despair. Drawing on his working knowledge of the front-line, Nash designed instead a highly sophisticated image that encapsulates the spatial disjunctions which governed the empty battlefield. By subtly dividing the canvas into three broad bands – a deep foreground of water-filled craters, the lateral axis of the road in the middle band, and the shattered landscape in the distance – he drew out the different directional properties in each of the three zones without losing either the phantasmagoric properties of the emptied landscape, nor the nullity of a place that had been relentlessly stripped of its former identity.[88]

As so often in Nash's war work, the foreground is crammed with insurmountable obstacles – pools of water that cannot easily be crossed, pyramidal blocks that bar the way into the interior space of the painting, piles of debris that clutter the ground plane.[89] All of these serve to frustrate our vicarious approach into the heart of the

---

85 Nash to Gordon Bottomley, *Poet and Painter*, 16 July 1918, p.99.

86 Nash quoted in King, p.85.

87 Paul Nash, *The Menin Road*, 1919. Oil on canvas, 182.9 x 317 cm. IWM:ART 2242. The painting was originally to be called 'A Flanders Battlefield', Nash recording it as a scene near Gheluvelt in the 'Tower Hamlets District' of the Salient. It was commissioned by the museum in April 1918, and Nash worked on it between June and February 1919.

88 Richard Cork, 'Images of Extinction: Paul Nash at the Western Front', in Jane Howlett and Rod Mengham (eds.) *The Violent Muse: Violence and the Artistic Imagination in Europe, 1910–1939* (Manchester: Manchester University Press), p.60.

painting's narrative. Cleverly, Nash plays games with the viewer. Between the concrete blocks and the pools there is a narrow strip of flat ground: it comprises the only pathway through the mess of the picture's foreground. But here, instead of offering us a point of entry into the painting he place a visual barrier – a single rectangular shape like a *louvre* shutter or serrated board – which effectively blocks any progress either into or out of the painting's chaotic interior. As if to underline the symbolic value of this blockage, Nash ensures that it does not align with the dominant forty-five degree diagonal that is the sub-structure of the picture's design and dictates every other angle in the painting, from the shafts of light in the sky to the shadows of the trees and the litter heaped around the craters. It is a small, perhaps insignificant device, intuitively positioned by the painter as a vital reminder that one needed very particular skills to decode and navigate the battlefield. Only the initiated could negotiate its troubled interior.

These subtle games of pictorial movement are played out again in the central band. Here, the surface of the road is painted in broad strokes of boldly applied paint, handled with an adroitness that belied his newness to the medium and his previous indifference to painting method. The shell-holes that puncture its surface are spaced – like giant foot-steps in deep snow – at regular intervals, and the avenue of trees on either side lent the road a sense of lateral movement endorsed by the two figures scuttling from left to right. But once again, Nash deliberately upsets the directional sense: on the left of the picture sharp diagonal shadows distort the road surface, on the right several trees are placed to offset the symmetry of the avenue, debris litters the flat surfaces constantly interrupting the lineal coherency of the middle band. Here, Nash has found pictorial means to show that freedom of movement is no longer guaranteed, mobility is controlled, progress in any direction is hazardous, escape is almost impossible.

The latent danger implied in the foreground and middle zone of the painting becomes horribly real in the third pictorial zone beyond the line of decapitated trees. Two soldiers take refuge from huge explosions which give off great plumes of smoke that mimic the forms of verdant trees. In an ironic twist these tree-plumes offer the illusion of protection and cover. However, like the Upas Tree they offer little but danger.

Where many war artists might have drawn the battlescape as an infinite series of parallel bands disappearing into the distance, Nash attempts something altogether more daring. Beyond the line of trees

89 This analysis was first articulated in Paul Gough, 'The Empty Battlefield: Painters and the First World War', *Imperial War Museum Review*, no.8 (London: Imperial War Museum, and Leo Cooper, 1993) pp.38–47.

he describes seven water-filled ditches; each one meanders sluggishly into the distance only to stop short of the horizon. Each of the ditches invites the eye to travel to the horizon, to explore the furthest reaches of the battlefield. But frustratingly, each ditch, in turn, fails to open up the view and ends either in a lazy serpentine coil or is abruptly blocked by some dam-like impediment. With a masterly understanding of the peculiar properties of the so-called 'empty' battlefield, Nash has condensed into one painting three types of pictorial movement: the awkward, obstructed path across the foreground; the delicately balanced lateral sweep of the road; and the unfulfilled progress into the distance where the 'Promised Land' of the horizon is unreachable, locked in some unimaginable future.

Although dwarfed by the scale of desolation, the figures play a pivotal role in *The Menin Road*. The two larger soldiers are, after all, at the very symmetrical centre of the huge painting. For an artist most often associated with unpeopled nature, Nash's landscapes are heavily imbued with the presence of man. He knew how to populate emptiness: his work expresses 'an intense "awareness" of man, not in his person but in his effects, in the presence of the absent'.[90] Bertram has calculated that some thirty of his eighty war pictures contain people. Ten of these have the figure as the main subject, though in a drawing such as *Leaving the Trenches*, all we see are their backs and tin helmets bobbing along the twisting trenches. Unlike his brother, Paul Nash was rarely at his most assured when rendering figures but he knew that they played a critical role in lending scale to his panoramas of devastation. There is a pitiable helplessness about the animals running amok in *The Mule Track*[91] or the tiny figures scattered across a duckboard track in *Void*, hunched diagonally as if marching doggedly into a howling gale, caught up in the 'black drama' of war's void.[92] Amidst the turbulence, however, there is also something stilled and muted; despite the painted shell bursts, the busied surfaces, and the tumbling figures, this suite of paintings has the power to remain silent as eloquent witnesses often are. And equally, there is something sensuous about the paint itself. One can sense Nash's enjoyment at coming to terms with this new material, handling the wet and fluid paint with a maturity that belied his years, all so very different in temperament from the detached linear

---

90 From Bertram (1955) p.99.

91 Paul Nash, *The Mule Track*, 1918. Oil on canvas, 61 x 91.4 cm. IWM:ART 1153.
On the occasion of Nash's work being included in a show in the USA, Bottomley was animated by 'the Mule Track' painting, writing to Nash that he was as glad to have it in reproduction 'as eight Nevinsons, and 'Spring in the trenches' as thirty-two Orpens', adding 'I am happy to see you making such a brave and vital and convincing show in the new world'. Bottomley to Paul Nash, *Poet and Painter*, 11 June 1919, p.107.

92 See: Paul Nash, *Men Marching at Night*, 1918, Lithograph on paper, 51.5 x 42.1 cm. IWM:ART 1605. The phrase 'black drama' is used by Eates, *The Master of the Image*, p.24. The Menin Road is now the N8, the junction that once formed Hellfire Corner is now a roundabout shared with the N37.

stricture of line, pen and wash.[93]

Upon reflection Nash considered *The Menin Road* to be the best thing he had ever done. He was right. His subsequent commission for the Canadian government, the slightly smaller canvas of *A Night Bombardment*, is impressive for its sparseness and its taut design, but it lacks the authentic complexity of vision that he captured so effortlessly in canvases produced only months earlier.[94] Perhaps, like many combatant-artists, Nash was exhausted by the war. The asthmatic condition that would bring about his premature death in 1946 had been exacerbated by his weeks in the trenches. Making the paintings was equally frustrating:

> How it ever got painted I don't know for I have experienced every sort of interruption, disappointment & delay since the day I started to work. It has been painted in four different places being begun in the country in a large shed, then moved to a bungalow, then shipped to London where I painted most of it in a tiny room & could only step back a few yards from the canvas – finally I got it into a decent sized room where it was finished.[95]

Yet, these irritations aside, Nash had emerged from the war as by far the most important and original young British painter of the period.[96] The war had accelerated his development as a painter, fusing his 'early pastoral vision with the forces of modernity',[97] fuelling his painterly imagination, and launching him to a status he could never have anticipated. His name was known, his work was selling, his pictures were widely reproduced, and his network of supporters and admirers extended further than he could have imagined three years earlier when, on New Year's Eve, he had stood on the edge of the year and wondered at the 'crowded life' that lay before him.[98]

---

93 My thanks to fellow painter David Haste for a number of the ideas raised in this section.

94 Paul Nash, *A Night Bombardment*, oil on canvas, 1918–1919. 182.9 x 214.4 cm. National Gallery of Canada, Ottawa. Transfer from the Canadian War Memorials, 1921.

Nash spent five weeks in France as an Official War Artist; four for the British War Memorials Committee, and a further week – much to his joy at the brief extension – working for the Canadian War Memorials Committee in the Vimy Sector. He returned to England on 7 December 1917.

Nash made little financial gain from his period with the Ministry of Information. In addition to their wanting him to finance his own exhibition, he was also required to sell his paintings at a forty per cent discount. King reckoned that Nash made only £10 from his Leicester Galleries exhibition. (King, p.85)

95 Nash to Gordon Bottomley, *Poet and Painter*, letter received by Bottomley, 25 April 1919, p.103.

96 Eates, *The Master of the Image*, p.27.

97 King writes at length about Nash's fusion of his early pastoral vision with the 'forces of modernity' (p.88).

98 Several of Nash's war pictures were reproduced in *Country Life*, and fifteen issued as Volume III of the publication *British Artists at the Front*, sponsored by Wellington House. It included a pencil portrait by Rothenstein, an introduction by C.E. Montague and a biographical essay by Jan Gordon (under the pseudonym Jon Salis). Despite the prestige of the publication, Nash was dismissive of what he considered Montague's over ripe prose: 'All that talk by Montague in the prevace [sic] is nonsense of course. Wire does and did grow as it is shown here [in the picture *Landscape* 1917], and I was neither mad nor drunk or trying to show an abnormal vision when I drew it.'

99 *Outline*, p.218.

At the age of thirty he returned to the 'Old World' crammed with the vivid impressions of war and peace, his innocence and idealism strained, if not shattered, in the trenches of the Western Front. Ahead, he wrote ominously, lay the 'struggles of a war artist without a war'.[99]

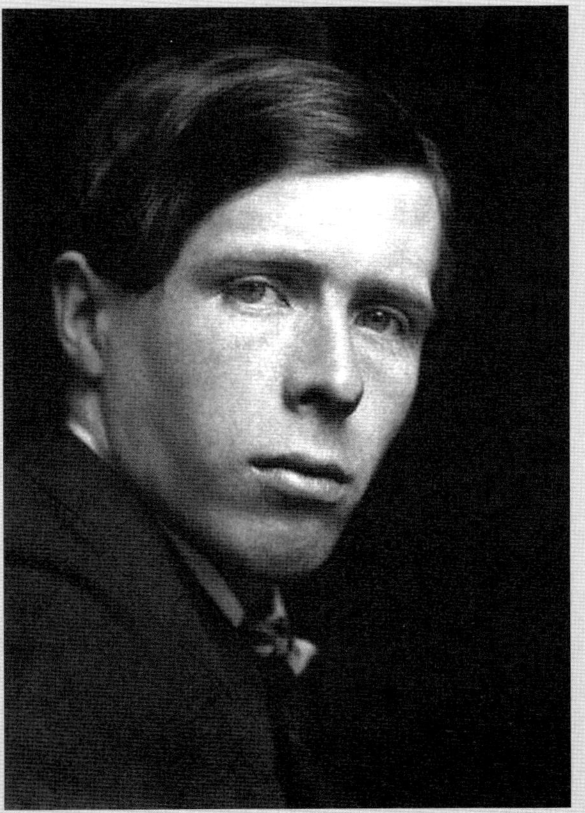

William Orpen

An onlooker
William Orpen – le petit majeur

On 10 June 1917, as Paul Nash was being evacuated from the Front to an English hospital, the portrait painter William Orpen was contemplating his reflection in a large mirror in an attic-room at Cassel, the fashionable hill-top town that commanded the flat Flanders plain.[1] Reflected in the mirror was the thirty-nine-year-old painter bedecked, somewhat unseasonally, in cold-weather trench gear: khaki greatcoat, shaggy goatskin jerkin, and steel helmet, its strap tugged tightly under his angular chin. Gathered around him is the equipment essential for his work – and his play – whisky bottles, soda-syphons, books, cigarettes, paintbrushes and canvases. Out of the open window can be glimpsed the roofs of the pleasant town which was a haven for British war correspondents, visitors and painters. Orpen has stressed its French qualities, accentuating the local colour and decoration of the room's interior, using a relaxed *Nabis*-like handling of the surfaces in and around the mirror. The artist himself is posed – as was his wont – in mid-glance, admiring himself in his newly-assumed garb, enjoying the unexpected thrill of his role as war artist. The eyes, though, are unblinking; his features hard and pointed, and his skin is reddened from long days painting on the barren battlefield of the Somme.

---

1 William Orpen, *Ready to Start: Self-portrait*, 1917. Oil on panel, 60.8 x 49.4 cm. IWM:ART 2380.

Six months later, Orpen painted yet another self-portrait.[2] Still the same flat steel-helmet and chunky trenchcoat, now augmented by a woollen scarf and black balaclava to keep out the chill. Gone, though, is the open-eyed self-absorption; the cheeks are puffier; sagging skin under the eyes betrays late nights and long days. There is compassion in his steady gaze, a sense that the painter has witnessed much, and yet knows that he has much more to see.

Orpen was one of the most prolific artists ever to be sent to the British sector of the Western Front and he stayed the longest of all official painters, enjoying special privileges because of his status in Edwardian high society and close friendships amongst the most senior figures in the British army. He was considered quite a catch. On the eve of the Great War, he ranked as one of the most commercially successful British painters of any period. Immensely talented as he was, socially advantaged and with boundless energy and personal drive, his work fetched high prices and his hard polished style of painting set the benchmark for two generations of boardroom portraits.[3] Yet, his unerring ambition to become a war artist, and his determination to unquestioningly serve his adopted country, was gained at the expense of his health, financial standing and his social status. Orpen's is one of the more complicated – perhaps most perplexing – tales of the arts during and after the Great War.

ORPEN, VIRTUOSO PAINTER

Orpen was born into a Protestant family near Dublin in 1878, where he grew up in idyllic, prosperous and carefree surroundings, the much-indulged youngest of four sons. His precocious talent for drawing saw him accepted into Dublin Metropolitan School of Art at the age of just thirteen, progressing to the Slade School in London six years later. Under the scrutiny of Frederick Brown, Philip Wilson Steer and Henry Tonks, he became the undisputed leader of the student body,[4] quickly mastering oil painting and developing an uncanny ability to mimic the Old Masters – especially Rembrandt and Velasquez – while allowing in sufficient acidic colour and flat surfaces to flavour his paintings with a veneer of stylish modernity.[5]

2 *Self-portrait*, 1917. Oil on canvas. 76.2 x 63.5 cm. IWM:ART 2382.

3 See Denis Farr, *English Art: 1870–1940* (Oxford: Oxford University Press, 1978) p.193.

4 One of his companions at the Slade School later wrote: 'When I was at the Slade, it was a one-man show; that man was Orpen.' Quoted in *The Artist*, August 1901, cited in John Rothenstein, *Modern English Painters*, Volume 1 (London: Eyre and Spottiswoode, 1952) p.243. Rothenstein further argued that the painting of 'the play scene in Hamlet' completed at the age of 21 was the culmination of Orpen's career. From this point the history of his life as an artist is the history of decline. *Modern English Painters*, p.244–45.

5 For a fuller discussion see an on-line review of *William Orpen: Politics, Sex and Death* at the Imperial War Museum, London (27 January–2 May 2005) by Bunny Smedley http://www.socialaffairsunit.org.uk/blog/archives/000312.php/ (posted 7 March 2005).

Recognised as a brilliant draughtsman, a consummate water-colourist and virtuoso painter, Orpen would soon command four-figure fees for his portraits of the wealthy, the powerful and (at times) the merely vainglorious in Edwardian society. Not that he was on his own. He was competing for the work with rival luminaries John Lavery and Augustus John, but he had two advantages over them: first, he was favoured by John Singer Sargent, who all but anointed him as his successor, and secondly, he refused to rely on a limited repertoire of painterly mannerisms and stock devices. Orpen's facility as an artist could easily have led to laziness (as, indeed, eventually overcame Augustus John) but he seems instead to have been driven by a relentless creative daemon. He experimented obsessively with pictorial illusions, using mirrors and *tromp l'oeil* devices to create images within images; making paintings with 'false' painted frames; self-portraits surrounded by fragments of pretend and actual collage. These devices, says Peyton Skipwith, he used like a conjuror, 'not just to show off his almost indecent technical skill, which they do, but also as a smoke screen, dazzling the viewer with his dexterity but leaving more questions unanswered than answered – now you see me, now you don't'.[6]

And when meeting the man, what *would* you have seen? In stature and in manner, Orpen cuts a curious figure in the elegant largesse of Edwardian London. Short (in fact, little more than five-feet tall), slightly built and dapper, not especially good looking, with a staccato speech and stoic disposition, he was prone to occasional bizarre practical jokes, and was impish by inclination. He had, wrote one memoirist, 'few prejudices and no opinions'. Even his supporters remarked on his restricted intellectual curiosity, his indifference – even scorn – for the life of the mind. At his best, he had a sense of fun, mischief and irreverent humour; his spontaneity and enthusiasm gave him a disquieting physical and mental energy.[7] Yet, even his few close advocates regretted his tendency to trivialize, to be unnecessarily self-mocking in the face of life's tribulations, and to be needlessly mawkish, a trait that he committed to paint through numerous

6 It might be argued that Orpen was simply next in line. Henry James said of Sargent that he 'never penetrated nor was penetrated by his subject' (in Arnold, p.106.) Bruce Arnold sees the transition from Sargent to Orpen as the inevitable transition from grandeur and greatness required of the Victorian society portrait painter to the humanity increasingly required of the Edwardian painter. However, not even Arnold is sure that Orpen was able to master the psychological portrait; to be able to read the 'mind's construction in the face'. (Bruce Arnold, *A Mirror to an Age*, p.106). Peyton Skipwith, 'An artist's reflections', *Apollo*, 4 January 2005.

7 See P.G. Konody and Sidney Dark, *Sir William Orpen: Artist and Man* (London, 1932) p.41. Less charitably, Wyndham Lewis noted Orpen's 'croaking and quavering Dublin patter, which he had taken good care never to get rid of' (in Percy Wyndham Lewis, *Blasting and Bombardiering, Autobiography 1914–1926* (London: Eyre & Spottiswoode, 1937) p.169. Arnold recounts some extraordinary practical jokes that nearly went wrong (Arnold, p.258) but largely regards Orpen's sense of humour, the self-mocking and visual teasing so often displayed in his self-portraits, as an endearing quality (Arnold, p.281). He is also sympathetic to Orpen's habit of often referring to himself in the third person as 'little Orps', or 'Ikkle Orps', or even 'Orpsie Porpsie'.

self-portraits in which he was inevitably dressed in some self-dramatising, even bizarre, garb – as a racing jockey, as a stalker dangling a dead ptarmigan, as a dandy in spats and bow-tie. Such guises may have been an unintentional protective device to keep people at bay, for there is a sad solitariness about the man; a celebrity painter with 'a wilderness of acquaintances and few friends'. He had, though, a magnetic appeal for women. His marriage, to Grace, was supplemented by a succession of very public affairs with some of the most renowned (and statuesque) beauties of the day. Typically of Orpen, these relationships were rarely unproblematic or discreet. He was embroiled for years with American-born millionairess Mrs Evelyn St George, a striking woman, over six feet tall, slender and admired for her magnificent style. The two became known in fashionable society as 'Jack and the Beanstalk'. A parallel affair during the war, with the 20-year-old Yvonne Aubicq, was marred by a silly story devised by Orpen to needlessly dramatise a portrait of her as an alleged 'Belgian spy' – an elaborate bout of horseplay which did little to endear him to the military authorities in France.[8]

Driven by jealousy, by irritation at his clowning around, perhaps even by disappointment in watching such talent restricted to society portraiture, his detractors (and there were many during his lifetime and many more after his premature death) regarded him as a meteoric figure who had sold out for social success. They dismissed his work as flippant, derivative and passé. He missed greatness, argued one observer, because he was 'in favour of mastery, that was a mastery without a compelling purpose'. Appraising his life's work, John Rothenstein, Director of the Tate Gallery, dealt a body blow that consigned Orpen to the invisible tiers of British art history. He first lauded Orpen (who was actually his uncle by marriage) for his singular gift of incisive draughtsmanship and his effortless competence as a painter in oils. Such superabundant talents, argued Rothenstein, ought to have produced memorable works, but instead, he accomplished 'scarcely anything' because his portraits were mechanical rather than meaningful, superficial rather than psychological. Even his grand figure compositions painted just after

---

8 The full tale of Mrs St George, the 'Belgian spy' and 'the refugee' incidents is recounted in Meirion Harries and Susie Harries, *The War Artists: British Official War Art of the Twentieth Century* (London: Michael Joseph, in association with the Imperial War Museum and the Tate Gallery, 1983) pp.31–33, and pp.70–72. Orpen painted dozens of self-portraits between 1907 and 1921, yet these do not chart a programme of self-discovery or self-realisation. Instead, observes the normally supportive Arnold, they capture little but 'resignation in the face of waste ...upon it the patina of self-mockery.' (in Arnold, p.260–63) See also Frank Rutter, 'Orpen's Self-Portraits', *The Studio*, Vol.LXXX, No.18, 1932, pp.268–77. On 9 December 1925 *Punch* magazine published a caricature of Orpen pointing his paintbrush like a fencing foil, with this caption:

> Bill Orpen's rapier thrust is great;
> He'll paint your portrait while you wait
> But, though he doesn't want it known,
> He much prefers to paint his own.

the war, which attempted to combine an emotional force with a heartfelt indignation, 'failed because he was unable to understand the nature of the events which so deeply moved him'.[9] These were harsh words indeed, and there were more to come as his reputation slid into obscurity.

Yet, Orpen's war pictures cannot be so easily written off: after all, he produced one of the largest bodies of paintings by any official artist. He worked unhesitatingly and loyally for the government, churning out portrait after portrait of generals, statesmen and politicians. He seemed to be driven constantly (and eventually self-destructively) by an innate sense of guilt and inadequacy in the face of a war fought by younger, braver men. He gave all his war work to the government for free, even though its donation brought hardship to someone whose income in 1915 from portraits alone was £7,700.[10] By 1917, because of his obligation to the government, this had fallen to £500, his private work had tailed off, and gone were the days when limousines queued outside his opulent Chelsea studio while their owners lined up to have their faces painted. Instead, Orpen was performing what he considered his patriotic duty, trudging the baked chalklands of the Somme or the miserable mud around Ypres seeking out new compositions in the service of the nation. Ironically, it was his stock-in-trade work that would be most useful to the war effort: his head-and-shoulder portraits of Sir Douglas Haig and General Trenchard, commander of the Royal Flying Corps (RFC), were reproduced widely by the Department (later Ministry) of Information as pictorial propaganda, leading to further and further demands on him to capture the likenesses of dozens of generals, entire cabinets of politicians, and, perhaps most movingly, the youthful looks of the 'aces', the fighter pilots in the RFC, the newest branch of the armed services.

It is, now, almost impossible to have a balanced view of Orpen's life and work, so thoroughly vilified has he – and his like – been in the past fifty years.[11] However, it was another war-artist (and possibly the least likely of these) who wrote the most perceptive note on

9 John Rothenstein, *Modern English Painters,* Volume 1 (London: Eyre and Spottiswoode, 1952) p.254. Arnold's defence of Orpen in the face of Rothenstein's crushing appraisal is well made, and is predicated on the counter-assertion that the war paintings – especially the emotional roller-coaster of the 'Peace' paintings and the 'Unknown Warrior' saga – should not be regarded as typical of the life's work. Although Arnold elsewhere accepts that Orpen could at times become little more than a mechanical brain, he argues that Rothenstein's essay distorts his whole life's work by concentrating on just four years' output, and even then Rothenstein completely misses the point (see Arnold, pp.401-404).

10 Orpen's earnings and prices make fascinating reading. In 1906 his rate card was 'Head and shoulders £120; Half-length £150. Full length £200. Small full length ½ or ¼ size life size £150' (all in Arnold, p.184). Four years earlier, to give some sense of comparison, Orpen was paid £25-0-0 for three weeks teaching work at Metropolitan School of Art in Dublin. That same year he earned £390 from sales of pictures. Arnold points out that in 1907 a General Practitioner could expect to earn £600 a year to be comfortably off, of this a third would be spent on private education for his children, the family would enjoy a month long summer holiday in Britain, and he and his wife would take a spring holiday on the continent. (Arnold, p.211)

Orpen. Richard Nevinson – himself the subject of controversy, envy and vitriol – published an essay in 1933 (two years after Orpen's death) which perhaps comes closest to understanding those final decades:

> In the public auction-room, or knacker's yard as artists call it, where public opinion is expressed more forcibly than elsewhere, and subject counts most, it has been seen that pictures of other people's relatives merely dressed in Victorian or post-Victorian costume, have no appeal, no matter how superb the draughtsmanship, the technique, or the characterisation. It is therefore inevitable that a proportion of Orpen's output will suffer severely. He himself was conscious of this, and rightly considered it of no importance. It was inevitable, nevertheless, that portrait painting should play such an important part in Orpen's artistic life, as his dexterity, shrewdness, uncanny sympathy and love of the particular were all part of his character, and no matter how often he complained of doing nothing but portraits in the latter years of his life, he could never resist doing another...[12]

'A SPECIAL CASE'
Orpen and Wellington House

In December 1915, Orpen was commissioned into the Army Service Corps and reported to Kensington Barracks where, according to one amused bystander, he wore himself out saluting the Adjutant, Captain T.T. Aikman. Orpen already knew several of the most senior figures in the British army; the Quartermaster General, Sir John Cowans had recently sat for a portrait and he had access to General Haig through Philip Sassoon, his private secretary. Knowing little about drill or soldiering, Orpen soon found himself at the centre of a lobby, orchestrated by his friends, supporters and patrons to make him a war artist, a lobby that almost backfired as their strenuous efforts nearly cancelled each other out. However,

---

11 The portrait of Haig is inscribed 'G.H.Q. 30th May 1917'. Oil on canvas. 74.9 x 63.5 cm. IWM:ART 324. That of Trenchard is inscribed 'HEADQUARTERS RFC 13th May 1917'. Oil on canvas. 76.2 x 63.5 cm. IWM:ART 325.

Orpen faced some fierce artistic rivals, especially Augustus John whose mercurial personality made Orpen appear rather dull and slow. John was recalled by all who met him as gregarious, fluent, colourful and charming; attributes that Orpen revealed only slowly, if ever. Although close as painters, even friends, John later vilified Orpen ruthlessly, especially after his death. Other artists such as William Rothenstein were awe-struck by John's striking looks, his lithe physique and legendary ardour, but it is worth noting Robbie Ross's memorable aphorism that people always came into the Carfax Gallery and 'prostrated themselves before a John but went off with an Orpen.' In William Rothenstein, *Men and Memories 1872–1938*, ed. Mary Largo (London: Chatto and Windus, 1978) p.118 and p.129. There are interesting parallels between Orpen's sincere but superficial patriotic responses and those of Noel Coward's, whose privileged background and reputation as a sentimental show-off is examined by David Cannadine, *In Churchill's Shadow* (London: Penguin, 2002) pp.244-278.

12 C.R.W. Nevinson, 'Sir William Orpen', essay in *The Post-Victorians* (London: Nicholson and Watson, 1933).

at the end of January 1917 the *Daily Mirror* announced news of a 'Unique Honour for Irish Artist', attesting that no less a figure than Haig had 'conferred' on Mr W.I.A. Orpen R.I.A. [sic] the status of official artist with the Army in France.[13] Struggling to stay in control of the appointment process, the Department of Information realised too late that this had been a 'private wangle' which might later lead to all sorts of problems. At Wellington House Masterman advised his colleagues that as Orpen was 'Irish and 'artistic'... it would be impolite to 'rag' him', and urged caution, warning 'he has friends in high places'.[14]

Matters then moved fast. By February 1917 Orpen was promoted from second lieutenant to major and his former superior, Captain Aikman, became his *aide* in France, with the wide-ranging duties of 'Manager, to inspect and make all military arrangements'. Masterman and Buchan at Wellington House were informed of these unique privileges in peremptory notes from the Quarter-master General's office, Cowan adding for good measure that he was 'willing to make arrangements to have a car placed at his disposal on his arrival in France'.[15] Wellington House staff could only look on as very senior officers involved themselves in Orpen's planning. Chief of Intelligence at GHQ, General Charteris told Masterman to regard Orpen as 'one of the special cases', who should be allowed an extended stay in France. Unlike other artists, whose primary aim was to gather visual material for propagandist work, Orpen was not to be limited to the customary three weeks, and he would retain his rank and salary of major throughout the war. Muirhead Bone, by contrast, had been a mere second lieutenant.

Freed of the usual petty constraints, and equipped with his own transport, chauffeur, batman, and indispensable personal manager, Orpen took full advantage of his appointment. His reputation preceded him and he enjoyed the better hotels in Amiens and Paris, unfettered freedom of movement, and the privileges of rank and social status. However, the burden of expectation was huge and Orpen did not treat his mission lightly. Crossing from Folkestone on a khaki-packed troopship he was understandably a little unsettled by the prospect and stood in awe of the soldiers heading for the front. 'My stomach,' he wrote in his war memoir, 'was twitching with nerves. What would I have been like had I been one of them?'[16] This sense of inadequacy, of a deep guilt at his privileged status

---

13 *Daily Mirror*, 30 January 1917.

14 For detailed background on the 'appointment' of Orpen see Harries and Harries pp.29–33. Robert Crawford, Director General of the Imperial War Museum, wrote in the Foreword to Robert Upstone *et al*, *William Orpen: Politics, Sex and Death* (London: Philip Wilson Publishers, 2005), p.4, that Orpen used his connections with the upper echelons of society to evade the formal strictures of his appointment but 'was always considered the star amongst the roster of official war artists.'

15 Cowans to Masterman, 24 March 1917. Orpen files, Imperial War Museum.

in the face of the obvious privations of the soldiers, would gnaw at his confidence in the coming years.

Disembarking on a bitterly cold Easter weekend, he had by Monday already completed his first drawing of one of the most memorable sights on the Western Front – the leaning Madonna and Child dangling perilously from the ruined belfry of Albert Cathedral.[17] From that moment on, Orpen was engrossed by the war, moved by the soldiers he met, impressed by the industrial scale of operations, fascinated by its ever-changing light and form. Raptured and awed, he described it as 'a new world'. In fact, Orpen had arrived at a pivotal moment in the course of the war: the Germans had withdrawn to the Hindenburg Line, allied spring offensives had brought a new urgency and fluidity to the static front, change was in the air. Four days after he arrived, the Battle of Arras began in snow and rain: nineteen thousand German prisoners were taken. On the British side alone some 132,000 casualties were sustained. Weeks later the Battle of Messines opened with the simultaneous detonation of nineteen enormous underground mines. The blast changed forever the contour of the ridge, causing an explosion that, as mentioned in the previous chapter, awoke the Prime Minister in Downing Street, and so loud it was heard in Dublin.[18] Driving where it was possible across the toxic waste, Orpen witnessed the country at its most abject:

> Miles and miles of Shell Holes bodies rifles steel Helmets gas Helmets and all kind of battered clothes German and English, and shells and wire... not a living soul anywhere near, a truly terrible peace in the new and terribly modern desert.[19]

Journeying further north to Ypres he saw little but 'the mud, the cold, the noise, the misery'.[20] Yet after a sluggish start he began to churn out new work, completing a portrait of Haig and another of 'Boom' Trenchard, painting aeroplane dog-fights over Cassel, and drawing German prisoners at Ballieul, an awesome task as he was faced with some 3,500 German soldiers locked in one vast cage, 'some nude, some half-nude, trying to clean the lice off themselves'.[21] His line drawings of these scenes are taut and concise, the work of a disciplined hand effortlessly describing history on an epic scale.

---

16 William Orpen, *An Onlooker in France* (London, Williams and Norgate/Ernest Benn, 1923), p.12. So successful was Orpen's lavishly illustrated memoir of his time at the front that a second revised and enlarged edition was published in 1924. All page references here are taken from this edition.

17 Orpen, *Albert*. Pencil on paper, 45.7 x 36.2 cm. IWM:ART 3024.

18 General Plumer, whom Orpen painted later in the war, is alleged to have told his staff the evening before the attack at Messines: 'Gentlemen, we may not make history tomorrow, but we shall certainly change the geography.'

19 Orpen to Tonks, undated, cited in Harries and Harries, *The War Artists*, p.66.

20 Orpen, *An Onlooker in France*, p.18.

21 This quote is from Orpen, *An Onlooker in France*, p.33.

When Orpen turned his back on Cassel, Ypres and the wet Flanders plain and headed south, his vision of war changed radically. 'Never shall I forget my first sight of the Somme in summer-time,' he wrote with a genuine thrill:

> I had left it mud, nothing but water, shell-holes and mud – the most gloomy dreary abomination of desolation the mind could imagine; and now, in the summer of 1917, no words could express the beauty of it. The dreary, dismal mud was baked white and pure – dazzling white. White daisies, red poppies and a blue flower, great masses of them, stretched for miles and miles. The sky a pure dark blue, and the whole air, up to a height of about forty feet, thick with white butterflies: your clothes were covered with butterflies. It was like an enchanted land...[22]

After murky Ypres, raw daylight burst into his world; not the even northern light so usually associated with the Low Countries, but an unusually piercing, acute and intense light that deflected off the seared white chalk casting bizarre shadows and extreme shifts in tone and colour. To an artist more accustomed to the dusky opulence[23] of cavernous Edwardian drawing rooms it came as a revelation. As he wandered over the recently emptied downlands of the old Somme battlefield everything shimmered in the heat; abandoned clothes were baked into weird combinations of colour, 'white, pale grey and pale gold. The only dark colours were the deep red bronze of the "wire", wild flowers sprouted everywhere... in the evening, everything golden in the sunlight'.[24] Apart from his small entourage, his only companions on these sojourns were distant burial parties who were patiently digging up, identifying, and re-burying thousands of bodies. Orpen passed one such group near Thiepval Hill, resting from their unpleasant work, and trying to identify the dead from their meagre finds – a few coins, pocket knives, an occasional identity disc – garnered from their long labour. Although Orpen does not make much of it in his letters, he knew he was trudging across boneyards; the killing grounds for vast numbers of men, and the former homes of many thousands of displaced villagers. It has been easy to dismiss his work at this time as insensitive and uncaring, the whimsical decorations of a zealous tourist, but this does not do justice to his earnest intentions, nor his actual work. Orpen was an astute observer; in April he had closely watched the 'endless stream of men, guns, food lorries, mules and cars' pressing along the great artery of the road from Albert to Bapaume, and he had been deeply impressed by the restless energy of the vast armies. Some time later he witnessed

22 Orpen, *An Onlooker in France*, p.36.
23 Andrew Graham-Dixon, *A History of British Art* (Berkeley: University of California Press, 1996) p.204.
24 Orpen, *An Onlooker in France*, pp.37–38.

its other face, watching with dread fascination as small bands of men limped back from the lines: 'some sick; some with trench feet; some on stretchers; some wounded; worn, sad and dirty – all stumbling along in the glare... Their eyes were wide open, the pupils very small...'[25] On his own, deep in the toxic wastes of the old battlefield, he saw for himself harrowing evidence of the consequences of battle:

> A hand lying on the duckboards; a Boche and a Highlander locked in a deadly embrace at the edge of Highwood; the 'Cough-drop' with the stench coming from its watery bottom; the shell-holes with the shapes of bodies faintly showing through the putrid water – all these things made one think terribly of what human beings had been through.[26]

Even in the safer towns to the rear, Orpen tried to see through the superficial appearance of things, noting that Peronne was 'now like a polished skeleton – very clean, but very brittle: a little breeze, and whole houses would tumble to bits'. Trying to comprehend the enormity of the violence around him, Orpen wrote long letters to his wife and friends in England. Decorating these with witty, self-deprecating cartoons he also enclosed short poems, in which he hoped to encapsulate the gravity of his surroundings. The resulting verse was intended to be soothing, even optimistic, but was often hopelessly naïve. In 'A Memory of the Somme', a poem about a British corpse seen in the old No Man's Land near Beaumont Hamel, Orpen eulogised the shuffling rats, the battered trench remains, the baking heat, and the strange odours wafting from the deep steps of a blackened dug-out. Yet, despite the evidence, he concluded that where once this had been Hell, 'now all is Peace' and the skeletal corpse has now achieve a state of purity; '...the sun has made him Holy and Pure... bleached white and clean. A daffodil is by his head, and his curly, golden / Hair is moving in the slight breeze... Here he lies, Pure and Holy'.[27]

It is not easy to defend such mawkishness. Not even his most sympathetic supporters could empathise with Orpen's misplaced tone of voice. But that was not how Orpen saw it. He may have taken a somewhat simplistic view of the war, one which glorified the 'valiant' fighting man and demonised the frock-coated politicians, but for him (as a recent biographer points out) being a war artist was not merely about making a neutral or an aesthetic record of one's experiences. Orpen was faced with a dilemma which would have tested any artist. How could he reconcile the demands of pictorial propaganda with such vivid and direct experiences of war?

25 Quoted in Harries and Harries, *The War Artists*, p.66.
26 Orpen, *An Onlooker in France*, p.20.
27 Orpen, *An Onlooker in France*, pp.23–24.

Propaganda was 'peremptory, organized and voracious in its appetite';[28] artists were mercurial in their reactions, spontaneous and hated to be told what to do. Although Orpen came from the most privileged tier of society, he liked to rebel against a programme of patronage that he (and others) regarded as unnecessarily strict, over-controlling and prone to neutering adventurous and renegade views. Although he had seen nothing of the fighting, had not been shelled or bombed, Orpen felt seared and exposed by its grim aftermath. War had become, and would remain forever, a deep and shattering, but strangely energizing, emotional experience.

A DEPLETED LANDSCAPE

Orpen recalled one officer scoffing at his ambition to draw the battlefield:

> Paint the Somme? I could do it from memory – just a flat horizon-line and mud-holes and water, with the stumps of a few battered trees.[29]

To which Orpen replied, 'but one could not paint the smell'. And it is true: the strange and sickly odours that wafted across the old battlefields were pungent and repugnant. They lay beyond the scope of telling and beyond the visual range of representation, although the acrid colours of some of Orpen's Somme paintings – with their scarlet edges, viridian shadows, and unflinching cobalt skies – cannot be excused as manifestations of his mild colour-blindness. His bold and at times near-discordant colour scheme is always matched by a searing blast of wilting sunlight that seems to corrode the very fabric of the land, oxidizing the remaining detritus of the trenches. Drawings such as *No Man's Land*[30] rely on the slightest indication of an outline to describe a dishevilled pile of clothes, or the single leather boot from which a wretched fragment of bone protrudes. There is an extraordinary balance in these drawings between what is actually depicted and the large tract of depleted white space that surrounds it and seems to depict nothingness.

Largely ignorant of the many stages of decay and putrefaction that befell the unburied and exposed corpses on a battlefield, Orpen

28 Arnold, *A Mirror to an Age*, p.316. Wyndham Lewis wrote of a chance meeting with Orpen in the hill-top spa at Cassel, where, surrounded by red tabs and brass-hats, Orpen was, according to rather snide remarks by Lewis, little more than a 'posh portraitist living on the fat of the land.' 'Upon hearing that I was with a battery in the Salient, he gazed in a half-mocking stare, twisting his eyebrows and smiling his wry Irish mockery at me... "Ah yes, it must be hell!" he said. He pronounced hell, "hail".' Lewis dismissed Orpen's 'watercolours and things of the War' as 'pallid and sentimental'. (Lewis, *Blasting and Bombardiering*, pp.169–170)

29 Orpen, *An Onlooker in France*, p.20.

30 Orpen, *A Trench, Beaumont Hamel*, pencil with touches of watercolour, 42 x 53.4 cm. IWM:ART 2393.

was seeing only a land that had been calcified, an enchanted place of extreme tonalities and saturated colour, a boneyard where the very earth 'glared with light'. Many others shared these same vivid sensations:

> To shelter from the glare rising off this totally tortured ground, I scrambled down in this hetacomb, where like the dead staring at the roof of the blue sky I felt separated from the world.[31]

Orpen rapidly evolved pictorial strategies to meet the unusual conditions: he dispensed with mid-tones, those subtle half-shades that denote the transition from darkness to light. In his drawings this resulted in figures that appear to hover in mid-air or are anchored to the earth by pools of deep shadow. It lends his paintings an odd theatricality as if they are powerfully lit by artificial beams. Perhaps this is most evident in his canvas *Dead Germans in a Trench*[32] with its masterful foreshortening and unblinking treatment of the long dead. Without half-tones the grisly scene is one of extremes; life and death, light and dark, black and white. How far removed are such paintings from the dusky interiors of refined Knightsbridge? What an extraordinary achievement for an artist who had never enjoyed painting outdoors, having always found it 'very difficult to work before nature'.[33]

In Orpen's work on the barren Somme battlefield light is no longer a force for the good. At the start of the war, a popular recruiting poster could proudly assert that the Englishmen's *Road to Triumph* 'travelled through Darkness to Light'. But just a few years later on the Somme, daylight was corrosive and revelatory, illuminating the very worst aspects of war: bones of man and beast, clods of decayed body and scraps of wasted cloth, evidence of terrible hand-to-hand fighting.[34] Even the living figures in this suite of drawings seem trapped by the light, rather than energized by it. *Man in the Glare*[35] depicts a young soldier almost pinned to the wall of a deep trench by the intensity of sunlight, his eyes squinting under an over-sized helmet, while around him the supporting walls are bleached away. Orpen understood the corrosive power of the battlefield sun. Whereas many artists drew the rough architecture of smashed trenches as a geometric tangle of torn wire and splintered timbers, Orpen drew the land in a state of advanced atrophy, where sandbags ooze earth

---

31 Paul Maze, *A Frenchman in Khaki*, pp.154–55.

32 Orpen, *Dead Germans in a Trench*, 1918. Oil on canvas, 91.4 x 76.2 cm. IWM:ART 2955.

33 Orpen, reflecting on the difficulties of painting outdoors in Clonsitta in 1910, quoted in *Landscape Painting in Britain, 1850–1950* (eds. Frances Spalding, Ian Jefferies) Arts Council of Great Britain, 1983, p.112.

34 Orpen, *An Onlooker in France*, p.18.

35 Orpen, *A Man in a Trench*. April 1917. Pencil and wash on paper, 48.4 x 38.1 cm. IWM:ART 3030.

WILLIAM ORPEN
Ready To Start. Self Portrait
(1917)
oil on panel, 60.8 x 49.4 cm
IMPERIAL WAR MUSEUM, LONDON
GIFT OF THE ARTIST, 1918

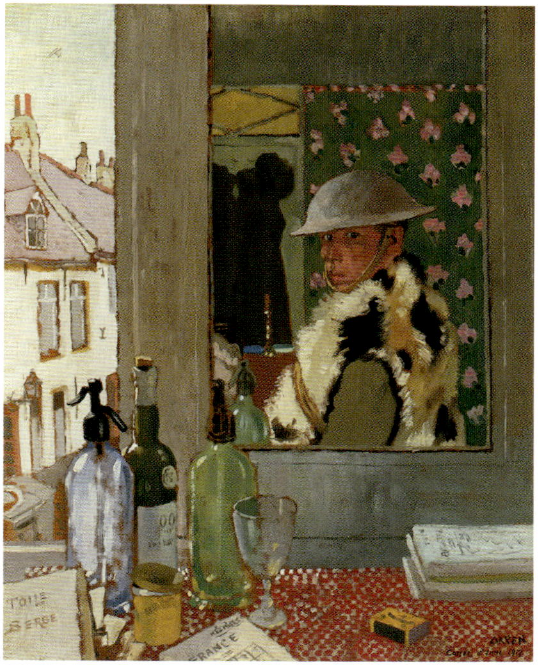

WILLIAM ORPEN
Self Portrait
(1917)
oil on canvas,
76.2 x 63.5 cm
IMPERIAL WAR MUSEUM, LONDON
GIFT OF THE ARTIST, 1918

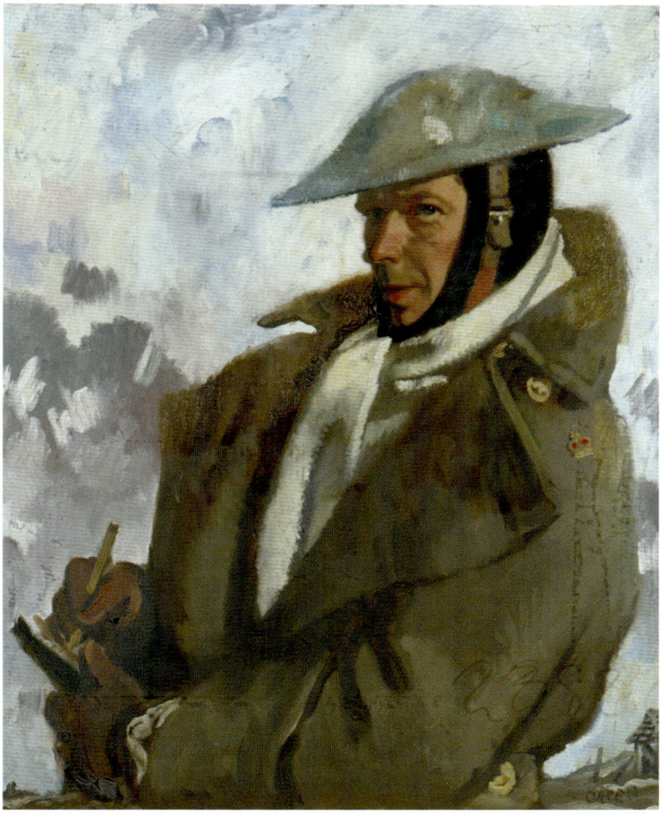

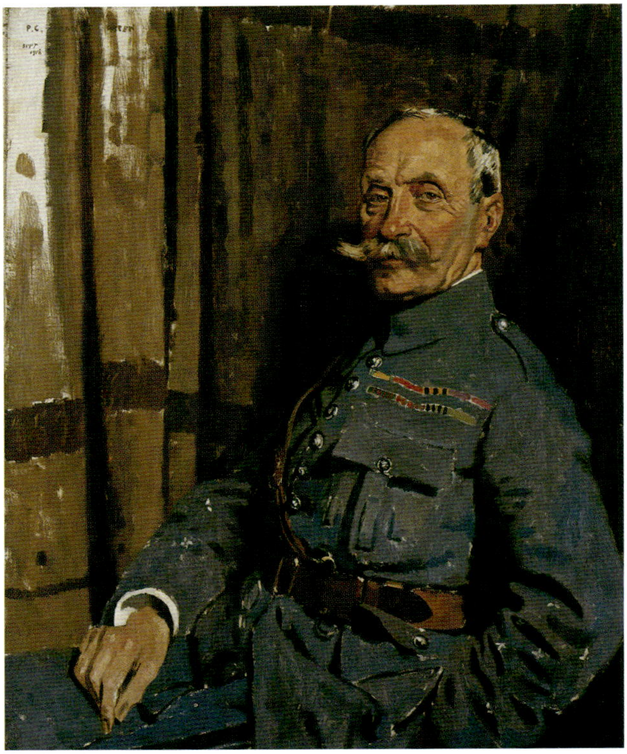

WILLIAM ORPEN
***Marshal Foch,* OM**
(1918)
oil on canvas,
91.4 x 76.2 cm
IMPERIAL WAR MUSEUM, LONDON
GIFT OF THE ARTIST, 1918

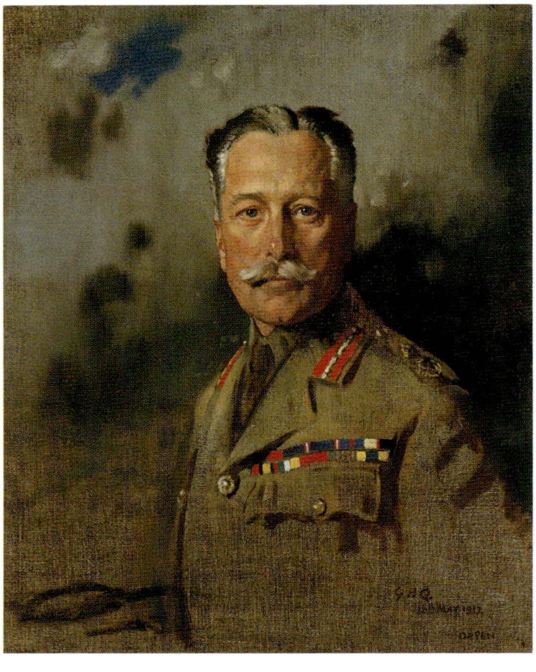

WILLIAM ORPEN
Field-Marshal Sir Douglas Haig,* KT, GCB, GCVO, KCIE *Commander-in-Chief, France, from December 15th 1915.Painted at General Headquarters, May 30th 1917
(1917)
oil on canvas,
74.9 x 63.5 cm
IMPERIAL WAR MUSEUM, LONDON
GIFT OF THE ARTIST, 1918

WILLIAM ORPEN
An Airman: Lieut RTC Hoidge, MC
(1917)
oil on canvas,
91.4 x 76.2 cm
IMPERIAL WAR MUSEUM, LONDON.
GIFT OF THE ARTIST, 1918

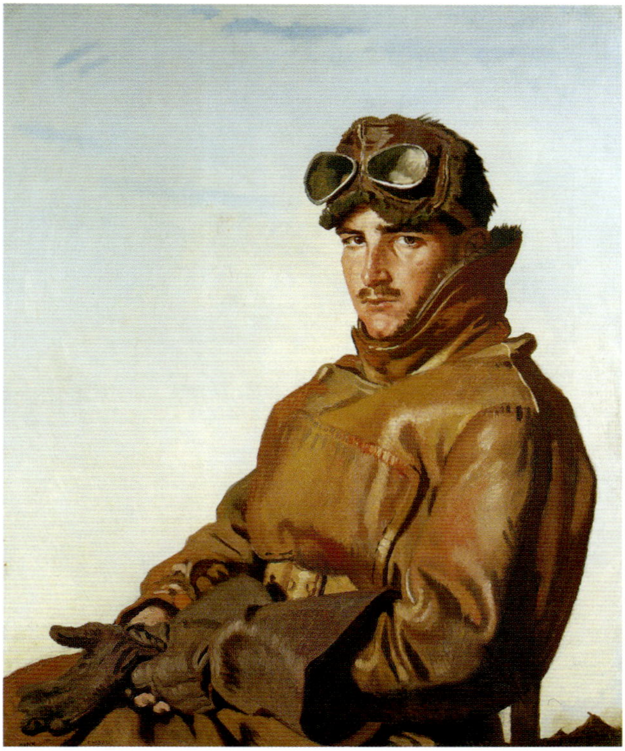

WILLIAM ORPEN
Lieut APF Rhys Davids, DSO, MC (1897–1917)
(1917)
oil on canvas,
91.4 x 76.2 cm
IMPERIAL WAR MUSEUM, LONDON
GIFT OF THE ARTIST, 1918

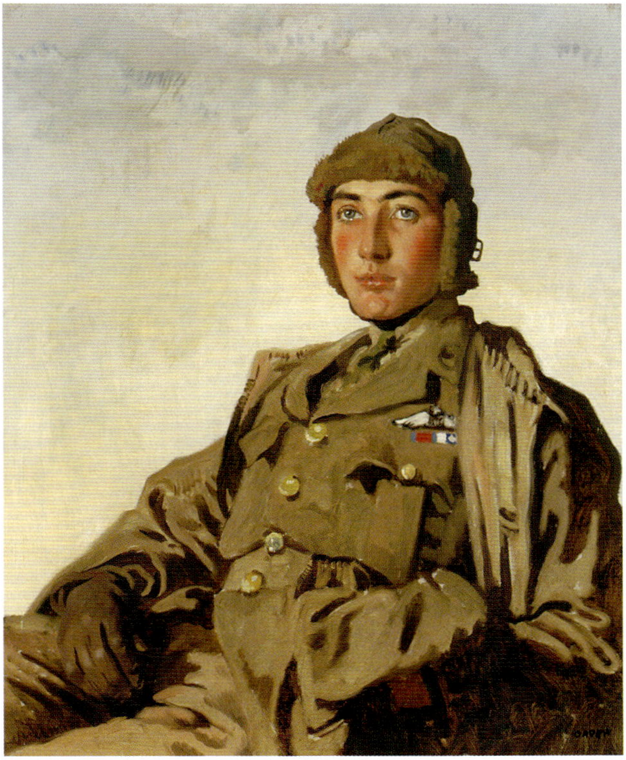

WILLIAM ORPEN
Dead Germans in a Trench
(1918)
oil on canvas,
91.4 x 76.2 cm

IMPERIAL WAR MUSEUM, LONDON.
GIFT OF THE ARTIST, 1918

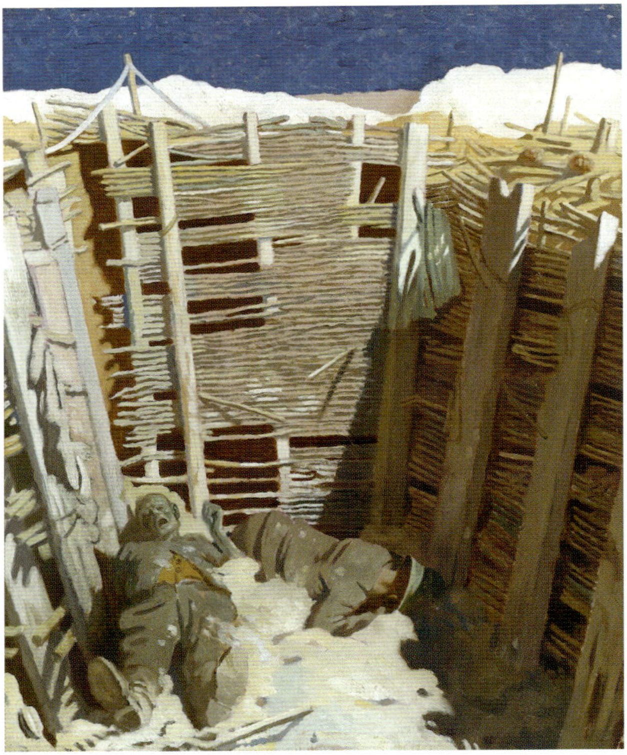

WILLIAM ORPEN
The Mad Woman of Douai
(1918)
oil on canvas,
91.4 x 76.2 cm

IMPERIAL WAR MUSEUM, LONDON
GIFT OF THE ARTIST, 1931

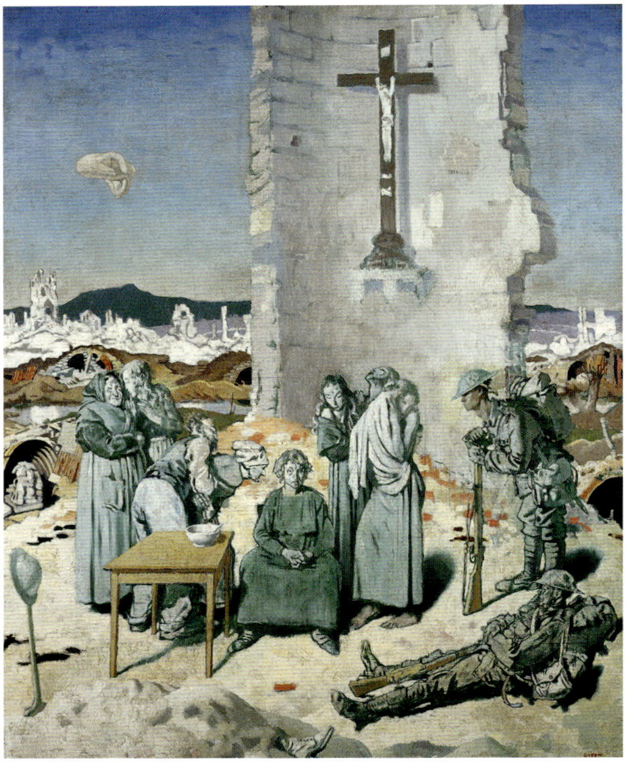

WILLIAM ORPEN
A Highlander Passing a Grave
(1917)
oil on panel,
60.9 x 50.8 cm
IMPERIAL WAR MUSEUM, LONDON
GIFT OF THE ARTIST, 1918

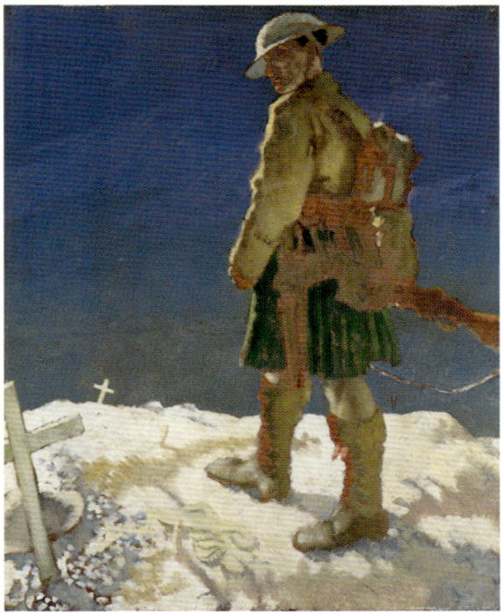

WILLIAM ORPEN
A Peace Conference at the Quai d'Orsay
(1919)
oil on canvas,
124.4 x 101.9 cm
IMPERIAL WAR MUSEUM, LONDON

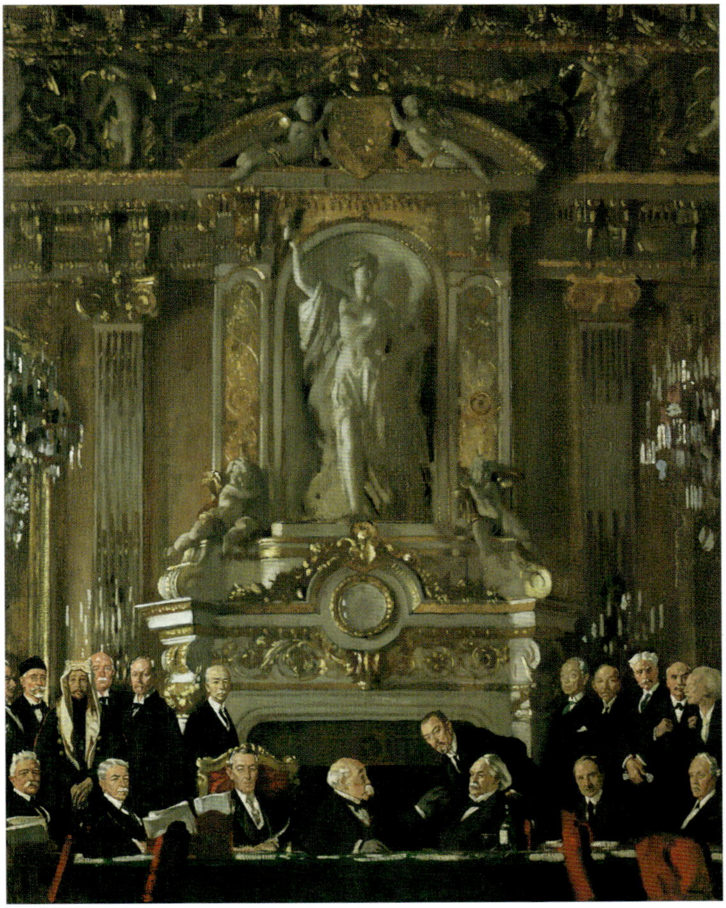

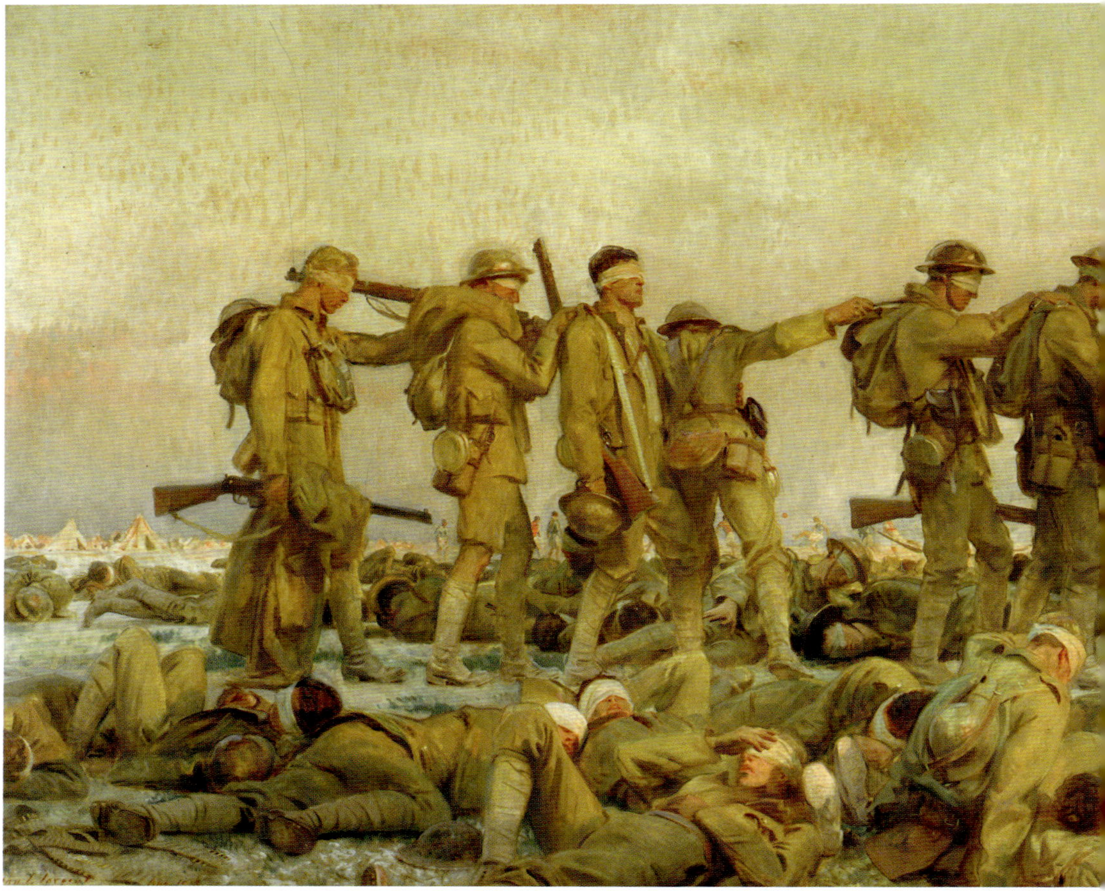

JOHN SINGER SARGENT
Gassed
(1919)
oil on canvas, 231 x 611.1 cm
IMPERIAL WAR MUSEUM, LONDON

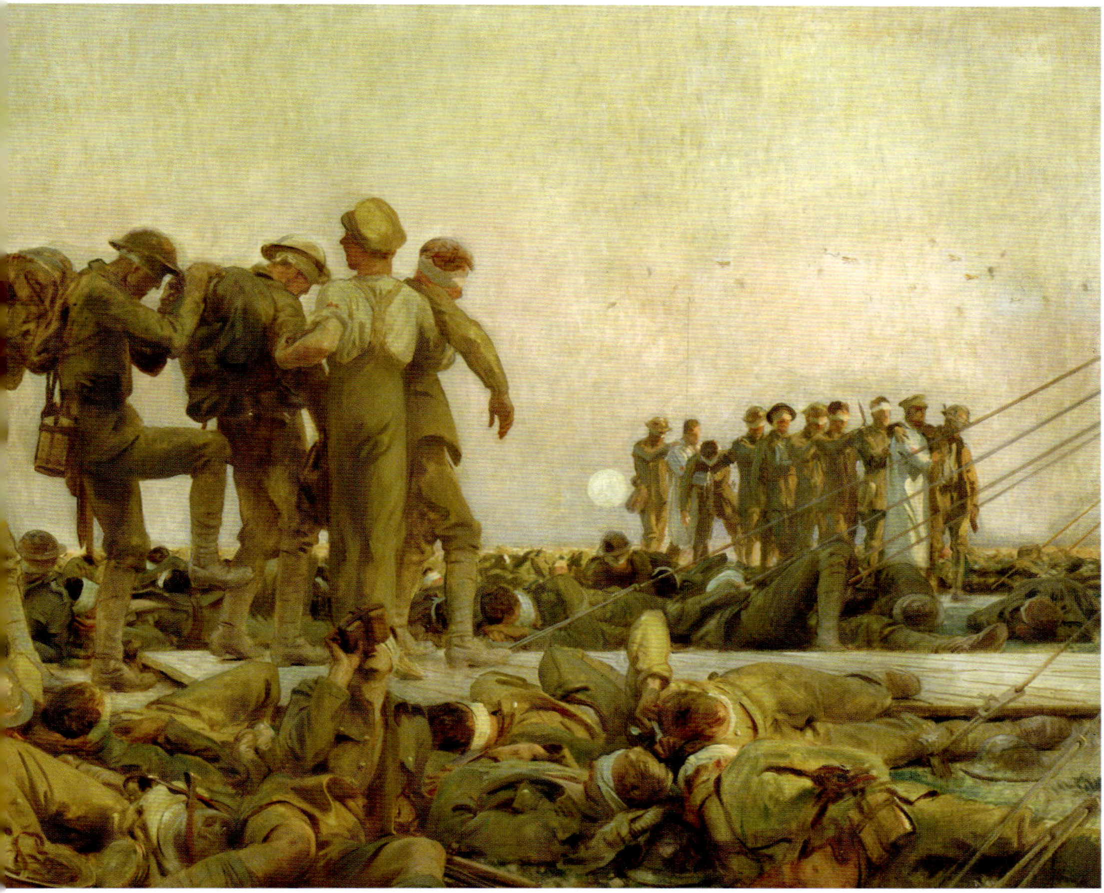

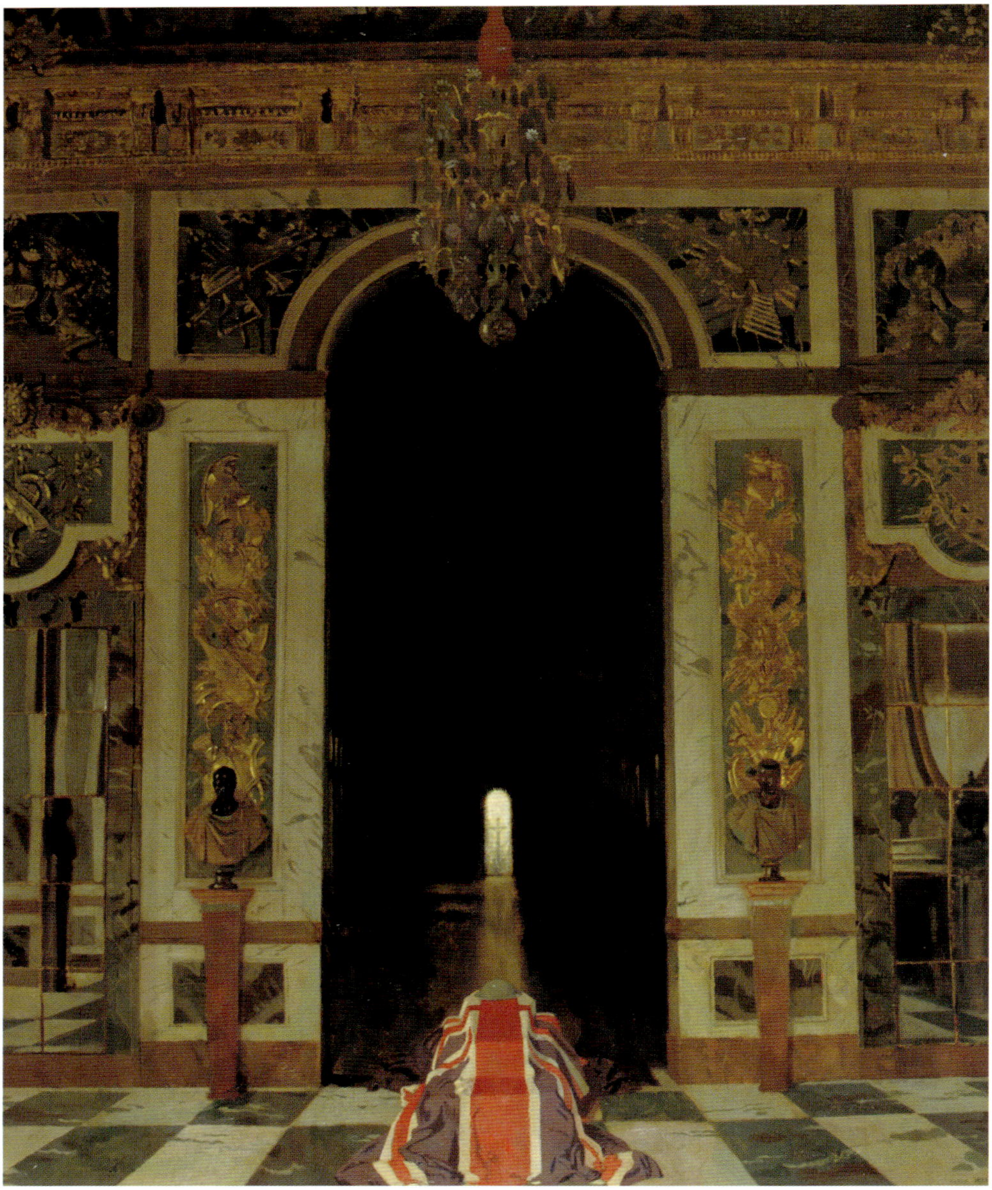

WILLIAM ORPEN

To the Unknown British Soldier in France

(1921–28)

oil on canvas, 154.2 x 128.9 cm

IMPERIAL WAR MUSEUM, LONDON. PRESENTED BY THE ARTIST IN MEMORY OF EARL HAIG, 1928 like pus, parapets seem to melt under the searing light, trenches are reduced to a glutinous fatty pulp; it is as if the land has been rendered to molten wax. The sweet odour of death and decay is almost palpable. In these works Orpen has painted 'the smell'.[36]

ORPEN'S SITTERS

Tramping the Somme was exhausting. Its shabby appearance and wincing odours wore at the painter's perseverance; its terrible recent history haunted the mind and played odd tricks. Nor could Orpen settle into any given pattern; his days spent working outside were interspersed with long car journeys to Paris or Amiens to paint yet more portraits. It was often a relief to return to the emptied battle-field. But after months in France the pressure was beginning to tell. He recalled one strange incident that occurred when he was painting the remains of a British and a German soldier – little more than 'skulls, bones, garments' – in the trenches near the shattered remnants of Thiepval:

> I was all alone. My faithful Howlett was about half a mile away with the car. When I had been working about a couple of hours I felt strange. I cannot say even now what I felt. Afraid? Of what? The sun shone fiercely. There was not a breath of air. Perhaps it was that – a touch of the sun. So I stopped painting and went and sat on the trunk of a blown-up tree close by, when suddenly I was thrown on the back of my head on the ground. My heavy easel was upset, and one of the skulls went through the canvas.[37]

Orpen recovered his senses and even carried on painting, but he was clearly unsettled and the incident wore at his nerves. Surely it would have been easier to do what he did best, to stay indoors painting portraits, to rely on tried and trusted formulae? But portrait painting makes its own peculiar demands on the painter. Not only does it require prolonged concentration, but the painter has to remain alert to the subtle nuances of expression that help capture the essentials of character; he must be brisk without being hasty, aware that only so much time can be expected from each sitter, only so long when the light stays constant, and only a finite time before the clothes and posture sag, the skin sets and the expression becomes a rictus of discomfort. Capturing a likeness is, for many painters, relatively simple. Finding a characteristic pose, judging the typical angle of a

---

36 A very fine example of this method of drawing is: Orpen, *A Trench, Beaumont Hamel.* Pencil with touches of water-colour on paper, 42 x 53.4 cm. IWM:ART 2393.

37 Orpen, *An Onlooker in France*, p.39–40.

head, and matching skin colour are the basic requirements for a portrait head. The setting, lighting and the pose also contribute towards the total effect. With its twenty-foot ceiling, massive chandelier, and natural light cascading from both north and south windows, Orpen's studio in South Bolton Gardens was well-designed for painting portraits, although he kept it sparcely furnished – even spartan – apart from the heavy drapes behind the raised 'throne' where he posed his sitters. He had a strict regime for capturing a likeness. First he laid down a translucent brown wash, then he would rapidly draw the face in monochrome with the fine point of the brush concentrating 'on the triangle of eyes and mouth' giving particular attention to the correct rendering of the cheekbones. One of his studio assistants described his method:

> What he observed seemed to go in through his eyes, be analysed and arranged in his brain, and written down with inevitable rightness by his unerring hand, as one complicated movement of his will. He painted at an incredible speed without alterations or erasures, and then, if not exactly what he wanted, he simply wiped it out and began again – but that was seldom... He taught that sufficient paint to create the illusion of light and shade, of tone and colour was enough, and laughed at touch, impasto, heureux salete, and, to use his own words, 'all that sort of tosh'.[38]

If history has not been especially kind to 'Orpen the portrait painter' this is due in part because for so long he worked in the shadow of the magisterial John Singer Sargent. No portraitist was more successful in reviving what was known as the 'swagger portrait' than the American painter. A 'swagger portrait' is one in which the sitter is shown, usually full-length, in ostentatious and self-conscious display. Sargent drew on the methods of the Old Masters, conjuring up a cold, objective technical brilliance to freeze on canvas the opulent vivacity of the *nouveaux-riches* families who formed his clientele, and whose sons and daughters would soon queue up to be rendered in their finery by his natural successor, Orpen. He, too, brought an objective realism to the task, although he liked to believe that he could also catch something of 'the mind's construction in the face', as Sargent had done, by matching psychological perceptions with his dazzling technical achievement.[39] It was not the case. Orpen might have

---

38 Sean Keating, 'William Orpen: A Tribute', *Ireland Today*, Vol.2, 1937, quoted in Robert Upstone *et al*, *William Orpen: Politics, Sex and Death* (London: Philip Wilson Publishers, 2005), p.28. The observations about portraiture are drawn from notes accompanying the exhibition *John Singer Sargent and the Swagger Portraits*, held at Tate Britain in 1993, devised by curators Alison Smith and Heather Birchall. See also: Andrew Wilton, *The Swagger Portrait: Grand Manner Portraiture in Britain from Van Dyck to Augustus John, 1630–1930* (London, Tate Publishing, 1992).

39 Arnold is especially penetrating in his analysis of Orpen's limited success at psychological portraiture, see Arnold, pp.106–107.

been a master of external appearances, but he was not especially interested in the minds of his subjects. Portrait painting was for him a professional, even mechanical, task and he struggled to overcome his natural reticence with strangers and gain any level of empathy for those 'parked' in front of him. As the war continued, the list of those queuing up outside his hotel room-cum-studio seemed to grow longer and longer.

Of the ninety-six illustrations reproduced in Orpen's 'war memoir' *An Onlooker in France*, nearly half depict stern and rather important middle-aged men in seated pose.[40] Many of these are little more than accomplished sketches, ragged around the edges of the canvas, with fleetingly-painted uniforms and the most cursory indication of setting or location. Many of their names are now obscure, their contribution to public history best located in footnotes to the war and its aftermath, the Peace Conference in Versailles, where Orpen was sent as the official recorder. His diaries are crammed with a treadmill of appointments and sittings; some more taxing than others.

On one of his frequent forays to the hotels and chateaux in the rear zones he was tasked with painting Marshal Foch, the head of the French forces. Protracted negotiations took place with the French Army's Chief of Staff. 'He would certainly sit. How long did I want him for?' Orpen recalled of their negotiations, 'An hour and a half each day, for four of five days? Certainly. When did I wish to start? The next day? Certainly. He would sit from 7 a.m. to 8.30 a.m. for as many mornings as I wished. Might he smoke while he sat? Yes! Bon!'[41] And so, for the following week without any fuss Foch sat, sucking expertly on his pipe, in the well-lit library, while a steady flow of reports from the battlefield were relayed to him by attentive aides-de-camp. 'If it was good,' reported Orpen, 'he would say "Bon!" If it was bad, he just made a strange noise by forcing air out through his lips'. A model sitter – calm, courteous, compliant – Foch was clearly a master of self-control. Orpen's study of the great general tries to pierce the calm exterior of the old soldier, attempting to locate 'the responsibility of it all – hidden in the brain behind those kind, thoughtful eyes'. He does not fully succeed; after all, he had little more than a few hours to try to know the man and to see through his mask-like surface. Instead, we have an assured pose of the veteran soldier in uniform, one hand thrust deeply into his pocket; his head cocked towards the viewer, his ear ever alert to the stream of news from invisible emissaries to stage-right.

Whereas Foch was reckoned by Orpen to be 'the most mentally

---

40 Of ninety-six reproductions of his work in the book, forty-two are portraits.

41 Orpen, *Marshal Foch O.M.*, 1918. Oil on canvas, 91.4 x 76.2 cm. IWM:ART 3046. The tale of the sitting is recounted in Orpen, *An Onlooker in France,* p.80.

calm and complete thing' he had ever attempted to paint, his brisk rendition of the President of the United States, Woodrow Wilson, depicts an outwardly genial, but more 'nervous and twitchy' character. Orpen had at first been refused access to the President, but through his network of contacts he secured a sitting at the Astoria Hotel in Paris where he had to face the anxious authority of the President's bodyguard, two large men and one 'enormous one' who seemed intent on bossing him around as he tried, in the thirty minutes before Wilson walked in, to arrange his palette and prepare the room for the sitting. Short, stringy and determined, Orpen was not accustomed to being told how to behave and working himself up to 'desperate action' he 'uttered one short, thoroughly English word, but one which has a lot to it' and the room was soon cleared, leaving the way for painter and sitter.[42] Wilson's relaxed but stately pose, one arm resting easily on the back of the chair, belies the complexities of the peace conference he was then embroiled in. Orpen, always an astute, even 'deadly observer' of appearances,[43] noted with grim satisfaction that President Wilson had already 'made a great hit in the Press with his smile. He was pleased at that, and after this he never failed to let you see all his back teeth'. Painted in a single hour snatched in the gaps between the interminable peace talks, Orpen's portrait finds little of the smile, instead there is a rather stern fixedness about his features, distant and shrewd, recognizing perhaps the failure of his noble aspirations for peace, 'the idealist who had lost his way'.

During 1918 the list of sitters seemed interminable, but as always Orpen worked diligently on behalf of the government. When he was finally secured by the incorrigible Lord Beaverbrook to work for the Canadian War Memorials Committee, he was instructed to paint nothing but portraits of the senior echelons of the Canadian military. Obediently, perhaps a little mechanically, he painted them: Generals Currie, Lipsett, Watson, Bustell, Loomis, MacDonnell, and for good measure, Currie's *aide-de-camp*, Major O'Conner. In the 'grip' of the Canadians, Orpen confessed to a fellow artist that he would like to run away to 'some old Battlefield to get some peace' because he was sick of having to 'sit down and do a "face" just as if one were in London'.[44]

Some faces, however, were worth painting. Perhaps the finest of the portraits are those of the young fighter pilots made during the autumn of 1917. One of the 'aces' Lieutenant R.T.C. Hoidge MC and Bar, had the temerity to turn up an hour and half late for his sitting with Orpen, but offered the 'irresistible excuse'[45] of having narrowly

---

42 This tale is told at length in *Onlooker*, p.103.

43 The phrase is from Arnold, *Mirror to an Age*, p.362.

44 Orpen to William Rothenstein, quoted in Arnold, *Mirror to an Age*, p.331.

escaped death in a dog-fight only hours earlier. Supping nonchalantly at a soft drink he recounted the tale: 'Let a damned old Boche get on my tail... I was so intent on an old two-seater I was chasing I never noticed the blighter – if old Beaumont hadn't come up and chased the blighter off I was for it – he put one bullet through the box by my head, blew off ½ my tail and cut 3 stays... but the morning wasn't wasted I got 4 Bosche afterwards.' In awe of such heroics, Orpen commented, 'Here was this youth the calmest thing in the world drinking his lemon squash...'[46] Hoidge's portrait depicts an alert young airman, with unflinching stare – 'bird's eyes' wrote Orpen – and a battle-ready demeanour. It has none of the disarming dreaminess of Orpen's other fine portrait of a 'a great youth', the fighter ace A.P. Rhys-Davids DSO MC who had been Captain of Eton from 1915–1916 and was already credited with bringing down twenty-two German planes, including the infamous Verner Voss. In these paintings there is less of the loose handling that characterises his portraits of frock-coated politicians made during his months at Versailles. Instead, the drawing is crisp; the bulky volumes of the flying coats suggested by lush shadows and rich colours. The paint surfaces have a generous creaminess and a porcelain-like delicacy, as fragile as the string and canvas flying machines driven by these young warriors. However, Rhys-Davids did not live to see his portrait varnished and framed; he was shot down soon after he sat for Orpen, the slim volume of William Blake poetry that he kept in his tunic in case he was captured and imprisoned, left unread.[47]

ORPEN'S 'WAR' EXHIBITION
May 1918

Only nine of Orpen's portraits were to be included in his huge show of 125 pieces simply entitled 'War' that opened at Agnew's

45 The story is well told in Harries and Harries, *The War Artists*, p.69. The portrait is *An Airman: Lieutenant R.T.C. Hoidge MC and Bar, 1917*. Oil on canvas, 91.4 x 76.2 cm. IWM:ART 2996.

46 Orpen to Rich, 17 November 1917, British Museum, Add.Ms 42711, in Harries and Harries, *The War Artists*, p.69. Orpen repeats the tale of Hoidge's late arrival in *Onlooker* p.52, adding that he had a face 'wonderfully fitted for a man-bird. His eyes were bird's eyes.' Orpen abandoned the first sitting to take lunch in silence with Hoidge, during which the pilot slowly revealed his extraordinary tale. 'Then,' concludes Orpen, 'we went upstairs and he sat like a lamb'.

47 Orpen, *Lieut. A.P. Rhys Davids DSO MC, 1897–1917*. Oil on canvas, 91.4 x 76.2 cm. IWM:ART 3004. Voss's death came after a bloody encounter with one of the 'premier squadrons' of the Allied air force, no. 56 squadron, B and C flights, whose pilots included James T B McCudden, A.P. Rhys Davids, R.A. Maybery, G.H. Bowman, R.T.C. Hoidge and K.K. Muspratt. His Fokker Dr I. was a much slower aircraft than the British SE 5a. Another 'ace' James McCudden described Voss's end: 'By now the German Triplane was in the middle of our formation, and its handling was wonderful to behold. The pilot seemed to be firing at all of us simultaneously, and although I got behind him a second time, I could hardly stay there for a second. His movements were so quick that none of us could hold him in sight at all for any decisive time... the triplane was still circling round the midst of six SEs, who were all firing at it as the opportunity offered, and at one time I noted the triplane in the apex of a cone of tracer bullets from at least 5 machines.'

in London on 3 May 1918. Its sheer diversity impressed an expectant public and over 9,000 people went to see it in the first four weeks, amongst them Queen Mary and Lady Cynthia Asquith. Having already been widely reproduced in the illustrated press, the 'khaki portraits' were very popular, as were the representations of artillery in action and images of individual combatants such as *Highlander Passing a Grave* and the widely reproduced *Thinker on the Butte de Warlencourt*.[48] But possibly the most newsworthy aspect of the exhibition was Orpen's unprecedented offer to donate the entire body of work – and any future pictures made of the war – to the British government.[49] Although his earnings had fallen drastically during the war years, his donation was born of a conviction that he should not profit unduly from the terrible suffering he had witnessed. Orpen set two strict conditions: that the collection should be kept together as a single *corpus* – possibly at the National War Museum – and that all his work should be presented in the white wooden frames that had stood out so dramatically on the deep red velvet walls of Agnew's. Orpen's exhibition toured to Manchester and then on to the United States. A proposal to have it shown *en masse* at the National Gallery in Dublin came to nothing as it was judged ill-advised to exhibit war paintings in the city at that time, especially those by an Irishman now permanently resident in England.[50] However, in the birthday honours list that June the painter was made a Knight Commander of the Civil Division 'for services in connection with the war' and he busily prepared himself for a speedy return to Flanders.

Despite there being little enthusiasm in some quarters to have Orpen back, he casually pulled strings in high places and was in France by early July 1918. Much to his *chagrin*, Major Lee at Intelligence GHQ who had opposed his return, was breezily informed by Haig's ADC that Orpen should be given every freedom to continue his good work. Yet the last few months of the war were confusing times for Orpen. Wracked by erratic ill-health and still maintaining his hectic social and professional duties, a new, and at times disturbing, zeal entered his thinking. He pleaded in near desperation to Beaverbrook for more support:

---

48 Orpen, *Highlander Passing a Grave*, Oil on panel, 61 x 50.8 cm. IWM:ART 2995.
Orpen, *Thinker on the Butte de Warlencourt*. Pencil and water-colour on paper, 51.4 x 41.9 cm. IWM:ART 2984.

49 In 1921 Orpen's gift – some 138 pieces – was officially valued at £28,000. In the long term, Orpen's generosity may have back-fired on his reputation, as it prevented a wider dispersal of his work and an opportunity lost for those outside London to see and appreciate his impressive body of paintings and drawings.

50 The debates about Orpen's politics and religious leanings are discussed in the catalogue essays that accompanied the exhibition at the Imperial War Museum in London. Robert Upstone, Roy Foster, and David Fraser Jenkins: *William Orpen: Politics, Sex and Death* (London: Philip Wilson Publishers, 2005). Orpen's friendship with Colonel A.N. Lee was particularly complex given the latter's part in the Easter Rebellion in 1916 and his role as Brigade Major in arranging the executions of many Republican prisoners.

> A great tract of country on the Paris front has been recaptured – another great tract on the Amiens front. This means that new work, years of it, has opened out for me on this most vital hundred miles stretch of land in the world. And I want to do it... The question is will you allow me to go on doing it? The truth is I have seen this regained country and I cannot bear to lose the chance of trying to represent some of it, and the men who have regained it. I will give everything I do.[51]

Turning down an opportunity to visit and paint the fighting in Italy, Open embarked on a final, almost self-destructive mission to record the heart of the war. However, his restless urgency was beginning to occlude his judgment. Under the self-inflicted pressure to describe the teeming fullness of the war and to witness its every aspect, Orpen's draughtsmanship – always so precise and considered – became loose and ragged, his once taut graphic line lapsed too often into weak caricature. His compositions, while not lacking in tonal drama, now appeared forced and melodramatic, even when seen together as a suite of connected stories. Despite their heartfelt sense of empathy, compositions such as *Bombing: Night* and *Adam and Eve at Peronne* seem laboured in their moralising, mannered in their pictorial arrangement.[52] On occasion, however, he was capable of producing quite extraordinary individual pieces.

In the British canon of war art there are, for example, few such harrowing images as *The Mad Woman of Douai*, an elaborate and garish canvas, which seems focused on German brutality but is in fact a thinly veiled representation of the aftermath of a rape.[53] 'There she sat,' noted Orpen with a mixture of disgust and fascination, 'silent and motionless, except for one thumb which constantly twitched.'[54] There is no comfort in the faces and postures of those who stand around peering pitilessly at her, their compassion as irreparably shattered as the ruins that surround them. As if to emphasise the point that Flanders had endured not one but two invading armies the soldiers are rendered in a very different painterly language than the other figures; they are like intruders arbitrarily borrowed from other pictures and 'set like cut-out figures in a scene of misery to which they don't belong'. Despite its awkward

---

51 Orpen's plea to Beaverbrook was further evidence of a sincere wish to help further the war effort. Orpen's income had plummeted from £9,355 in 1916 to just under £900 – an army major's pay – out of which income tax had to be paid.

52 Orpen, *Bombing: Night*. Oil on canvas, 76.2 x 63.5 cm. IWM:ART 2994.
Orpen, *Adam and Eve at Peronne*. Pen, pencil and water-colour, 58.4 x 45.7 cm. IWM:ART 3008.

53 Orpen, *The Mad Woman of Douai*. 1918. Oil on canvas, 91.4 x 76.2 cm. IWM:ART 4671. This painting – donated by the artist to the Imperial War Museum in 1931 – is the largest of Orpen's battlefield narratives and, interestingly, is exactly the same dimensions as most of the official portraits (of Haig, Trenchard, Foch, Plumer, Lee, etc).

54 Orpen, *An Onlooker in France*, p.93. 'Bunny Smedley' is especially insightful about this strange canvas, see http://www.socialaffairsunit.org.uk/blog/archives/000312.php (posted on 7 March 2005).

theatricality, in this painting Orpen was attempting to describe a face of the war that few others were willing to witness, let alone broach in paint.

Every way he turned now he was faced with appalling dilemmas: the collapse of moral order, the commonplace ubiquity of death, the uncomfortable intimacy between sex and violence. On one strange day he witnessed three young French prostitutes 'all dressed up, silk stockings and crimped hair', plying their trade over the bodies of soldiers being readied for burial. He shuddered at the sight of them offering passers-by 'a little love'.[55] There is little doubt that Orpen, exhausted and increasingly unwell, was at the very edge of his self-knowledge as a painter, looking for guidance perhaps from the work of Callot and Goya, while trying not to relish the macabre, mad and morbid temperature of the war as it reached its crazy crescendo. He tried to re-imagine some of the more bizarre incidents of war in a series of 'parable paintings' such as *Armistice Night, Amiens* and *The Official Entry of the Kaiser.*[56] In these narrative pieces he was clearly grappling with the black humour of 'victory', borrowing from Hogarth examples of irreverent display, and relying on a strict tonal structure to hold in place the crazy behaviour of wild crowds and marauding soldiers. Not all the pictures succeed. Even the tender images of loss, such as *A Death Among the Wounded in the Snow* is compromised by mawkish posture, a pallid palette and an 'innate staginess'.[57] In his suite of 'Victory' pictures, it is as if Orpen were sketching events from the front row of the theatre stalls, the painted figures little but jobbing actors, and the shattered ruins backlit drops hoisted into place for effect. Despite its disarming power, *The Mad Woman at Douai* is over-stylised and clumsily designed, although in its treatment of indifference and lack of compassion it is an extraordinarily resonant and contemporary image. It still haunts us because it addresses fundamental concerns in our human condition, and to his credit, Orpen did not flinch from tackling such major themes. In these bitter paintings – never to surface again in his lifetime – Orpen had shoved aside the residue of high Victorian portraiture, temporarily abandoning his infatuation with the glittering opulence of Edwardian wealth. His palette, once tonally subdued and expertly controlled, had gained 'a lurid, acidic, even unwholesome quality that was wholly of the twentieth century'.

55 Orpen, *An Onlooker in France*, p.93. The idea that France had been invaded by two armies: British and German is made in Gordon Williams, Review of Bruce Arnold, *Orpen: Mirror to an Age*, in *Trivium: Literature and the Arts*, Vol.18, May 1983, p.108.

56 *Armistice Night, Amiens*, 1918. Oil on canvas, 91.5 x 71 cm. Private Collection.
The Official Entry of the Kaiser, 1918. Oil on canvas, 91 x 71 cm. Private Collection.

57 Orpen, *A Death Among the Wounded in the Snow*, c.1918. Pencil and watercolour on paper, 45 x 58.4 cm. IWM:ART 2985. The phrase 'innate staginess' is from Richard Cork, *A Bitter Truth: Avant-Garde Art and the Great War.* (New Haven: Yale University Press, 1994) p.195.

WILLIAM ORPEN
A Trench, Beaumont Hamel
(1917)
pencil on paper,
41.9 x 53.3 cm
IMPERIAL WAR MUSEUM, LONDON
GIFT OF THE ARTIST, 1918

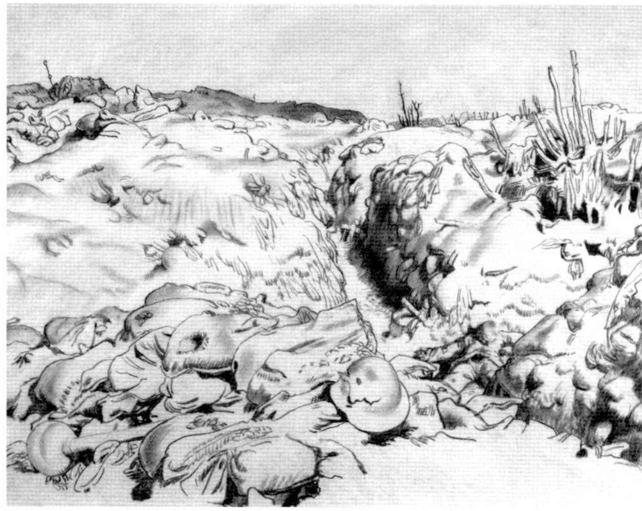

WILLIAM ORPEN
Sketch for 'Adam and Eve at Péronne'
(c.1918)
ink pencil watercolour
on paper, 58.4 x 45.7 cm
IMPERIAL WAR MUSEUM, LONDON
GIFT OF THE ARTIST, 1918

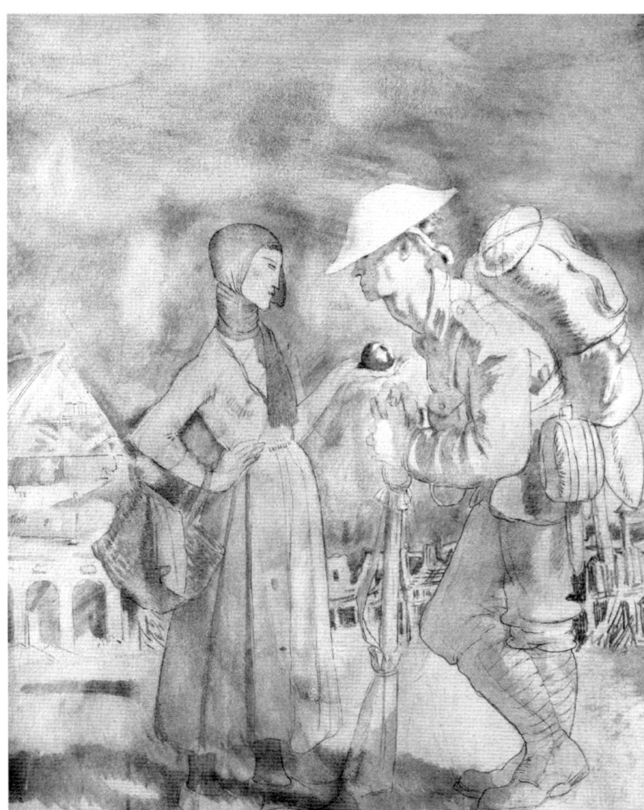

However, his renditions of these strange weeks of 'victory' remained incomprehensible to many and paved the way for the manic energy that he brought to his last batch of war art: the Peace Conference at Versailles.

PEACE AND PAIN

Orpen's illnesses remain mysterious, their cause now impossible to diagnose. He had his first bout in Cassel in late 1917, which started as a skin infection initially considered to be lice, but then thought to be scabies. After rudimentary treatment Orpen discharged himself from hospital believing that he had blood-poisoning, although its outward signs suggest something far more alarming. As well as the rash, he had a deep sore in one foot, and a second in his throat which he graphically described to his wife as 'a white hole with a black band around it, and all the flesh for about six inches beyond a deep scarlet'.[58] By November 1918, worried and worn-out, he completely collapsed, spending much of the winter out of sight, nursed (it has to be assumed) by his mistress, Yvonne Aubicq. In late November he sketched himself wrapped rather comically in bandages with a large sticking plaster patching up the wound in his neck, which had still not healed. Barely surviving the Spanish influenza epidemic Orpen dragged himself into 1919 ever ambitious to serve his adopted country. He wrote to his wife Grace: 'My heart is about the only thing I have left whole – all my other organs are not past repair – but they are a bit 'joggly' – but I'm well on the mend now and the Doc says I'll be able to act like an ordinary mortal in four or five months...' The Armistice bought little succour. Writing about the very hour that the fighting stopped, Orpen noted wearily that 'on this day, looked forward to for years:

> I must admit that ... I found something wrong – perhaps, like all great moments expected, something is sure to fall short of expectations. Peace was too great a thing to think about, the longing for it was too real, too intense. For four years the fighting man had thought of nothing except that great moment of achievement: now it had come, the great thing had ceased, the war was won and over. The fighting man – that marvellous thing that I had worshipped all the time I had been in France – had ceased actively to exist. I realised then, almost as much as I do now, that he was lost, forgotten.[59]

---

58 Orpen to Grace, cited in Arnold, *Mirror to an Age*, p.332. During the 1920s Orpen wrote in confidence to Colonel A.N. Lee suggesting that the sores, boils and abscesses that still plagued him were due to syphilis, possibly in its secondary stages. See A.N. Lee papers, Department of Documents, Imperial War Museum, London. Cited in Robert Upstone *et al*, *William Orpen: Politics, Sex and Death* (London: Philip Wilson Publishers, 2005), p.42–43.

Yet, as always, Orpen stirred and readied himself for more work. Only days after the Armistice, Alfred Yockney at the Imperial War Museum had written to the French Ambassador to set out Orpen's credentials for the coming Peace Conference, asserting 'that no British painter is so well equipped to paint such an historical picture for the Nation'.[60] It was to be another arduous undertaking. Orpen moved to Paris, where, between late January and mid-July, he embarked on a series of individual portraits of every political leader (and many of their senior colleagues) attending the conference. As he diligently painted each head, his official commission was radically changed. Instead of a single historical picture for the nation, he was told to paint three large paintings, a huge undertaking whose only incentive might have been the fee of £6,000. However, Orpen was becoming increasingly disillusioned. After weeks and weeks of observing the long drawn-out political wrangling, his confidence in the peace process was ebbing away:

> From my window-seat it was easy to see how self-important the majority of these little black 'frocks' thought themselves. It was like an opera bouffe, after the people I had seen, known and painted during the war; and these, as the days went by seemed to be gradually more and more forgotten. It seemed impossible, but it was true. The fighting man, alive, and those who fought and died – all the people who made the Peace Conference possible, were being forgotten, the 'frocks' reigned supreme. One was almost forced to think that the 'frocks' won the war. 'I did this,' 'I did that,' they all screamed, but the silent soldier man never said a word, yet he must have thought a lot.[61]

Orpen finished only two of the large canvases. They were unsatisfactory pieces and he knew it. For someone who was glibly dismissed by other painters as 'the pet of the bourgeoisie', 'a posh portraitist living on the fat of the land',[62] who was jealously despised for courting the rich and the influential, Orpen had answered back, even if the riposte was not especially barbed. In the first of the large canvases – *A Peace Conference at the Quai d'Orsay* – Orpen squashed the eighteen world leaders into less than a quarter of the painting, the remaining portion is dominated by the ornate decoration of the chamber.[63] Subjugated by the interior space, each figure is rendered in a stiff and implacable posture, isolated from their neighbour, and

59 Orpen, *Onlooker*, pp.98–99. On those same blackened streets that night, Orpen recounts meeting a Tommy who threatened to murder him because 'of his misery'. Orpen took him home to his billet and talked him out of it, assuring the soldier that 'he would have a great time in the future.'

60 Yockney to Orpen, cited in Arnold, *Mirror to an Age*, p.368.

61 Orpen, *Onlooker*, pp.103–104.

62 See Wyndham Lewis, *Blasting and Bombardiering*, p.170.

63 Orpen, *A Peace Conference at the Quai d'Orsay*, 1919. Oil on canvas, 124.4 x 101.9 cm. IWM:ART 2855.

painted as though incapable of conversation or dialogue. It was a clever painterly ruse orchestrated by Orpen to mock the protracted and manipulated peace process. The second painting – *The Signing of the Peace* – was even larger, some 60 inches by 50, but at least its awkward collation of isolated portraits is relieved a little by the reflections in the vast mirrors that lined the hall.[64] Like Velasquez peering into the court of Philip IV of Spain, Open's reflected silhouette – split in half by the junction of two mirrors – can be clearly spotted behind the stately, but diminutive, figures of Lloyd George, Clemenceau and Woodrow Wilson.

Wearily, Orpen embarked on the third panorama of principals and politicians, and spent a further nine months painstakingly building a panoply of statesmen and servicemen gathered under the gilded surroundings of the Hall of Peace. Then, without warning the museum, he painted them all out. 'It all seemed so unimportant somehow,' he told the *Evening Standard*. 'In spite of all these eminent men, I kept thinking of the soldiers who remain in France for ever.'[65] Methodically, he obliterated the thirty-six figures, painting in their place 'a coffin covered with the Union Jack, two semi-nude soldiers guarding it and two cherubs in the air above'.[66] Exhibited at the Royal Academy in the summer of 1923, with the title *To the Unknown British Soldier in France*, it was voted 'picture of the year' by public ballot.[67] The left-wing press was jubilant; the *Daily Herald* called it 'a magnificent allegorical tribute to the men who really won the war', but *The Patriot* thought it 'a joke and a bad joke at that'. Nor was it much liked by the Trustees of the Imperial War Museum, who after much procrastination rejected it, noting with untypical temperance that '…it does not show what we wished shown'.[68] To make their point, the final instalment of his fee was withheld from Orpen.

It is a curious picture, well-intentioned but mawkish in Orpen's inimitable way. The figures are familiar to those who know his war paintings, being related to the family of emaciated, rather feminised soldiers who wander in and out of his war narratives. These two are taken from his drawing *Blown-Up – Mad*.[69] As a rule, the British did not produce much effective anti-war painting, though clearly there

---

64 Orpen, *The Signing of the Peace in the Hall of Mirrors, Versailles, 28th June 1919*. Oil on canvas, 154.2 x 127.0 cm. IWM:ART 2856.

65 *Evening Standard*, 7 May 1923.

66 Orpen to Ffoulkes, 19 February 1922.

67 Orpen, *To the Unknown British Soldier in France* (first version) 1922. Oil on canvas, 172.4 x 128.3 cm. Altered later. Imperial War Museum, London. The painting was selected by public ballot to be the Royal Academy's 'Picture of the Year, 1923'.

68 *Daily Herald*, 8 May 1923; *The Patriot*, 5 October 1923; *Sunday Express*, 20 May 1923. The painting's official record is: Orpen, *To the Unknown British Soldier in France*, 1921–28. Oil on canvas, 154.2 x 128.3 cm. IWM:ART 4438.

69 *Blown-Up*, 1917. Pencil and watercolour on paper, 58.4 x 43.1 cm. IWM:ART 2376.

was a post-war groundswell of smouldering bitterness that this large ungainly canvas seem to satisfy. The *Liverpool Echo* ridiculed the War Museum's decision and defended the painter's boldness:

> Orpen declines to paint the floors of hell with the colours of paradise, to pander to the pompous heroics of the red tab brigade. The IWM may reject the picture, but the shadow legions of the dead sleeping out and far will applaud it with Homeric hush.[70]

For his part Orpen appears to have made no further public comment, leaving the painting to tell its rather odd tale. There is, though, a final coda to this strange story. Five years later, in 1928, Orpen approached the War Museum offering to repaint the canvas as a tribute to Earl Haig who had recently died. With permission, he painted out the gaunt, insane soldiers, the cherubs and the garlands, leaving only the draped coffin and the marble halls. 'Nothing is left,' commented one observer, 'but a nameless dead soldier in a cold emptiness. It is a disturbing picture'.[71] Disturbing indeed, but no longer vitriolic. Orpen had transformed it once from an acerbic comment on political vanity into his homage to magnificent soldiery, and then back again into a tribute to an equally vaunted and vilified British army commander. Few other artists could have given one painting such a convoluted history. It is a palimpsest that parallels the many twists and turns of Orpen's long war; the dim outlines of each successive layer still evident in the *pentimenti* of the picture's apparently immaculate surface.

THE KEY STONE: 'GASSED'
by John Singer Sargent

In one of the strange ironies of British war art, it was not to be the work of its longest serving artist that would hold the public's imagination in the decades, perhaps even the whole century, after the Great War. Orpen had served his country unstintingly from the moment he signed on in 1915 to his last brushstroke in 1923. His gift of over 150 paintings and drawings was unprecedented; the range of work unrivalled by any other official artist. By rights his authority ought to have been unchallenged. And yet, apart from one or two small drawings, a landscape or two perhaps, there is no

70 *The Liverpool Echo*, 10 May 1923. Charles Ffoulkes, secretary at the Imperial War Museum, held the view that the museum should take 'this last picture of Orpen's as 'a final commitment under our agreement with him, as it is not only a very remarkable specimen of his work, but it would be the only symbolic picture in our collection…' (Quoted in Arnold, *Mirror to an Age*, p.378).

71 Samuel Hynes, *A War Imagined: The First World War and English Culture* (London: Bodley Head, 1990) p.460.

magnum opus to rival, for example, Paul Nash's *The Menin Road,* or Stanley Spencer's *Travoys*. Orpen was not even included in the final list of work for the grand Hall of Remembrance that was to be lined with seventeen 'super-pictures' representing and commemorating all aspects of the war.[72] Instead, the laurels were to be granted to his rivals in the New English Art Club and the Royal Academy. And incredibly, the corner stone of this impressive architectural scheme was to be painted by none other than John Singer Sargent, an individual so removed from the realities of warfare that on his only visit to the battle zone he asked whether there was any fighting on Sundays.[73]

Held in exceedingly high esteem by the British War Memorial Committee, the sixty-two-year-old Sargent was even sent a letter by Lloyd George personally inviting him to join the war artists' scheme. His brief (ideally suited to Sargent's American nationality) was to find a subject that encapsulated British co-operation with her most powerful ally. Like so many fellow painters who had recently alighted on the Western Front and knew little of its intrinsic history or unique properties, Sargent struggled to locate a subject: 'The further forward one goes the more scattered and meagre everything is', he complained. 'The MOI expects an epic – and how can one do an epic without masses of men?'[74] Instead Sargent homed in on a succession of subjects that epitomized the odd disjunctions of the war: a camouflaged field; peasants at harvest with a crashed bi-plane in the meadow beyond; a set of gigantic wheels in a smashed vault; the light falling across the picturesque ruins of Arras Cathedral. They are beautifully rendered watercolours, displaying a lightness and deftness of touch that belies Sargent's reputation as a painter of formal portraits.[75]

Roaming the battle zones in the company of Henry Tonks,

---

72 According to Harries and Harries, *The War Artists* (p.99) Orpen discounted himself from the super-pictures scheme by refusing to travel to Italy to attempt an Anglo-Italian subject. He wrote to Yockney on 18 April 1919 to disassociate himself from any suggestion that he might be persuaded to paint 'an elephant-like 20 ft x 10 ft' – a waspish comment on Sargent's 'super-picture'.

73 Sargent's query about fighting on Sunday was made to a General Fielding. His companions, Tonks and Sir Philip Sassoon gave up trying to make the sixty-two-year-old painter understand anything of the war and its realities. See Charles Merrill Mount, *John Singer Sargent* (London: The Cresset Press, 1957) p.293.

Sargent was recruited by the British War Memorial Committee as an official war artist in May/June 1918, travelling from Charing Cross Station on 2 July 1918 to Boulogne where he was attached to the Guards Division; their HQ was at Bavincourt, south of Arras. He moved with the Guards to their battle line HQ at Berles-au-Bois, and was joined by Henry Tonks on 16 July. Sargent returned to London in late October 1918 and commenced painting in his Fulham studio. In addition to sketches made at the Advanced Dressing Station in France, Sargent employed clothed models in his studio.

74 Sargent to Hon. Evan Charteris, 11 September 1918, quoted by Evan Charteris, *John Sargent* (London: Heinemann; New York: Charles Scribners, 1927), p.214. Lloyd George's letter to Sargent, to contribute to 'a series of immortal works' is reprinted in full in Charles Merrill Mount, *John Singer Sargent*, pp.290–291.

75 The Imperial War Museum has a fine collection of these watercolour studies, amongst them: *A Street in Arras*, August 1918, IWM:ART 1607; *A Crashed Aeroplane*, 1918, IWM:ART 1610; *Camouflaged Tanks, Berles-au-Bois*, 1918, IWM:ART 1618.

Sargent eventually located 'three fine subjects with masses of men':

> One a harrowing sight, a field full of gassed and blindfolded men – another a train of trucks packed with chair a cannon – and another frequent sight a big road encumbered with troops and traffic. I daresay the latter, combining English and Americans, is the best thing to do, if it can be prevented from looking like going to the Derby.[76]

Ultimately, he abandoned his search for British and US troops working side-by-side, and chose instead the memorable image of several hundred gassed men he had seen at le-Bac-du-Sud, on the road south-west of Arras. The painting that resulted from this traumatic sight is a vast frieze of pain; a work of compassionate engagement that eclipses much of Orpen's uneven *opus*.[77] Sargent mustered all his creative genius for this vast strip of a painting, some twenty feet long by ninety inches tall, and compiled it slavishly from piles of preparatory drawings and on-the-spot notes. To add further flavour to the memory, Sargent had recent experience of family death from enemy action and, while in France, had spent a week in a field hospital after contracting an intense bout of 'flu. He later described 'the accompaniment of groans of wounded, and the chokings and the coughing of gassed men' as a 'nightmare'.[78]

The effects of mustard gas appeared some two to three hours after exposure to just one part gas in ten million parts of air. The most common effect was a painful swelling of the conjunctiva and eyelids, but it was rarely permanent and successful counter-measures were

76 Sargent to Hon. Evan Charteris, 11 September 1918. Tonks and Sargent witnessed the gassed men at Le Bac du Sud on 21 August 1918 just as the sun began to set. In a letter to Yockney, 4 October 1918, Tonks remembered that 'After lunch we started out in Sargent's car together along the road to Doullens... The dressing station was situated on the road and consisted of a number of huts and a few tents. Gassed cases kept coming in, led along in parties of about six just as Sargent has depicted them, by an orderly. They sat or lay down on the grass, there must have been several hundred, evidently suffering a great deal chiefly I fancy from their eyes which were covered up by a piece of lint... Sargent was very struck by the scene and immediately made a lot of notes.'

Charteris also offers an uncredited account (possibly written by Tonks) which noted how Sargent 'began making sketches and a little later asked me if I would mind his making this essentially medical subject his, and I told him I did not in the least mind. He worked hard and made a number of pencil and pen sketches which formed the bases of the oil painting... It is a good representation of what we saw, as it gives a sense of the surrounding peace. I regret he did not put in something I noticed, a French boy and girl of about 8 years, who watched the procession of men with a certain calm philosophy for an hour or more, it made a strange contrast.' Charteris, *John Sargent*, p.212.

77 Sargent, *Gassed*, 1918–1919. Oil on canvas, 229.8 x 609 cm. IWM:ART 1460. In the IWM Concise Catalogue, 1963, there is a fuller caption: 'The Dressing Station at le Bac-de-Sud [sic], on the Doullens-Arras Road, August 1918. Gassed cases arrived in parties of about six men, led by an orderly. They sat down or lay down on the grass, and there were several hundred patients when the artist made his sketches. The gas used in this attack was known as mustard gas, and it caused temporary blindness' (p.265).

78 Sargent to Isabella Stewart Gardner, n.d., quoted by Charteris, *John Sargent*, p.216. See also Richard Cork, *A Bitter Truth: Avant-Garde Art and the Great War*. (New Haven: Yale University Press, 1994) pp. 220–221. Sargent's painting also conveys a rich allegorical meaning through the intertwined ideas of 'the blind leading the blind' and the allusion to the 'eye for an eye' (see Graham Shaw, PhD thesis, *Sights of Battle: Art and War in Britain*, 2007, p.146).

devised that reduced death from gas attack to three per cent, while 93 per cent returned to duty. The short-term impact, though, was catastrophic; mustard gas worked on human vapour, causing swollen lips, loss of taste, blisters a foot long, and blindness that might last up to three days. In more severe exposures men might cough up a cast of their mucous membrane, lose their genitals or be burnt through to the bone.[79] Sargent's painting captures an air of discomfort but not the full gamut of pain; the bandages are clean, the wounds discreet, even polite; the statuesque Tommies are fit, whole and cared for, although their suffering is palpable. A single figure appears to lean over to vomit, but not in the direction of the viewer; another lifts his leg in a comically exaggerated fashion to climb an unseen step, having been forewarned by a shirt-sleeved orderly. Although fighter planes can be spotted in the extreme right of the painting, the war is a distant distraction, less boisterous than the game of football taking place in the radiance just beyond the reclining wounded who sprawl across the foreground of the vast canvas. There is little doubt that *Gassed* is one of the great monuments of the conflict, a testament to the pity of war, but also an elegy to redemption and recovery, and it is justifiably revered as a tribute to the endurance of the fighting men as well as an effective icon of anti-war propaganda.[80]

Despite the unblemished success of Sargent's *magnum opus*, the last word must be William Orpen's. Although he was clearly stung by Sargent's achievement, describing it with faint praise as an 'awfully long strip of a picture',[81] he may have gained some comfort from the abject failure of Augustus John to produce his much-vaunted war painting.[82] Whatever his feelings, Orpen felt important lessons had to be learned and he wrote to the commissioners at the war museum

79 These facts are from Denis Winter, *Death's Men*, pp.122–123. Soldier and writer M.R.D. Foot chose to exclude Sargent's painting from his book on art and war not merely because he considered it sentimental and hackneyed but because he felt it gave the wrong impression. 'My own father', he wrote, 'once stood in one of those pathetic-seeming queues of men blinded by mustard gas, each with his hand on the shoulder of the man in front; [and] was back in action with his battery a week later.' Foot's father argued that it was 'a humane weapon'. M.R.D. Foot, *Art and War: Twentieth Century Warfare as Depicted by War Artists*, London: Headline, 1990). The typescript of Foot senior's recollections are held in the IWM Library, (86/57/1) as 'Once a Gunner…'

80 Richard Cork, *A Bitter Truth*, pp.220–221, and Harries and Harries, *The War Artists*, p.99. John Thomas, in his appreciation of Sargent's painting, explores the distinction between those casualties laid out on the floor and those in line, suggesting that *triage* was in operation, with those more severely injured and closer to death being kept further away from the treatment tent located to the right of the picture frame. Arguing that the symbolic readings of the painting have been undervalued, Thomas also notes that the football game is an officially organized game being played in proper kit only 'yards from where the players' comrades are writhing in agony or dying.' John Thomas, '*Gassed* and its detractors: interpreting Sargent's major war painting', *Imperial War Museum Review*, No.9, 1994, pp.46–47.

Charteris summarises the painting thus: 'There is no striving after the picturesque; dramatic account has been entirely dispensed with. It is stated in its starkest terms, it is more than merely descriptive. He has given a spiritual value to realism, and dignity and solemnity to the facts.' Charteris, *John Sargent*, p.215.

81 Orpen to Yockney, 4 October 1918. Orpen file, Imperial War Museum.

to roundly admonish them: 'One thing I think you must have learned by now & that is – don't tell an artist what to do… instead of "America & France" you have *Gassed* by J.S.S. & *Query* by Aug. E.J.' And he concluded bitingly, 'So much for ordering artists about'.[83] Until his premature death, few of the many patrons who commissioned his work would ever find themselves in a position to order him about. In the 1920s his energy remained largely undiminished, the commissions poured in, and his facility to capture likenesses never deserted him, but his health quickly did. By 1931 he was dead, aged just fifty-three, his reputation built on countless virtuoso portraits of tyrants and tycoons, politicians and premiers, and only in the last few years has his impressive body of war art started to gain the recognition that it really deserves.

82 Orpen was continuously, and often disparagingly, compared with Augustus John. Wyndham Lewis, dining with Lord Beaverbrook in 1917, was asked by the press baron whether Lewis would rather go round the world with John or Orpen. 'We both agreed,' wrote Lewis, 'that the former experience would be more full of incident'. Lewis, *Blasting and Bombardiering*, p.191.

83 Orpen to Yockney, 18 April 1919. Orpen file, Imperial War Museum.

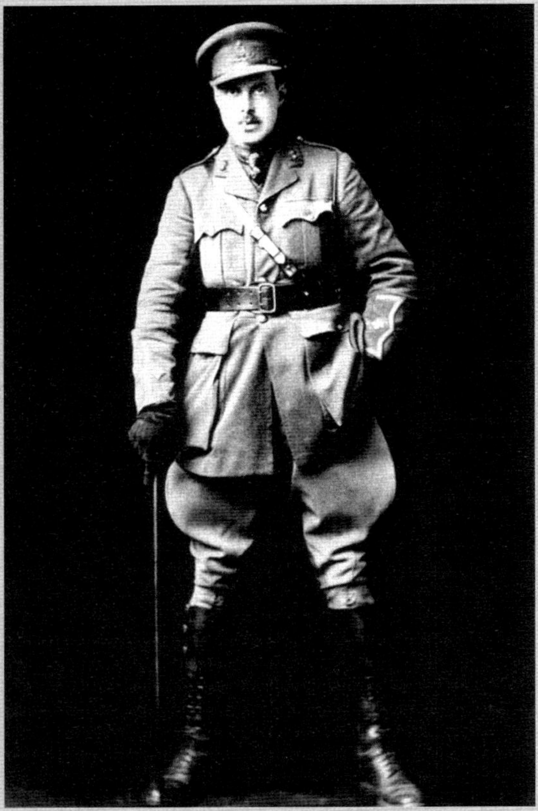

Wyndham Lewis

Wyndham Lewis
'A very dangerous type of spectator'

INTRODUCTION
The Gunner's War

> A gunner does not fight. He merely shells and is shelled. He discharges a large metal cylinder, aiming it by means of a delicately-adjusted mechanism, to fall at a certain spot which he cannot see, in the hope that he may kill somebody he hopes is there.[1]

So wrote the artist, polemicist, and one-time gunnery-officer Percy Wyndham Lewis, reflecting on his experience of the Great War. In the years immediately before the conflict, Lewis had gained a distinctive reputation as a painter, writer and leader of the Vorticists, a radical arts movement that scandalised (and to a degree, also entertained) Edwardian society. Vorticism, as we shall see, gained notoriety not only because of its uncompromising visual identity, but because it poured a withering anger on the philistinism and lethargy of middle-class values and ideals. Lewis epitomised the vitality and rawness of the Vorticist ethos: he was edgy and acerbic, a brilliant mind with a caustic turn of phrase, an engaging leader with an extraordinary capacity for generating polemic.[2] He was also a superb draughtsman, and like the roboticised figures in his drawings,

---

1 Percy Wyndham Lewis, *Blasting and Bombardiering, Autobiography 1914–1926* (London: Eyre & Spottiswoode, 1937) p.158.

2 Denis Farr, *English Art: 1870–1940* (Oxford: Oxford University Press, 1978) p.210.

he loathed inaction and cultivated an image of untrammelled energy and drive.

Even before 1914, conflict and violence played a considerable part in his imaginative life. Always on a war footing, he liked to believe that others were so disposed, and his invective is littered with the language of 'operations, offensive and defensive'.[3] Indeed, to understand Wyndham Lewis's art we need to gain some insight into the closed world of guns and cannons, mortars and machine-guns, in which he served for many months. He would later recreate the sights and sounds of heavy artillery in dozens of drawings and paintings, and also in some of the most evocative prose to come out of the siege warfare on the Western Front:

> '...a great barrage was laid upon the German trenches. A Field Artillery officer was up there with me and we waited down in the trench for the barrage zero hour. We got up just before the storm broke. Then, to the second, there was the muffled crash of massed artillery, and over came the barrage – every type of projectile, groaning, panting, bumbling, whistling and wheezing overhead. Down they plunged upon the German trench, a chain of every type of burst, and a screen of smoke and earth defined, as far as one could see on either hand, the German line.[4]

'MONSTROUS ANGER...'

For much of the time, the Great War was a war of position, a prolonged duel fought from long-distance by huge cannon. It was the quintessential artillery war. While front-line soldiers dreaded the prospect of hand-to-hand fighting, of having to engage an enemy with bayonet and grenade, it was the awesome power of artillery that was the real killer.[5] A wounded man was three times as likely to die as a result of a shell wound to the chest as of a bullet wound. Not only could distant guns pound a specified tract of earth for hours, sometimes days, on end, but a direct hit from a heavy

---

3 For Lewis on a constant war footing: see John Rothenstein, *Brave Day, Hideous Night*, 1966, p.42, quoted in Jane Farrington, *Wyndham Lewis*, exhibition catalogue, Manchester City Art Galleries (London: Lund Humphries, 1980), pp.66–67. As Herbert Read notes, Lewis's comrade-in-arms, T.E. Hulme, was also a militarist 'by faith and acted upon his beliefs with a rare enthusiasm' devoting his energies to the technical problems of artillery practice and to wider military strategies. See T.E. Hulme, *Speculations: Essays on humanism and the Philosophy of Art*, editor Herbert Read (London: Routledge and Kegan Paul, 1924) pp.x-xi. *Speculations* also contains his essay 'Reflections on Violence', pp.249–260.

4 Lewis, *Blasting and Bombardiering*, p.158.

5 Some 59% of all wounds inflicted on British soldiers came from shellfire; machine gun and rifle bullets accounted for 39%. See Gary Sheffield, *Forgotten Victory: the First World War Myths and Realities* (London: Headline/Review 2001) pp.110–111. As John Terraine wrote: 'The war of 1914–18 was an artillery war. Artillery was the battle winner, artillery was what caused the greatest loss of life, the most dreadful wounds and the deepest fear.' John Terraine, *White Heat: the New Warfare, 1914–1918* (London: Sidgwick and Jackson, 1982) p.95.

metal shell would completely obliterate the body, reducing a living being into little more than a putrid whiff of air.[6] To troops under sustained heavy shelling, artillery destroyed not only the body, but the mind, inducing new depths of fear by its precision and its random anonymity.

There were two types of weapon: the howitzer, which lobbed a large shell in a lazy arc over objects in its way, and the gun, a rapier rather than a cudgel, firing lighter shells on a flat trajectory with high muzzle velocity.[7] Guns were categorised by projectile weight in pounds, while howitzers were listed by calibre in inches.[8] The static nature of much of the war on the Western Front, and on so many other fronts from Macedonia to Gallipoli, resulted in mass concentrations of siege cannon. Often positioned only yards apart, many were designed to bombard thick fortress walls and made short work of the flimsy shelters scraped into the Flanders clay or Salonikan sand. Cold statistics help give an idea of the massive proportions of these artillery pieces. The German 420 – a howitzer that took a shell seventeen inches wide – weighed twenty tons and had to be moved by nine tractors. It squatted in a gunpit that took four days to excavate and had to be lined with steel walls. Twelve men were needed to load and fire each one-ton shell, a light railway and crane had to be used to manoeuvre it into position. When fired, the mammoth machine lurched on its base, recoiling backwards, emitting a sound like a jet plane taking off. Its five-metre gunflash eclipsed the daylight and set fire to the undergrowth for yards around. Moving at 1,700 mph, a shell could cover a distance of six miles horizontally, reaching a height of several thousand feet. Upon impact the projectile would blast a hole large enough to bury a house; the Great Crater in the village of Athies, which Muirhead Bone drew in 1917, was the result of one such blast.[9]

The agonies wrought by artillery began well before the explosion. As veterans recount, it was the sound that was unsettling. A skilled ear could identify each different gun, its calibre, the path of the shell

6 'A small gust of putrid air' is a phrase used by Peter Conrad, *Modern Times, Modern Place: Life and Art in the Twentieth Century* (London: Thames and Hudson, 1999) p. 215. The statistics about shell wounds is taken from Geoffrey Noon, 'The Treatment of Casualties in the Great War', in Paddy Griffith (ed.) *British Fighting Methods in the Great War* (London: Cass, 1996) p.90, pp.101–102.

7 The howitzer allowed a steep angle of descent and, as a result, could strike targets that were protected by intervening obstacles. Howitzers of the Great War period were also valued for their ability to fire shells that were about twice as large as shells fired by guns of the same size. They could fire larger amounts of explosive with considerably less barrel wear than the gun. Thus, while a 75-mm field gun that weighed one ton or so was limited to shells that weighed less than 8 kilograms, a 105-mm howitzer of the same weight could easily fire shells that weighed 15 or 16 kilograms. The German army began the war with a far greater proportion of howitzers than the French. See H.A. Bethell, *Modern Guns and Gunnery*, (Woolwich: FJ Cattermole, 1905, 1907, 1910); and O.F.G. Hogg *Artillery: its Origin, Heyday and Decline* (London: C Hurst & Co, 1970).

8 This method of classification and nomenclature had been adopted in the nineteenth century. But the system broke down in the 1930s with the introduction of gun-howitzers.

9 Muirhead Bone, *The Great Crater, Athies*, May 1917, IWM:ART 2164.

(which might be spotted momentarily like a meteorite), and the probable point of impact. The firing of a small field gun gave a crack 'like a fat man hitting a golf ball', the medium artillery piece sounded 'like a giant newspaper being torn, its shell a farm cart coming down a steep hill with its brakes on'. The heavy gun went off like a blow on the skull, its giant metal projectile rolling in a leisurely arc across the sky, 'for a time the listener felt he could run beside it. Then it speeded up like an express train rushing down a tunnel'.[10] Shells emitted different sounds: a near miss might whistle or roar; shells crossing dense woods or wide valleys gave off a deceptive echo; those that fell in enclosed places gave a double bang and no warning at all. As Denis Winter notes, the strain of listening for all these sounds did something to the brain: 'A man could never be rid of them'.[11] In his book *Anatomy of Courage*, subaltern Moran remembered how he was too stunned to think during one bombardment, noting how the shelling took its toll on his nerves later on:

> I was to go through it many times in my sleep. I used to hear all at once the sound of a shell coming. Perhaps it was the sound of the wind in the trees to remind me that war had exacted its tribute and that my little capital was less than it had been. There were men in France who were ready to go out but who could not meet death in that shape. They were prepared for it if it came cleanly and swiftly, but that shattering, crudely bloody end by a big shell was too much for them. All their plans for meeting death with decency and credit were suddenly battered down. Self-respect had gone out of their hands. They were no longer certain of what they would do. It frightened more men away from the trenches than anything else.[12]

For his part, the artilleryman was regarded by front-line infantry as a distant figure, fussing over his complicated equipment and obsessed with the mathematical calculations that determined the effectiveness of his work. A battery of siege artillery was a hermetically sealed unit of eight guns, with its own supply and signal system, a complex paraphernalia of telescopes, maps and ranging gear used for locating the enemy, and wagon-loads of supernumerary possessions – armchairs, suitcases, and blankets – that were the envy of passing infantry, who by contrast, carried everything they owned in their shoulder packs. It was, nevertheless, 'rough and heavy work' and

10 These phrases are taken from Denis Winter, *Death's Men* (London: Allen Lane, 1978) pp.116–117; a number of Winter's similes draw from George Orwell's *Homage to Catalonia* (London: Secker and Warburg, 1938) p.83.

11 Denis Winter, *Death's Men*, p.116.

12 Lord Moran, *Anatomy of Courage*, cited in Winter, p.119.

it required rough and heavy men – 'coal-miners, Rugby footballers, heavyweight boxers and outsize navvies'.[13] A gunner's outlook was diametrically different to the infantryman's. Where his was a close-up world of marches and trenches, the artilleryman was interested only in registering a target in the far distance, his vision locked in a calculable future.

WYNDHAM LEWIS

'Mad, bad and dangerous to know'[14]

Born in 1882 in a yacht off Novia Scotia, of an American father and English mother, Percy Wyndham Lewis was to become a key figure of the British intellectual, literary and artistic *avant garde* in the first half of the twentieth century – one of the *enfants terribles* who savaged middle-class values and sensitivities in the years before the war. He was a striking figure, with 'deep, dark, Italian eyes, looking out of a fuzz of hair flanking on either side the upturned collar of an Inverness cape'.[15] Along with the cape went a broad-rimmed hat, a sharply clipped moustache, and an air of dashing intrigue. Commenting on his self-portrait of *The Artist as the Painter Raphael*, Lewis told a fellow painter that there were no highlights on the eyeballs because it would give the wrong kind of life to the head. Glinting eyes would hint at an unstable inner psyche,[16] and Lewis deplored self-doubt, instability and vacillation. He believed that man could only rise above the beasts by classical detachment and self-control, and he divided the population into those who could achieve this level of command – the 'natures' – and the vast majority who could not, whom he dismissively categorised as puppets or automata. His existentialism was powerfully self-assured, never anguished or troubled by the thoughts or feelings of others.[17]

His art training began, like so many in that rich chapter of British painting, at the Slade School of Art where he studied on a three-year scholarship from 1898. His literary career began in France soon after, during a six-year sojourn in Europe where he started the jottings that

13 Lewis, *Blasting and Bombardiering*, p.96.

14 Angela Weight, Foreword, in *Wyndham Lewis: Art and War* (London: Wyndham Lewis Memorial Trust and Lund Humphries, 1992) p.9.

15 This description of Lewis is by Violet Hunt, quoted in John Ferguson *The Arts in Britain in World War One* (London: Stainer and Bell, 1980) p.12.

16 These comments were made to the painter Michael Ayrton, and cited in Walter Michel, *Wyndham Lewis: Paintings and Drawings* (Berkeley and Los Angeles: University of California Press, 1971), p.337; also cited in Jane Farrington, *Wyndham Lewis*, exhibition catalogue, Manchester City Art Galleries (London: Lund Humphries, 1980), p.85. For many years, Lewis nurtured an air of intrigue by using the Pall Mall Deposit Company as a forwarding address, and creating elaborate ruses to disguise his real age and the date of his birth.

17 These thoughts on Lewis and existentialism are taken from www.fluxeuropa.com/wyndhamlewis-art_and_ideas.htm

would soon lead to a succession of iconoclastic publications. Having exhausted his family allowance Lewis returned to London where he was soon exhibiting with the Camden Town Group, the Allied Artists' Association, and the Second Post-Impressionist Exhibition staged by Roger Fry who also persuaded him to join the Omega Workshops. It was not a happy arrangement: the Bloomsbury aesthetic did not appeal to Lewis who later ridiculed the Workshop as little more than a 'curtain and pin factory in Fitzroy Square'.[18] His few art-works from that time are untypical of his maturing style, being decorative rather than declamatory. Lewis refused to play second fiddle to Fry and after an unfortunate and rather public squabble, he and three others broke away in October 1913, never to return.

The seeds of Lewis's dissent had been planted some months earlier. With fellow painter Richard Nevinson, he had hosted a visit by the Italian Futurist Filippo Tommaso Emilio Marinetti, a self-aggrandizing and eccentric character, accompanying an exhibition of fellow-Futurists at the Sackville Gallery in central London. British culture was ill-prepared for the invasion. With little warning it detonated in the fashionable West End; going off, exclaimed the eminent painter Walter Sickert, like a 'sudden explosion in Sackville Street, next door to Whistler's tailor…'. Having declared the death of 'Past-ism' and the birth of Futur-ism in 1909, Marinetti's movement demanded that 'A clean sweep should be made of all stale and threadbare subject-matter in order to express the vortex of modern life – a life of steel, fever, pride and headlong speed'.[19] It was to be an art that celebrated machines, speed, electricity, and glorified war as a cleansing power; their favoured techniques were fragmented picture surfaces, dynamic sensations, and a sense of unstoppable movement. Their creed was strident and unambiguous: 'There is no more beauty except in strife. No masterpiece without aggressiveness… We declare that the world's splendour has been enriched by a new beauty; the beauty of speed… a roaring motor-car, which seems to run on machine-gun fire, is more beautiful than the Victory of Samothrace'.[20]

---

18 Lewis's views on Bloomsbury and on Fry in particular are to be read in *Blast 2* (July 1915) quoted in Charles Harrison, *English Art and Modernism*, (New Haven CT and London, Yale University Press, 1981, revised edition 1994) p.101.

19 For these and other reflections on Marinetti, Lewis, and the emergence of the Vorticists see: W.K. Rose (ed.) *The Letters of Wyndham Lewis* (London: Methuen, 1963); Richard Cork, *Vorticism and Abstract Art in the First Machine Age* (London: Gordon Fraser Gallery, 1976); Andrew Wilson, 'Introduction' to *Wyndham Lewis, 1882–1957* (London: Austin/Desmond Fine Art, 1990).

Most art historians regard it important not to underestimate the influence of Marinetti on modern conceptions of art in Britain. He radically challenged and overturned conventional ideas of literature, he invented the idea of the artistic manifesto, and originated the idea of an 'avant garde' in art. By the publication of *Blast 2*, however, Lewis correctly predicted that 'The War will take Marinetti's occupation of platform-boomer away. The War has for the moment exhausted interest in booming and banging.'

20 These are taken from declarations in Marinetti's 'Initial Manifesto of Futurism' published in *Le Figaro*, 29 February 1909.

Impressed by their fascination with the modern world and by their feverish clamour for revolutionary change, Lewis was bemused and intrigued by the noisy lectures, provocative manifestos, and beating of drums that seemed to herald every public appearance by the fanatical Marinetti.[21] During one memorable dinner at the Florence Restaurant in Rupert Street Lewis and thirty fellow artists paid three shillings for the privilege of hearing the Italian denounce English art, condemn British customs, trash its traditions (and much else besides) whilst Nevinson provided a suitable militant accompaniment standing behind a curtain banging a drum ceaselessly, while the band downstairs played *You made me love you, I didn't want to do it...* over and over again. 'It was grand,' wrote Nevinson, 'if incoherent.'[22]

Although the press would forever after call him a 'Futurist painter', Lewis soon tried to distance himself from the Italian's ideology, even if he borrowed much of his polemical style. Amidst the clamour, hearing his own inner voice was not that easy, and Lewis smouldered with frustrated energy. Even when he created a Rebel Art Centre in March 1914, and ensconced himself as the chief rebel, the self-appointed 'enemy of the art establishment', he struggled to distinguish himself from the Italian movement, his thinking almost drowned out by Marinetti's tub-thumping and drum-bashing.

Then, in the summer of 1914 Lewis and his youthful supporters burst decisively into the sluggish Edwardian art scene just as future howitzer shells would soon do in Flanders. The onslaught came in the form of an iconoclastic publication called *Blast* – an over-large, lurid, puce-covered manifesto with a loud typeface and provocative writing.[23] Like its principal author, it was strident and sarcastic, mocking and mendacious, savaging the nineteenth century and the legacy of the Victorians, cursing the 'abysmal inexcusable middle class', and scorning (for good measure) both the aristocracy and the proletariat. It 'BLASTED' those it despised or pitied, and 'BLESSED' those it revered. The opening salvo proclaimed:

---

21 A good summary of the 'fanatical Marinetti' is in Denis Farr, *English Art*, p.208. Marinetti and Nevinson's manifesto contained a rounding indictment of 'The pessimistic, skeptical and narrow views of the English public'.

22 C.W.R. Nevinson, *Paint and Prejudice* (London: Methuen, 1937) p.77.

23 *Blast* had two editions, the first published on 2 July 1914, and the second a year later. The first edition was printed in folio format, with the title 'BLAST' displayed diagonally across its bright pink soft cover. The opening twenty pages of *Blast 1* contain the Vorticist manifesto, written by Wyndham Lewis with assistance from Ezra Pound and signed by Lewis, Edward Wadsworth, Pound, William Roberts, Helen Saunders, Lawrence Atkinson, Jessica Dismorr and Henri Gaudier-Brzeska. David Bomberg and Jacob Epstein chose not to sign the manifesto, although their work was featured. It also contained articles by Ezra Pound, Rebecca West, Gaudier-Brzeska and an extract from Ford Madox Hueffer's novel *The Saddest Story*, which later became known as *The Good Soldier* (published under his pseudonym Ford Madox Ford). The first edition also contained Vorticist-style illustrations by Epstein, Lewis and others.
The second 'War Number' edition featured one of Lewis's woodcuts on the cover and carried a short play by Ezra Pound, and T.S. Eliot's poems *Preludes* and *Rhapsody on a Windy Night*. An article by Gaudier-Brzeska *Vortex (written from the Trenches)* described his understanding of the Vorticist aesthetic.

BLAST First (from politeness) ENGLAND
CURSE ITS CLIMATE FOR ITS SINS AND INFECTIONS
DISMAL SYMBOL, SET round our bodies,
of effeminate lout within.
VICTORIAN VAMPIRE, the LONDON cloud sucks
The TOWN'S heart.

Although its style was indebted to the anarchic typography and free-word poems of Marinetti and the Italian modernists, Lewis knew that in launching the 'hugest and pinkest of all magazines' with its 'portentous dimensions and violent tint',[24] he had to exaggerate the differences between his nascent art movement and the Futurists, whose modernity he blessed but whose blurred pictorial technique he blasted. He also had to distance himself from the Cubists. Although he admired their formal structures and fractured language, he was quickly bored by their mundane subjects. 'However musical or vegetarian a man may be,' scoffed Lewis, 'his life is not spent exclusively among apples and mandolins'. From the German Expressionists he learned visual intensity and power, but he was not really interested in their raw, interior emotions, demanding instead something more physical and concrete. 'Give me the *outside* of all things,' he instructed his followers, 'I am a fanatic for the external of things'.[25] The result was Vorticism, a distinctively British art movement and possibly the one serious artistic philosophy to originate in Britain in the first half of the twentieth century. It was Lewis who gave it expression in paint, Gaudier-Brzeska and Epstein its sculpture, but it was Ezra Pound who formulated its poetry and concocted its title, defining the vortex as 'a radiant node or cluster from which, and through which, and into which, ideas are constantly rushing'.[26]

In truth, Vorticism was never easy to define. The term was meant to suggest 'suction, whirlpool, maelstrom, a state of exaltation, spiritual daring, aggressive intellectual action'.[27] But Lewis had a habit of defining it by a systematic process of exclusion and rejection, summarily casting aside most of European art, the Paris School, the jazzed-up histrionics of the Italians, and the rigidity of Dutch painters such as Mondrian. Yet, Vorticism was much more than the sum of things it ridiculed; for every negative there was a positive:

24 Lewis's phrase 'portentous dimensions' is from *Rude Assignment*, p.125. Marshall McLuhan later suggested that the typography for *Blast* had been set up by an alcoholic printer 'exactly as Lewis required in return for large supplies of liquor.' Marshall McLuhan, *Counterblast* (London, 1970) p.5.

25 See Wyndham Lewis, *Tarr* (1st publication 1918, 2nd edition rewritten 1928; Calder and Boyars: Jupiter Books, 1968) pp.279–280.

26 Ezra Pound, 'Vorticism', *Fortnightly Review*, 1 September 1914.

27 From Werner Haftmann, *Painting in the Twentieth Century: an Analysis of the Artists and their Work* (New York: Praeger, 1965) p.153. Lewis told his friend Douglas Goldring in 1943 to think of Vorticism as a 'whirlpool... At the heart of the whirlpool is a great silent place where all the energy is concentrated. And there at the point of concentration, is the Vorticist.' D. Goldring, *South Lodge*, (London, 1943) p.65.

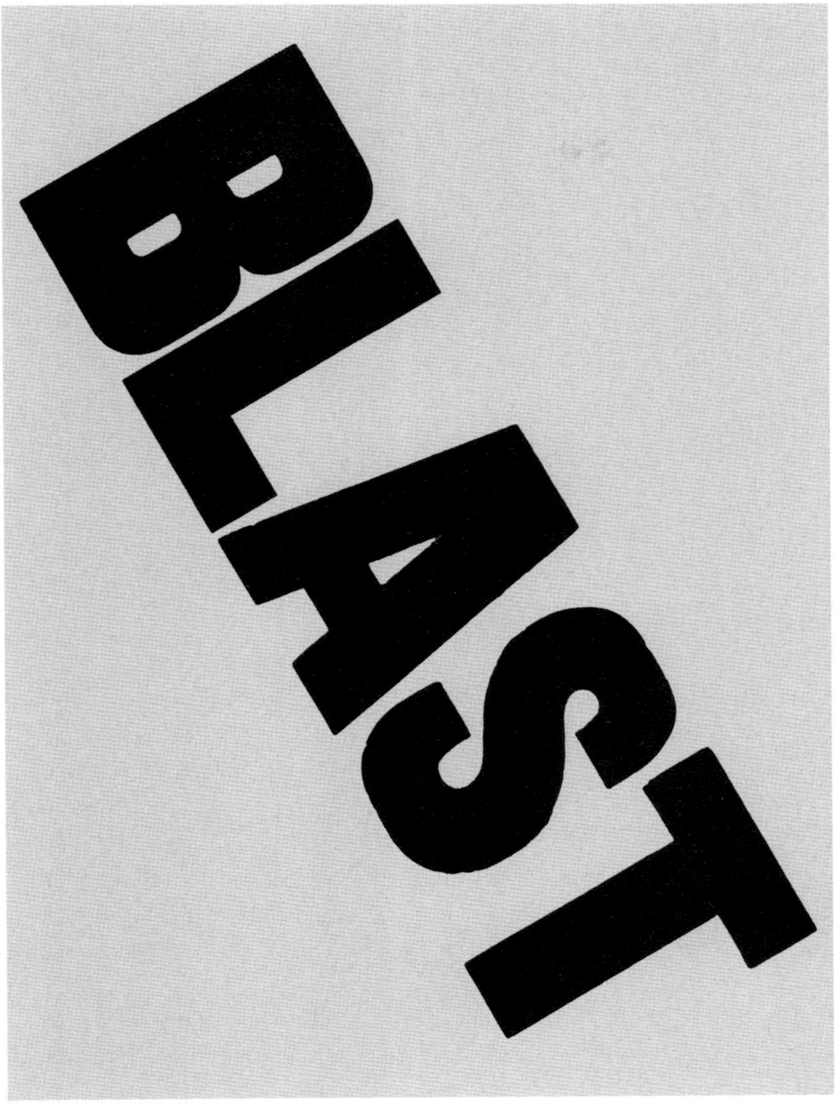

cover of *Blast*
(1914)

1

BLAST First (from politeness) **ENGLAND**

CURSE ITS CLIMATE FOR ITS SINS AND INFECTIONS

DISMAL SYMBOL, SET round our bodies,
of effeminate lout within.

VICTORIAN VAMPIRE, the LONDON cloud sucks
the TOWN'S heart.

A 1000 MILE LONG, 2 KILOMETER Deep

BODY OF WATER even, is pushed against us
from the Floridas, TO MAKE US MILD.

OFFICIOUS MOUNTAINS keep back DRASTIC WINDS

SO MUCH VAST MACHINERY TO PRODUCE

THE CURATE of "Eltham"
BRITANNIC ÆSTHETE
WILD NATURE CRANK
DOMESTICATED
POLICEMAN
LONDON COLISEUM
SOCIALIST-PLAYWRIGHT
DALY'S MUSICAL COMEDY
GAIETY CHORUS GIRL
TONKS

11

page from *Blast*
(1914)

> By Vorticism we mean (a) ACTIVITY as opposed to the tasteful PASSIVITY of Picasso; (b) SIGNIFICANCE as opposed to the dull or anecdotal character to which the Naturalist is condemned; (c) ESSENTIAL MOVEMENT and ACTIVITY (such as the energy of the mind) as opposed to the imitative cinematography, the fuss and the hysterics of the Futurists.[28]

Visually, these essential ingredients resulted in a hard-edged, coldly beautiful aesthetic[29] producing drawings, prints and paintings that depict massive human forms trapped in jagged, bold black and white designs, amidst heavy architectural structures that teeter madly on stressed diagonals. Through their art the Vorticists embraced the modern machine-world, seizing the static rigidity and mechanical surfaces of machinery and engines to create bold and memorable images. Lewis could not achieve all this on his own, and his friend, the philosopher T.E. Hulme, helped him shape this system of ideas by drawing on a wide reading of northern European thinkers, while Ezra Pound fleshed out its terms of reference. It was Lewis, however, who was its figure-head, the vortex of calm at its epicentre.

Aged thirty-two when *Blast* was first launched, Lewis's magnetic personality attracted a crowd of the capital's most adventurous painters, writers and sculptors. William Roberts, just nineteen years old and still a student at the Slade, was one of the youngest. Fifty years later he painted from memory a characteristic gathering of the Vorticists at the Restaurant de la Tour Eiffel (off Tottenham Court Road in central London) in spring 1915.[30] As Roberts recalled, 'In my memory *la cuisine francaise* and Vorticism are indissolubly linked'. Arranged around the presiding figure of Lewis are Cuthbert Hamilton, Ezra Pound, William Roberts, Edward Wadsworth; in the doorway are Jessica Dismorr and Helen Saunders; while Joe, the waiter, dispenses champagne and Rudolph Stulik, the proprietor of the restaurant from 1908 to 1937, offers a dessert that threatens to distract Frederick Etchells, who is holding the first issue of the virulently-pink broadsheet.

---

28 Lewis, 'Note' to the catalogue of 'The First Exhibition of the Vorticist Group', opening 10 June 1915, at the Dore Galleries, London.

29 Cited in Andrew Graham-Dixon, *A History of British Art* (Berkeley: University of California Press, 1996) p.209. Lewis commented upon his close relationship with T.E. Hulme in his first autobiography: 'what he said should be done, I *did*. Or it would be more exact to say that I did it, and he said it' (Lewis, *Blasting and Bombardiering*, p.106).

30 *The Vorticists at the Restaurant de la Tour Eiffel, Spring 1915*, 1961–2. Oil on canvas, 183 x 213.5 cm. The Restaurant de la Tour Eiffel, at 1 Percy Street, London W1, was a haunt of the Vorticist painters. Roberts's comment on the evenings at the restaurant was published in *The Listener*, 21 March 1957. The painting was purchased from the artist by the Tate Gallery (T00528, Chantrey Purchase, 1962).

Roberts contested Lewis's claim to be the leader of the Vorticists, making a number of counter-claims some 40 years later, in a series of pamphlets published between 1956 and 1958: W. Roberts, *Cometism and Vorticism: a Tate Gallery catalogue revised* (1956); *The Resurrection of Vorticism and the Apotheosis of Wyndham Lewis at the Tate* (1956); *A Press View of the Tate Gallery* (1956); *A Reply to my Biographer, Sir John Rothenstein* (1957); *Abstract and Cubist Paintings and Drawings* (1957).

For a brief intense moment Vorticism penetrated all the arts, making an impact on theatre, photography, literature, the plastic arts, typography and design. Underpinning its every manifestation was Lewis's vituperative intellect and his stubborn belief in the 'integrity of the defined, single object':

> Anything living, quick and changing is bad art always... Deadness is the first condition of art: the second is absence of soul, in the human and sentimental sense. With the statue its lines and masses are its soul, no restless inflammable ego is imagined for its interior: it has no inside: good art must have no inside.[31]

Lewis saw Vorticism as the still centre in the maelstrom of modern life, a 'unifying element in a chaotic and diverse environment'.[32] But to see the work that resulted is to see drawings and designs that shimmer with a tensile energy, paintings that pulse with staccato movement, sculptures such as those by the young Frenchman Henri Gaudier-Brzeska that combine savage primeval life forms with the dynamic diagonal that became its trademark. Although Lewis demanded an art that was static and permanent the two pieces of art that best summarise the short-lived movement gained their energy from mechanomorphic forms in agitated motion. David Bomberg's painting *The Mud Bath*, was first shown in 1914. It took its inspiration not from the technologies of heavy industry nor the 'steep walls of factories', but the public baths in East London which Bomberg sometimes frequented. (In actuality, it was a steamy and sedentary place in the Whitechapel Road.) Except here on the canvas, the figures have morphed into cavorting diagonals that orbit rather crazily around a central black pillar. Humans – if that is what they are – have been stripped down to simple angular shapes and their colour distilled to the bare minimum. Perhaps the other most memorable single work was Jacob Epstein's *The Rock Drill*, which merged a robotic man with an immense machine, creating the century's first 'tribal-mechanical deity, phallically potent, a centaur for the machine age'.[33]

---

31 For an elaboration of these concepts see Lewis, 'The Melodrama of Modernity', p.144, and Lewis, *Wyndham Lewis the Artist, from 'Blast' to Burlington House* (London: Laidlow and Laidlow, 1939).

32 Cited in Denis Farr, *English Art: 1870–1940* (Oxford: Oxford University Press, 1978) p.214.

33 *The Mud Bath*, 1914. Oil on canvas, 152 x 224 cm. Tate Gallery. Bomberg's subject was Schevzik's Vapour Baths, Whitechapel, East London.

Rock-Drill, destroyed. Epstein's *Torso in Metal from the 'Rock Drill'*, 1913–1914. Bronze, 70.5 x 58.4 x 44.5 cm. Tate Gallery, London.

Quoted in Andrew Graham Dixon, *A History of British Art* (Berkeley: University of California Press, 1996) p.208.

WAR

Did the work of the Vorticists somehow anticipate the onset of war? Scanning Europe in 1914 we can now detect forebodings of the conflict. People would later recall the self-destructive, raucous hysteria of the months that led up to the fatal shots in Sarajevo, describing the season of 1914 as 'a positive frenzy of gaiety' tainted by an overwhelming urge to attack and destroy.[34] Belligerence was tempered by black humour, but the boisterousness had an unyielding edge to it. Wyndham Lewis sharpened it into a blade, exhorting his followers with the cry:

> Well then! This is what it is time to do.
> We must kill John Bull.
> We must kill John Bull with art![35]

But the war tore the group to pieces. Gaudier-Brzeska died in an infantry charge on the front. T.E. Hulme, critic and philosopher was killed by shell blast near Nieuport. Roberts, reduced to penury, had to enlist in the artillery; Bomberg joined the Royal Engineers, only to suffer the ignominy of a self-inflicted gunshot wound two years later. Epstein had been conscripted a Private in the Fusiliers after what he believed to be a 'deliberate conspiracy in the press'.[36] Wadsworth was in the Mediterranean, an intelligence officer in the Royal Naval Volunteer Reserve until he was invalided home.[37] Lewis himself joined the Royal Garrison Artillery, drawn to the 'Romance of the big guns' and in the apparently comforting knowledge that Napoleon had once been a gunner.[38]

Sensing that he originated from a military caste, Lewis had considered volunteering for the army as early as the summer of 1915. With typical brio, he wrote to Mary Borden Turner:

> I must join the Army. I have as little reason to be shot at once and without a hearsay as any artist in Europe, but have certain accomplishments

34 See Richard Cork, *A Bitter Truth*, pp.28–29.

35 See *Blast 1*, and Walter Michel and C.J. Fox (eds.) *Wyndham Lewis on Art: Collected Writings, 1913–1956* (London: Thames and Hudson, 1969).

36 Epstein believed there had been a conspiracy in the popular press, orchestrated by Augustus John, to have him sign up; see Epstein to Quinn, quoted in Michael Holroyd, *Augustus John*, Volume Two, cited in Harries and Harries, p.89. The press 'campaign' is documented in Stephen Gardiner, *Epstein: Artist Against the Establishment* (London: Flamingo, 1993) pp.166–168.

37 Having served a quiet war on the Mediterranean island of Mudros, Wadsworth was eventually invalided home where he gained employment in Bristol and Liverpool supervising the dazzle camouflage of ships. It was the academic marine painter Norman Wilkinson who pioneered this extraordinary method of marine camouflage. Although Wadsworth went on to paint one of the iconic images of the war *Dazzle-Ships in Drydock at Liverpool*, 1919 (for the Canadian War Memorial Scheme) he appears to have had only a very limited part in the origination and development of the innovative designs. See Paul Atterbury, 'Dazzle Painting in the First World War', *Antique Collector*, April 1975.

38 Lewis, *Blasting and Bombardiering*, p.96.

> (such as an unusual mastery of French) that might be of more use to pen-polyglot allies than my trusty right arm, which, I flatter myself, is rather a creative than a destructive limb.[39]

Despite his extensive knowledge of foreign languages he failed to secure a place in the Intelligence Services, and set his sights on joining the artillery. He laid down two conditions. One, that any unit he joined had nothing to do with horses, the second that he promptly gained commissioned rank. After all, he argued 'I felt it was due to the editor of *Blast* to be his own master to some extent. Once I had a 'pip' I could go on being a "crowd-master"'.[40] At the Field Artillery Cadet School in Exeter he studied ballistics and geometry, each week narrowly avoiding loss of life in the mandatory riding lesson. At Trowbridge Cadet School he proved adept at mathematics and calculus, and passed out fifth from the top of his class.

> I bought two well-cut suits of old-gold khaki, in Savile Row, a cane, a revolver, and a sumptuous British warm. I was now an 'officer', whom hundreds of thousands of men still living have saluted – have trembled at the sight of, if they were half-seas over. I passed into a more abstract class.[41]

A photograph taken at the time shows Lewis in his new garb: a cigarette hanging from his mouth, cap raffishly askew, a gloved hand clutching a whip. Looking every inch the dashing – if somewhat fierce – subaltern in jodhpurs and high leather boots, he is caught in sharp relief against an impenetrable black background, poised – or more truthfully, 'posed' – for action.[42]

THE ROMANCE OF WAR
May 1917[43]

Lewis arrived in Belgium on 24 May 1917 to join a siege battery of six-inch 26-cwt howitzers near Wytschaete, just south of the Ypres

39 Lewis to Mary Borden Turner. quoted by W.K. Rose (ed.) *The Letters of Wyndham Lewis* (London: Methuen, 1963).

40 Lewis, *Blasting and Bombardiering*, p.97. The Royal Regiment of Artillery was created in 1722 and was based at the Royal Arsenal in Woolwich (before relocating to Highbury in north London the Woolwich Arsenal was a works football team made up of workers in the arsenal). The regiment traditionally wore blue uniforms and had its own names for ranks (privates were gunners, corporals were bombardiers, etc). In 1899, the Royal Artillery was split into the Royal and Horse on one side and the Garrison (which included the Mountain Artillery) on the other. The Royal Garrison Artillery was in charge of the guns on forts, mainly huge muzzle-loaded guns. During times of peace or naval warfare, the RGA operated coastal guns, but when the Army needed to march on heavily fortified positions the RGA would mount the heavy guns on wooden carriages.

41 Lewis, *Blasting and Bombardiering*, p.98.

42 The original photograph, taken in December 1916, is held by the Rare Books Department, Cornell University Library.

43 Sub-title to 'Part III – A Gunner's Tale', of *Blasting and Bombardiering*.

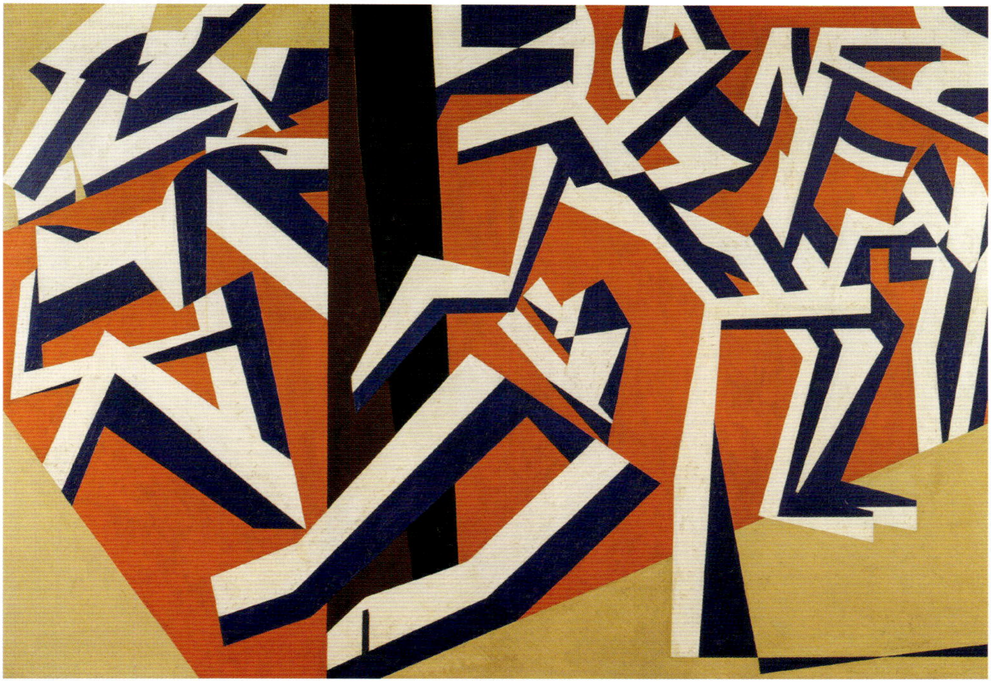

DAVID BOMBERG
The Mud Bath
(1914)
oil on canvas, 152.4 x 224.2 cm

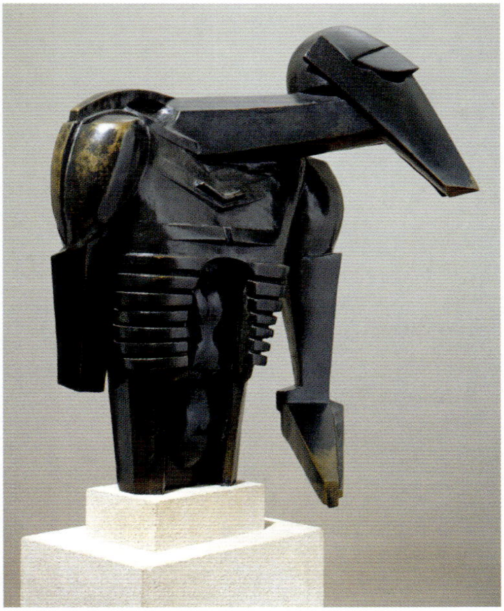

JACOB EPSTEIN
Torso in metal from 'The Rock Drill'
(1913–14)
bronze, 70.5 x 58.4 x 44.5 cm

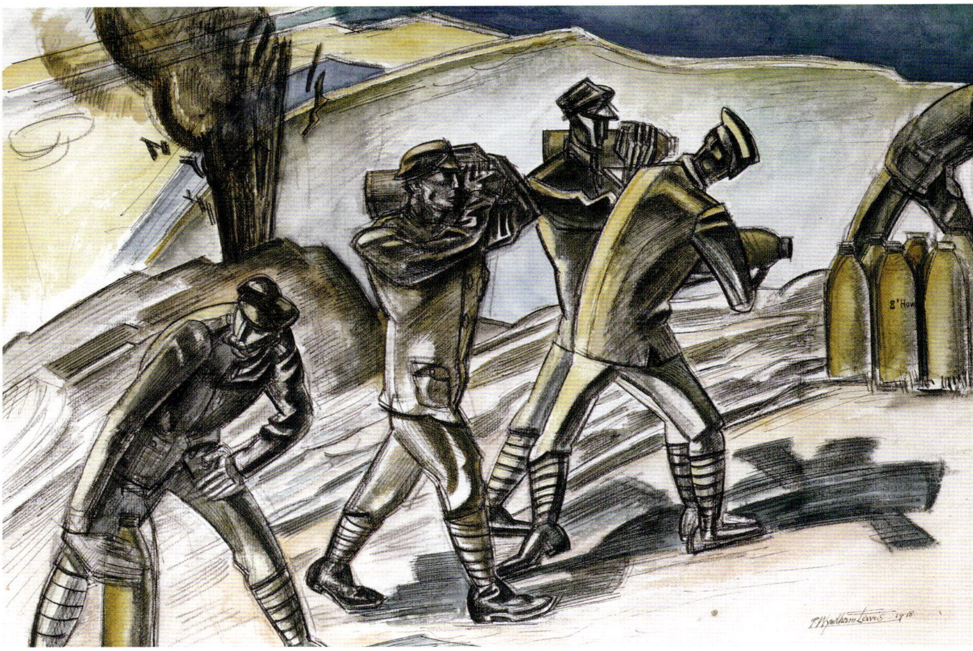

WYNDHAM LEWIS
Howitzers, or Shell-humping
(1918)
watercolour, 31.5 x 47.3 cm

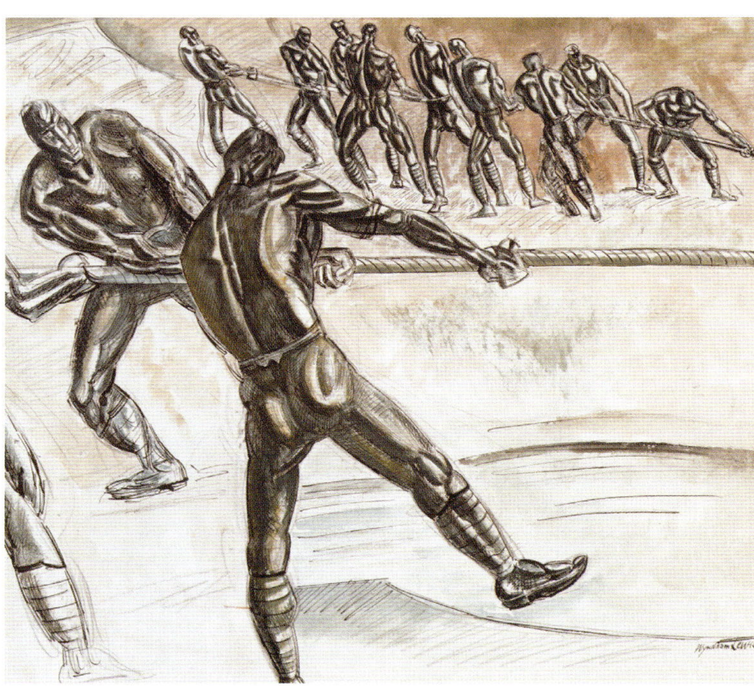

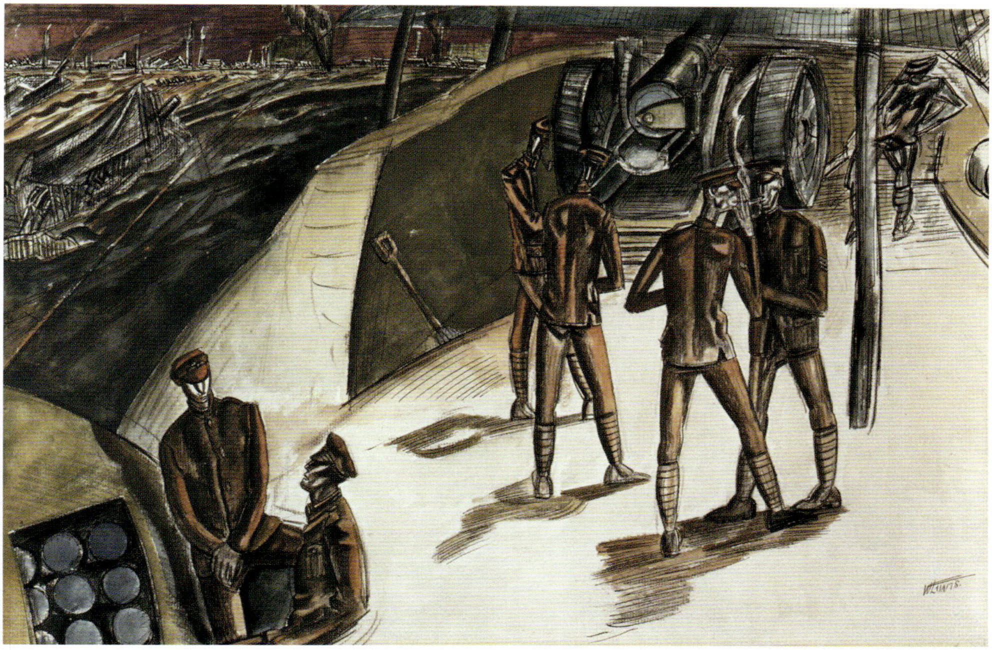

WYNDHAM LEWIS
Drawing of The Great War No. 1 (The Menin Road)
(c.1918/19)
watercolour on paper, 29.8 x 46.6 cm

WYNDHAM LEWIS
Drag Ropes
(c.1918)
pencil, pen and black ink and watercolour, 35.5 x 41.5 cm

WYNDHAM LEWIS
A Canadian Gun-pit
(1918)
oil on canvas, 304.8 x 363.2 cm

NATIONAL GALLERY OF CANADA, OTTAWA
(PHOTOGRAPH © NATIONAL GALLERY OF CANADA);
TRANSFER FROM THE CANADIAN WAR MEMORIALS, 1921.

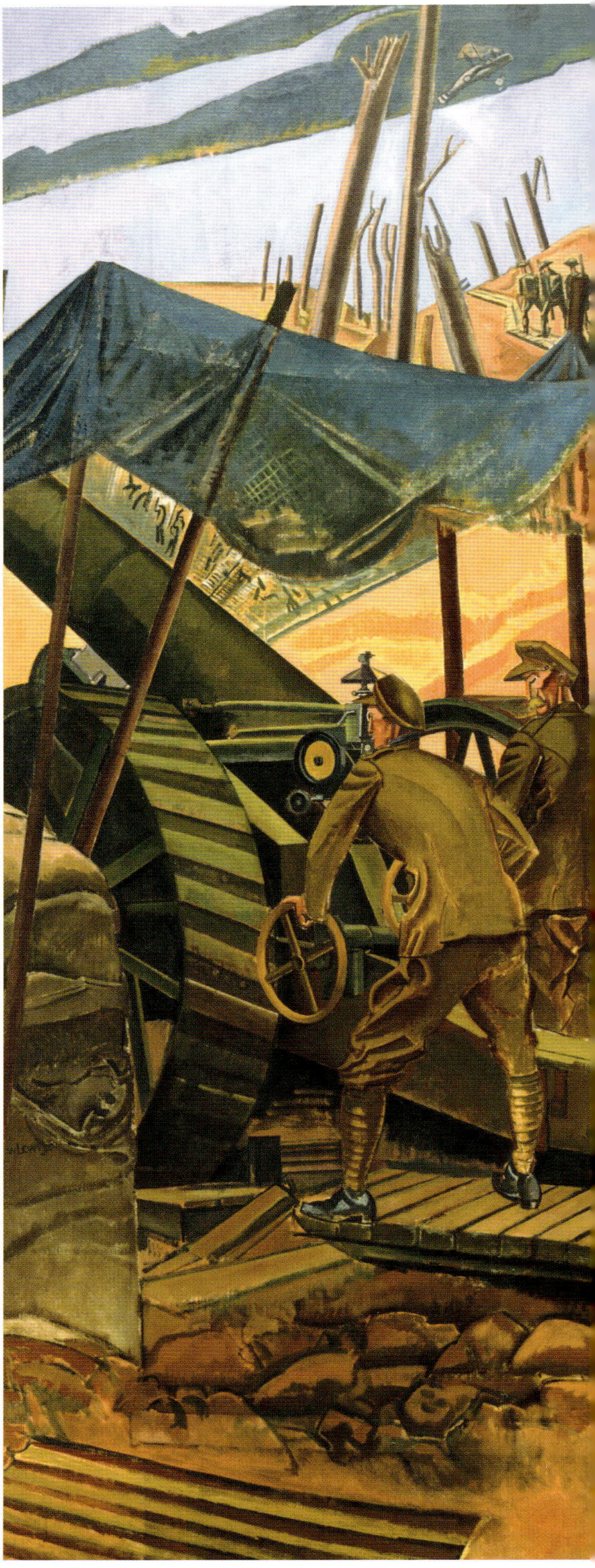

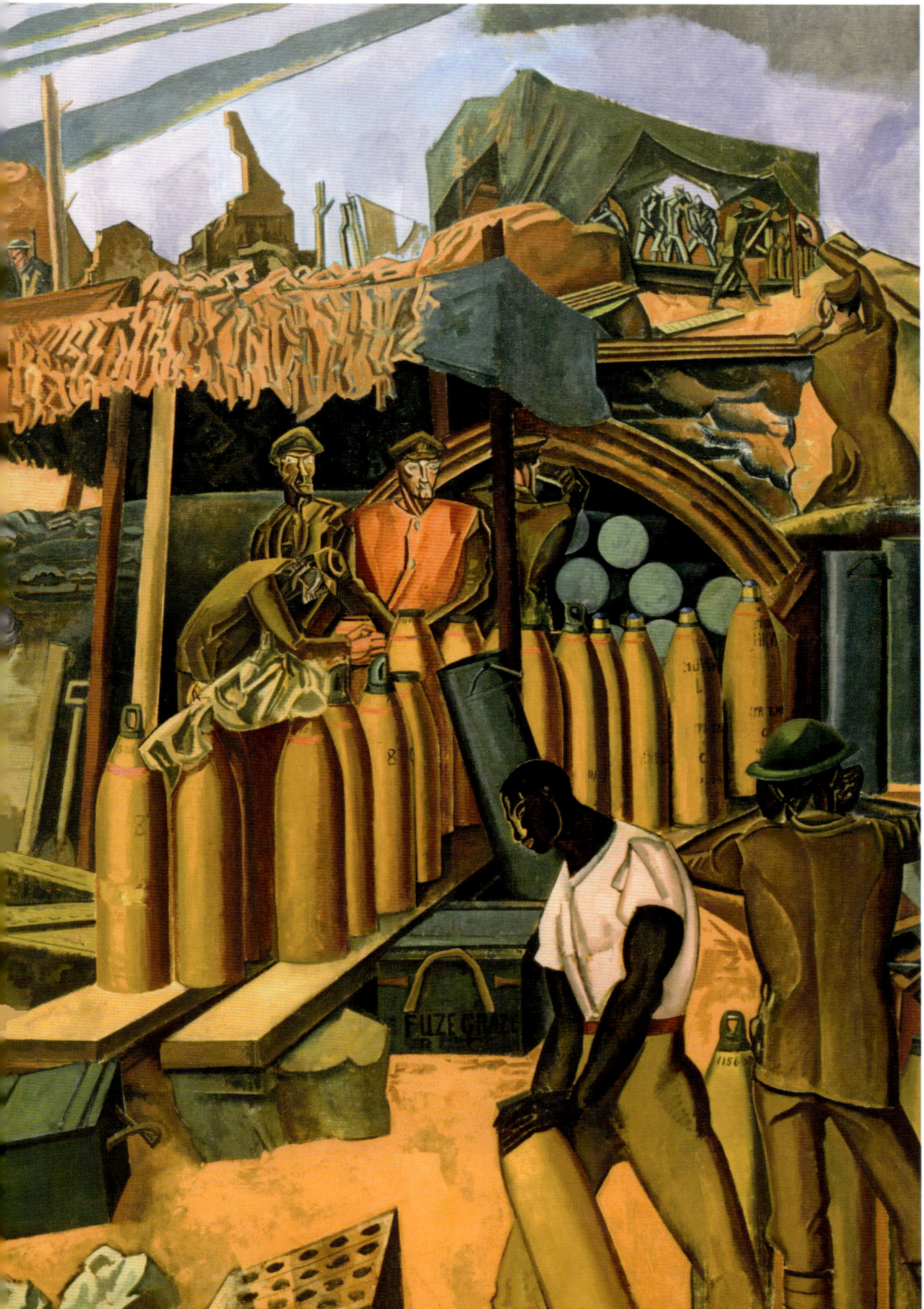

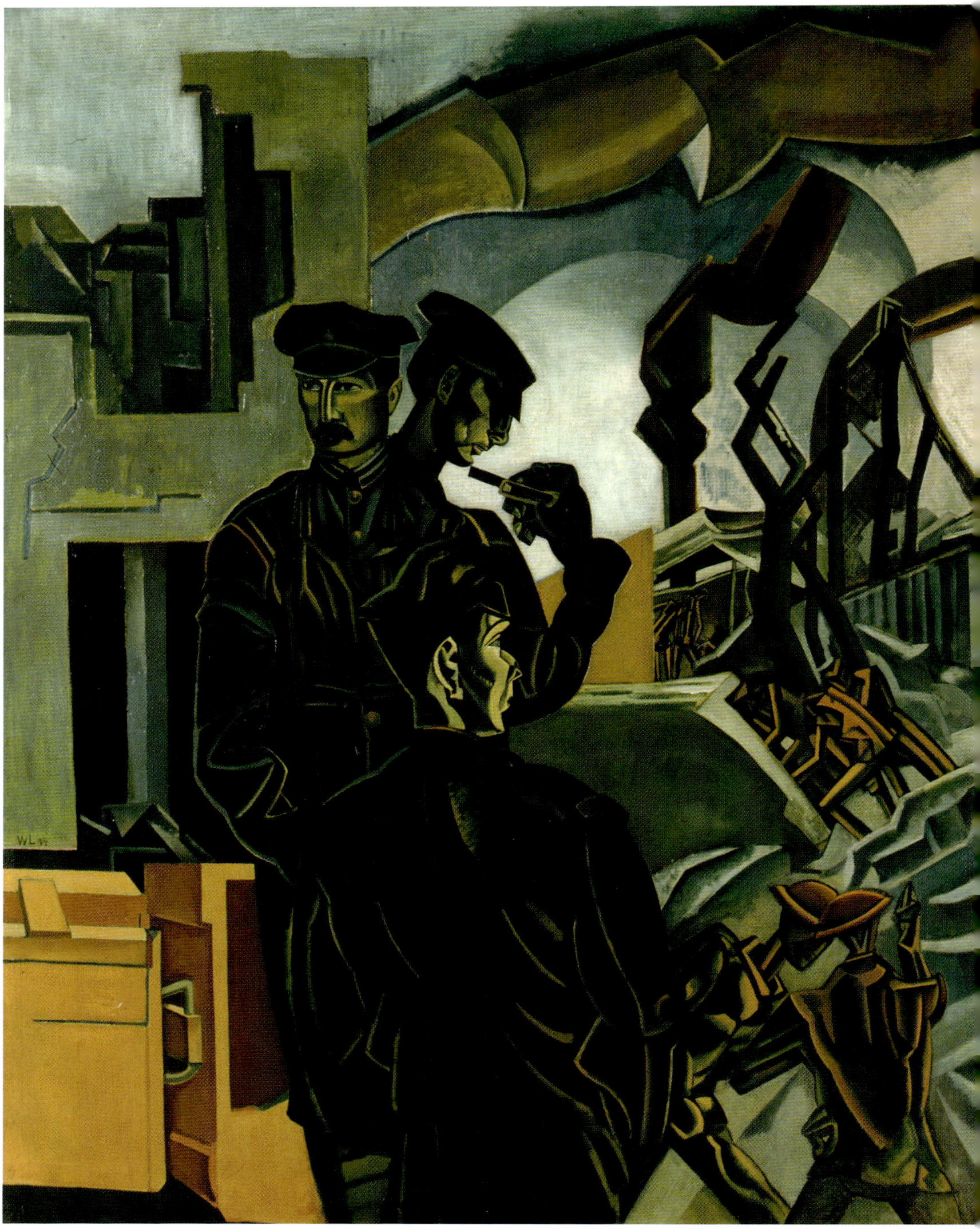

WYNDHAM LEWIS
A Battery Shelled
(1919)
oil on canvas, 182.8 x 317.5 cm
IMPERIAL WAR MUSEUM, LONDON

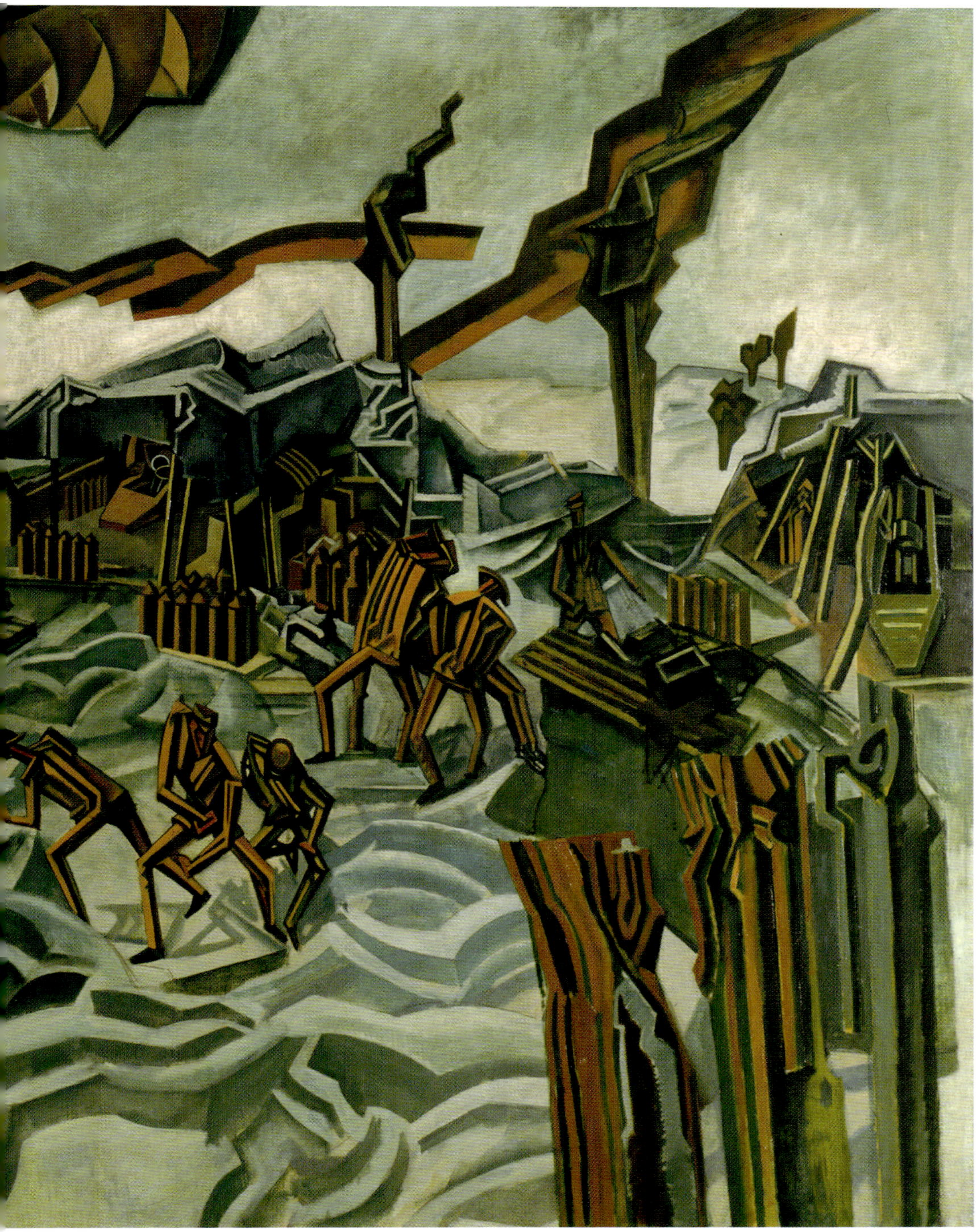

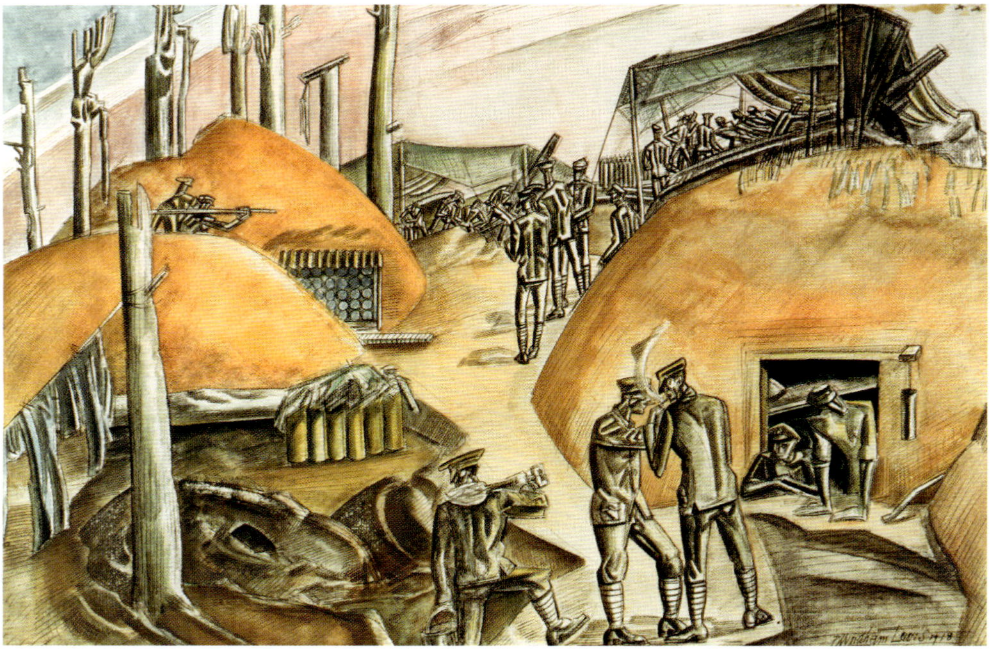

WYNDHAM LEWIS
A Battery Position in a Wood
(1918)
ink watercolour on paper, 31.7 x 46.9 cm
IMPERIAL WAR MUSEUM, LONDON. GIFT OF SIR MUIRHEAD BONE, 1919.

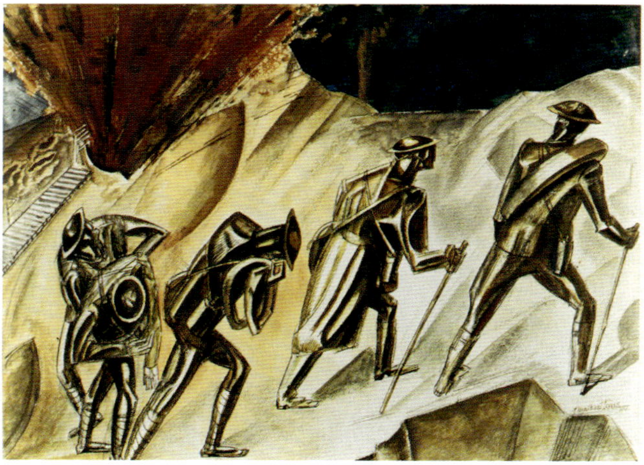

WYNDHAM LEWIS
Officers and Signallers, 1918
(1918)
ink watercolour gouache on paper, 25.4 x 35.6 cm
IMPERIAL WAR MUSEUM, LONDON.

Salient. Despite the 'sinister expectancy' of the Front, he regarded war as an oddly romantic affair:

> We arrived at railhead at night and a battle was in progress... There was no moon or stars – all lights had been turned down for the performance. Only the unseen orchestra thundered away, before an unseen stage. We had to imagine the actors which we knew were there, crouching in their sticky labyrinths... With great suddenness – as we stood, very impressed as newcomers in the midst of this pandemonium – in a neighbouring field a battery of large howitzers began firing... So we plunged into the romance of battle... if your mind is of a romantic cast, there's nothing for it, I am afraid. The likelihood that you will get your head blown off cannot weigh with you for a moment. You must not miss a war, if one is going! You cannot afford to miss that experience.[44]

Lewis used the term 'romantic' very carefully and rather reluctantly. Here, it is tinged with a sense of droll irony, but in the same breath he also felt that 'a care for truth compels me to use it'.[45] Lewis understood 'romanticism' as an accumulation of sensations: the violent sounds of the 11-inch guns with their dramatic flames and their interminable, monotonous percussion; the desolate lunar panoramas of the Salient which he imagined were like the first glimpses of the Pacific 'as seen by the earliest circumnavigators' and many mysterious things that could not be seen, which lurked in its darkest shadows, or could only be felt. 'The truth is,' he asserted, '...it is not what you see, at all, that makes an event romantic for you, but what you feel. And in war, as you might expect, you feel with considerable intensity'.[46] Lewis refused to believe he himself was a romantic, nor did he like war, and he apologised for having to admit that the conflict, even on the Western Front, had an 'exceedingly romantic character'. He recognized, though, that it suited those of a subjective inclination: 'you have not lived if you have not been present at a battle, of that I can assure you'.[47] Such attitude may seem at odds with the image of Lewis as hard-edged Modernist, the self-proclaimed abstractionist, the advocate of rational order. But such

44 Lewis, *Blasting and Bombardiering*, p.112. A Battery was usually lettered A to D; each of the Batteries numbered 198 heads at full establishment. Each was commanded by a Major or Captain, with a Captain as Second-in-Command, and 3 Lieutenants or Second-Lieutenants in charge of 2 gun sections. The Battery establishment also included a Battery Sergeant-Major, a Battery Quartermaster-Sergeant, a Farrier-Sergeant, 4 Shoeing Smiths (of which 1 would be a Corporal), 2 Saddlers, 2 Wheelers, 2 Trumpeters, 7 Sergeants, 7 Corporals, 11 Bombardiers, 75 Gunners, 7 Drivers and 10 Gunners acting as Batmen. See O.F.G. Hogg, *Artillery: its Origin, Heyday and Decline* (London: C. Hurst & Co, 1970).

There were two models of 6"-Howitzer in use in 1916: the 30-cwt 1896 pattern and the 26-cwt 1915 model. Other than the weight, the key differences were that the 1915 model had a greater maximum range: 11,400 yards against 7,000 [3.9 miles] for the older model.

45 Lewis, *Blasting and Bombardiering*, p.114.

46 Lewis, *Blasting and Bombardiering*, p.115.

47 Lewis, *Blasting and Bombardiering*, p.114.

responses would have been very familiar to the Romantic philosophers and poets of the eighteenth century who understood the intensity aroused by contradictory stimuli and the enjoyment felt when dangers 'tauten our fibres'. This is most pithily summarized by a single passage in a treatise by Edmund Burke:

> Whatever is felt in any sort to excite the ideas of pain, and danger, that is to say, whatever is in any sort terrible, or is conversant about terrible objects, or operates in a manner analogous to terror, is a source of the Sublime; that is, it is productive of the strongest emotion which the mind is capable of feeling.[48]

Savouring danger – at a reasonably safe distance – was the guiding ethos of the Sublime. Poets, painters, and writers sought out the 'darkest and most imperfect parts' of the map to find gut-wrenching and awe-inspiring experience. In its pursuit, Samuel Taylor Coleridge embarked on reckless alpine adventures to assuage his appetite for the sublime majesty of mountain scenery. Upper-class young men crossing the dreaded Alps on their obligatory Grand Tour transformed what had always been considered a hazardous rite of passage 'through strange, horrid and fearful crags', into a journey of enormous moral and aesthetic significance which they then recorded in epic poetry and rendered in moody watercolours.[49] Guided by the tenets of High Romanticism, underpinned by the philosophy of the Sublime, young British aesthetes went out of their way to encounter fearful mountains, deafening waterfalls and precipitous crags in the hope of achieving an intense communion with Nature and, by extension, the ultimate Deity. In craving experiences so seeped in awe that they were veritably 'awe-full', Coleridge, Burke and Schiller would have instantly recognized Lewis's vision, sharing and relishing his ecstatic fear:

> You only have to think a moment: the dark night, with the fearful flashing of a monstrous cannonade – all the things that do not come into the picture, which are not seen, in other words, but which are suggested in its darkest shadows – what could be more technically 'romantic' that that, if it is romance that we must talk about? ...By definition, romance is always inside and not outside. It is, as we say, subjective. It is the material of magic. It partakes of the action of a drug.[50]

---

48 Edmund Burke, *A Philosophical Enquiry into the Origins of Our Idea of the Sublime and Beautiful*, 1757. Introduction by James T. Boulton (London: Routledge and Kegan Paul, 1958). See also: Morton C. Paley, *The Apocalyptic Sublime* (New Haven and London: Yale University Press, 1986) who categorized three components to the Sublime: 'Its chief source was power, its chief subject matter, terror, its identifying response, astonishment.' (p.2) Another useful reference is: Samuel H Monk, *The Sublime: a Study of Critical Theories in xviiith England* (Ann Arbour: University of Michigan Press, 1935/1960).

49 Coleridge described himself as 'no novice in mountain mischiefs'. See for example, Coleridge's letters to Thomas Wedgewood, 9 January 1803 cited in E.L. Griggs, (ed.) *Collected Letter of Samuel Taylor Coleridge* (Oxford: Oxford University Press, 1956–59) Vol. ii, p.483.

What they would have understood less well was that danger in modern war was more pervasive and more penetrating in its reach than it had been a century earlier. Burke had qualified his peroration on the power of terror-tinged experience by adding that if danger or pain pressed too closely 'they are incapable of giving any delight, and are simply terrible'.[51] Lewis appreciated this too. Although he was at times thrilled by the cacophonous 'orchestral accompaniment' of heavy artillery in full throttle, he knew too well that these same guns – the 'startlingly romantic accessories' – could plough up the ground till it looked like nothing on earth. They could transform a smart little township, inside an hour, into a romantic ruin (worthy, as he noted, of Turner or Claude Lorrain), causing irreversible shell-shock, and inflicting spectacular wounds.[52] Being hit by a bullet, warned Lewis, 'even a dum-dum', was nothing when compared with the impact on flesh of a red-hot iron shell splinter. War might be romantic, it might even have moments of sublime transcendence, but only ever at a safe distance and only when protected by many feet of well-filled sandbags or several inches of armour-plated metal. Such comforts could not often be guaranteed in the trench world. Lewis knew that to stare into the negative sublime of the Western Front was indeed the prerogative of 'a very dangerous type of spectator'.

CHANGING BATTERIES

> I am here (in firing line) since yesterday. Battery split up, and I have come as reinforcements. My address is now 224 Siege Battery RGA, BEF, France. Whizzing, banging and swishing and thudding completely surround me, and I almost jog up and down on my camp bed as though I were riding in a country wagon or a dilapidated taxi. I am in short, my dear colleague, in the midst of an unusually noisy battle.[53]

Lewis's writing about the war offers a rich blend of colourful incident, droll anecdote and astute insight into the daily behaviour of a diligent (if somewhat jaded) forward observation officer (in army lingo, the F.O.O.). His main duty was to occupy an observation post, often in sight of the enemy line, and direct the fire of his battery's guns which might be located far behind him.[54] In order to direct the fire of the blinded guns, the F.O.O. 'registered' the battery by

50 Lewis, *Blasting and Bombardiering*, p.115.

51 Burke, p.40.

52 See footnote (3) and also Geoffrey Noon, 'The Treatment of Casualties in the Great War', in Paddy Griffith (ed.) *British Fighting Methods in the Great War* (London: Cass, 1996).

53 Lewis to Ezra Pound, 6 June 1917, in T. Materer, *Pound/Lewis: the Letters of Ezra Pound and Wyndham Lewis* (London: Faber and Faber, 1985) p.73.

selecting a conventional point on the map, observed the burst of fire as it landed and advised the guns by field telephone to 'shorten' or 'lengthen' according to whether the shell fell beyond or short of the object aimed at. This is called 'bracketting'. Lewis was required to do it often, experiencing the occasional satisfaction of reducing to dust the puny remains of an emptied and ruined village. However, it was very dangerous work as German gunners were equally set on blinding the 'eyes' of the enemy artillery. In this hazardous duty he was accompanied by a section of signallers who had the even more disagreeable task of checking and mending the telecommunication wire which was strung out between the observation post – the O.P. or O. Pip to give its military call sign – and the distant battery. The wire could seldom be concealed in the ground and was easily snagged, snipped, or torn up by enemy artillery. A single break in the line would end all communication, leaving the O.P. stranded as if it were a vessel lost and adrift in the ocean. It would then be at the mercy of counter-fire directed by the diligent German spotters hidden in equally obscure O.P.'s or dangling in baskets from balloons suspended over the British lines. One of Lewis's subsequent drawings depicts a section of officers and signallers observing the fire of their own batteries; one uses a trench periscope, another field glasses, a third checks the range of fire on a grid-lined chart, while the tortured land beyond their post is torn up by shell-bursts of all shapes. A diagonal parapet line separates them in their studious concentration from the barrage, a feeble barricade that offers only a modicum of security.[55]

When not observing, much of the time was spent waiting around and occasionally coming under counter-battery fire by well-aimed German artillery. Lewis detested the bouts of languid inactivity, when there was very little to do 'except hang about and smoke cigarettes' and he knew they were over-manned – especially with those giving orders. 'We had six officers in this battery. Five too many.'[56] This state of prolonged tedium punctuated by terrifying fear, became the norm; it is evident in the languid figures of many of his later drawings, and its disadvantages soon became obvious to Lewis, who described how the gunner:

> ... was always 'in the Line', he had no spells of rest 'behind the Line'. Where he slept, often for a year on end, was in the midst of nests of batteries which were one of the main objectives of the enemy shelling.[57]

---

54 Lewis gives an account of the role of the F.O.O. in his first autobiography, remarking that he 'had never engaged in personal combat with a German in a trench or anywhere else. So I have not 'fought' the Germans except in the abstract sense that I have been responsible for the dispatch of unlimited number of shells in their direction, and as a result of the explosion of these shells (when they were not duds) I may have done these men more injury than I could ever have done, I am sure, with my strong right arm.' (*Blasting and Bombardiering*, p.125).

As a siege-battery subaltern, Lewis reckoned that half his time was spent at the observation post, although 'quite ninety per cent of that time was wasted'. The other ten per cent was inevitably lively. On an active front, enemy spotters would detect an observation post in less than thirty minutes and 'shell it to pieces'. 'They even shelled anything that *looked like* an observation post', remarked Lewis. 'A half-dozen stumps of trees in what was once a wood they would never let alone.' He left a vivid account of one foolhardy foray into no-man's-land to establish a new post at the behest of a superior officer – a small commercial gent in Civvy Street ('perhaps a garage proprietor,' speculated Lewis drily, 'or employee in a Shipping Office'), who appeared hell bent on taking back a Military Cross to Balham.[58] Pointless and perilous, the escapade took Lewis closer to the battlefield than he had ever before been. He later wrote of his awe at the sight of this 'parched, hollow, breathless desert':

> At this point civilization ended... beyond this battery was a short stretch of shell-pitted nothingness – for we had entered upon that arid and blistering vacuum; the lunar landscape, so often described in the war-novels and represented by painters and draughtsmen, myself among them, but the particular quality of which is so difficult to convey. Those grinning skeletons in field-grey, the skull still protected by the metal helmet: those festoons of mud-caked wire, those miniature mountain-ranges of saffron earth, and trees like gibbets – these were the properties only of those titanic casts of dying and shell-shocked actors, who charged this stage with a romantic electricity.[59]

A few weeks later, in the second half of June, he contracted trench fever, suffering a grossly swollen neck and face, and sporting a lurid green tongue. He was sent down to 46th Stationary Hospital at Etaples by the coast, where his case was judged critical, and then on to a convalescent home at Dieppe. It was not the most glorious opening to his war and he spent seven weeks out of the line. He rejoined his original Battery at Nieuport on the coast. For two months they installed and manned four large-calibre 7½-inch naval

---

55 Lewis, *Great War Drawing* no.2, 1918. Pen and ink, watercolour. 38.1 x 54.2 cm. Southampton Art Gallery.

56 Lewis, *Blasting and Bombardiering*, p.123.

57 Lewis, *Blasting and Bombardiering*, p.120.

58 Lewis's account of this escapade is in *Blasting and Bombardiering*, p.117–125.

59 These passages are taken from Chapter IV 'A Day of Attack'. Lewis and his fellow officer established that there was no fixed front-line as yet, but determined that an old German dug-out would serve as an excellent O.P. On their return journey they came under further fire as more German batteries were now being brought into action, and encountered an infantry party moving forward to man the new front-line 'their eyes turned inward as it seemed, to shut out this too-familiar scene.' Lewis recounts with ill-concealed pleasure that the excitable Major 'got into hot water' for his rash roaming into the battlefield, not caring for his officious zeal. 'But I daresay,' concluded Lewis, 'they gave him an M.C. anyway, just to keep him quiet.' (*Blasting and Bombardiering*, pp.135–136)

guns bought forward in readiness for an attack on the German-held ports that autumn. Apart from the periodic fall of small gas-shells, which meant that every man had to sleep for weeks on end in their gas masks, it was an uneventful time. The guns were never fired; the attack never came. They were shelled but did not retaliate. On several occasions Lewis only narrowly missed being maimed by shell fragments. He and his brother officers would feign a nonchalant air as the odd 'large viciously-hissing splinter passed at headlong speed immediately between our noses, which were about a foot apart'. On another less lucky occasion No.4 Gun, which Lewis commanded, took a direct hit that killed his trusted sergeant and six men, injuring six more. In their next battery position, again when he was off duty, his same gun team sustained a direct hit from an air attack. Lewis was aware that he was courting extreme danger, a truth driven home by the news that T.E. Hulme, serving nearby with the Marine Artillery, had been killed.[60]

As 1917 wore on Lewis's battery was moved south, fitted out with four 6-inch Mark XIX guns, and became embroiled in the Battle of Third Ypres, now commonly known as the Battle of Passchendaele.[61] The climax of the war, and Lewis's part in it, was approaching. Not that it felt much like that for most of the time. Unable to draw, and debilitated by being constantly on duty, he became increasingly fatalistic and complained of being moved about at random upon 'this muddy board'. His battery was positioned five hundred yards south of Hellfire Corner on the Menin Road where they lent support to the 1st Anzac Corps' attacks on Polygon Wood, Zonnebeek, and the Broodseinde Ridge.

> There were 'zero hours', for which we waited with our eyes on our wristwatches, there were days of attack, or rehearsals for attack, practice barrages, sudden alarms and excursions, which died down ten minutes after the first flare up. I cannot tell you what any of these things were. All that I know is that I moved hither and thither over this sea of mud and have since been told that it was a fool who was moving me.[62]

Much of his time was spent in observation posts looking down at apparently deserted German lines, registering targets and calling

60 Lewis recounts how Hulme died in the same bombardment in 1917 that killed the sergeant of his own gun and made casualties of most of his crew. See Lewis, *Wyndham Lewis the Artist: from Blast to Burlington House*, 1939, pp.68–69.

61 Passchendaele, wrote Lewis, was the most appropriate name of the battle-bog of Third Ypres. 'The very name, with its suggestion of *splashiness* and of *passion* at once, was subtly appropriate. This nonsense could not have come to its full flower at any other place but at *Passchendaele*. It was pre-ordained.' (*Blasting and Bombardiering*, p.151)

62 This quote is from *Blasting and Bombardiering*, p.152. One of the most recent accounts of the military operation in which Lewis's unit was involved is in Frank Bostyn, *Passchendale 1917: The Story of the Fallen and Tyne Cot Cemetery* (Roesalare: Roularta, 2007) See Part One: Six 'The Battle of Broodseinde: 4 October 1917. New Zealand Division', pp.87–97.

down fire from batteries concentrated around the rim of the Salient. As noted earlier, he recorded his impressions in graphic prose.[63] Lewis later translated these sights, and sounds, into a series of tough drawings which revealed an extensive repertoire of explosions. These ranged from great plumes of blackened cumulus and inverted pyramids of dense charcoal, to a double helix of delicate pencil lines and highly stylized rolls of smoke wafting over a gun position, like telescopic tubes of highly-polished pewter. Most of his drawings of 1918 feature a detonation of some form or another. In one drawing, *Officers and Signallers*, the five figures shy away from the terrific shell-burst falling nearby, their polished metallic bodies about to be peppered with falling debris from the triangular blast of dung-coloured mud.[64] In another watercolour, *Action* (or *Artillery*),[65] a single shell-burst punctuates the horizon; like some vast and towering tree it rises dramatically out of the tossing quagmire of the battlefield.

By this stage in the battle, O.P.s were in isolated and extremely dangerous positions. Lewis believed that they had become a 'snare and a delusion', maintained more out of a moral imperative and duty than for their use in registering nebulous enemy targets. He wrote a vivid account of a particularly perilous trip to man one such post on an exposed ridge-line. Crossing diagonally the rolling waste of the deserted battlefield, he and his small party of signallers became ruefully aware that a German sausage-balloon hung over the O.P., 'surprisingly low down and shockingly far forward' as he grimly recalled. For the next five hours the spotter hunted Lewis and his men, 'potting' at the stranded figures with no less a 'fowling piece' than a battery of German 5.9 howitzers.

> He had doubtless been watching us for some time. He had seen us pulling our legs, with a sodden pop, out of the mud of the sunken road: he had seen me enter the Anzac telephone pill-box; and he had remarked with a savage grin of glee, the signaller-corporal point to the famous O. Pip in the distance, as we started upon our last lap. 'Na na... So kommt doch! Kommt docht her, Ihr Soldatchen! Wir warten schon! Habt keine Angst, wir werden nicht roh sein. Also!'[66]

In a war notorious for its anonymity, where death could be arbitrary and instantaneous, Lewis later regarded this encounter as an extra-ordinary duel between two unsighted artillery officers, which he eventually won. However, at the time, he took it very personally:

---

63 Lewis, *Blasting and Bombardiering*, p.158.

64 Lewis, *Officers and Signallers*, 1918. Pen and ink, crayon, watercolour, 25.4 x 35.6 cm. IWM:ART 5932.

65 Lewis, *Action* or *Artillery*, 1918. Watercolour and ink line, 35.2 x 50.9 cms. Cooper Art Gallery, Barnsley.

66 Lewis, *Blasting and Bombardiering*, p.162.

> I should think you could count on the fingers of your hands the soldiers who have been fired at in the personal way by weapons of such dimensions – and a whole battery of them… First, a sausage-balloon sitting with impunity up in the air above you, upon a nice clear day: secondly, the Observer in the balloon with plenty of time on his hands, and in the mood for a little sport; and thirdly, two men practically underneath it, in an empty landscape. Again, were it a larger collection of people, then it would no longer be personal.[67]

WAR ARTIST
December 1917–1919

As Passchendaele ground to a standstill, Lewis went on leave to London where he was encouraged by a friend, Captain Guy Baker, to apply to join Lord Beaverbrook's Canadian War Memorials Scheme, an ambitious enterprise to decorate the new Parliament Buildings in Ottawa with large paintings of the war. Lewis had first become aware of the privileges granted to official artists when he happened across William Orpen dining with hordes of 'brass-hats' at a restaurant in a pleasant spa behind the Salient. 'The glimpse of this posh portraitist,' snarled Lewis, 'living on the fat of the land at Cassel made my mouth water'. In turn, Lewis's proposal was accepted and he was released from his duties as a gunner, returning to the Western Front as an official war artist on 13 December 1917.[68] He had mixed feelings about leaving his battery, expressing a sigh of 'half relief, half regret' at bidding farewell to his 'untidy little batman' and the 'squalid, insanitary, little rat-hole where I slept'.[69] Despite being elated at the congenial prospect of 'twirling' his brush once more he ruminated for a moment on the bombed and 'battered rivulet' that had been his home, asking himself: 'what is the claim that such places, such conditions, have upon one's desires, that no Ritz suite or castle-palace can compete with?' Indeed, he found his official residence as a 'Canadian' artist at times a little discomforting:

> We lived in a large chateau. Our life there was uneventful – quiet, dignified, and aloof. The contrast to the squalid mud hovels of the

67 Lewis, *Blasting and Bombardiering*, p.165.

68 Lewis appears to have held the architect of the Canadian scheme, Lord Beaverbrook, in high esteem, considering him 'the brightest of the Press Barons', who must have had a very remarkable instinct for public affairs to 'have got rich so young, to have pushed politicians about just as he wanted to, and to have created far and away the best cruiserweight newspaper in England, the *Evening Star*.' (Lewis, *Blasting and Bombardiering*, p.191). Lewis was rather surprised that it was Beaverbrook's official war art scheme that had 'saved' all of England's artists from military servitude. 'We do not associate,' he reflected, 'the land of the "Mounties" and of Montcalm with the fine arts…' (*Blasting and Bombardiering*, p.190).

69 Lewis's views on Orpen are recorded on pages 170–171 of *Blasting and Bombardiering*. His regret at leaving his batman is expressed on pages 194–5.

> Front was a little startling. And we had a staff car at our disposal which reported for duty every morning.
>
> I ran down to my battery in the car – to my new Canadian battery. It was a '6 inch How' battery. I had nothing to do with it, of course, except to paint. It stood by itself, in the great open spaces of the Vimy Ridge. There was nothing near it.
>
> This battery seldom fired. Everything was different in this part of the line – so different that to start with I could I could scarcely believe my eyes, or ears.[70]

Quite why Lewis needed to be back at the Front is not clear; his contractual obligations as specified by the Canadians were rather loosely worded and he boasted that he could draw any artillery piece with his eyes closed. He also exposed himself to unnecessary danger, such as a time on the Vimy Front when a shell exploded overhead. 'It was,' he wrote with measured indignation, 'just as if the Germans had got wind of my activities, and had said, "Ha! We will put a little shellfire into this picture".' So rare were these incidents, however, and so quiet the Front that Lewis mused (with uncharacteristic charity) that 'the gun probably went off by mistake while they were cleaning it'. So Lewis spent much of his time drawing the preparatory and peripheral work of a battery: gun laying and pit digging; observation and reconnaissance work, and the back-breaking work of moving and storing ammunition. In drawings such as *Battery Position in a Wood*,[71] Lewis also captured the lassitude of a battery awaiting fire orders. A lethargy laced, however, with latent tension. Although some of the gunners languish in their dug-outs they are alert to the sounds of incoming fire; others stand around in groups chatting and smoking, but remain close to their guns, ready to bring them into action at short notice. The laundry suspended from a shattered tree may hang limply in the still air, but the washing-line itself is taut; its rigidity echoing the many other stressed diagonals in the composition.

Lewis was a masterful draughtsman, arguably one of the greatest of the twentieth century. His war drawings are full of surprises, abrupt changes of pace and tone, and he had an unerring sense of design knowing exactly where to place the motif on the sheet of paper for maximum effect, how to 'take a line for a walk and make it go somewhere original and unexpected'.[72] Particularly powerful are his drawings of the battlescape as if it were a liquefied and muddy ocean, an uncharted zone that was shapeless and without form, where mortar rounds would send ripples across the soggy surface, and where detonations would crash like gigantic breakers

70 Lewis, *Blasting and Bombardiering*, p.200.
71 Lewis, *Battery Position in a Wood*, 1918. Pen and ink, crayon, watercolour, 31.7 x 46.9 cm. IWM:ART 1672.
72 Angela Weight, Foreword, *Wyndham Lewis: Art and War* (London: Lund Humphries, 1992) p.8–11.

on the sandbagged wall of the trench. 'A direct hit on our pill-box,' exclaimed one combatant, 'rocked the place like a boat caught in the trough of the sea.'[73] Another soldier observed a battlefield under fire as 'the skyline heaved and smoked, throwing up fountains and jets of soil and grey smoke as if it were a dark sea breaking heavily on a reef'.[74] Lewis devised a system of short animated pencil strokes to represent the squally choppiness of this 'sea of mud', and his stranded gunners and signallers are often shown struggling to reach *terra firma*, like poor swimmers caught in a rip-tide.[75]

Most of these subtleties of design were lost in the large painting completed for the Canadian war art scheme. Lewis was disappointed by his canvas, *A Canadian Gun-Pit*, which he regarded as a compromise between his experiences, his intentions and the restrictions of the brief. Indeed, he dismissed the work as 'one of the dullest good pictures on earth'.[76] In fact, the brief was rather loosely worded and laid down few constraints. Chief artistic adviser to the Canadian scheme, Paul Konody, had declared in 1917 that 'apart from having the broad outlines of his subject made clear to him... each artist is given the fullest liberty to do whatever may best suit his temperament so that the artistic quality of his work may not suffer from irksome constraint'.[77] Lewis knew, however, that Konody was at times a fickle client. He had been irritated by the artistic licence taken by two of his fellow Vorticists and had raged at David Bomberg for producing what he condemned as a 'futurist abortion' of a painting, demanding that he repaint *Sappers at Work: A Canadian Tunnelling Company* in a more naturalistic style.[78] Mindful of Konody's temper and his power to summarily reject an artist's work, Lewis produced a faithful rendition of an 8-inch howitzer being prepared

---

73 Carroll Carstairs, *A Generation Missing* (London: William Heinemann, 1930) p.103.

74 'Charles Edmonds' (Charles Carrington), *A Subaltern's War* (London: Davies, 1929) p.33.

75 In his hair-raising account of the duel between him and the German spotter in the sausage balloon, Lewis describes at one point how his small team of intrepid explorers reached the 'final bog of bogs' and set out across the single duck-board track: 'The last of our party had left *terra firma* a few yards behind him when the first shell came down. It whooped out of the air and into the mud some yards to the side of us'. Further shells landed, isolating them, and then shattering the duckboards ahead. 'At this I turned and found that one of the hindmost signallers had already reached *terra firma*, and a second one was in the bog. I shouted out to get back and we returned to the 'shore' at the double.' (*Blasting and Bombardiering*, p.163)

76 Lewis to Read, 17 December 1919, cited in W.K. Rose (ed.) *The Letters of Wyndham Lewis* (London: Methuen, 1963) p.102.

77 Lewis was a little wary of Konody, having crossed him at least once before the war. But, according to Lewis, he was received with open arms: 'When I asked him if he had among his artists an artillery-artist, to paint howitzers, he shouted NO! When I said I knew all about howitzers – how would it be for me to paint one – he screamed OF COURSE!!! With his dramatic miteuropean accent he gave this suggestion such a rich Austrian welcome as no suggestion ever before or since.' (*Blasting and Bombardiering*, p.190)

78 Alice Mayes, 'The Young Bomberg, 1914–1925', memoir dated 1972, Tate Gallery Archive. For a full account of Bomberg's difficulties with Konody see Richard Cork, *A Bitter Truth*, pp.229–231. However, Sue Malvern argues that these difficulties are easy to exaggerate, and owe more to misunderstanding and bad timing than 'any sort of conspiracy to undermine the artist.' (Malvern, *Modern Art, Britain and the Great War*, p.115–116)

for firing.[79] It is a busy scene, dutifully rendered by Lewis with near-deadpan precision. He even provided Konody with documentary records to prove that every detail was correct. We see that the howitzer is being 'laid' (that is aimed for firing) and that the carrying-caps on the high explosive shells are being replaced by 'graze' fuses, which will detonate at the slightest deflection. We can identify the fibre cartridge cases, which hold the bagged powder charges, and the intricate webbing of the camouflage netting. We can read how each piece of ordnance is inscribed and marked with numerals and stencilled codes. As an index of artillery, it is a convincing inventory but it is less convincing as a piece of modernist art. There is none of the startling spatial ambiguity that marks much of Lewis's work at that time, nor any of the wilful distortion of appearances that were his trademark. In its place, however, we have a powerful command of rectilinear form, constructed around the counterpoint of timbers, duckboard slats, metallic treads, and upright shells that fill the centre of the picture's space. It is also a well balanced and harmonious piece of pictorial construction, especially in the syncopated arrangement of warm and cool complementary colours – mustards and ochres in the foreground, giving way to viridians and light blue in the upper half of the painting, picked up in the shells, the canvas awning and the streaks of sky – which lend it a decorative, even playful, air. Only the angular faces and the small robotic figures in the top-right corner remind us that Lewis was still the titular head of a radical art movement, even if, by now, the momentum had dissipated.

'ALL SCOOPED OUT AND VERY EL GRECO'

'A Battery Shelled', 1919[80]

Two sensations might strike us when viewing Lewis's war art: the first is the strong distinction between the figures and their surroundings; while the figures that populate his compositions are rigid in pose and stylistically formalized, the surroundings are often more naturalistic, almost at odds with the robotic mannerisms of the chisel-faced figures. Secondly, we cannot help but be impressed by Lewis's peculiar knack of rendering the fluidity of the battlefield, its innate sogginess, and its tendency to take on the tossing indeterminate form of an ocean upon which the guns, the cement O.P.s, and the gunpits seem more like barren islands stranded in heavy seas than places of military significance.

79 *A Canadian Gun Pit*, 1918. Oil on canvas, 304 x 363 cm. The National Gallery of Canada, Ottawa.
80 Lewis, *Blasting and Bombardiering*, p.170.

Both characteristics are evident in the largest painting he made during the war. *A Battery Shelled* was to be one of the seventeen super-pictures intended for the Hall of Remembrance. At a little over six feet by eleven its scale exactly mirrored the huge dimensions of Uccello's sixteenth-century masterpiece *The Rout of San Romano*, which was hanging in the National Gallery, London, and had been chosen by the British War Memorials Committee (along with the smaller *Surrender at Breda* by Diego Velasquez) as a template for the paintings that would line the walls of the proposed memorial building. Few models could have been more suited to Lewis's artistic temperament:

> Uccello's battle piece is a magnificent still-life, a pageant of armours, cloths, etc., the trappings and wardrobe of War, but in the line and spirit of it, as peaceable and bland as any tapestry representing a civic banquet could be. It does not borrow from the fact of war any emotion, any disturbing or dislocating violence, terror or compassion – any of the psychology that is proper to the events of War... The principal thing is that this is a purely inhuman picture, in the sense that the artist's attitude was that of the god for whom blood and death mean no more than bird's plumage and the scintillations of steel.[81]

Any artist who shared this aloof and cool demeanour, continued Lewis:

> ...would approach any disturbance or calamity with a child-like and unruffled curiosity and proceed to arrange Nissen huts, shell-bursts, elephants, commanding officers, aeroplanes, in patterns, just as he would proceed with flowers in a vase, or more delectable and peaceful objects.[82]

Dispassionate, organized, rather cold, Uccello's art appealed to Lewis's rationalizing frame of mind. It also somehow echoed the military practices that he had come to learn in the artillery: its insistence on measurement and control, the need for precision and shared order. Those, for example, who manned each of the four guns in a battery had an exactly prescribed role. Each of the gun crew had a number, each a particular function. The No.4 was the man who laid the gun; he established its proper position after each firing, while the No.2 actually fired it, jerking the lanyard to produce the series of detonations that caused the discharge.[83] This rigid organisational structure allowed the most efficient use of the team. It also ensured their safety, with each one knowing his designated place and role in the complex procedure of loading, firing and re-setting the massive

81 Lewis's Foreword to 'Guns', The Goupil Gallery, February 1919.
82 Lewis's Foreword to 'Guns', The Goupil Gallery, February 1919.

machines once they had juddered back into place. If gun drill is not strict, even stiff, wrote one ex-officer, 'men round the gun get hurt'.[84]

This may, in part, explain the physical appearance of many of the figures in Lewis's drawings, their cipher-like, near-robotic appearance, the way they work together in tightly choreographed groupings. Of course, he was not overly concerned with literal representation; the figure was a metaphor for far more wide-reaching notions about the human condition, their individual likenesses subservient to a broader set of ideas about the relationship of man to the machine. Lewis was clearly fascinated by the function of the gunner: captivated by his highly-disciplined role in the gun-team, which required singularity of purpose and exacting standards of behaviour, just as he was enthralled by his intense symbiotic rapport with the machine itself. There was something in the precise logic of the gun team that recalled Pound's earlier admiration of the compressed and economic power of the machine: 'its ability to perform its function with clean precision and without any emotionalism or fuss'.[85] Without reneging on the brief set by the Canadians, and later the British War Memorial Committee, Lewis was trying to present a complex set of ideas that concerned the plight of the individual caught up in a grotesque factory of war.[86]

And to do so Lewis had to turn his back on the near-total abstraction that he and his followers had embraced in 1913. It was not a comfortable transition but, for his own well-being, Lewis knew it had to be made. In 1950 he reflected on the reasons and offered a fuller rationalization:

> The war was a sleep, deep and animal in which I was visited by images of an order very new to me.... The Geometrics which had interested me so exclusively before, I now felt were bleak and empty. They wanted filling. They were still as much present in my mind as ever, but submerged in the coloured vegetation, the flesh and blood, that is life... War, and especially those miles of hideous desert known as 'the Line' in Flanders and France, presented me with a subject-matter

83 The gun layer had to go through a precise series of checks known as 'laying procedures', to ensure the weapon was on the proper firing azimuth, this was the angular distance along the horizon between a point of reference, usually the observer's bearing, and another object. Once the howitzer was reported 'laid', they were ready to fire rounds at a specified target.

A similar regime existed for large and smaller team weapons: a .303 Vickers Gun Team, for example, had six members, each with prescribed roles: 'Number One was leader and fired the gun, while Number Two controlled the entry of ammo belts into the feed-block. Number Three maintained a supply of ammo to Number Two, and Number Four to Six were reserves and carriers, but all the members of the team were fully trained in handling the gun.' George Coppard, from *With a Machine Gun to Cambrai* (London: Her Majesty's Stationery Office, 1980).

84 M.R.D. Foot, *Art and War* (London: Headline, 1990) p.67.

85 Richard Cork, 'What is Vorticism?' in Jane Farrington, *Wyndham Lewis*, p.25.

86 This idea is articulated in Catherine Wallace, 'Art for Posterity? The Commissioned War Art of Percy Wyndham Lewis', *Imperial War Museum Review*, pp.51–62, p.59.

> so consonant with the austerity of that 'abstract' vision I had developed, that it was an easy transition.[87]

A Battery Shelled is the fullest expression of these new ideas.[88] It depicts a battery position under enemy fire amidst geometrically-ruined buildings. Arranged around a semi-circular pit of gouged-up earth are dugouts, duckboards, piles of shells, and two guns heavily camouflaged with netting. In the centre of the painting, groups of semi-mechanized figures go about their grim business with a curious syncopated gait, while overhead tubular columns of smoke billow across a steel-grey sky. Surveying the busy scene are several black-clad figures in soft caps, who present three aspects of the human form. One stands full-face looking out of the frame. A second in three-quarter view, his hands stuck deep in his pockets. The third is seen in profile, his pipe-stem balanced on his chin, a striking silhouette against the arcs of orange and light-grey that dance and jig across the picture surface. Their studied indifference, their utter lack of interest in the events all round them, contrasts dramatically with the determined industriousness of the insect-like creatures gadding about in the pit below. There, the earth convulses in crests and waves of steely grey-blue 'water' rolling in and around the cipher-like gunners. Even the heavy guns appear to bob about precariously in the deep troughs of mud, while the triumvirate gaze out as though from the bridge of a ship.

It is a most perplexing painting. There is no obvious reason why the inscrutable demeanour of the black-clad figures should be so very different from the frantic dance of the orange stick-figures. Furthermore, Lewis seems to have deliberately muddled the spatial layout of the painting's composition; the geometrical plumes of smoke merge with the barrel of the cannon on the right-hand side; in the centre they float independently of the battery, and on the left the smoke segues into the stiff limbs of a shattered tree. The painting teeters on the edge of incoherence, a confused jumble that is compounded by its disjointed space and its dislocated narrative. But, somehow it works. *A Battery Shelled* is one of the major artworks of the Great War, bringing together in one enormous panorama the crazy contradictions that were part of the gunner's life: the bouts of wearying inactivity, the languid nonchalance affected by the officer-class, the endlessly rehearsed gun-drill that required exact precision and co-ordinated effort, but above all, the innate tragedy of the war portrayed so movingly in the 'tired and lifeless stare' of the figure looking out and away from the chaotic mess of the fighting.[89]

---

87 Lewis, *Rude Assignment* (London: Hutchinson, 1950) pp.128–129.

88 Lewis, *A Battery Shelled*, 1919. Oil on canvas, 182.7 x 317.7 cm. IWM:ART 2747.

It is also a *tour-de-force* of painting as a plastic art. Lewis manages rather effortlessly to combine two opposing pictorial styles: the geometricised abstraction of the tree-stalks, the convulsing wedges of mud, and the vortices of rusty smoke, with the literal representation of the three spectating figures. The geometrics have been 'filled' to make an impressive and legible work, yet as John Rothenstein realized, they still remain geometrics, and hardly affect the realism of the painting.[90] It is an impressive balancing act. Despite the strictures of the commission, Lewis has compromised nothing and, in not doing so, had created possibly the most radical statement of all the official war art schemes.

Lewis later regretted his part in the war, complaining that it had denied him four years of artistic growth. It had also effectively ended his *avant-garde* art movement, nipping Vorticism in the bud before it had a chance to flower, denying for decades a British dalliance with pure abstraction. Yet, decades after, he concluded it had not been all bad. 'In the long run,' he reflected, 'the War helped my career 'but it was a long run all right'.[91]

The last word – and some of the very best words in his electrifying war-memoir – has to be from Lewis himself, in his triple role of painter, polemicist and writer, telling the hair-raising tale of a tactical withdrawal at the height of the battle around Passchendaele.[92] As always, it is trenchant prose – evocative, poetic, even sublime:

> That evening we evacuated our pill-box under a perfect fusilade of shells. I lost my pipe as we went steeplechasing in and out of trenches. In the distance I turned to look back at this obnoxious death-trap, as one turns to look back at a mountain whose top one had just visited, once one is down below. The sunset had turned on its romantic dream-light and what had been romantic enough before was now absolutely operatic. A darkening ridge, above a drift of saharan steppe, gouged and tossed into a monotonous disorder, in a word the war-wilderness; not a flicker of life, not even a ration-party – not even a skeleton; and upon the ridge the congeries of 'bursts', to mark the spot where we had been. It was like the twitching of chicken after its head had been chopped off. We turned away from this brainless bustle, going on all by itself, about an empty concrete easter-egg. In a stupid desert.[93]

---

89 There is a sensitive appreciation of the painting by Catherine Wallace, *Wyndham Lewis: Art and War*, pp.38–41.

90 John Rothenstein's thoughts about Lewis's geometrics is contained in Jane Farrington, *Wyndham Lewis*, p.10.

91 'The War', recalled Lewis, 'had robbed me of four years, at the moment when, almost overnight, I had achieved the necessary notoriety to establish myself in London as a painter.' It also caught him before he felt he had considered his training. However, he also felt that 'the War' (Lewis always chose to capitalise it) was neither bad or good, 'because if it had not occurred I should certainly have wasted my time in a hundred ways'. (*Blasting and Bombardiering*, p.213)

92 It was Rothenstein who suggest that Lewis was a 'triple personality'.

93 Lewis, *Blasting and Bombardiering*, p.159.

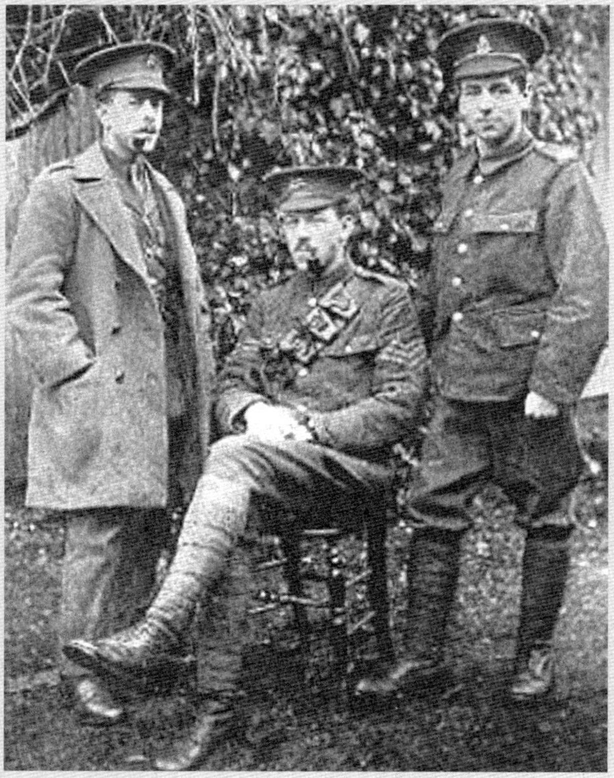

Three brothers (*left to right*):
Sydney, Percy and Stanley Spencer

Stanley Spencer
'A genius pitched in the mud'

THE 'FORGOTTEN FRONT'

Our visual register of the First World War is dominated by images of the Western Front: line after line of crude entrenchments stretching from the North Sea to the Alps and described by Wyndham Lewis as 'an epic of mud'. Many of the lasting images of the war were created by soldiers such as Nash, Owen and Sassoon who found an uncomfortable inspiration in the 'squelching mire' and noisome troglodyte world of dug-outs, heavy artillery and barbed wire.[1]

By comparison, the Mediterranean theatre of operations is regarded today – as, indeed, it was then – as a mere sideshow to the main event in north-west Europe. Although many have heard of the ill-fated Gallipoli campaign or the heroic escapades of T.E. Lawrence in the Middle East, few will know that the Allied forces were embroiled for many of the war years in northern Greece, preventing an aggressive Bulgarian army – steeled by German troops – from occupying the entire Balkan region.[2] An olden land of wild mountains, deep valleys and poor communications, it had been

---

1 'Epic of mud' was a term coined by the soldier-artist Percy Wyndham Lewis. See his *Blasting and Bombardiering, Autobiography 1914–1926* (London: Eyre & Spottiswoode, 1937).

2 Even in the most expansive histories of the war there are few if any references to 'Macedonia', 'Salonika', or 'Bulgaria'. In Jay Winter and Blaine Baggett's epic survey of the period *1914–1918: the Great War and the shaping of the 20th Century* (BBC, London, 1996) there is not a single mention of the Macedonian campaign. Earlier histories, such as S.L. Mayer and A.J.P. Taylor's *History of World War One* (London: Octopus, 1974) give a slightly more rounded view of the global conflict but, as many historians have suggested, the Western Front still dominates the historiography of the war.

fought over during the Balkan Wars of 1912 and an uneasy truce was held between the three neighbours – Bulgaria, Greece and Serbia – although all agreed that the city of Salonika should remain a free port. Of ancient Greek origin, nurtured under Ottoman rule, and populated by Turks, Greeks and Jews, the city's strategic importance lay in its location as the only sea outlet for Greek Macedonia, the fertile region sandwiched between the port and the Serbo-Bulgarian border some 40 miles to the north.[3]

On the eve of the Great War Salonika retained an Asiatic appearance, characterised by mosques and minarets, Byzantine churches and an air of exotic dilapidation. Outbreak of war convulsed the region. While Serbia sided with the French, the Bulgarians allied with the Germans. Greece chose to be neutral but its leaders remained divided, a state of affairs that further confused the complicated political allegiances in this volatile part of southern Europe. In 1915, having witnessed the collapse of the much-feared Imperial Russia, the Bulgarian army lent their considerable weight to the Austro-Hungarian forces attacking Serbia by sweeping through its army's weakened eastern flank. As the Serbs retreated, they invoked their promised support from France, who in turn demanded military input from a rather reluctant British government. In response, two brigades of British and French regular troops landed in Macedonia, having been offered the use of Salonika by the Greek government. But just as they disembarked that October, the Greek cabinet collapsed and the new government proved less amenable to the compromising of Greek neutrality. In any case, the Allied support came too late. Advancing south, massed Bulgar forces had already routed the Serbian army, wreaking slaughter and chaos, forcing them back through neutral Albania and into exile on Corfu. Some 200,000 Serb soldiers perished in the severe winter snows. With their collapse, the small French and British force had to fall back on the port to spend many idle months behind a deep defensive bastion around Salonika, a line so dense with wire it became known as 'the birdcage'.[4]

While the rampant Bulgarian army dug into strong positions in the mountain ridges that lined the Greek frontier, the allied governments assembled a multi-national – some called it 'motley'

3 Salonika was named after Thessaloniki, Philip of Macedon's daughter and Alexander the Great's half-sister, and founded in the fourth century BC to commemorate Philip's triumph over Thessaly and Greece. It thrived as a port because it was perfectly situated for trade between the Mediterranean and the Balkans, between Europe and Asia, and enjoyed a prominence in Roman times. Later, the city stood alongside Constantinople as a bastion of Byzantium's orthodoxy. After the First Balkan War, in 1912, Greece reclaimed her from the Ottoman Empire. Today – as Thessalonika – she is Greece's second city. See Mark Mazower, *Salonika: City of Ghosts* (London: Harper Collins, 2004).

4 The 'Birdcage' was described, rather facetiously, by the Germans as the greatest internment camp in Europe.

– contingent of reinforcements from France, Britain, Italy, India, and even Russia. They took up position across the width of the peninsula, establishing a front that ran roughly along the northern frontier of present-day Greece.

British forces held the eastern section of this arc, a sector of some thirty miles bounded at each end by two mighty rivers, the Struma and the Vardar. Rising sharply above them was the Kerkini mountain range, dominated by two peaks, the Grand and Petit Couronnes, which formed both an impressive obstacle and an impassable military stronghold. Dug deep into its ravines and promontories were the well-equipped Bulgarian and German troops. They enjoyed an uninterrupted view of the British trenches and gun emplacements strung out along the malarial valleys far below.

100066 PRIVATE SPENCER S, ORDERLY RAMC

Stanley Spencer was twenty-three years old at the outbreak of war. One of the golden generation that had graduated from the Slade School of Art in London, the boyish-looking painter would become famous (and occasionally infamous) for two things in his intense and rather complicated life: the celebration and immortalisation of his home town of Cookham – his 'heaven on earth' as he lovingly called it – and the fusion in his paintings of sex and religion, love and dirt, the heavenly and the ordinary.[5]

Spencer's visionary imagination was realised through many hundreds of paintings, drawings and thousands of letters. They exposed a complex understanding of his world and an unrivalled ability to transform the menial and the banal into intense images of joyous delight. Through hundreds of highly-wrought narrative images Spencer transformed Cookham into a visionary paradise where everything was imbued with the utmost importance whether it be 'a conversation in the grocer's shop' or the idea that Christ might once have carried His cross through its streets. Cookham became a whole world in miniature where he and his family and neighbours would daily rub shoulders with Old Testament figures, and where it seemed entirely appropriate that the Resurrection should take place in its churchyard.

It took an extraordinary individual to create such visions and there was little about Spencer that was ordinary. In appearance he was somewhat unprepossessing. His brother, Gilbert, described him at the Slade School as 'boyish, being little more than five feet tall,

5 Kenneth Pople, *Stanley Spencer: a biography* (London: Collins, 1991); Fiona MacCarthy, *Stanley Spencer: an English Vision* (New Haven and London, 1997); Kitty Hauser, *Stanley Spencer* (London: Tate, 2001). See also the short essay 'Brother Stan', reprinted as an appendix in *Gilbert Spencer R.A.: Memoirs of a Painter* (London: Chatto and Windus, 1974) pp.219–221.

wearing Norfolk jacket, Eton collar, jersey, breeches and long stockings. His youthful image was emphasised by his tousled black hair, fresh, rosy complexion and general untidiness'.[6] So acute was his unworldliness that he had at first to be accompanied to the Slade by his father until he gained enough confidence to travel alone. He was particularly perturbed by the prospect of crossing the Euston Road. Once inside the art school, he promptly earned the nickname 'Cookham' for his incessant high-pitched chatter about his home town, and just as quickly gained a reputation as a draughtsman of extraordinary skill, winning many of the School's drawing and composition prizes and he left in 1912 in 'a blaze of glory'.[7] Gregarious, magnetic and engaging in the right company, Spencer sought out and attracted a succession of mentors and patrons. The painter Henry Lamb was one such individual who would play an important part in Spencer's war. Eight years older than Spencer, Lamb assumed the role of worldly patron to Spencer's 'provincial innocent', the sun to Spencer's planet.[8] At first both basked in the relationship, although over time Lamb developed an ambivalent view of the younger man's complex personality, ever admiring the painter but at times wary of his peppery side, and increasingly irritated by his obsessive pre-occupations with his complex domestic and personal circumstances. Like many of the older men that Spencer would seek out and befriend during the course of his adulthood, Lamb was a remarkably tolerant and enabling patron, offering money, advice, accommodation and professional support that was not always appreciated, or even acknowledged, by Spencer. Despite his effusive charm, Spencer's company was often exhausting, the endless self-referential chatter (to say nothing of his 'unblinking candour')[9] made him a wearying – although always engaging, if sometimes prickly – companion, and Lamb failed twice to finish a portrait of the younger artist largely on account of Spencer's inability to sit still and stop talking.

6 Richard Carline; 'Stanley Spencer: his personality and mode of life', in *Stanley Spencer R.A.*, Royal Academy, 1980, p.11. This story is also told in Gilbert Spencer, *Stanley Spencer by his brother Gilbert* (London: Gollancz, 1961) p.107, reprinted, Bristol: Redcliffe Press, 1991; and cited in Maurice Collis, *Stanley Spencer* (London: Harvill Press, 1962) pp.37–38.

7 Maurice Collis, *Stanley Spencer*, p.39. Spencer won the Melville Nettleship Prize at the Slade which was awarded for figure compositions. William Roberts was also a prizewinner.

8 Stanley Spencer to Henry Lamb in 1919, quoted in Keith Clements, *Henry Lamb: the Artist and his Friends* (Bristol: Redcliffe Press, 1985) p.214. After his first visit to meet Henry Lamb, Stanley wrote to the Raverats, 'I like him & do not feel him to be a low worm. I do not think his work is interesting except sometimes.' (15 December 1913, Tate Gallery Archive [TGA] 8116.32).

9 This phrase is Ken Pople's, who has a fine and sympathetic reading of Spencer's complex character. Author's conversations with Ken Pople, 2004–05. Lamb's biographer, Keith Clements, has little time for Stanley's egocentricity. 'On the surface [Stanley] seemed content to be subservient, but his subservience was manipulative and masked an astonishing determination and near arrogance: qualities that contributed greatly to the power and extent of his output as a painter but rather detracted from his personal relations.' Keith Clements, *Henry Lamb: the Artist and his Friends*, p.214.

LEAVING COOKHAM
July 1915

In 1915, having slept virtually every night of his twenty-four years under the same roof, Spencer left the 'pullulating bosom' of Fernlea, his protective homestead on the High Street, to serve first as a medical orderly in a converted asylum in Bristol, and then as part of a Field Ambulance Unit on the Macedonia Front. Spencer served on the British sector until the Armistice, joining an infantry regiment in the latter stages of the war. Some seven years later Spencer translated his war experience into an extraordinary series of murals on the painted walls of a private memorial chapel in Hampshire, southern England. It is perhaps the most complete memorial to peace and redemption ever completed in the aftermath of the First World War. There is nothing like it anywhere in northern Europe. Across the painted walls of the chapel, three tiers of images depict his tedious duties as a medical orderly in Bristol; his field ambulance work near Salonika, and then on a vast end wall – some five metres wide by eight metres high – an epic panorama of recovery and redemption, the 'Resurrection of the Soldiers'. For nine months Spencer toiled on this wall, his small, tweed-suited figure lost high amongst the scaffolding in the dozens of painted Spencer-esque figures. After the chapel was opened in 1932 a visitor was heard to exclaim: 'My dear, the Resurrection is not in the least like that!'[10] They were wrong. Spencer's idea of resurrection was not one of judgment, or of the revival of the dead, or the re-appearance of Christ. Instead, it embraced the more holistic idea of the Resurrection of the body and the mind. Spencer's social background and his concern for the 'common man' (and woman) meant that his interest lay in an egalitarian and inclusive notion of the body, one that was indifferent to social hierarchy and ignorant of external trappings and trophies of wealth and position. In Spencer's mind, the Oratory at Burghclere was not a resurrection solely of the dead, nor for that matter a resurrection merely of the soul, rather it was 'resurrections of his state of mind at different times'.[11] It was a time of 'release & change' whereby even the mules & the tortoises enjoy redemption, a re-finding of themselves from their earthly experiences, and an opportunity to return what is now no longer needed. Freshly resurrected, the soldiers emerge from the untroubled earth and hand back their crosses to the tiny Christ figure, just as they once returned their blankets and trench coats to the Quarter-Master Sergeant.

---

10 Quoted in George Behrend 1965. For a full account of the Burghclere chapel see Paul Gough, *Stanley Spencer: Journey to Burghclere* (Bristol: Sansom, 2006).

11 Adrian Glew (ed.) *Stanley Spencer: Letters and Writings* (London: Tate Publishing, 2001).

LEAVING BRISTOL
May 1916

Spencer felt trapped in Bristol. His ten months in the Beaufort Military Hospital felt like a prison sentence. Its rough camaraderie and brutal regime shattered the stillness and unity of his enclosed world, but, ironically, also stimulated the enquiring and curious side of his mind that had remained dormant until that moment. In his eighty-eight notebooks, his thirteen diaries and nearly one thousand extended pieces of reflective prose, Spencer often ruminated on the impact of the 'Beaufort' on his subsequent career as an artist. Sometimes he remembered the hospital fondly, especially after dark 'with the feeling of night, night, slippers, go quietly, terrible operations, uncanny supernatural atmosphere'. Other times he remembered the hospital as a vile, degrading place where the 'utterly selfish spirit' of his fellow-orderlies made him 'wild'.[12] It was some small comfort that his brother, Gilbert, served as an orderly in the same institution, and on occasion he was able to visit newly made friends, such as Desmond Chute, in the city of Bristol: friends who would exert a powerful influence on his thinking about art, religion and the imagination.

Gilbert had described the asylum as a place where 'anything less likely to provoke creative art would be impossible to imagine',[13] but Spencer's status as an 'artist' became public knowledge in late 1915 when his name appeared in the national press. Scrubbing the floor of the hospital dispensary one morning he was cornered by a one-legged Gallipoli veteran who demanded to know if this slight, scrubbing figure were the same 'Stanley Spencer' so lavishly praised in the newspaper – *The Times* – that he was dangling in front of his nose and demanding, 'Is that you, you little devil?'[14]

Spencer was rightly astonished. He had no idea that his paintings, amongst them *The Centurion's Servant* which had been selected by Tonks for the New English Art Club autumn show in London, would be so well received. As he later wrote, 'I had almost forgotten my fading past. It made a strange impression on me'.[15] So remarkable

---

12 Spencer, TGA 8116.58. Stanley to the Raverats, August (?) 1915, TGA 8116.55. Stanley first made a record of his war experience in 1919 (TGA 733.3.28). This draft formed the basis of a notebook written as he developed his ideas for the Oratory at Burghclere. (TGA 733.3.84). This notebook was typed up in 1948 (TGA 733.3.85). A section was later added to this typescript (TGA 733.3.128).

13 Spencer, Gilbert, *Stanley Spencer by his brother Gilbert* (London, Gollancz, 1961; reprinted, Bristol: Redcliffe Press, 1991) p.136.

14 Spencer, Reminiscences, Glasgow 1945–47, TGA 733.3.86. Spencer recorded the episode with the Gallipoli veteran in a letter to Sir William Rothenstein written but never posted in May 1938. 'I had been a Tommy for nearly six months then, so that a reminder of my former life came like an apparition of myself. I have often felt how much that little notice meant to me right through the war.' (cited in Collis, *Stanley Spencer*, pp.46–47)

15 TGA 733.3.86. Tonks later acknowledged Spencer as 'having the most original mind of anyone we have had at the Slade and he combines it with great powers of draughtsmanship'. Cited by Andrew Causey, 'Stanley Spencer and the Art of his Time', in *Stanley Spencer RA*, catalogue of the Royal Academy Exhibition, 1980, p.23.

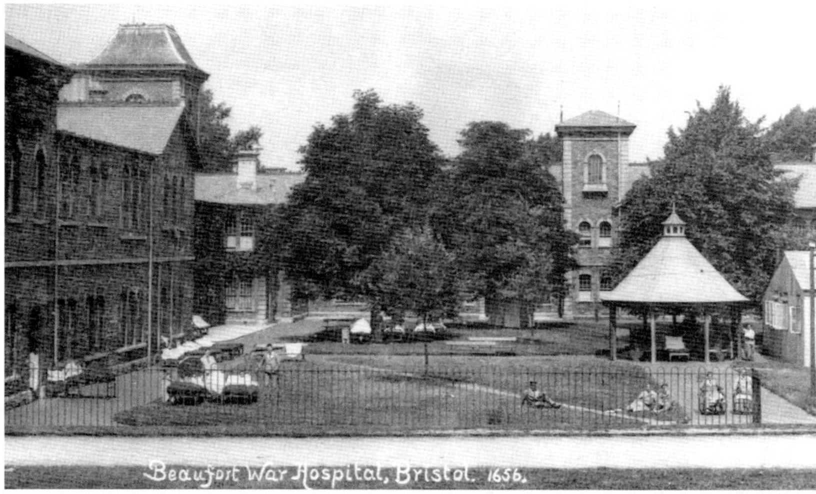

Beaufort Military Hospital, Bristol

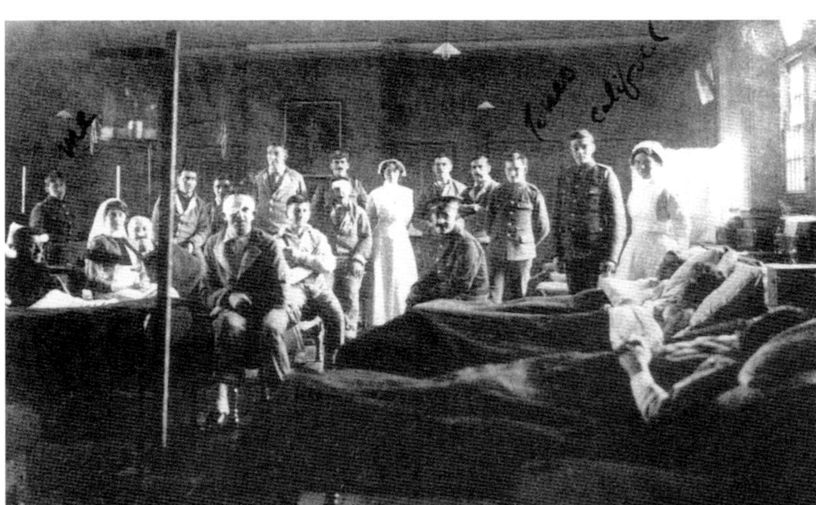

A medical ward at the Beaufort Military Hospital, c.1915
(Stanley Spencer marked up on left as 'me')

was this revelation amongst his comrades that the news quickly spread the length of the vast hospital. The effect was extraordinary:

> The matron, a tall gaunt creature before whom Queen Mary looked quite a crumpled thing, came down the ward with a veritable sheaf of dailies under her arm determined to track down this great unknown. Even she looked a little less grim and gaunt. These notices were very welcome to me. I had been terribly crushed. They gave rise to such teasing remarks from the Sisters as, 'When are you going to get that commission, orderly?' having scented I was a bit different, or thought I was.[16]

As his reputation as a 'famous artist' spread around the Beaufort, Spencer was asked to draw his fellow orderlies and patients. Few drawings have survived, he gave most of them away, and he felt rather rusty at first. Even on overseas and active service he would be pestered for drawings. He was glad to oblige:

> I do anything for these men. I do not know why but I cannot refuse them anything & they love me to make drawings of photos of their wives & children or a brother who has been killed. A diary of a man who was killed chronicled the weather day after day & as you read these monosyllables it gives you an intensely dramatic feeling.[17]

However, there was little relief from the grinding routine of the hospital and Spencer applied for overseas service in late autumn 1915, but it was not until mid-May the following year that he finally left Bristol. At short notice, the small draft of volunteers left the Beaufort on 12 May 1916 just as the British Expeditionary Force in France approached the final stages in its preparation for the 'big push' – the offensive on the Somme planned for late June. Spencer swept the ward out for the final time with his ward chum George Saunders. 'I felt a bit sad,' wrote Spencer to Desmond Chute, 'Poor old George was so upset.'[18]

MACEDONIA
'Just like being in the Bible'

After the carbolic grimness of the military hospital, Spencer was stunned by the sights he saw from the troopship as it steamed up the

---

16 Spencer, TGA 733.3.85. This is Spencer's only mention of the royal visit of September 1915, a visit that was a highlight for most at the hospital, but only a sideshow for the painter.

17 Chute correspondence, Stanley Spencer Gallery, Cookham.

18 Spencer to Chute, 13 May 1916, Stanley Spencer Gallery, Cookham. George Saunders was one of the inmates who earned an occasional penny from the hospital orderlies for undertaking menial tasks such as boot-polishing.

Mediterranean. 'It makes me tremble down in my inside,' he wrote, 'every time I look at yonder coast.' His letters teem with exotic sights; of great sandy mounds on the Tunisian seaboard, a coastline dotted with white buildings that seemed to be palaces or mosques, and peculiarly shaped hills 'like the wrinkles on the back of a bullock's neck – most wonderful'.[19] In another he described the view of the coast off Algeria as mysterious: 'It was just like being in the Bible. Now it is a white ghost-like sea with a dark dusky blue horizon which clears towards the top & the mountain tops appear above'.[20] At some point in the Mediterranean, he and his brother Gilbert 'dipped flags' when their ships passed on their separate ways as Gilbert sailed off to join the Expeditionary Force in Egypt.

However, by the time the troopship arrived in the Gulf of Salonika, the troops were lethargic, morale was low and military discipline had to be firmly re-enforced. 'The sergeants,' noted Spencer, 'seemed to find their voices again'. Upon disembarkation he found himself parted from the last contact with Bristol when he and a musician friend Lionel Budden were marched off to different camps. He noted wryly that 'because of the laws of the army one of which is 'tallest on the right, shortest on the left' in single rank size we were separated beyond all hope. It was our only difference. So we were marched off to different camps. We grinned as we solemnly marched past to our several destinies...'[21]

Spencer's destiny turned out to be eighteen months of hard labour with the field ambulance. During this time, to judge from his copious letters to Chute and to his sister Florence, his tasks had little to do with administering medical aid; they were mostly menial in character – carrying, lifting and fetching. Accustomed to the vagaries of service life, Spencer was not unduly disappointed, though perhaps a little nonplussed at the turn of events. Thirty years later he remembered how he had lain out under the stars on a hillside in Macedonia ruminating on his decision to join the medical corps:

> When at Bristol... I thought in a dreamlike way of the life in field ambulance. The word 'field' had a nice unhospitally sound, & ambulance suggested cart wheels & possible shouldering thereof. It was outdoors & there might be patches of it here & there pretty free & unmilitarised. But these were romantic pictures in my bed pan fetching mind. Impossible romanticising...[22]

Spencer left the depot after only a few days and found himself posted not to a field hospital but up the line to the Doiran Sector as part of

19 Chute correspondence, Stanley Spencer Gallery, Cookham.
20 Spencer to the Raverats, probably September 1916, TGA 8116.62.
21 Spencer, Notebook 1945–47, TGA 733.3.86.

a detachment heading for the 68th Field Ambulance. A twenty-mile train journey took him to the rail-head at Karasuli, a village lodged between two large lakes. Spencer was transfixed by what he saw. He wrote later of being enraptured by the landscape: its unusual, but strangely familiar, colours, the peculiar light and visual incident, the whitewashed buildings, solitary peasants, the goats and donkeys, tall cypresses and deep ravines. The total effect seemed to bring into unexpected reality everything he had so cherished in the early Italian paintings that he studied so earnestly at the Slade. It was as if the visions of his youth had become fact; his imagined Biblical landscapes had found their proper Renaissance setting. The impact was profound.

> I sat on the wooden seats [of the troop train from Lembet] & was entranced by the landscapes from the window. Low plains with trees & looking through trees to strange further plains, or fields, & here & there a figure in dirty white. It was not landscape; it was a spiritual world.[23]

THE ATTACK ON 'MACHINE GUN HILL'
September 1916

Travelling by foot and ox-cart the small section of RAMC men ventured up the line along the narrow supply road which hugged the line of hills by Lake Ardzan. Spencer grew to cherish this track, likening it to a favourite walk near his home in Cookham, and declaring that each step was 'a part of my soul. When I think of the places along it and the different parts of this continuous hillside, for me to describe them is to describe something of myself'.[24]

After a few weeks his unit moved from the village of Corsica (a rough Anglicisation of 'Chaushitsa') nearer the line to Kalinova

---

22 Spencer, TGA 733.3.86. Spencer's field ambulance unit was part of the 22nd Division, a New Army Division (made up of three brigades: 65th, 66th, and 67th) that had crossed to France in September 1915, but in October had embarked for Salonika. It remained in the theatre for the rest of the war. Spencer's unit, the 68th Field Ambulance had been one of the few British units involved in the Retreat from Serbia in December 1915. In addition to divisional engineers and artillery, the Division had two other Field Ambulance Units, the 66th (to which Spencer was later transferred) and the 67th. 22nd Division troops were involved in four battles: Horseshoe Hill (10–18 August 1916); Machukovo (13–14 September 1916); Doiran (24–25 April, and 8–9 May 1917); and the Battle of Doiran 18–19 September 1918. An Armistice with Bulgaria was signed on 30 September 1918, and the Division ceased to exist by the end of March 1919. The Official History records that the Division suffered casualties of 7,728 killed, wounded and missing.

23 Spencer, Notebook 1945–47, TGA 733.3.86. Ken Pople brilliantly captures Spencer's sense of being transported to the quattrocento (see Ken Pople, *Stanley Spencer*, p.132). Spencer noted that Mount Olympus, to the south of his first encampment, dominated the prospect from Salonika. He described how it emerged from a five-day seaborne sandstorm: 'As the sun rose, it was grand, ... in shape rather symmetrical, a sort of wounded eagle shape, wings out and flopping on the ground. In the centre, just a small peak and the great shoulders reaching out either side; there were one or two stratas of mist that obscured the base; the upper bands were a pale emerald green, then blue-red and then the main widest band was magenta of a warmish tinge...' Underestimating its distance from the city, Gilbert Spencer actually tried to walk to Olympus (Gilbert Spencer, *Stanley Spencer*, Redcliffe, Bristol, 1991).

24 Spencer, Notebook 1945–47, TGA 733.3.86.

– by now little more than the uninhabited shell of a Greco-Turkish village destroyed in the Balkan Wars.[25] From here he was to be pitched into the assault on a notorious vantage point known to the British as 'Machine Gun Hill'. The aim of the attack was to deprive the enemy of their observation posts overlooking the French sector west of Vardar, and to occupy the German front-line that dominated the high ground. Success would transform the British front-line along the Karasuli-Kalinova Ridge into a much-needed reserve line of defence. However, much of the land to be fought over was tough, impenetrable scrub that looked green and lush from a distance, but was in fact thick with low thorny bushes that concealed deep gullies, dried-up water-courses and razor-edged stone ridges.

British commander General Milne chose the moonlit night of 13 and 14 September 1916 for the assault. Support units – including Spencer's 68th Field Ambulance – were moved west a few kilometres to take shelter behind the ridge just behind the front line. Assault battalions – drawn from Liverpool (King's Own) and Lancashire regiments – protected on the left flank by Welch Fusiliers, succeeded in climbing through steep ravines and routing the German infantry. By early morning Machine Gun Hill had been captured. However, although the Allies also took the Serbian town of Monastir, they failed to fully penetrate the strong Bulgarian and German defences, and the hill was lost the following day to overwhelming counter-attacks.[26]

It was Spencer's first experience of battle. His orders were to help evacuate the British wounded to the dressing station in the abandoned village of Smol about two thousand yards behind the front line. Usually by night, he had to accompany stretcher-bearer parties of some ten or twenty orderlies into the Sedemli Ravine, one of many river-beds cut into the face of the hills north of Kalinova. There, they would meet the regimental stretcher-bearers who brought down casualties from the front-line, a routine that was accompanied by a curious 'clanging sound' like bars of steel being knocked together.[27] Spencer's first task was to transfer these casualties from hand-held stretchers to the mule-drawn 'travoys' that would become his everyday companions during his period with the RAMC. This rather cumbersome activity would be memorably recorded in a drawing of travoys traipsing along the Sedemli Ravine that was made from memory in 1919.[28] The travoy, or *travoi* (to use its proper

25 The names of most of the places Spencer knew have changed: Salonika is now Thessalonika; the River Vardar is now the Axios; Karsuli is Polikastro; Sidemli as it was known to British forces, was actually Chidemli, and is now Metamorfosi; Smol: Mikro Dasos; 'Corsica': Chaushitsa; 'Basili': Bajirli; 'Kil-Kut', where Spencer met up with Henry Lamb, was probably Kilkush, now called Kilis.

26 According to the Official History, 70 Germans were taken prisoner and nine machine guns destroyed during the attack on the position. British losses – killed, wounded or captured – were 586 men.

27 Spencer, Notebook 1945–47; TGA 733.3.86.

28 See *Travoys passing Up Sedemli Ravine on the Way to Le Naze*, 1918, pencil and wash, 22 x 26 cm. IWM:ART 3878; and *Stretcher-bearers, Macedonia*, 1918, 22.4 x 15 cm. IWM:ART 3879.

French designation) was a form of mountain sledge, a mule-drawn contraption comprising two wooden shafts steel-tipped at one end, onto which precarious frame was strapped the canvas stretcher – hence the 'clanging sound' of grinding steel. As a consequence of this controlled dragging, which was both uncomfortable and ungainly, the casualty invariably slid to the foot of the stretcher, jolted there by the treacherous conditions of the tracks and by the vagaries of the mule, which was led by an Army Service Corps driver. Spencer's only option was to support the casualty by gripping him under the armpits, but his short stature made this an exhausting method and it did not always prevent the invalid from being pitched headlong into the stony ground.[29]

As orderly, Spencer's role was much less glamorous than that of the regimental stretcher-bearers. With their 'SB' brassard, bearers had invariably volunteered for front-line duties in search of a more varied life than that of orderly. SBs were excused fatigues, were exempted from some of the more petty aspects of military authority, and often lived apart in relative comfort when out of the line. However, their work was quite often dangerous, and there were only thirty-two stretcher-bearers for every one thousand front-line soldiers. One senior officer is reputed to have remarked that had he thousands of Victoria Crosses to distribute, 'all would go to stretcher-bearers'.[30] By contrast Spencer's accomplishments went largely unrecognised, his most testing moments were spent trying to prevent the wounded soldiers from spilling out of the sagging and unwieldy travoys, a task ill-suited to his diminutive frame. The obstinacy and unpredictability of the mules caused untold annoyance. He often complained that his arms used to ache while trying to pull them around to prevent them from lying down and falling into a deep (and rather unmilitary) slumber.

For so many of those who toiled behind the front-lines, military life was primarily an intensification of industrialised shiftwork; a matter of loading and unloading, fetching and carrying; 'Before the battle, shells; after, stretchers.'[31] To compound this labour, every piece of equipment was heavy: iron plate, rough hewn wood, unwieldy canvas, and inflexible khaki greatcoats. Rather miraculously, in his subsequent drawings and paintings Spencer managed to lighten the load of the past, to transform the malarial grubbiness of the Salonika campaign into something more poetic and spiritual.

---

29 There were other variations on the 'travoy': the 'doolie' required the shafts to be slung between two mules, and was used to overcome marshy ground. The cacolet (or 'cacklet' as the British troops called it) was a sort of chair slung either side of the mule in a rather haphazard, even hazardous, fashion. Spencer depicted this type in one of the arched panels at Burghclere.

30 See Denis Winter, *Death's Men* (London: Penguin, 1978) p.196.

31 As Geoff Dyer suggests 'Things get lighter over time. The future may not be better than the past but it will certainly be lighter. Hence the burden, the *weight* of the past'. Geoff Dyer, *The Missing of the Somme* (London: Penguin, 1994) p.60.

No.418112, PRIVATE SPENCER
C Company, 7 Royal Berkshire Regiment, Macedonia, October 1917

Spencer changed units several times during his service with the RAMC in Salonika. Such changes – brought about by periods of illness and hospitalisation – were unwelcome to most soldiers; friends were lost, equipment displaced, rations refused. It caused Spencer real distress: he was highly dependent on familiar routines and any sudden change disoriented and troubled him. In December 1916, barely two months since arriving in Salonika, he had to spend a short period in a field hospital, from whence he was posted to a different ambulance unit. By March 1917, he was again in hospital with a recurrence of malaria bought on when nasal catarrh developed into bronchitis. Upon his release he was again posted to a different unit, the newly formed 143rd Field Ambulance, where his role seemed to be little more than to 'round up mules, young ones, fresh, alert eared, that were here & there breaking away & striking out on their own'.[32] Although Spencer's untested unit had been sent to a relatively quiet part of the front it was not easy or safe work: on one occasion they came under artillery fire and he witnessed the extraordinary sight of a sun-lit rose bush pulverised into a cloud of dust by the direct hit of a 'dud' shell.

Meanwhile, the war trundled on. Despite courageous efforts by British assault troops – including a desperate attack by Spencer's county regiment, the 7th Royal Berkshires – the 'spring offensive' was a failure and the opposing lines congealed. A long and uncomfortably hot summer beckoned. Spencer's reputation for being 'artistic' earned him the dubious privilege while with the 143rd at Todorova, of decorating the doors of the latrines. He was required to paint the letters that indicated the men's and the sergeants' cubicles, and he 'tried his magic' by marking the latter with a 'big letter S for Sergeants & painted some dog roses round it'.[33]

It was here at a place called Kil-Kut that Spencer eventually caught up with Henry Lamb, then a captain in the 30th Field Ambulance who was stationed nearby. It was a momentous reunion with his

32 Spencer to the Raverats, TGA 8116.61.

33 Spencer, Notebook, 1945–47, TGA 733.3.86.

34 Spencer to Florence, 2 September 1917, TGA 733.1.756. After withdrawing his name from military service in late August 1914, on account of a troublesome pile condition, Lamb trained in medicine at Guy's Hospital, working overseas in France in early 1915 and then enlisting under the Lord Derby recruiting scheme in the summer of 1915, eventually reading for the lowest medical qualification to gain a temporary commission in the Royal Army Medical Corps. In August 1916 he was commissioned as a subaltern in the special reserve of the RAMC and posted with the Northumbrian Field Ambulance to Macedonia. In late 1917 he was transferred to the 30th Field Ambulance, attached to the 5th Royal Inniskilling Fusiliers, and later posted to Palestine, and then in May 1918, via Egypt to France where he won the Military Cross for conspicuous gallantry for removing wounded while under heavy shellfire. He was gassed in October 1918 and recuperated in London until demobilisation as unfit for further service in early 1919. He was then aged thirty-six.

friend and mentor, 'like coming across a cool running stream after a hot day's march'.[34] Here, perhaps, Spencer expressed his disillusion with the Field Ambulance, and soon after the meeting he decided to quit the medics. In August 1917, spurred on by notices displayed at Mirova Camp asking for volunteers to join the somewhat denuded infantry, he put his name forward for transfer to the 7th Battalion, Royal Berkshires. His transfer was confirmed in October 1917. Spencer embarked on the second phase of his personal trinity – medical orderly, soldier, patient – and this phase would definitely be the most hazardous.[35]

Spencer saw out the war with the infantry, as 418112 Private Spencer, C Company, 7 Royal Berkshire Regiment. He manned outposts, went on the occasional patrol, and was marched hither and thither with often no idea why or where he was being sent. By day he performed the menial tasks so fittingly known as 'fatigues'; a daily grind of carrying, fetching and humping provisions and siege-equipment, but at all times keeping low and concealed; by night he set off for the outposts – 'new moon-shaped ruts in the ground' – and patrolled the wire. It was hazardous but often quite thrilling work: 'We formed up, in the evening just before sunset, outside the dugouts... taking two bombs each from a box as we did so. It was always suspected by the Bulgars as being the time to start a barrage... The shells dropped uncomfortably near and I was glad when... getting to the outposts, we were able to take cover in a communication trench.'[36]

Hazards lay everywhere. On one occasion when moving up the line, Spencer chose – quite properly – to avoid the exposed position of a high ridge and slipped down the banks of a gently sloping ravine, only to find himself entangled in a mass of barbed wire that he had not spotted. 'I had to extricate myself very carefully and not get flustered and the feeling of being caught in every way was alarming.' A memory of this incident would find its place on to the end wall at the Oratory at Burghclere, with one of the central figures cocooned in a fine mesh of coiled wire.[37] Throughout this period, discomfort

---

35 During the spring offensive of April 1917, the British forces – by then massed in considerable force of two corps – attacked with three Divisions (the 22nd, 26th and 60th) around Doiran and on the Vardar as a diversion from the main Franco-Serb attack further west. Both attacks failed. Although a stalemate set in, British troops in the Struma Valley adopted highly mobile forms of disruptive action using cyclists, cavalry and foot patrols to deny the Bulgars and Turks a foothold in any of the villages and strongholds. However, both armies usually evacuated the valley in the summer, owing to the prevalence of disease. 10th Division historians record that during a two-week period in the previous autumn (30 September to 10 October) hospital admissions for wounded were 836 and 554 for illness, usually related to malaria.

Spencer's decision to join the infantry may have had an ulterior motive. He may have guessed that front-line soldiers would be demobilised before support troops, but his primary motivation was a spiritual one: he craved the familiar landscape and ambience of the Vardar Hills where he had heard that the Berkshires were posted.

36 Spencer, numbered writings 1936, TGA 733.2.25.

37 Another member of Spencer's unit commented drily, 'You'll get yourself into trouble' in Richard Carline, *Stanley Spencer at War*, p.94, and numbered writings 1936, TGA 733.2.25.

and danger seemed to be omnipresent. Even tea-time, when his section were provided with a dixie of tea and a portion of bread – an occasion that he usually savoured for its feelings of happiness and rest – became associated with 'a terrible sinking feeling and loss of spirits' because it was immediately after this that the men had to 'stand-to' outside the dug-outs and 'then the going into the outposts'. Of another dangerous task – attaching a piece of ribbon-wire to the Bulgars' defences – Spencer dryly commented that it was 'a job about which one could say nothing polite at all'.[38]

The absolute nadir of his war service came on the eve of a night-attack to clear the Bulgars from entrenched positions on the Dorian Front. It was to be a frontal assault on 'Pip Ridge', a 2,000-feet high, heavily defended mountain with fortresses built on some of its higher peaks. Having been ordered forward with his unit, Spencer's anxieties reached a new pitch as he steadied himself for his first battle. Then, at the last minute the Berkshires were stood down and relieved by troops from the Oxford and Bucks Light Infantry. Overwhelmed with relief, Spencer and his platoon returned to their start position, only to be inexplicably ordered back up the front line later that night. 'With a ton weight on my spirit,' he dragged himself forward, 'and it was horrible as I approached to hear the infernal shouting of orders'.[39]

The reason for this sudden reverse of fortunes was soon obvious. Losses on the opening morning of the attack had been appalling: in the British sector alone some 160 officers and 3,000 men had been killed, wounded or taken prisoner within the first 48 hours. One battalion – the 12th Cheshires – is said to have simply disappeared, while another, the 7th South Wales Borderers, could only muster one officer and eight other ranks at the end of the battle. As one embittered veteran wrote some twenty years later: 'The very name of the battle is unknown to most. Yet, in singularity of horror and in tragedy of defeated heroism, it is unique among the records of British arms':

> Imagine, if you can, what it means to fight up a hillside under a deadly fire, wearing a hot mask over your face, dimly staring through a pair of clouded goggles, and sucking the end of a rubber nozzle in your mouth. At the same time heat is pouring down on you from a brazen sky. In this plight you are called on to endure the blast of machine-gun fire, the pointed steel or bursting shell of the enemy. Nor are you called on to endure alone; you must vigorously fire back, and vigorously assail with

38 Spencer, numbered writings, 1936, TGA 733.2.25.

39 The offensive on the Vardar Front began on 1 September 1918, but was delayed on the British sector until the 18th of that month, as they faced the best of the Bulgarian troops and some of the strongest fortified positions.

> your own bayonet. It is as much like hell as anything you can think of. Welch Fusiliers got as far as the Hilt, only half a mile below the central fortress, before being driven back by a fierce Bulgarian charge. Every officer was killed or wounded.[40]

Struggling to maintain any momentum, all British infantry were pressed into service. The Berkshires had to set off immediately, marching from three in the afternoon until midnight, halting at the familiar Sedemli Ravine, and then warned to be ready to move to the 'start line' at two in the morning. By extraordinary coincidence it was during a short rest that night that letters from home were distributed and Spencer received a note from one of his dearest friends in England, Gwen Raverat, congratulating him on his appointment as an Official War Artist – a vague possibility that had been mentioned months earlier but which Spencer assumed had come to nothing. His bewilderment was soon interrupted by fresh orders; instructed to tear up the letters, he was told to carry an additional bandolier of fifty rounds just as he learned that the last British attack had caused a thousand casualties.[41] Spencer's moment of reckoning as a soldier had come. 'I did not relish the prospect,' he later recalled:

> As I thought what, in an hour and a half's time, I should be experiencing it seemed to me inconceivable what would or might be happening to me…
>
> There was the most glaring fact staring me in the face that the place where yesterday if I had shown myself beyond the second belt of barbed wire for ten minutes in the dark, would have got a machine gun bullet through me and where shrapnel was almost a continuous occurrence. And here we were, who for two and a half years had not dared to make hardly one change at all in our front, going to suddenly calmly tread over our wire & over the Bulgar lines right bang in amongst them… I felt a kind of disagreeable gloominess & taciturness settle on my spirits as the night wore on.[42]

Spencer's confusion was compounded by the fact that he had only the dimmest idea of what was expected of him; 'Privates were usually not told anything.'[43] But suddenly and without warning the dreadful prospect of battle lifted: the Bulgars had withdrawn, indeed had apparently vanished. Spencer's sense of release was palpable:

> I looked curiously about the ground in front of me which I had only ever seen in the darkness of night. In the night I had gazed and strained my

40 A long account of this battle was drawn up anonymously by 'An Unprofessional Soldier' on the Staff of 28th Division, and published in 1938–39, as 'I saw the Futile Massacre at Doiran.' Issue 46 of *I Was There*.

41 Spencer, numbered writings 1936, TGA 733.2.25.

42 Spencer, numbered writings 1936, TGA 733.2.25.

43 Spencer, numbered writings 1936, TGA 733.2.25.

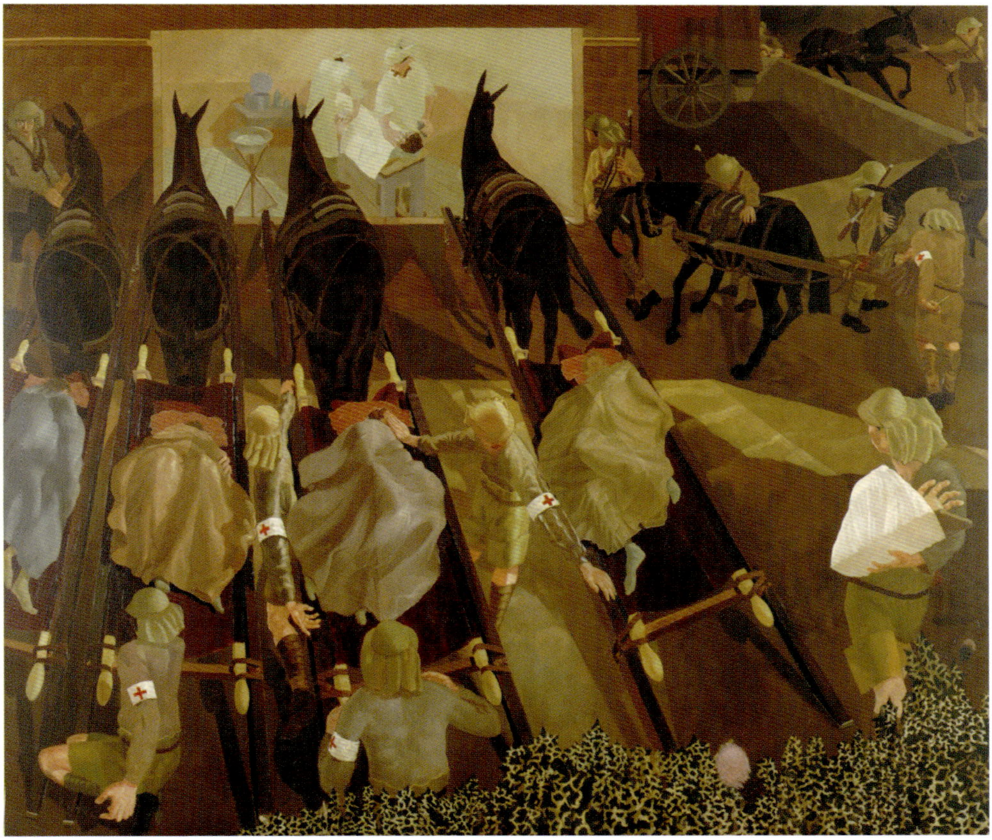

STANLEY SPENCER
Travoys Arriving with Wounded at a Dressing-Station at Smol, Macedonia, September 1916
(1919)
oil on canvas, 182.8 x 218.4 cm
IMPERIAL WAR MUSEUM, LONDON

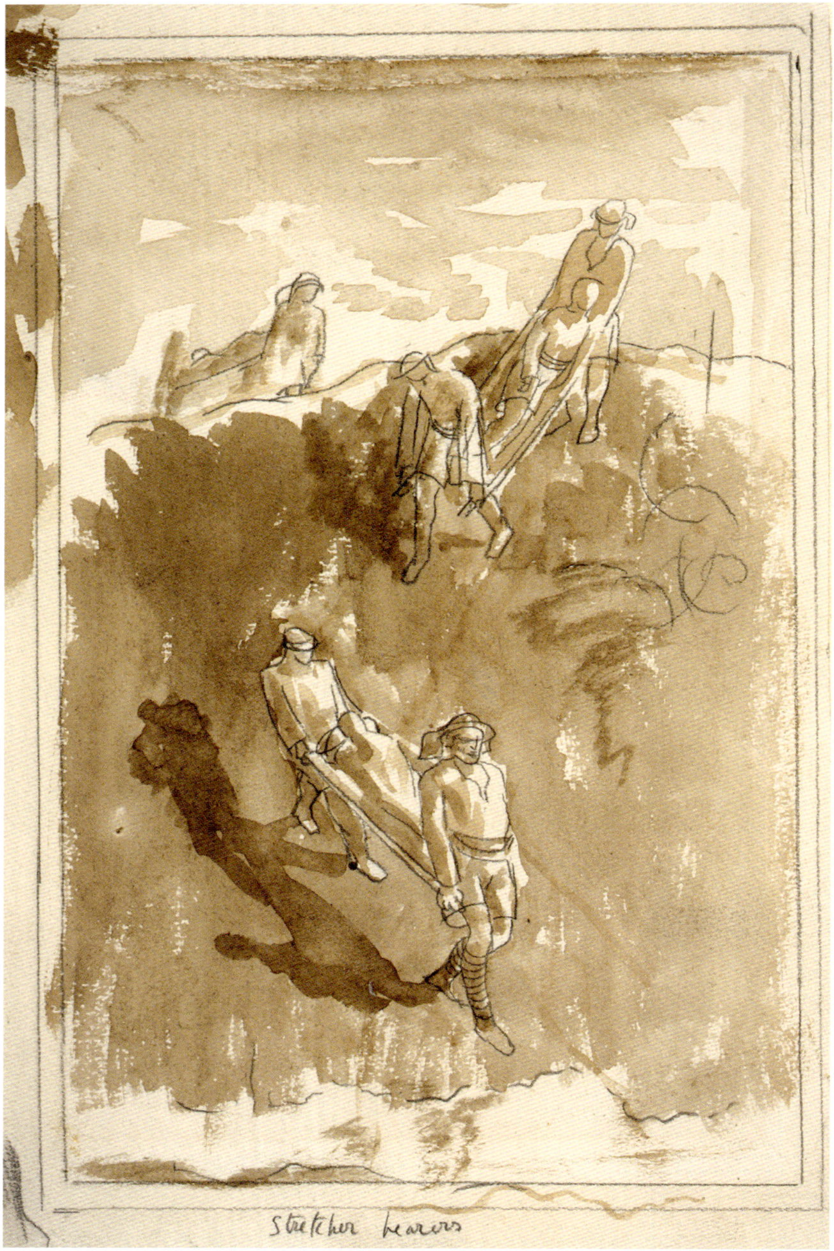

STANLEY SPENCER
Stretcher-bearers, Macedonia
(1919)
pencil and wash

IMPERIAL WAR MUSEUM, LONDON

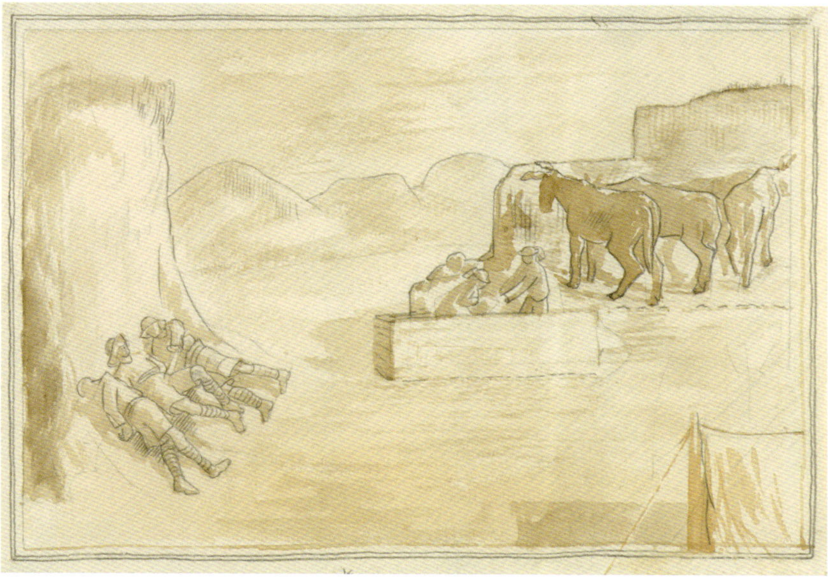

STANLEY SPENCER
A Study of Soldiers and Mules
pencil wash on paper,
18.3 x 25.1 cm

IMPERIAL WAR MUSEUM, LONDON

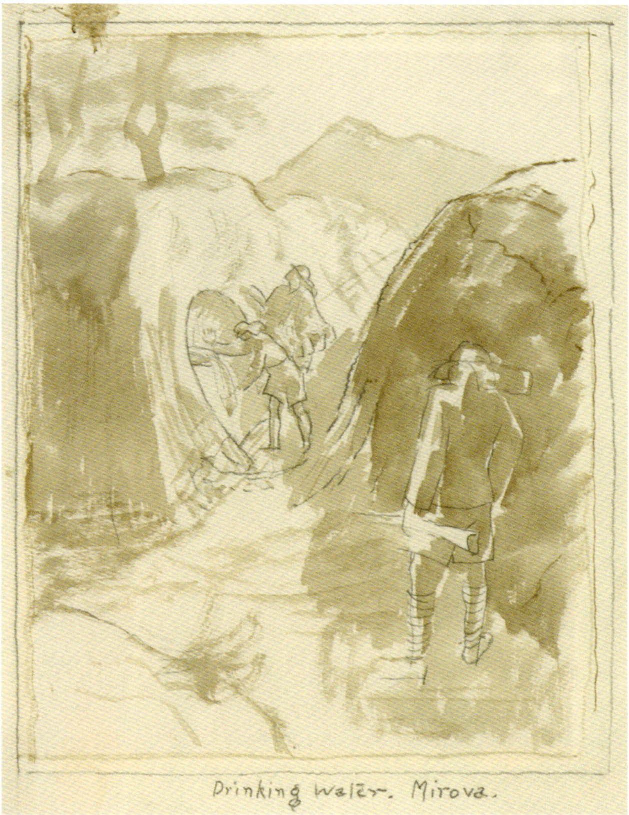

STANLEY SPENCER
Drinking Water, Mirova, Macedonia
pencil wash on paper,
25.3 x 17.5 cm

IMPERIAL WAR MUSEUM, LONDON

STANLEY SPENCER

The Resurrection of the Soldiers

Sandham Memorial Chapel, Burghclere

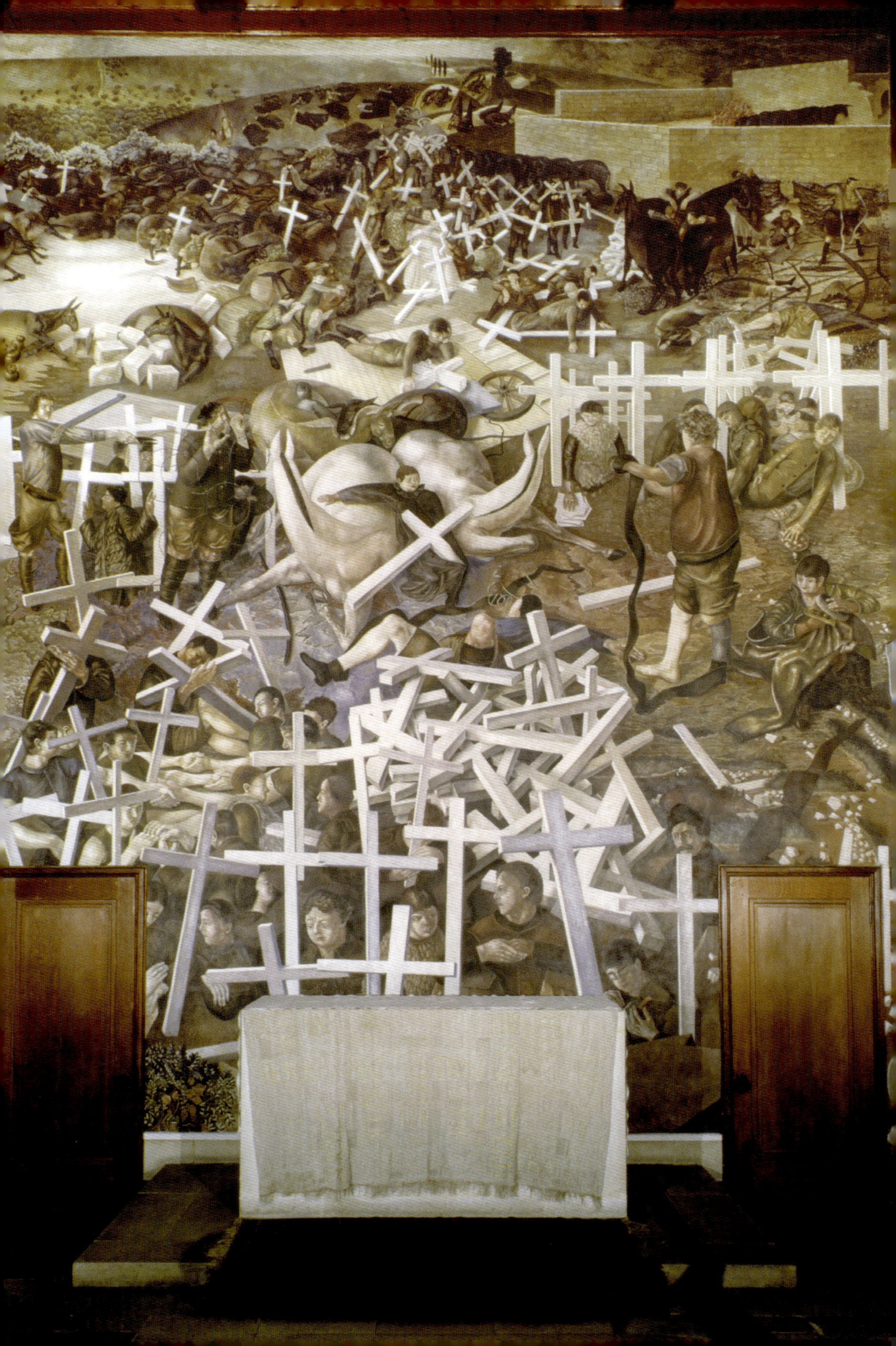

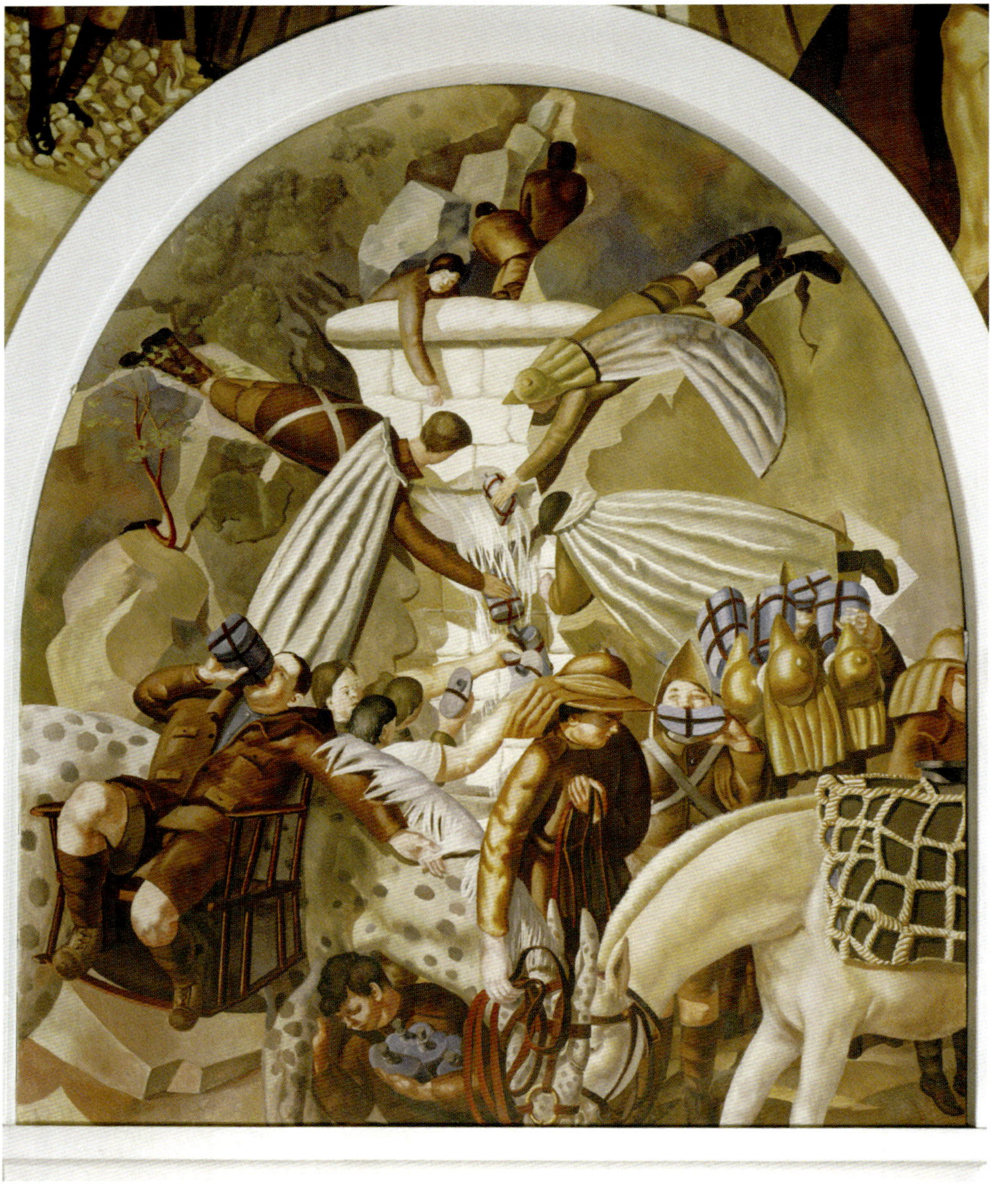

STANLEY SPENCER
Filling Water-Bottles
(1926)
Sandham Memorial Chapel, Burghclere

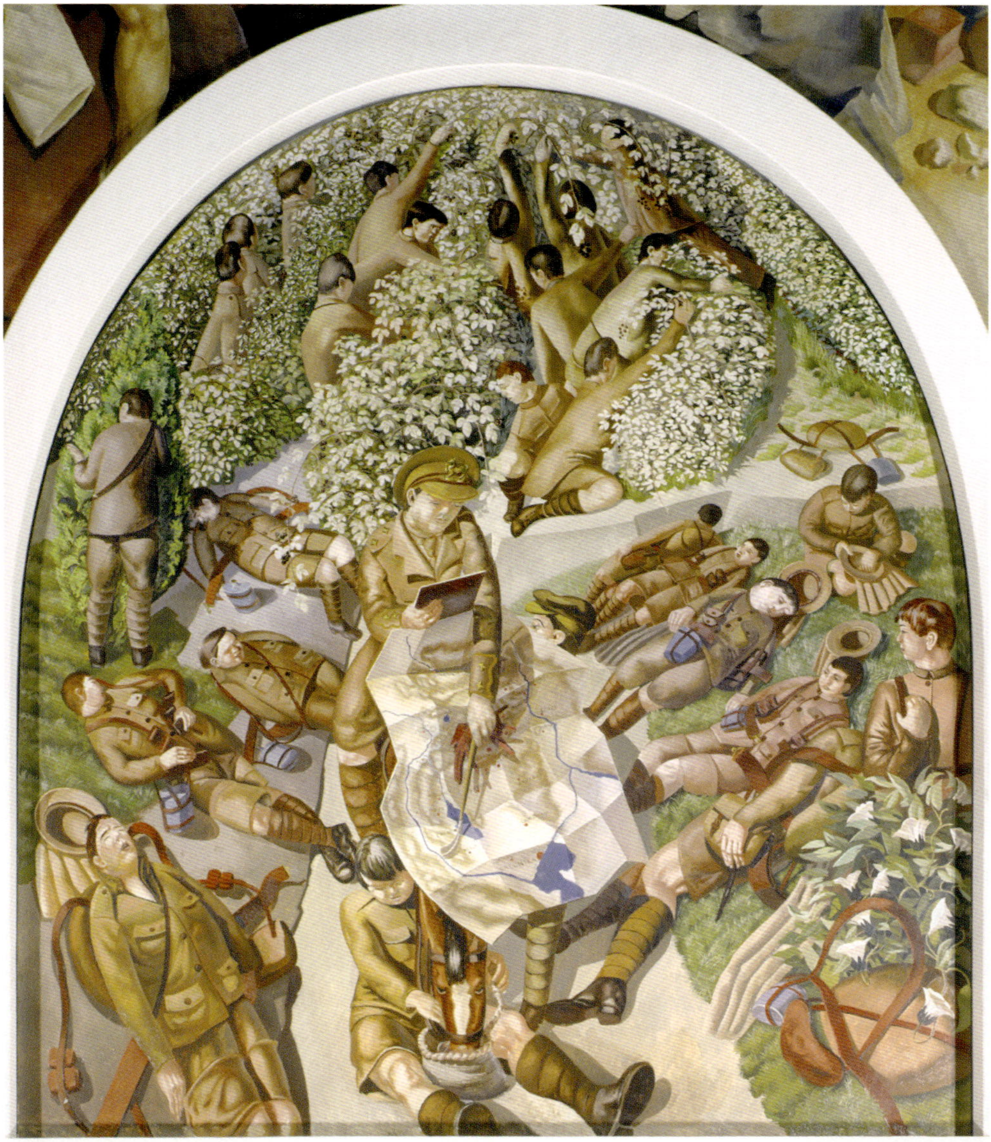

STANLEY SPENCER
Map-reading
(1928)
Sandham Memorial Chapel, Burghclere

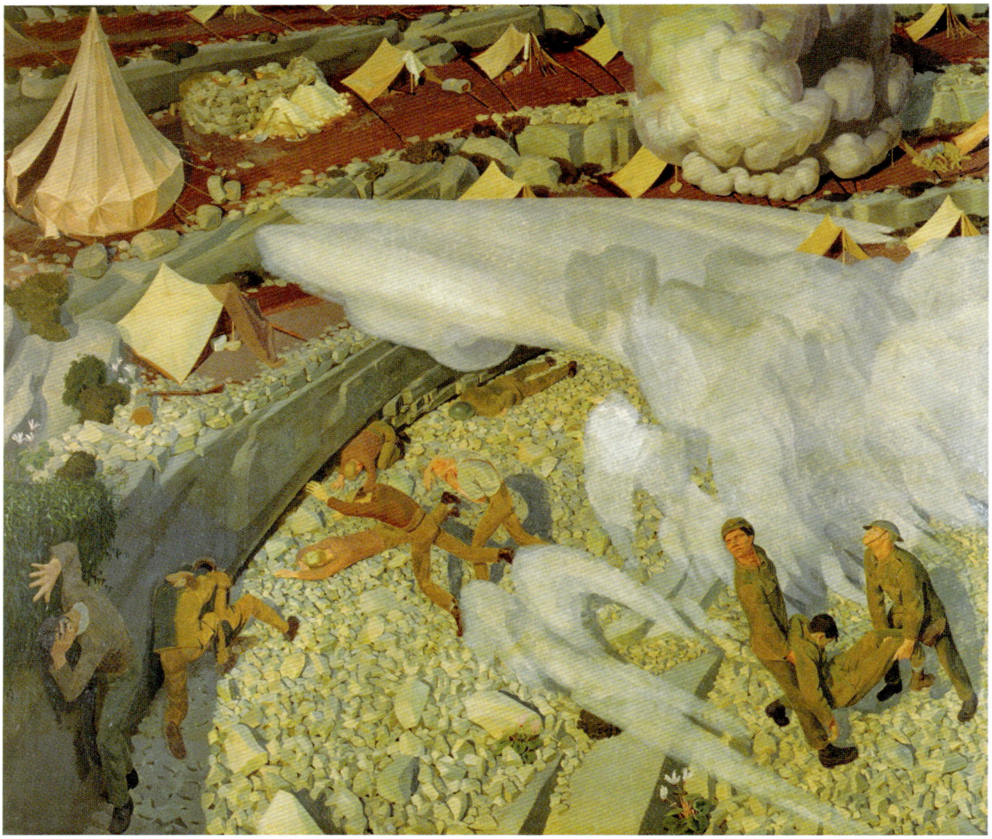

HENRY LAMB
Irish Troops in the Judean Hills surprised by a Turkish Bombardment
(1919)
oil on canvas, 183 x 218.4 cm
IMPERIAL WAR MUSEUM, LONDON

> eyes to see what some object was on the left, and now I could see that it was just the straggling remains of a tree and the slight rise of ground on which it stood. Away to the right, the two hills, one bigger, one smaller, [these were the Grand and Petit Couronnes] which had presented such an eerie appearance at night when the Bulgars had been sending up Very lights, looked just another bit of Macedonian country now.[44]

This sudden withdrawal by the enemy was a prelude to their eventual collapse, as the Bulgarians were chased and harassed back through the mountains by British and Allied troops. The Berkshires were in the vanguard of this action and Spencer was to come under fire a number of times, but he saw out the Armistice in hospital having suffered a relapse of the malaria that had spread as an epidemic through the British forces. From his hospital bed in Salonika he yearned for 'something nice', a chance 'to do some fine paintings or to read some fine literature or hear grand music'.[45] He wrote to his sister Florence a few days later expressing his determination to learn fresco painting, and expressed his vision to 'build a church & the walls will have on them all about Christ. If I don't do this on earth I will do it in heaven'.[46] His release from Macedonia was accelerated when he was placed on the 'Y' list for the repatriation of serious malarial cases. He returned via Italy and France in late November 1918 with a mixture of relief and foreboding:

> When I was returning from Macedonia after all the years out there & never expecting to return. As I approach the lighthouse off the Isle of White [sic] in the dark & the light swinging round & round now on our ship now not: its wonderful. I the 'unborn babe' still in the ship – am having a chat with a sort of angel who is giving me advice & some notion of what this life of mine in England is going to be like. In this imaginary converse I now & then get a little concerned at the future possibilities being foretold & raise my unborn eyebrow & say 'nothing precipitate I hope?'[47]

One can only guess at the intense sense of relief that Spencer felt upon arriving home – 'I begin to think that I have been killed & that now I am in heaven' – and as he re-acquainted himself with cherished places in the town it seemed as if he 'were performing a miracle every time I beheld the familiar spots'.[48] However, it was not all comfort.

---

44 Spencer, TGA 733.3.85.

45 Letter to Henry Lamb, 6 October 1918, TGA 945.41. Spencer spent his last few days before being sent to hospital, in a state of near collapse; even light duties such as carrying blankets exhausted him.

46 Spencer to Flongy (Florence), 10 October 1918, TGA 733.1.757. On 16 October 1918 the Bulgarian army requested an Armistice; three days later it came into force.

47 Stanley Spencer to Daphne Robinson (Spencer's niece), January 1951. Correspondence courtesy of Daphne Robinson, through an arrangement with Dr Jeremy Harvey.

To add to his own exhaustion and the nation-wide sense of loss and numbness after four years of war, he discovered that his beloved brother Sydney had been killed the previous September on the Western Front in France, news that had not reached him in Macedonia. It deeply soured the joy of his homecoming.

'TRANSFIGURATION'

Stanley Spencer, Official War Artist, 1918–1919

Six months before the Armistice, Spencer's name had come up in a list of artists being considered by the Ministry of Information's War Artists' Advisory Committee. The young painter was championed by the Scottish etcher and draughtsman Muirhead Bone, a forceful and influential advocate of young painters and himself an official war artist.[49] Bone's role in Spencer's career is easily overlooked, but like Henry Lamb's, it should not be under-estimated, as the letter of May 1918 from the Committee Secretary, Alfred Yockney, made clear:

> Mr Muirhead Bone, who takes a great interest in your work, has suggested that you could paint a picture under some such title as A Religious Service at the Front [or] any subjects in or about Salonika, which could be painted by you before your return home.[50]

Like many artists serving on the front line, Spencer leapt at the chance of official employment. He told Henry Lamb that he had promptly replied 'to say that I am ready to enter an agreement for the purpose of doing this work', adding that his imagination teemed with pictures, some of which he had already been able to commit to paper:

> I am aching to paint ideas I have for men asleep in a tent, that bivouac idea I showed to you. Of men at drinking water... 2 pack mule pictures, a picture of a lecture on mosquitoes, 2 mule line pictures. A picture of one limber wagon bringing grub.
>
> I am as much influenced by this particular Sector as I was by Cookham in peacetimes I do believe.
>
> I want to do some ravine pictures.[51]

---

48 Spencer to the Raverats, December 1918, TGA 8116.81. Stanley's first words upon returning unannounced at Fernlea on 16 December were ' Where is Sydney?' Tragically Sydney had been killed on 24 September 1918 during a German artillery barrage. He had been awarded the Military Cross on 8 August 1918.

49 Bone's generosity was backed up by the offer of a one-off fee of £120 if Spencer could give his son, Stephen, painting lessons for a year. Although Stephen decamped to Paris, Spencer ended up living with the Bones at Steep for four months. (Cited in Maurice Collis, *Stanley Spencer*, p.71)

50 Spencer, numbered writings, September 1918, TGA 733.2.30.

51 Spencer, numbered writings, September 1918, TGA 733.2.30.

On the same day he wrote to his friend in Bristol, Desmond Chute: 'If I get this job, I shall be able to show God in the bare 'real' things, in a limber wagon, in ravines, in fouling mule lines... This place has a great hold on my mind.'[52] By 27 June 1918 he wrote in mounting anticipation to Florence that 'I have no further news of my prospective job, but I expect to hear in a few days'.[53] However, by September, having heard nothing from London, he had given up all hope, and this explains his astonishment when he read of his 'appointment' as an official artist as he lay awaiting the night attack on the Bulgarian lines near Doiran. Once again, he was to be disappointed. In October 1918, after many agonies at the front and another bout of malaria, Spencer complained to Henry Lamb that he had 'no news at all about the Min. of Inf. Job. I am afraid they have forgotten all about it. I have written twice to Yockney. It will be a cruel disappointment to me if I can't do any painting'.[54]

Repeated letters to Salonika GHQ went unanswered. There is some suspicion, now impossible to verify, that Spencer's superior officers – anxious to keep hold of all the fighting men they could – withheld crucial correspondence from the Ministry or delayed responding to their calls for redeployment. Not all artists could be transferred. Spencer's painter friend Darsie Japp – then a Major in the Royal Artillery also serving on the Macedonian Front – could not be spared, especially on the eve of a planned offensive. Despite intercessions on his behalf Spencer remained with the infantry. Even Henry Tonks joined the lobbying: 'Spencer is, I should think, not much good as a private soldier though I am sure very willing, a genius pitched in the mud.'[55]

Dejected at not being released from his battalion, Spencer left a poignant note of that period of miserable trepidation:

> As the war drew to an end it became agonising to me wondering if I should be snatched away. Apart from greed for life I felt I had got a lot up my sleeve that I wanted to produce before I died, & every day I was being detailed off for worse & worse dangers. As an infantry man what would have been the use of this insignificant fragment of gun fodder that I was if I had said to the sergeants 'I have a picture at home [Swan Upping] & I just want to finish it before going into this attack'. In any case I was in the Vardar Valley preparing for a big offensive while my picture as I hoped was where I left it at home in Cookham... I was optimistic also & seemed to see in all that looked peaceful, something

52 Stanley to Desmond Chute, quoted in Richard Carline, *Stanley Spencer at War*, pp.95–96.
53 Spencer to Florence, 27 June 1918, TGA 756.41.
54 Spencer to Henry Lamb, 6 October 1918, TGA 945.41.
55 Henry Tonks to Alfred Yockney, 12 October 1918, Imperial War Museum, Department of Art, Stanley Spencer file.

> which suggested that peace was near, that we were on the edge of it. This made the sudden appearance of fresh supplies of ammunition & orders for the beginning of a new offensive insupportable to the spirit.[56]

And he concluded this painful fragment of memory with the forlorn – but ironic – thought: 'Oh no, it is not proper or sensible to expect to paint well after such experiences.'

So it was not until he was back in Cookham in the middle of December 1918, that he took up his official commission under Scheme Two. He was offered the not inconsiderable sum of £200 to produce a single canvas measuring 72 inches by 86 inches, one of many required to line the walls of a grand Hall of Remembrance intended for central London.[57] Although the memorial hall scheme would end in failure, Spencer began his official painting in January 1919 having first completed his *Swan Upping* canvas – the 'picture at home' – that had lain untouched in his bedroom for four years.[58]

Ignoring the suggested title of 'A Religious Service at the Front', Spencer took as his subject a memory of an Advanced Dressing Station (or A.D.S.) that had been set up behind the front on the Doiran-Vardar Sector in 1916. An A.D.S. was one part in the chain of medical support that lay immediately behind the battle lines. He had in mind a dressing station located in Smol (a small village with a mosque and minaret, on the flanks of the Sedemli Ravine) that had been established to cope with the anticipated casualties from the attack on Machine Gun Hill in September 1916.

Spencer, who was then serving with the 68th Field Ambulance near Corsica Camp, recalled the scene some years later:

> I was standing a little away from the old Greek church which was being used as a dressing station, and arriving there were these rows of travoys crammed with wounded men… In the top of the picture mules look in at the enlarged window… inside of which an operation is in progress. The mules and travoys are coming from the direction of the hill away to the right and lining up outside this old disused church… The wounded have their faces covered in little squares of mosquito netting for the moment.[59]

He reconstructed this scene from memory. All his sketches, including an original drawing for the painting, had been left behind, with virtually all his personal property, in a military bath-house while

56 Spencer, numbered writings (possibly 1936) TGA 733.2.44.

57 The memorial hall project ended in failure for many reasons, not least a lack of public will to raise funds for such a vast building project. A similar scheme for Ottawa, Canada also foundered.

58 Spencer was also keen to finish *Swan Upping* as he wanted to re-establish contact with two possible buyers, Louis and Mary Behrend. They did indeed buy the painting and became Spencer's major patrons after the war supporting him in realizing the Sandham Memorial Chapel in Burgchlere.

59 Spencer, TGA 733.3.1.

the regiment prepared for the final offensive of the campaign. Despite Yockney's best efforts none of the work was ever recovered, and Spencer was forced to concede that '...some Macedonian peasant now has my drawings'.[60]

Because of the required size of the painting, he hired Lambert's Stables at Moor Hall in Cookham as a temporary studio. For someone accustomed to working in a warm corner of his large family house, the stables were a chilly and uncharitable place and Spencer felt the cold terribly. There was little to remind him of its previous occupants, the horses having been requisitioned as remounts for the war effort, nothing left 'save for their noble names emblazoned in gold and crimson above their empty stalls'.[61]

He did not regard the commission as a war painting at all. It was intended instead as an image of calm and recovery, of peace and hope. Such sentiments were often swamped by the rhetoric of victory that pervaded the atmosphere of remembrance in the post-war years. But Spencer wanted the wounded to be located in a place of peace so that they could realise a 'stillness of the spirit', not merely a release from conflict. He was always fascinated by the sense of detachment that could be gained in the midst of maelstrom. Whether caught up in the mayhem of battle or the bustle of the Beaufort, he strove always to reach a state of psychological refuge. He had recognised it in some of the patients in the Beaufort Hospital who were blissfully unaware that there was a war on:

> In the midst of the war there was a species of peace made and sustained by the state of those in it but not of it... one would have thought the scene was a sordid one, a terrible scene, but I felt there was a grandeur about it... All those wounded men were calm and at peace with everything, so that pain seemed a small thing to them. There was a spiritual ascendancy over everything... Like Christ on the Cross [the wounded] belong to a different world than those tending them... I have tried to express the fact that these men on stretchers and the orderlies attending them are inserting peace in the face of war by means of the way I display them in the composition, so that in spite of what is going on and although they are conforming to the conditions they are in...[62]

Immersed in this 'communion of peace', Spencer wanted to drown out the suffering and pain that hung around the aid post, to create instead a peaceful atmosphere, a place of hope and reconstruction. He selected certain memories to achieve that result, recalling how he had been:

60 From 'Mosaic', an unpublished Spencer family record, Berkshire County Records Office, Reading, Berkshire.

61 Quote in Pople, p.184.

62 Spencer, TGA 733.3.1 in Pople, p.189.

> ... impressed with the calm way the wounded men spoke to each other – about some cabbages they had been trying to grow for instance... A homely atmosphere was being preserved in spite of what was happening... [The place was] not a scene of horror but a scene of redemption from it and I was right in making it a happy picture, as the early painters were right in making the Crucifixion a happy painting.[63]

By 6 February 1919 Spencer reported to the museum that the picture 'is begun and goes apace' and by June, both Bone and Yockney visited Cookham to find it completed. They were impressed with what they saw. *Travoys Arriving with Wounded at a Dressing-Station at Smol, Macedonia, September 1916*, is extraordinarily bold in design.[64] A small yard is seen from a high vantage point, as though the painter were hovering above the travoys laid out in a fan-shape radiating from the bare operating theatre. Its harsh bulb light casts complex shadows into the yard, which is crowded with mules, travoys, drivers and orderlies. The casualties form misshapen bundles huddled under voluminous, dull-coloured blankets; more casualties are being delivered from the top right-hand corner of the painting, creating a sweep of movement that pulses through the composition. But for all its busy-ness this is not a confused or over-crowded painting. The hustle and bustle of the yard is instantly becalmed by the concentrated silence within the chapel-like operating room where the two figures administer to a patient. 'This picture is not,' wrote Spencer to the museum staff, 'in any material or practical sense a truthful representation of the scene it is supposed to depict.' As was always the case in his art, the painting is multi-layered, spiritually ambitious beyond the sum of its many parts, a scene not of horror but of redemption:

> '...[it] is intended to convey a sense of peace in the middle of the confusion. The figures on the stretchers treated with the same veneration and awe as so many crucified Jesus Christs and not as conveying suffering but as conveying a happy atmosphere of peace. Also like Christs on Crosses they belong to another world from those tending them.[65]

---

63 TGA 733.3.1. As always, Ken Pople makes an effort to fully comprehend the multivalent levels of an image such as *Travoys*. He explores Spencer's use of metaphysical language – 'I felt there was a grandeur about the scene', 'pain seemed a small thing to them', 'inserting peace in the face of war', and concludes that there are too many possible meanings to such phrases, indeed as many meanings as there are readers. Spencer's understanding of peace, he concludes, is a stillness of the spirit, not merely an absence of war. It closely chimes with Stanley's phrase that the wounded, despite their uncomfortable predicament, 'all seemed to be taking part in some communion of peace.'

64 The full detail is: *Travoys Arriving with Wounded at a Dressing-Station at Smol, Macedonia, September 1916*, Oil on canvas, 183 x 218.5 cm. IWM:ART 2268. The Imperial War Museum catalogue has an accompanying text: 'About the middle of September, 1916, the 22nd Division made an attack on Machine Gun Hill on the Doiran-Vardar Sector and held it for a few nights. During this period the wounded passed through the dressing-stations in a constant stream, by means of the mountain ambulance transport shown in the picture.'

65 Spencer, TGA 733.3.

The monumental boldness of the composition owes something to Spencer's earlier desire to paint an operating theatre at the Beaufort, with the surgeon's implements radiating from the prostrate patient at the heart of the composition. His ideas for the official painting were first tested out in smaller drawings – one showing several travoys in procession along the Sedemli Ridge, another of wounded being carried by mules, and a further sepia sketch of the eventual composition – but despite their innate gracefulness, these are modest achievements when compared with the larger canvas.[66] In its mood and composition, *Travoys* predicts the fan-like design of both *The Resurrection, Cookham* and the end wall of the Oratory at Burghclere. In each of the three designs the splayed shapes of the stretchers, the tilted gravestones and the pyramid of white crosses lead to a sort of pictorial crescendo – the icon of the redemptive act performed by Christ, or God, or (as in this painting) the surgeon bowed over the patient.

In *Travoys* the eye is encouraged to work its way across a variety of foreground spaces, while the radiating forms of the stretchers spin around the epicentre of the composition. Each figure plays its part in moving the eye towards the pictorial goal, either through its posture or through a directed glance. Heads are always turned back into the picture's space, eye contact is averted, the patients and soldiers turn in on themselves, or are transfixed by the miracle being performed so diligently inside the makeshift operating theatre. The wounded figures in *Travoys* are caught in that indeterminate zone between life and death, balanced in a state of transubstantiation that would be explored more fully on the walls of the Oratory. As already noted, they belonged to 'a different world than those tending them,' suggested Spencer, 'in it but not of it'.[67]

One of the more curious elements of the picture is the painterly treatment of the patterned shapes at the foot of the canvas; the spikiness seems so at odds with the softer, more reassuring rounded forms in the rest of the painting. In the sepia sketch this space is rather unsatisfactorily filled by a strolling figure, who was excised from the final version. Instead, Spencer painted the native vegetation, a 'tall sort of holly scrub… an ancient Greek weed' that he found strangely appealing:

66 Amongst the related drawings are *Travoys passing Up Sedemli Ravine on the Way to Le Naze*, 1918, pencil and wash, 22 x 26 cm. IWM:ART 3878; *Stretcher-bearers, Macedonia*, 1918, pencil and wash, 22.4 x 15 cm. IWM:ART 3879; and *A Study of Soldiers and Mules*, 1918, pencil and wash, 15.4 x 24 cm. IWM:ART 3881.

67 Spencer, TGA 733.3.1. Stanley made this sense of self-absorption even more pronounced in the oil painting. Compare the portrayal of the figures with the sketch for *Travoys* of 1919 in the Imperial War Museum Collection in which all the figures face outwards or walk out of the picture frame.

This pictorial device seems to have become more pronounced in Spencer's work after the war: in none of his paintings based on his experiences as an orderly, soldier or patient (including the many dozens of figures on the wall of the Sandham Memorial Chapel) is there a single eye-to-eye engagement with the viewer.

> Along the bottom of the picture in the immediate foreground are great thistles. The leaves are large and have great spikes. They have milky lines all over them like variegated holly leaves have. The flowers are mauve and look like great maces. Whichever way the flowers go, the leaves form a kind of halo around them... The four wounded I think of as a separate group of nebulae. Each group has the same density but each has a different kind of density. For the feeling they give one, they might be four saints enthroned, the stretcher handles being so to speak ornaments.[68]

Spencer always associated his time in the Sedemli Ravine with particular sounds. For all combatants working near the front line, the ear became finely attuned to different noises, especially at night when sound was amplified and fears greatly imagined. Spencer keenly remembered the 'scrunching of the gravel' under the wheels of the Bulgar wagons as they moved after dark along the road to Machine Gun Hill, a road that he only ever heard, and never saw, and as a result became oddly magnified in his imagination:

> There was something so unreal about no man's land & still more about Bulgars land; I began to imagine that they were not real or rather that they belonged to a new kind of realness. Hearing that cart in the road was like listening to people talking in Hades. All my thoughts about the Bulgars led me into the night, there was 'day' in my Bulgarian world, but it was at the other end of night in a remote sense that our 'tomorrow' is. Their 'day' seemed to me a prolongation of our night. Our midnight comes at 12 o'clock, but their midnight never comes; they are always going towards it.[69]

Like the itch of an old war wound, Spencer would always associate the 'clanging' sound of metal on stone – like 'bars of steel coming together' – with the dread anticipation of the cumbersome mule-drawn sledges, the wounded men, and their bearer escorts.[70]

The aural calm at the centre of *Travoys* contrasts with the clamour of one of the few other official paintings of the Mediterranean campaign commissioned by the War Memorial Committee. It was painted by Spencer's friend and mentor Henry Lamb and was based on his experiences as a Medical Officer in Palestine. *Irish Troops in the Judean Hills surprised by a Turkish Bombardment* is not necessarily a partner to Spencer's painting, but it is designed to the same proportions and adopts the same high vantage point. Painting it in his studio on

---

68 Spencer to Edward Marsh quoted in Pople, p.185. See also C. Johnson, *English Painting from the Seventh Century to the Present Day* (London, 1932) p.330; and Maurice Collis, *Stanley Spencer* (London: Harvill Press, 1962), pp.38, 52, 67.

69 Spencer to Sir Michael Sadler, 30 November 1922, TGA 8221.2.173.

70 Spencer, notebook 1945–47, TGA 733.3.86.

the top floor of the Vale Hotel overlooking Hampstead Heath, Lamb wanted to create as faithful a record of the Inniskillings under fire as possible. To this end, he procured a full set of soldier's equipment and three somewhat unkempt soldiers from a Salvation Army Hostel who posed for him during the summer of 1919, each 'in turn leaned, crouched, and posed as though hurtling for cover among the paraphernalia of water bottles, entrenching tools and mess tins that littered the studio floor'.[71] The result was an impressive evocation of war: a near-aerial view of eleven figures caught in a sudden barrage and struggling desperately to reach the shelter of a slate-grey stone terrace. For an artist who had done little serious painting for five years it was a significant achievement, executed at breakneck pace to meet the Imperial War Museum's deadline. However, Spencer's painting *Travoys* was finished sooner, and it is likely that Lamb would have proffered advice on its progress (though it is equally likely that Spencer would not have heeded it).[72] Similarities in scale, design and finish suggest that the two had been developed in tandem. Indeed, it had been one of the ambitions of the memorial scheme to seek co-operation from pairs of painters so as to effect some visual unity between the component parts of the ambitious Hall of Remembrance. Artists Charles Sims and David Young Cameron, for example, had agreed a common horizon-line for their paintings of the Western Front, which were intended to hang either side of *Gassed*, the vast seven-feet by twenty-feet frieze by John Singer Sargent RA intended to be the keystone for the grand, but eventually doomed, scheme.

Although Lamb's painting would do much to establish his reputation, Spencer was less sure about his official offering. In a letter written a week before the first great Armistice commemoration in 1919, Spencer expressed some ambivalence about *Travoys*. He tended to agree with Tonks's verdict that the painting – which went on public show at the Royal Academy exhibition of the nation's war art in December of that year – 'has all my worst faults & some worse than that. But there are many things in it which I like as much as anything I have done'.[73] This mood seems to have set in soon after

---

71 Suzanne Bardgett, 'Henry Lamb and the First World War', *Imperial War Museum Review*, No.5, 1990, pp.42–57.

72 Perhaps a little unfairly, Keith Clements points out that it was equally unlikely for Spencer to have volunteered advice on Lamb's work in progress as 'he was usually too preoccupied with himself and his own work to help others'. *Henry Lamb: The Artist and his Friends* (Bristol: Redcliffe Press, 1985) p.226. The art critic of *The Burlington Magazine* found Lamb's work to be 'unsatisfactory as a whole, but extremely interesting' whereas *Travoys* was reviewed as the work of an artist of 'uncommon personal vision... [Spencer's] picture, one of the best in the exhibition, seems to be the result of inconsistent instincts, which lead him sometimes to the development of ingenious flat pattern, sometimes to three-dimensional construction.' ('A monthly chronicle', *The Burlington Magazine*, Volume 36, 1920, pp.94–95). Other reviewers were more enthusiastic about Lamb's painting; in the *New Statesman* (30 December 1919) one critic applauded its 'precision of structure', another (in the *Daily Chronicle*, 13 December 1919) thought it 'distinguished in colour.'

73 Spencer, TGA 8116.87. On the viewing day Stanley was initially turned away from the Academy by an attendant who thought him too scruffy to be an artist or an invited guest. (TGA 733.3.7).

the canvas was completed, but it had hardened by the time he wrote to Yockney bemoaning a total loss of direction and a sudden decline in his enthusiasm for war art:

> Somehow I seem to have lost the thread of my 'Balkanish feelings'... I still have hope in the next few years to do something good out of my Balkan experiences... It's off Mr Yockney... the thing is this Mr Yockney, as artists we can do just what we like (that sounds very nice) BUT WE MUST NOT DO WOT WE DON'T LIKE, [sic] woe unto us if we break this law.[74]

Despite the light-hearted tone, this was a firm and absolute rejection. Although he began work on a canvas of some soldiers in a ravine and another of a group pinning clothes to a tent, he 'could not do it and felt too muddled', and he gave up to once more engross himself in the Cookham atmosphere that was all round him.[75] Having handed *Travoys* over to the war museum and turned his back on Macedonia, Spencer thought he had achieved a final act of closure on his war experience.

And the Macedonian campaign itself; how has history viewed that distant, rather sorry Front? It is practically invisible in the popular histories of the war. Perhaps the greatest legacy of three long years was the high incidence of disease, especially malaria, of which there were 162,517 recorded cases in the British forces alone. Endemic malaria sapped the strength and morale of a poorly supplied army, whose legitimacy as a strategic force had been compromised by deals with the French government, the wavering neutrality of the Greeks and the political fall-out from the Gallipoli campaign. In Britain, the army in the Balkans was unfairly and inaccurately criticised as a waste of resources, a sideshow that merely repeated the mistakes of the Dardanelles. However, as is now recognized, the campaign brought about the defeat in the field of the Bulgarian army, liberation of Serbia and the protection of Greece, as well as the strategic exposure of both Austria and Turkey.

It was, of course, the malarial connection that provided the catalyst for the building of the great Sandham memorial chapel, and there are constant reminders in the paintings of the virulence of the disease, including a *vanitas* reference in the swarm of mosquitoes in the apex of the tent in the panel called *Reveille*. This obscure touch is the only concession to the illness that had

---

74 Spencer to Alfred Yockney, 27 July 1919 Imperial War Museum, Department of Art. In his numbered writings, possibly of 1936, Stanley concluded one passage of reminiscences about the end of the war by stating 'Oh no, it is not proper or sensible to expect to paint well after such experiences.' TGA 733.2.44.

75 Spencer, TGA 733.3.1.

blighted Spencer's time in Macedonia. Yet, without the chapel and Spencer's memorable paintings perhaps even less would be remembered about the dusty, malignant campaign fought by the 'gardeners of Salonika'.[76]

76 An ironic nickname earned by the allied troops in Macedonia, who were famously described by the French Premier, Clemenceau, as the 'Gardeners of Salonika' after he had learned that following another abortive attack on the Bulgarian lines the Allied troops were 'digging in'.

Gunners, bombers, sappers and the 'PBI'
William Roberts, Harold Williamson, John Nash and David Bomberg

Not all the Official War Artists were the product of the officer class. Nor were all from the upper tiers of British society who would naturally assume they were born to take command of others. There were some, like Wyndham Lewis, who never doubted their innate authority. 'I felt it was due to the editor of *Blast* to be his own master to some extent,' he crowed, 'Once I had a "pip" I could go on being a "crowd-master"'.[1] Others in his 'crowd' were less assertive, and perhaps less fortunate. As we have seen, Henri Gaudier-Brzeska became a rifleman with the French Army and died in an infantry charge on the Western Front. David Bomberg joined the Royal Engineers as a lowly soldier, only to suffer the ignominy of a self-inflicted gunshot wound two years later. After a long and rather public attempt to stay out of the army, Jacob Epstein was conscripted a Private in the Royal Fusiliers after what he regarded as a deliberate conspiracy in the press.[2] Stanley Spencer, during his three years with the colours, never rose above the lowliest ranks of the army. Reduced to little more than a menial labourer with the medical corps and then on gruelling active service with the Royal Berkshires in Macedonia,

1 Percy Wyndham Lewis, *Blasting and Bombardiering, Autobiography 1914–1926* (London: Eyre & Spottiswoode, 1937) p.97.

2 Epstein believe there had been a conspiracy in the popular press to have him sign up, orchestrated by Augustus John. See Epstein to Quinn, quoted in Michael Holroyd, *Augustus John*, Volume Two, cited in Meirion and Susie Harries, *The War Artists: British Official War Art of the Twentieth Century* (London: Michael Joseph, in association with the Imperial War Museum and the Tate Gallery, 1983), p.89.

he found it difficult to cope with the rough camaraderie of the men and was regularly on the receiving end of abusive behaviour, even an occasional beating, from surly NCOs. William Roberts, another of Lewis's coterie, joined up partly because he was penniless. Like Spencer, his years in service were hard, occasionally brutal. In fact, his 'final contretemps' with the army capped several years of uneasy association with authority. In his war memoir, he remembered the incident very clearly:

> Passing one summer evening [in 1919] by Wellington Barracks, as the Guards were marching back and forth across the parade ground, with rifles at the slope and bayonets fixed, I stopped among the sightseers to admire the troops as they moved in step to the martial music of their band. Absorbed perhaps in the memory of a similar parade on Horse Guards one spring morning some two years before, I had not noticed that the marching had stopped and the music had changed to the National Anthem until I felt a sharp tap on my shoulder from behind and heard a voice say 'Jesus Christ man stand to Attention.' Turning I saw the scowling face of a 6-foot sergeant of the Irish Guards.[3]

Something of this fearfulness is evident in much of Robert's impressive body of work that he produced for both the British and Canadian schemes. One of the simplest designs shows a group of red-tabbed generals swanning past two infantrymen, their bodies frozen in taut salute. To the red-striped officers, the soldiers are practically invisible, mere outlines lost in a miasma of yellow ochre, while the generals are fully modelled with animated gestures and well-cut uniforms. Few artists could rival Roberts for this level of satirical observation. Sue Malvern has described his work as the 'most acerbic and cynical' produced by any of the English artists employed under the government's schemes, bitter enough to rival the social realism of the German artists Otto Dix and George Grosz, and possibly in a class of their own for their portrayal of the arduous – and occasionally deadly – life in the firing lines.[4] Roberts' story is one of degradation and danger, but also of extraordinary creativity and fortitude.

WILLIAM ROBERTS
4.5 inch howitzer gunner

Roberts was living in Chalk Farm, north London at the outbreak of war, not far from fellow Slade School of Art students David Bomberg

3 This and subsequent extracts are taken from Roberts' war memoir published in London, 1974 as *Memories of the War to End War 1914–18* (on the title page) or 4.5 *Howitzer Gunner* R.F.A. *1916–1918* (on the cover); the present text and title are taken from William Roberts, *Five Posthumous Essays and Other Writings* (Valencia, 1990) p.36.

and Bernard Meninsky. Already impoverished, his living conditions were not improved by the onset of conflict, but he managed to avoid Kitchener's recruitment campaign until early 1916 when he, and many of his friends, registered for service as part of Lord Derby's voluntary scheme to create a national reserve. With his fellow painters, Roberts had been busy during the early part of 1915, producing hard geometric drawings for the second edition of *Blast*, showing with them at the Doré Gallery, and later with the London Group at the Goupil Gallery in Regent Street. He had even been commissioned that year by the London *Evening News* to create a stirring vision of St George slaying the dragon. Quite what the sub-editors in Fleet Street made of the robotic figure of the knight and the heavily geometricised dragon is difficult to guess. Whoever wrote the caption was equally nonplussed, suggesting that most readers would regard the drawing as little better than 'a distorted jig-saw puzzle'.[5] To eke out his paltry earnings from sales, Roberts also worked at Tufnell Park munitions factory assembling bomb parts.[6]

Rejected by the Artists' Rifles as a potential officer, Roberts tried to join the Welch Regiment but was diverted to the artillery and received his call-up papers on 4 April 1916. For the next three years he was Gunner Roberts Number 123744 of the Royal Field Artillery. Having mustered at 4th Depot RFA Woolwich ('The Shop' as it was known) the recruits were transferred to cavalry barracks at Weedon, near Northampton, where for five months they undertook rigorous gun-drill on eighteen-pound guns. Drill took place on the vast parade ground at Weedon, and consisted of endlessly rehearsing the laying of the gun – that is preparing it to fire – and taking up correct position; tasks that were always performed at the double. The repetitive drill was interspersed with the customary 'fatigues': peeling potatoes, 'scrubbing the barrack-room floors with brick-dust, unloading and carrying large sides of meat to the cook-house', feeding the horses (a particularly hazardous undertaking that required deft movements to avoid being kicked by the excited beasts), and strenuous sessions of 'buttons, boots and spurs polishing in preparation

4 See Sue Malvern, *Modern Art, Britain and the Great War*, pp.122–132.

5 *Evening News*, St George's Day Celebration issue, 1915. For the newspaper Roberts produced an uncompromising, severe, and diagonal Vorticist design. St George has become a robotic figure astride a steel steed, his armour and lance is just discernible as a simplified sliver of black and white: the dragon's head little more than a triangle locked in the bottom of the uncompromising design. 'This drawing,' ran the rather bemused caption, 'will appear like a distorted jig-saw puzzle.' And the same might have been said of his designs for *Blast* No.2 which were equally abstracted; their very titles – 'Combat' and 'Machine-Gunners' categorically embraced the modern mechanical-world that so enraptured the Vorticists, a world in which the human figure magically morphed with motorized machine-parts and the human form is irreversibly entangled in a never-ending conflict. (For reproductions of these and other lost works, see Richard Cork, *A Bitter Truth*, pp.74–78).

6 Although Roberts was shocked to find that Lewis had unilaterally signed him up to the Vorticist manifesto, he appreciated that the resulting notoriety was a welcome boost to his nascent career. Later in life, he wrote of his fear of being manipulated by Lewis for his own political ends and published several repudiations of Lewis's leadership.

for the morning parade on the barrack square'.[7] It was dull, repetitive and bruising work. Physical violence was never far away. On one occasion when being interviewed – ineffectually, as it turned out – for a possible commission to become an officer, Roberts made the terrible error of resting his hands on the table in the hope of making his interrogation less formal and putting himself more at ease:

> Immediately there came a terrific explosion that caught me full in the face leaving me dazed. At the same time, from across the table, I heard a voice yell 'Stand to attention man when you address an officer.' I was then promptly dismissed.[8]

By August 1916 Roberts was in Flanders, still a gunner. His battery was part of the 51st Brigade RFA attached to the 9th Scottish Division, and consisted of six 4.5-inch howitzers. In trenches around Vimy Ridge he worked as a signaller, learning the trade by hauling heavy phone equipment and rolls of cable up the communication lines. Not far from where Wyndham Lewis was manning his own isolated Observation Post (the 'O.P.'), Roberts learned to lay wires between the O.P., the batteries and Brigade Headquarters, and perhaps more importantly to distinguish them from the infantry telephone cables. As he later wrote, it was exasperating work:

> These thin insulated cables of different colours, with their identity tags, crisscrossed the ground in all directions. They were continually getting broken or cut by shell bursts. When this happened, the line was said to be 'diss', and this meant signallers turning out. Putting the broken ends together again was hard enough in daylight, especially with 'Jerry's' shells dropping around. However, it was far worse to leave your dug-out at night and grope about in shell craters and mud, searching for the damaged wires with the 'D Battery 51st Brigade' label attached, while the enemy's guns did their best to destroy them again.[9]

In the New Year of 1917, Roberts's unit moved from Ypres to the Arras Front where much of his time was spent digging concealed gun emplacements, making camouflage screens out of strips of coloured material and painting large spreads of canvas with jig-saw patterns. On two occasions, Roberts had a slim opportunity to seek

7 *Memories of the War to End War*, p.5. Robert's war memoir is possibly the best thing he ever wrote. As his biographer writes his recollections are 'crystal clear', objective and absent of sentimentality. The historian A.J.P.Taylor described it as 'a little masterpiece. I know no book which conveys so well what the Great War was really like. You have said more in a few pages than others have done in long volumes.' Andrew Gibbon Williams, *William Roberts: An English Cubist* (London: Lund Humphries, 2004) p.34.

8 *Memories of the War to End War*, p.8.

9 *Memories of the War to End War*, p.11.

transfer to the Camouflage Section: on the first, a fellow student at the Slade, Colin Gill – now an officer with the Royal Engineers – came to inspect their work in the Roclincourt *mairie*. But Roberts could not summon the confidence to approach him. On the second, only a few days later, Leon Underwood, another painter he had known in London, was sent to instruct them in attaching the netting. But again, Roberts hesitated and the chance to renew the acquaintance was lost. It was his last opportunity. With the preparations for the Battle of Arras complete, Roberts rejoined his battery and saw some of the most violent action so far. He remembered in particular the death of two artillerymen:

> One was tall, gaunt Tom Gunn, the Limber-gunner of F. Sub-section. As we stood by his corpse someone lifted the blanket that covered his face. It was emaciated and the colour of pale ivory. The other man had died from shell shock. He stood upright by the wheel of his gun unmarked but quite dead. Just a short while before he had invited some of us to share in a parcel of food he had just received from home, but the party had to be cancelled.[10]

Violent death was never far from Roberts. On another occasion 'A' Sub-Section's gun-pit took a direct hit, smashing the gun and killing its crew. Amidst the chaos, Roberts recalled the strange sight of his commanding officer 'on his hands and knees among the ruins searching by candlelight for survivors'. Perhaps it was this incident that stimulated his later drawing *Burying the Dead after a Battle*.[11] It is one of the most moving renditions of camaraderie and loss to come out of the war. An extraordinarily poignant scene of a group of soldiers, heads bowed in soldierly respect, while in the near-distance a town burns, an aeroplane falls from the sky, and tanks pitch about under billows of shellfire. A jagged band of barbed wire separates the chaotic noise of battle from the private burial scene in the lower half of the drawing. 'We buried our own dead,' he wrote in his war memoir, 'together with some left over from the infantry's advance, shoulder to shoulder in a wide shallow grave, each in his blood-stained uniform and covered by a blanket. I noticed that some feet projected beyond the covering, showing that they had died with their boots on, in some cases with their spurs on too.'[12]

Although rather deadpan in tone, Roberts's memoir teems with characters who populated the battery: a boxer from Bethnal Green called 'Cockney' Sharpe, a Don Juan figure who liked to relate lurid

---

10 *Memories of the War to End War*, p.13.
11 *Burying the Dead after a Battle*, 1919, pastel on paper, 50.8 x 45.7, IWM:ART 15594
12 *Memories of the War to End War*, pp.17–18.

details of his sexual exploits while singing the same fragment of song over and over again; the cook whose face and uniform were almost black from the constant use of creosote used to light his fires; the Sergeant-Major (Spud) Murphy, a disciplinarian who patrolled the wagon-lines; the battery commander Major Morrison, an imposing, handsome, square-jawed man, who was 'every inch a regular soldier'; and Roberts himself, somewhat hapless, a civilian-soldier of limited aptitude for the military, and such a poor cook that he had to be relieved of his light duties as an officer's batman. There were a few small compensations. He read Flaubert avidly; he wrote long and anguished letters to his girlfriend Sarah, and he reminisced about his joyous days at the Slade. He was ever alert to the visual incidents of the front – the abstract patterns of the camouflage screens, the jagged lines created by the sections of duckboard laid across the sodden ground, the insignia on the officers' uniforms and a hundred other small details which he later wove into a suite of trenchant drawings and watercolours. As a writer, Roberts observed incidents from several angles: he tells a story of how soldiers might find notes written by the munitions girls tucked into the shell boxes, recalling that they often carried their names and addresses or a photograph of themselves with a note inviting a reply. For those lucky soldiers who opened such a case, Roberts recalled, 'there was the likelihood of a stimulating correspondence, cigarettes, or a parcel of food, and who knows what else besides'. However, he and his fellow artillery men also knew that the boxes of ammunition would often contain a defective shell, a 'dud' or a 'premature' that would burst in the gun barrel, causing death and havoc all around. This happened to one of the guns in Roberts's battery during night firing on the Somme.

His familiarity with shells, their fuses, propellants and primers, and all the paraphernalia of high explosives stood him in good stead when he was eventually commissioned to paint a 'super-picture' for the Ministry of Information. But that prospect lay far away as the Battle for Arras came to an inconsequential end. By the late autumn 1917, the 51st Brigade were in the Ypres Salient, north of the Menin Road, indeed not far from Wyndham Lewis's battery of howitzers which was in position to the south of the same road.[13] As usual, Roberts found himself on hazardous sorties laying and repairing telephone wires, or leading horse-drawn wagons laden with ammunition towards the front. Detailed one night to take three wagons up to the battery the party lost its way in the dark, their

13 Lewis recounts his period on the Menin Road in *Blasting and Bombardiering*, p.152. His battery was positioned five hundred yards south of Hellfire Corner on the Menin Road where they lent support to the 1st Anzac Corps' attacks on Polygon Wood, Zonnebeek, and the Broodseinde Ridge. One of the most recent accounts of the military operation in which Lewis's unit was involved is in Frank Bostyn, *Passchendale 1917: The Story of the Fallen and Tyne Cot Cemetery* (Roesalare: Roularta, 2007) see Part One: Six 'The Battle of Broodseinde: 4 October 1917. New Zealand Division', pp.87–97.

track simply vanishing into the mud, nothing ahead of them but darkness, 'broken ground and shell-holes'.[14] To add to the spreading confusion, the enemy started to drop artillery shells amongst them, upsetting the horses, terrifying the men, and interrupting their task:

> A few yards away on our left there was a faint glimmer of light. We found it came from a hole in the ground partly covered with some cupolas, and lighted by two pieces of candle; squatting inside were two Australian 'Tommies' having a meal of pork and beans. Asked if they knew the whereabouts of D. Battery, they could give us no information. In this predicament, lost among a welter of shell craters and gloom, with the German guns 'searching and sweeping' and the horses going wild, the sergeant decided to unload the shells and dump them in the mud. To have taken back the ammunition we would have had to admit the failure of our mission.[15]

Much of Roberts's war experience ended like this: it begins with a simple plan and a sense of order, only to be abruptly overtaken by disruption and mayhem, culminating in fiasco or failure. What is so fascinating is that it is so closely echoed in the art that he made; the drawings often have a simple setting, usually based around a single and simple narrative – laying signal wire, trying on gas masks, turning out for a sudden battery action – yet the figures seem unable to act in unison. Instead they pour across the picture surface, they tumble out of dug-outs all jumbled together, making wild and exaggerated gestures; they trample on each other in their rush, a disorganised *mêlée* made up of bundles of interconnected figures; his soldiers are seldom drawn as distinct bodies, but often reduced to tubular ciphers sporting some strange grimace. Unlike Lewis's robotic artillerymen however, these gunners are more individualised – with shrieking mouths, straining bodies, and gawping expressions – but they rarely act in tandem, they lack the purposive choreography of Lewis's teams, who by contrast are almost clock-like in their precision and sense of purpose. In watercolours such as *Gunners: Turning Out for an SOS Battery Action at Night*, for example, Roberts catches something of the sense of panic and fear that must have lingered just under the surface but was held in check by days and weeks of essential drill.[16] In these remarkable sketches, as Malvern notes, there is a palpable tension between the 'external' world of physical, threatening forces and the 'internal' world of mechanical solidarity.[17] At its best, this creative tension produced dynamic,

14 *Memories of the War to End War*, p.21.

15 *Memories of the War to End War*, pp.20–21.

16 *Gunners: Turning Out for an SOS Battery Action at Night*, c.1918, pencil watercolour on paper, 32.3 x 32.3, IWM:ART.

17 See Sue Malvern, *Modern Art, Britain and the Great War*, p.124.

pulsating work of scintillating pace and vibrancy; resulting in quite brilliant sketches such as *Signallers* or *Tommies Filling their Water Bottles with Rain from a Shell Hole.*[18] When it was less good, it was usually because Roberts had become formulaic – as sometimes happens when drawings are mechanically re-scaled to fit a larger canvas – and they tend to be fussy, and over-decorative. But as a total body of work they are extremely powerful, the 'apocalyptic madness of the front' is undiluted and unrelenting,[19] and it haunted Roberts for decades, even surfacing some sixty years later in a small, neat drawing of Tommies strung out on the enemy's barbed wire.[20]

LEAVE

After seventeen months unbroken overseas service, Roberts was granted two weeks leave. He spent the first week with his parents in Hackney, but the remainder at the Hotel de la Tour Eiffel off Tottenham Court Road in central London, a haunt of his fellow-Vorticists in the years before. The sense of disjuncture between the dismal gun-pits and the brightly-lit, snug and sociable hotel and its crowded restaurant were disorienting, even bewildering. Night after night Roberts dined amongst old friends and acquaintances: Hope-Johnstone, on leave from Greece, Gerald Brenan, now a serving captain, and Augustus John (by then an official war artist with the rank of major), while the society hostess Nancy Cunard dined at a nearby table, amongst actors and their hangers-on. 'It was a novel experience,' he wrote, 'having for a year or more taken orders from sergeant-majors, sergeants, corporals, bombardiers, not forgetting gunners, to find myself associating with majors, captains, lieutenants, actors, and art critics'.[21]

All too soon he was back at the front, where he found D Battery entrenched amongst the sand dunes on a coastal position near the Belgian town of Nieuport. Despite its secluded air of seaside tranquillity and rather luxurious deep dug-outs, the position received frequent counter-battery fire from the Germans, often in retaliation for fire directed at the enemy lines by British warships prowling off the coast. After dark, the German fire was methodical and accurate.

18 William Roberts, *Signallers*, 1918, ink, pencil and watercolour on paper, IWM:ART 1167. William Roberts, *Tommies Filling their* Water *Bottles with Rain from a Shell Hole*, 1918, ink, pencil, chalk and watercolour on paper, 50.8 x 38.1 cm. IWM:ART 1169.

19 Sue Malvern, *Modern Art, Britain and the Great War*, p.124.

20 Sixty years after the war and inspired by George Coppard's unembellished war memoir *With a Machine Gun to Cambrai* (1969) Roberts made a drawing of British soldiers hanging 'on the wire'. *On the Wire*, c.1974, pencil, charcoal and water-colour on paper, Imperial War Museum.

21 *Memories of the War to End War*, p.22. A restaurant still stands at 1 Percy Street in the heart of Fitzrovia and only a few doors from Lewis's flat. In the late spring of 1915 Roberts moved from his parents' home in Hackney back to dwellings in 4 Fitzroy Street, a stone's throw from the restaurant. No.4 has now gone, but adjacent terraced houses survive.

On one such night he was detailed to be one of a four-man stretcher-bearer party tasked to take a wounded driver to an Advanced Dressing Station some distance away. After an arduous and awkward stumbling across half a mile of broken ground they reached the medical post only to be told by an angry orderly – resentful for what he saw as a cruel trick – that the driver was already dead. Roberts later gave shape to this grim episode in a vigorous drawing of soldiers manhandling a stretcher towards a curtained dug-out.[22] These were perhaps the toughest days for Roberts: he was morose and increasingly resentful at watching the war wipe out his creative past, and promising little more than a monotonous and miserable future. 'I believe I posses the average amount of hope and patience,' he complained to Sarah, 'but this existence beats me... I am feeling very bitter against life altogether just at present.'[23]

By late 1917 the British campaign on the Belgian coast had come to little. Roberts's battery, like so many in the British artillery, was moved south, as was Wyndham Lewis's unit which had also been stationed near Nieuport in readiness for a possible attack on the German-held ports that autumn. The 51st Brigade travelled slowly south towards the Somme to join General Gough's 5th Army, which was taking over long sections of line from the French forces. It was during this languorous journey down to the Somme that Roberts was contacted by Guy Baker with some startling news: 'Lewis is back here on leave, and has been made an Official War Artist. Do some drawings at once and send them to Konody, he is choosing artists to do war paintings for the Canadian War Records Office.'

Faced with the prospect of escape, Roberts seized the moment and despite the lack of materials he hastily produced a drawing on a sheet of newspaper. As he was finishing his design he was admonished by an officious officer but managed to find time to fold the drawing into an envelope and send it to Konody in London. Concerned that he might take fright at his reputation for abstract work, Roberts wrote to Konody assuring him that he would send on 'some more things that will have less 'Cubism' in them'. As was so often the case, he heard nothing for weeks, until in late December 1917 a letter arrived from the Canadian War Records Office, off Bond Street:

> With reference to your communication re your being transferred to the Canadians for the purpose of painting a Battle Picture for the Canadian War Memorial Fund, I would be glad to know whether, providing you are given the necessary facilities and leave, you are prepared to paint the picture at your own risk, to be submitted for the approval of the

22 William Roberts, *Died of Wounds*, 1919, Private Collection, reproduced in Sue Malvern, *Modern Art, Britain and the Great War*, Plate 100.

23 Andrew Gibbon Williams, *William Roberts: An English Cubist*, p.36.

> committee. The reason for this request is that the Art Adviser informs us that he is not acquainted with your realistic work and Cubist work is inadmissible for the purpose. If the picture, which would be 12 ft wide, is accepted you would be paid from 250 to 300 [pounds], in case of refusal you would be refunded for material and trouble.[24]

Although Roberts replied positively to its author, Captain J. Harold Watkins at the Canadian Records, he heard nothing for months and languished with his unit at Etinehem on the old Somme battlefield near Albert. Apart from losing his paybook – with the princely sum of fifty pounds recently sent by Ezra Pound who had sold two of his paintings on his behalf – it was a quiet time. However, in quick succession Roberts was given two unusual tasks that related to his pre-war past – the first was to paint an inscription on the shield of two German field-howitzers that had been heroically salvaged from the battlefield; the second was to accompany an officer to an O.P. in the front-line and make a drawing of the terrain beyond. He did not make a good hand of it, being unfamiliar with the graphic conventions that were required:

> From the OP I saw a completely featureless landscape, save here and there a few broken sticks of trees. I made a pencil drawing of this barren piece of ground, but what use my superiors would be able to make of this sketch I could not imagine.[25]

Roberts sensed he was being tested. In fact, the instructions to release him to the Canadians had already been received at Brigade Headquarters and they were setting him some tasks of their own. However, before he could be sent back to London his unit became caught up in the German Spring Offensive that broke on 21 March 1918, and had to retreat amidst scenes of pandemonium and instances of near mutiny. He came under repeated enemy fire, from machine-gun and artillery, and on one occasion was even ordered back to an evacuated position to rescue two puppies that belonged to one of the unit's officers, but had been forgotten during the retreat.[26] In early April, *en route* to a new battery position near Messines, Roberts was unexpectedly instructed to pack his kit. His days with the artillery were over, although he and his fellow crew were astonished that he should be dismissed from active service at the height of a major campaign. 'This was a time of crisis,' he later wrote, 'and those who

24 This event is recorded in detail in *Memories of the War to End War*, pp.22–26. The letter from The Canadian Records Office was dated 28 December 1917.

25 *Memories of the War to End War*, p.34.

26 Roberts recounts this frightening escapade in *Memories of the War to End War*, p.36. Gibbon Williams suggests that this reckless command was made out of spite by an officer who resented Robert's pending return home.

could use a rifle were being sent into the firing line from the base depots; storemen, clerks, even cooks. It seemed strange to be returning to England at this time.'

It was not until 20 April 1918 that Roberts fetched up at Victoria Railway Station, the only person to step off the leave train. His ten days at the base camp in Le Havre were spent carrying out the customary fatigues, including a bout of gas drill that required him to don a gas-mask, pass through a narrow covered trench blanketed at both ends and filled with poison gas. In his matter of fact way, Roberts records that these practice sessions helped 'to pass the time'.[27] They also provided the basis for a memorable drawing of the same topic with the soldiers' features hidden inside grotesque, insectile masks.

Upon meeting Paul Konody, he was presented with one list of the artists that had already been employed and another of their allotted subjects. All except one had been allocated and that was the first gas attack sustained by the Canadian Expeditionary Force in 1915. Recent familiarity with the noxious weapon notwithstanding, Roberts had no experience of the effects of cloud gas and told Konody so. This was to no avail as he was allocated the subject, transferred to the Canadians (or 'loaned' as he termed it) and set up in a studio in Flood Street, Chelsea.[28] Although the Canadians paid for the studio rent he continued to wear Royal Field Artillery uniform but lived as a civilian, free from military duties, and at his own expense.

THE FIRST GAS ATTACK

As Roberts started to research the background to his allotted subject he became increasingly aware of the scale of the tragedy he was being asked to depict. The attack had happened without warning on 22 June 1915 during the Battle of Gravenstafel Ridge in the Ypres Salient. The Germans released clouds of chlorine gas onto the front-line trenches manned by French troops, largely made up of Turcos and Zouaves from the 45th Algerian Division. Chlorine gas acutely irritates the lungs and bronchial tubes, causing vomiting, violent coughing and breathing difficulties. Heavy doses would cause the lungs to deteriorate in seconds, the victim would cough up blood

27 *Memories of the War to End War*, p.38.

28 This splendid purpose-built studio is located at 10 Chelsea Manor Studios, Flood Street, Chelsea, London. Roberts' meeting with Konody was followed by an equally difficult meeting with another adviser to the war art schemes: 'Next and last of my interviews was with Robert Ross, one time friend of Oscar Wilde. This took place at his flat in Dover Street. A small rotund, sallow complexioned man greeted me. Our meeting was brief. He asked what medium would I use to paint my picture, I replied: "Oil." Nevinson, he said, for his, was going to use marble medium. I remarked that this was a method new to me. After a pause, he glanced at me doubtfully and said; "You are William Roberts aren't you?" I assured him I was, and at this the interview ended. I never quite understood what part Ross had in the Canadian War Paintings scheme. He died soon after our meeting' (p.39).

and die in minutes, 'doubled up, fists clenched, in agony'.[29] On that dreadful day in 1915, after a long and heavy bombardment, a thick yellow cloud of the gas had carried across no man's land, wafted by a northerly wind that was blowing that morning. In the history of warfare no one had ever witnessed anything quite like it. A young territorial soldier from the Queen Victoria Rifles, Private Anthony Hossack, was watching from a distance:

> As we gazed in the direction of the bombardment, where our line joined the French, six miles away, we could see in the fading light the flash of shrapnel with here and there the light of a rocket. But more curious than anything else was a low cloud of yellow-grey smoke or vapour, and, underlying everything, a dull confused murmuring.[30]

Unprepared for this manner of warfare, the Algerians ran away in disarray, falling back through the support trenches occupied by the Queen Victoria Rifles and the reserve battalions of the First Canadian Brigade. With his own eyes smarting and recoiling from the pungent, nauseating smell Hossack watched with disbelief as galloping horse teams started streaming down the road; behind them over the fields came mobs of infantry 'running, falling, being enveloped by the cloud':

> Away went their rifles, equipment, even their tunics, that they might run faster. One man came stumbling through our lines. An officer of ours held him up with levelled revolver. 'What's the matter, you bloody lot of cowards?' says he. The Zouave was frothing at the mouth, his eyes stared from their sockets, and he fell writhing at the officer's feet.[31]

According to official accounts the Canadian soldiers who eventually held the line and repelled the German attack, were similarly 'amazed at the anguished faces of many of the French colonial soldiers, twisted and distorted by pain, who were gasping for breath and vainly trying to gain relief by vomiting'.[32] As the Canadians tried to stabilise the front, confusion was rampant; the Dominion reserves equally as unprepared for gas attack as the north Africans. Masks and other equipment to ward off gas would soon be devised and issued, but until then if there were another gas attack, the Canadians were simply instructed to protect themselves by urinating on their handkerchiefs or other strips of cloth and hold them across their mouths.

---

29 Peter Slowe and Richard Woods, *Fields of Death: Battle Scenes of the First World War* (London: Robert Hale, 1986) p.28.

30 Peter Slowe and Richard Woods, *Fields of Death*, p.30.

31 Peter Slowe and Richard Woods, *Fields of Death*, p.30.

32 *Canada in Flanders*, Volume 1, quoted in *Canadian War Memorials Exhibition*, London, Burlington House, 1919, entry 67.

Drawing on his extensive experience at the Front, Roberts chose to describe the moment the Canadian Field Artillery come into action to repel the expected German attack. In the Canadian line there is a semblance of order and discipline: the loaders reach for the ammunition, layers set the sights, a charge is hurriedly prepared, in front of the battery an officer tries to clear the way of fleeing Algerians so that the nearest gun can be properly aimed; in fact, the upright stick (or aiming point) planted a few yards in front of each gun is the solitary vertical line in the entire painting.[33] By contrast, the fleeing Zouaves pour down and across the vast canvas, flowing uncontrollably from the top right-hand corner of the frame, mingling with fleeing Canadian soldiers and causing untold mayhem as they force their way past the guns, clasping their eyes and clutching their convulsed bodies. And remember, this canvas is very large – ten feet by twelve – and the figures are almost life-size. In fact, Roberts managed to squeeze over twenty figures into this panoply of havoc. His mastery of composition is indeed impressive: there is a sense of controlled disorder, achieved largely by reducing cast shadows to the very minimum and by alternating the colour scheme so that the pervading warm hues – the khaki uniforms, the crimson pantaloons, the glistening flesh tones of the semi-naked gunners – are peppered intermittently with touches of cool blue and steel grey. These complementary colours rotate in an oval movement throughout the centre of the image – from the braces of the figure on the left, through the breech of the gun, and across to the right of the canvas via the cummerbunds and the puttees of the Zouaves, and then it loops back again into the picture across the light grey of the wheel rim, the second gun breech and the lilac tips of the three shells at the foot of the composition. This elliptical movement acts as a subtle counterpoint to the prevailing diagonal thrust of the picture, which so powerfully endorses the flight of the Algerians from top-right to lower-left.

In its grim magnificence *The First German Gas Attack at Ypres* is almost Baroque in scale and ambition, closer to the vast swirling narratives of Tintoretto or Veronese than the rectilinear jottings of the Vorticists. Others thought so too (though not John Singer Sargent who called it a 'hideous post-impressionist picture' fearing perhaps that it might outshine his own epic of gassed infantry). Laurence Binyon was almost overwhelmed by its impact, stunned at Roberts's 'torrent of Turcos and Zouaves pouring headlong down the canvas':

---

33 Roberts explains that the guns were sighted upon an upright stick or aiming point, called a night-line planted a few yards in front of each gun. The painting's title is: *The First German Gas Attack at Ypres*, 1918–1919, oil on canvas, 304.8 x 365.8 cm. National Gallery of Canada.

> ...the crimson of the French soldiers' uniforms mixed with the khaki makes a wild colour-pattern like a great bed of tulips. It is queerly compounded of stylistic elaboration and utter realism, and from a human point of view strikes me as rather horribly cold-blooded. Mr Roberts is still a very young artist but his great gift is undeniable and his future excites interest.[34]

MEN IN ACTION
Two NCO-artists

Roberts was, in fact, just twenty-three years old when he completed the picture, and for him it was the greatest achievement of what had been a miserable and vexing war, rooted at the lowest end of the army's rigid hierarchy. His sequel to the Canadian picture was an even larger canvas painted for the British War Memorial Committee. But he could not repeat his success. *A Shell Dump, France* has none of the pictorial innovation and sheer bravura of the Canadian painting. Instead it is a stiff and confusing tableau, chock full of information, yet choked of the visceral energy of his previous work.[35] In an excess of visual description Roberts itemizes the business of manhandling heavy metal shells (even making a special visit to Bramley ammunition dump, near Reading to refresh his memory), but his pains were to no avail. The picture is lifeless and attracted little attention or praise when hung in the Royal Academy show of British war art in late 1919. Luckily, the smaller drawings and watercolours he produced as he laboured over 'Shell Dump' have assured his place in the pantheon of British war artists.

There were others who, like Roberts, had had equally prolonged exposure to war's privations. Neither Harold Williamson nor John Nash were to make the officer class. Both endured prolonged duty at the front. Their work was later purchased by the government as a way of securing pictures by artists with authentic experience of the fighting.

Twenty-two at the outbreak of war, Williamson had served as a Corporal with the King's Royal Rifle Corps on the Western Front after having studied at Leeds School of Art and the Royal Academy Schools in London, where he won the Turner Gold Medal. Towards the end of the war he was championed by Royal Academician

34 Laurence Binyon, *New Statesman*, 8 February 1919.

35 William Roberts, *A Shell Dump, France*, 1918–19, oil on canvas, 182.9 x 317 cm. IWM:ART 2273. Roberts also made several studies for the shell dump painting, see IWM:ART 1889, and IWM:ART 1164. A reviewer in *The Burlington Magazine* was complimentary about Roberts's drawings, but dismissed *Shell Dump* as a congestion of 'meaningless puckers', which reduced the entire surface of the painting to 'a sort of energetic textile pattern'. Very different, wrote the reviewer, from the lucidity and space feeling of Mr Wyndham Lewis's *Battery Shelled*.' ('X', 'A Monthly Chronicle: The Imperial War Museum: Exhibition of War Paintings and Other Records', *The Burlington Magazine*, Volume 36, 1920, pp.94–95).

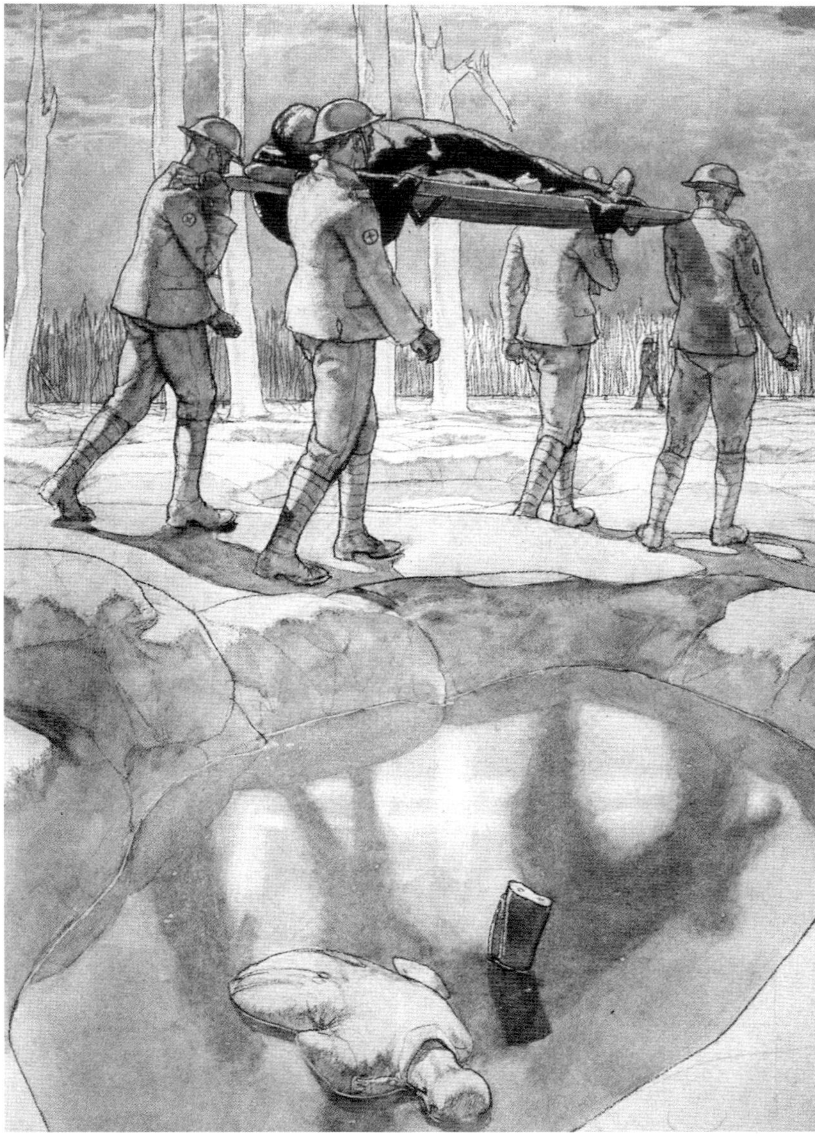

HAROLD WILLIAMSON
Stretcher-bearers
(1918)
black chalk and watercolour, 54 x 38 cm
IMPERIAL WAR MUSEUM, LONDON

Charles Sims, who hoped he might become an official painter. Sims wrote enthusiastically that 'The artists of your quality who have seen most of the fighting from the Somme to St Quentin can be counted on one hand, especially as privates'.[36] But Williamson did not secure work until the museum purchased his record of a German attack during the Spring Offensive of March and April 1918.[37] His large canvas captures the vaporous atmosphere of a wet morning on the Villers-Bretonneux sector; rain falls, puddles collect and a rather depleted line of British infantry prepares to ward off an attack by German troops who can be spotted through the murk. In an extensive background note, Williamson remembered the circumstances behind the painting:

> Before dawn, an intensive bombardment of our lines opened up, and was maintained for a couple of hours. In the gloom and rain the storm troops then came over, and smashed through our two first lines. The picture shows them moving with exact discipline and just appearing to the few men in reserve. The shell holes in the foreground show the accuracy of the preceding bombardment. The British are hopelessly outnumbered, but training and discipline keep them going, without thought of retirement. Two men are firing a Lewis gun. The wounded man has a poor chance of getting away; he must cross much open country swept by enemy fire, and go through a heavy barrage. At the last the few left were surrounded, but fought their way out, some wounded, some being taken prisoner.

Williamson was a masterful draughtsman and, like many in his generation who were rigorously instructed in drawing from the figure, he could effortlessly illustrate the clothed body in any variety of controlled poses. The frightened boy-soldier (actually a self-portrait of the artist) clutching his arm as he turns from the parapet is one such accomplishment, as is the team of stretcher-bearers who transport a casualty in another chalk-and-water-colour drawing. However, little in Williamson's art school training could have prepared him for the sight of prone figures sprawled across the trench floor, or bodies bobbing about face-down in a water-filled crater, the butt of their rifle protruding from the still surface. In his letters home, Williamson recalled the dreadful circumstances behind this image. Having just had news of his sister's premature death, Williamson spent a desperately bleak Christmas Day 1917 in a shell-hole, made

36 Charles Sims letter is in H.S.Williamson file, IWM Department of Art. It is accompanied by another supporting letter by Dr H.C. Orrin FRCS. A letter to the artist from Alfred Yockney, 18 July 1919, suggests that 'the black hair of the prone figure [in the large oil painting] might be modified slightly.' By any standards an unusual intervention from an administrator to any artist. Williamson had served with the King's Royal Rifle Corps since January 1916, and was wounded twice, by a grenade fragment at Delville Wood in September 1916, and at Villers-Brettoneux in April 1918.

37 Harold Sandys Williamson, *A German Attack on a Wet Morning, April 1918: a heavy attack in the neighbourhood of Villers-Bretonneux*, oil on canvas, 106.6 x 152 cm. IWM:ART 1986.

worse when an officer on his rounds of the improvised trench-line was shot by a sniper. 'Imagine it,' wrote Williamson, 'looking after a man 6 foot 3, in a bit of trench half the width of your kitchen... partly filled too with a fire step. I had to sit on the step, and hold him across my knees, while the stretcher-bearer dressed him. Our stretcher was broken, & with difficulty we got another, one bearer being shot through the head bringing it.' Eventually, they loaded the stricken Captain onto a stretcher and waited in the freezing snow for dawn:

> When daylight came we put out the Red Cross Flag (a mutual arrangement of that part of the front) & four men having been told off for the work, we hoisted the stretcher out of the hole & got him safely away. I heard afterwards that they carried him miles without incident, but only to have him die from exhaustion within sight of the dressing station.[38]

By comparison with Williamson's impressive education credentials, John Nash had no formal art school training at the outbreak of war. One year younger than Williamson he enlisted in the Artists' Rifles in September 1916, and found himself serving in France only two months later.[39] Attached temporarily to the 7th Royal Fusiliers at Oppy Wood until April 1917, he returned to the Artists' as a lance-corporal and was often in the front-line. He was later transferred to the Second Battalion to take charge of nine men in a bomber section, and took part in a disastrous attack on Marcoing in December 1917, at about the same time that Williamson was cooped up in his snow-filled shell-hole. One month later – after a determined campaign by his elder brother, Paul – Nash was released from active service and commissioned under the British War Memorial Committee's Scheme Two, as an honorary second lieutenant. This released him from active duty and paid a salary of £300 per annum (over and above his military pay) and, in return, required him to make available his total artistic output for the agreed period of employment, which was initially six months. These were less than generous terms and were invariably offered to younger artists of modest standing in the

---

38 The account of Captain Brownsword's wounding and death is in Williamson's letters and manuscripts held in the Department of Documents at the Imperial War Museum, letter to his parents 7 January 1918. Extracts from the letters are available on line at:
http://www.iwm.org.uk/upload/package/45/FatalSalient/index.htm

For examples of Williamson's work relating to this incident see *Removing the Wounded, 60 Yards from the Enemy*, 53 x 38 cm. IWM:ART 1477; *Stretcher-bearers*, black chalk and watercolour, 53.5 x 38.2 cm. IWM:ART 1476; and *A 'Crump': a Shell Exploding*, watercolour on brown paper, 35.6 x 51 cm. IWM:ART 1473.

39 Three months after the outbreak of war Nash was sworn in as Special Constable in Buckingham, then moved to London where he was employed making tents at the Mappin and Webb company in White City. His application to join up in early 1916 failed because of ill-health, but following the summer offensives in France he was accepted into the Artists' Rifles (28th London Regiment). In the intervening months he had done clerical work at the Ministry of Munitions, often staying with Edward Marsh, private secretary to Churchill, and a great advocate of young painters, including John's brother Paul Nash.

British art world. However, given the nature of his daily work in France, the offer was irresistible.[40]

By any comparison, John Nash was having a tough war: rooted at the foot of the rank structure, stuck in the 'poor bloody infantry', and constantly frustrated by his inability to secure a commission. Much of his work in the first months in France was little but heavy labour. He recalled a typical day of 'fatigues' spent unloading three trucks full of 80-lb sacks of oats. Others were wasted on repetitive domestic tasks:

> Got up the grub at 7 oc, cleaned the dixies, cleared out 3 messrooms & washed the tables, drew coal for the Company, emptied all the rubbish bins, drew day rations, got up lunch, cleaned dixies, emptied messroom 'trash boxes', drew tea, cleaned up messroom again, cleaned dixies – exhaustion – cleaned myself – coma...[41]

A talented amateur pianist, a self-taught reader of music and an avid botanist, Nash found some comfort in solitary walks in the French countryside. His letters are full of vivid descriptions of nature, the lie of the land, its colour, lines and mass, its potential for painting. His quick eye 'never missed a flower on the walls of a trench or in the splintered woodland' as he sought out life and growth amidst the dereliction.[42] On the odd occasion he was even able to sketch such sights, writing here about the 'yearly miracle' of spring:

> I saw a wonderful, almost awe inspiring sight today on the railway – a landscape. In the foreground was the glittering line coloured w[ith] red brick dust which we had just been throwing down – so a strip of red then a line of poplars in the shade, then the shaded merged into a sunny green field covered w[ith] pale bright reeds, then 3 rows in succession of poplars in the sun like bright bleached skeletons then the wood or forest above them on the hill in shade, a frowning red simple black; above all layers of fearful clouds... Today the fatigue ended at 10 oc & to our amazement we have been free all the rest of the day. So I slipped away alone & did some drawing & roamed in the woods & on the hill & saw many fine effects. I can't connect the spring w[ith] this continual struggle & could

40 A full account of Nash's complicated transfers while on active service is to be had in Allan Freer and John Widdowson (eds.) *Love Letters from the Front: John Nash to Christine Kuhlenthal, France 1916–1917* (Gloucester: Cyder Press, 2007). An equally full, and often candid, account of the convoluted marital and extra-marital activities of the Nash brothers and their wives and would-be lovers is to be had in Ronald Blythe's *First Friends: Paul and Bunty, John and Christine – and Carrington* (London: Viking 1997).

41 Letter IV, in *Love Letters from the Front*, p.13. For security reasons, or in some cases because they have been censored, none of the letters is dated, though it is just possible to guess an approximate date.

42 Allan Freer writes eloquently of John Nash's appreciation of nature, his long walks in France where 'like John Tradescant in the seventeenth century, botanizing amid the carnage of the battlefields of the Civil War, John Nash never missed a flower on the walls of a trench or in the splintered woodland... they afforded a link in the country world he had left behind and the English landscapes he had already painted'. *Love Letters from the Front,* Introduction, p.xxi.

> wish all our surroundings were bleak & bare till the war was over & so everything could then burst forth.[43]

Trench duty came soon enough. Nash showed such aptitude for soldiering that he was given more responsibility and sent on a succession of courses in machine-gunnery and trench mortar firing, where he became an expert in mortars and grenades, even composing his own hand-drawn instruction manual. On the eve of the Battle of Passchendaele in autumn 1917 he was extremely disappointed not to be sent to the Front with his mates but dispatched to the reinforcement camp to train others. 'I was very agitated at first,' he wrote to Christine, 'but ascertained from my CO that there was no stigma attached to this position, only in case of accidents someone must be here to train reinforcements.'[44]

Few painters have managed to capture the unique sensibilities of the trenches; the way the men had to huddle together for warmth, the apparent snugness of a dug-out but also its vulnerability, the thin coverings of corrugated iron sheeting and the oppressive weight of the turgid mud. In his oil painting *An Advance Post, Day*, the figures are folded into the earth and into one another as though rooted in the Flanders soil, only the very tip of the twelve-inch bayonet piercing the horizon line just inches above their vulnerable heads.[45] The drabness of the troglodyte trenches, the dingy dug-outs and saps was often compensated by brilliant skies and stunning night-time light shows. Nash was thrilled at such sights. He described one such near-sublime experience:

> On Sat night at 10 oc I wonder what you were doing. I was standing on the fire step w[ith] my gun & fixed bayonet by my side peering over 800 yds of tangled wire & grass trying to see if 'Fritz' was a-coming across to pay us a visit, while around about fell, flew & whistled respectively 5.9" shells, whiz-bangs, pineapples so called, & machine gun bullets, so that I never knew when I was not going to be blown to bits, but I do assure you, & I thought it curious myself, that my feelings were not of fear – what was unpleasant was the wet, it poured all night, sleepiness & continual looking into darkness & cramp. We were told that we experienced one of the worst nights for some time. A wonderful & awe inspiring experience. I was also so interested by the Boche's beautiful lights & star shells & the

---

43 Letter X, in *Love Letters from the Front*, pp.27–28.

44 Letter XXXVI, in *Love Letters from the Front*, p.89. Nash's disappointment is evident: 'Since I have been writing this I have been dispatched w.[ith] others to a reinforcement camp – all the rest are going up to do great things I hope [in the Battle of Passchendaele, late summer and autumn 1917]. I am chosen to stay behind. This always happens & you must see the reason, but why me? I dare say you will be relieved but I feel depressed nevertheless – I am here & my friends are or will be elsewhere, all among it.'

45 John Nash, *An Advance Post, Day*, 1918. Oil on canvas, 76 x 50.8 cm. IWM:ART 1157. See also: John Nash, *An Advance Post: Night*. n/d. Watercolour, 33 x 40 cm. IWM: ART 1158.

> general amazement of it all kept me from being afraid. Here I do think the educated mind gains upon the common soldier, who is like a child, until by time and usage he becomes a don't care – a philosopher – or so nervy that he is of more trouble than use. Then dawn broke behind a shattered wood & the larks began to sing. Another wonderful incident.[46]

Nash's astute observation and his intense experiences combined in his larger oil paintings to produce work of great singularity. He was extraordinarily adept at conjuring up the specific meteorological conditions of the skies directly above the trenches of northern France. Nowhere is this more brilliantly executed than in the large canvas *Oppy Wood, 1917 Evening.*[47] Nash had been sent to the zig-zag trenches in the wood as his induction to the front-line and to test his reactions. It was, recalled Nash sixty years later, 'an eerie place... a very ingenious trench system which had been dug by the Norfolks, who were there before us, by skilfully tunnelling under these vast trees which had fallen', a place where explosions of any kind resounded eerily around the remnants of the beeches.[48] In this almost magical painting, there is something quite transcendental about his representation of the sky, with its near-symmetrical clouds and radiant luminosity. Ten years later in Germany, Otto Dix would create a similar sky-scape high above the blighted and ancient battlefield in his painting called *Flanders*, though in place of Nash's crystalline light, Dix has wrought a scene of apocalyptic magnitude, replete with fossilized foot soldiers and clouds trailing like shredded pennants.

With justifiable reason Paul Nash feared greatly for his brother's safety on the front. After weeks of trying to track him down in late autumn 1917, Paul – now an official war artist with officer's rank, car and chauffeur – finally met up with his corporal brother. It was an emotional reunion. 'I found the dear old fellow at last after a day's search,' he wrote:

> Looking very well – a bronzed and tattered soldier with incredible hands all rough and overgrown with cuticle – his eyes, I thought less shy, very blue and bright, thin in the face but not worn or strained; his voice rather

46 Letter XXX, in *Love Letters from the Front*, p.69. In a subsequent letter (No.XXXIII) Nash writes with equal awe of the sight of 'our aeroplanes, firing w.[ith] their guns on the trenches late in the evening, the machine is silhouetted against the bright afterglow while from it proceed a straight chain of golden flashes like a fine chain pulled taut. Then all round it are bursts of black shrapnel which on explosion assume certain shapes in the smoke like a ball of wool pulled out. One's artistic or aesthetic pleasure is often enough shattered by a terrific 'crump' coming over a long diminuendo whine then bang & showers of earth like a fountain are tossed in the air. I think I c[oul]d do some drawing of it all – but not here.' Letter XXXIII, in *Love Letters from the Front*, p.79.

47 John Nash, *Oppy Wood, 1917 Evening*, 1918, oil on canvas, 183 x 213.4 cm. IWM:ART 2243.

48 John Nash, 'Artists in an Age of Conflict', Imperial War Museum, Department of Sound Records, Accession No.000323/05. Nash was interviewed by Joseph Darracott of the Imperial War Museum and David Brown of the Tate Gallery.

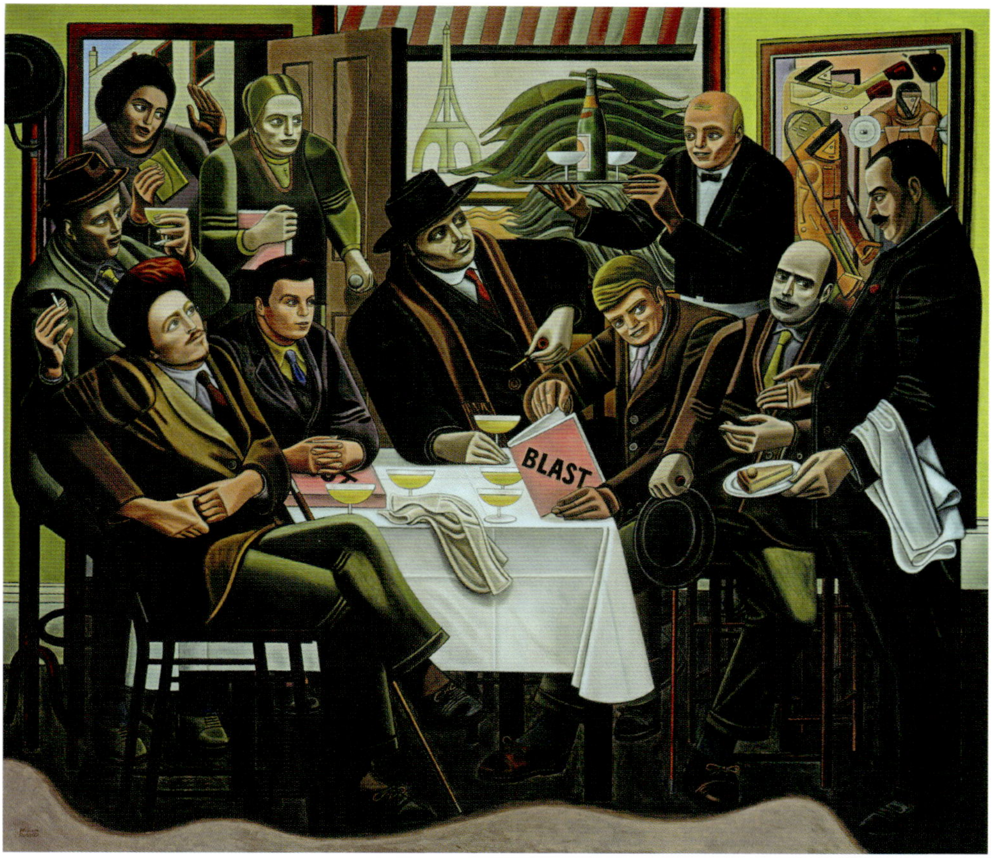

WILLIAM ROBERTS

The Vorticists at the Restaurant de la Tour Eiffel: Spring, 1915

(1961–62)

oil on canvas, 182.9 x 213.4 cm

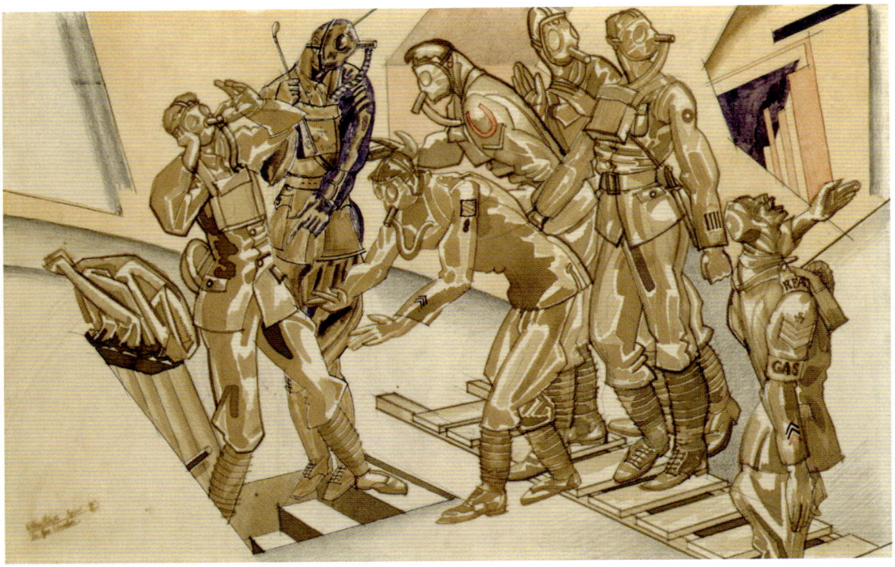

WILLIAM ROBERTS
The Gas Chamber
(1918)
ink watercolour on paper, 31.7 x 50.8 cm
IMPERIAL WAR MUSEUM, LONDON

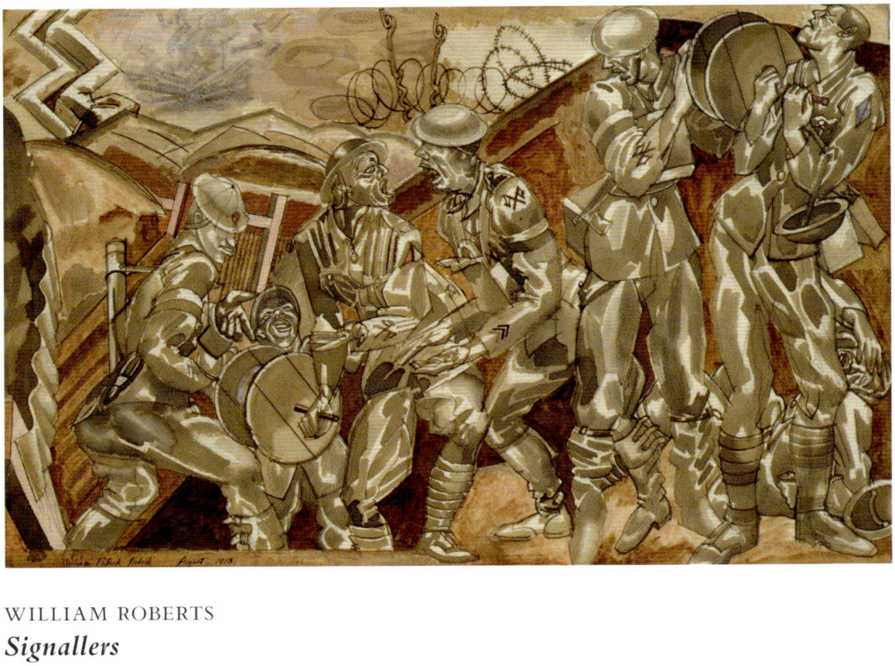

WILLIAM ROBERTS
Signallers
(1918)
ink pencil watercolour on paper, 31.1 x 49.5 cm
IMPERIAL WAR MUSEUM, LONDON

WILLIAM ROBERTS
Tommies filling their Water Bottles with Rain from a Shell Hole
(1918)
ink pencil chalk watercolour on paper, 50.8 x 38.1 cm
IMPERIAL WAR MUSEUM, LONDON

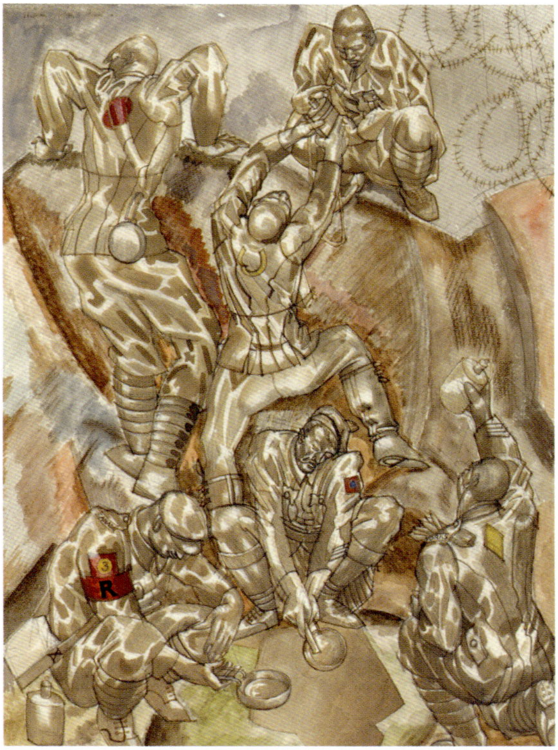

WILLIAM ROBERTS
Turning Out for an SOS. Battery action at night
(c.1918)
pencil watercolour on paper, 32.3 x 32.3 cm
IMPERIAL WAR MUSEUM, LONDON

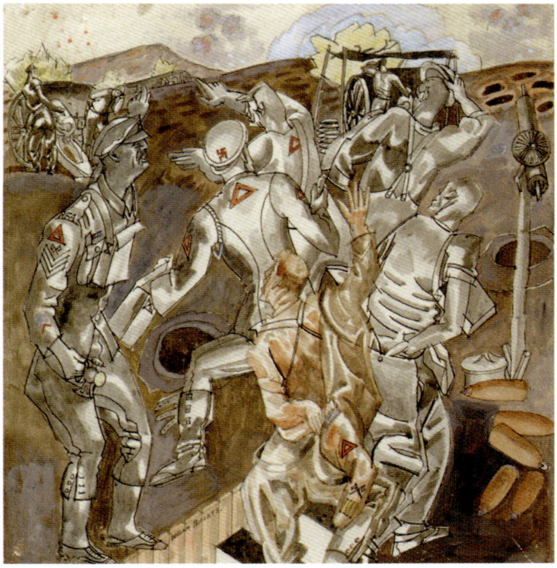

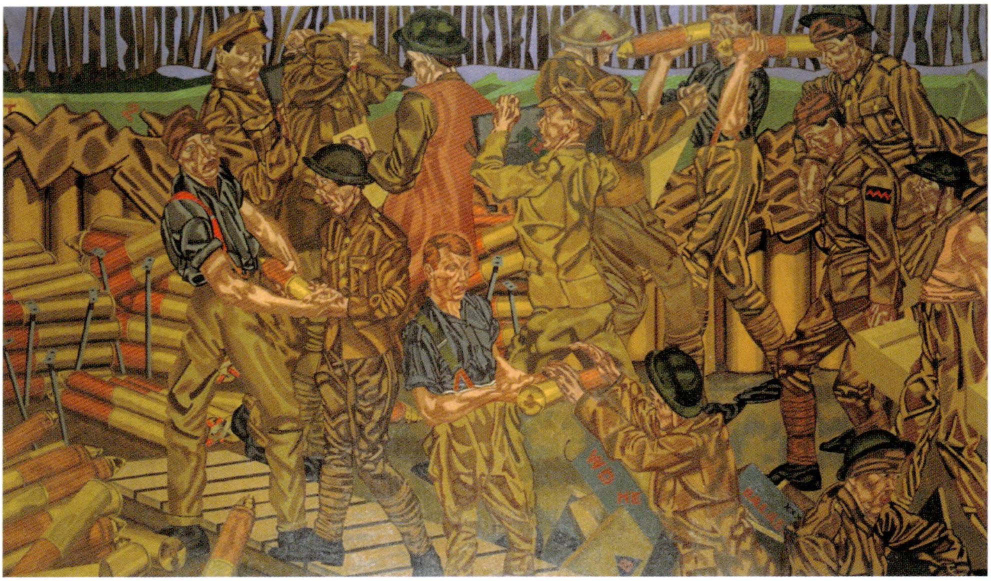

WILLIAM ROBERTS
A Shell Dump, France
(1918)
oil on canvas, 182.8 x 317.5 cm
IMPERIAL WAR MUSEUM, LONDON

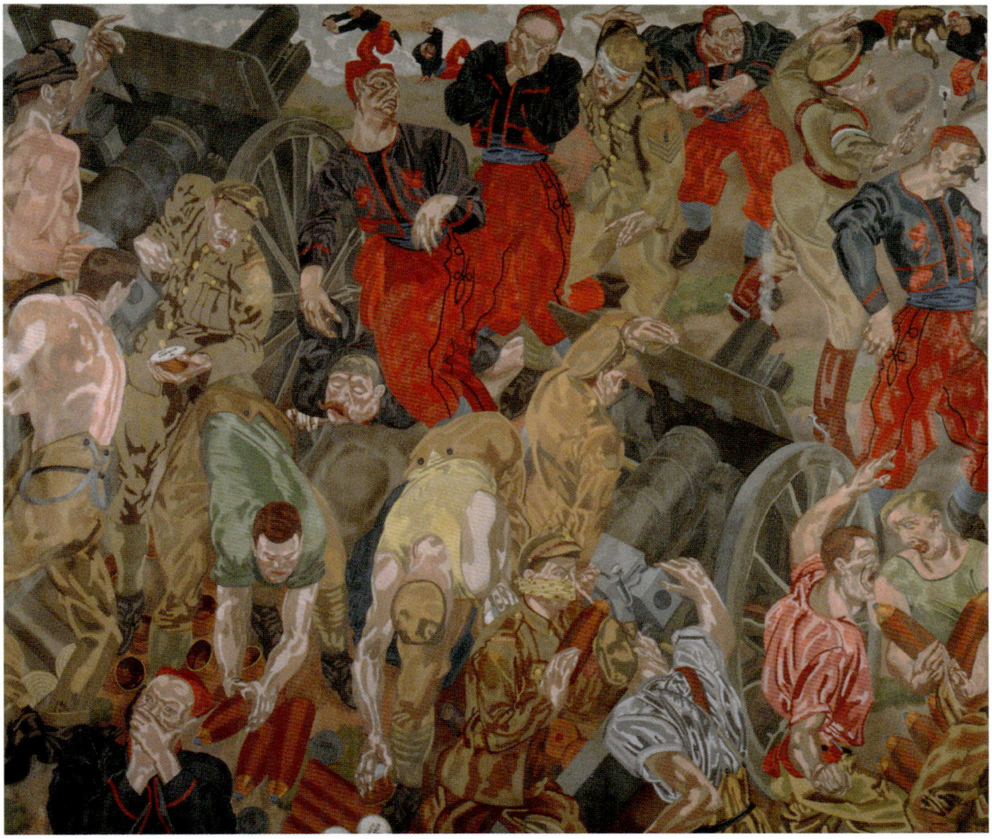

WILLIAM ROBERTS
The First German Gas Attack at Ypres
(1918)
oil on canvas, 304.8 x 365.8 cm

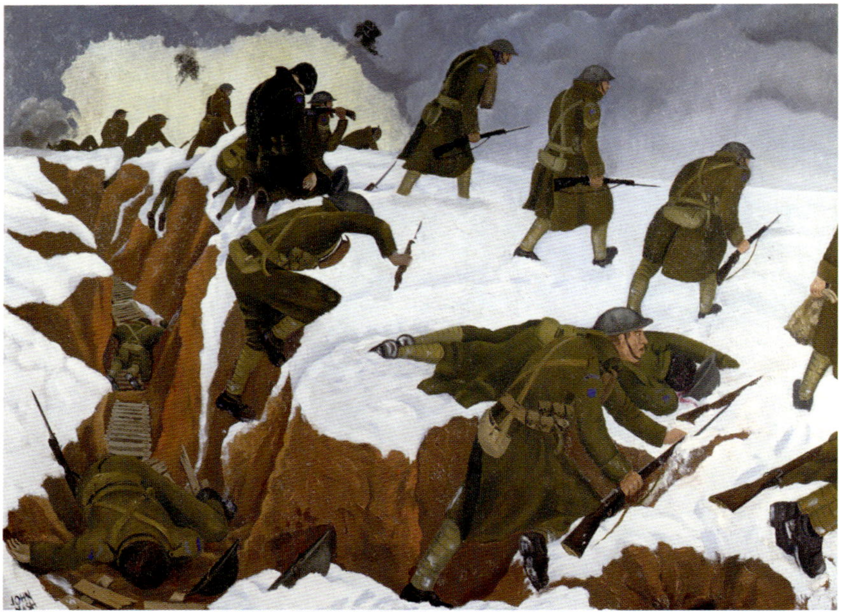

JOHN NASH
'Over The Top'. 1st Artists' Rifles at Marcoing, 30th December, 1917
(1918)
oil on canvas, 79.8 x 108 cm
IMPERIAL WAR MUSEUM, LONDON

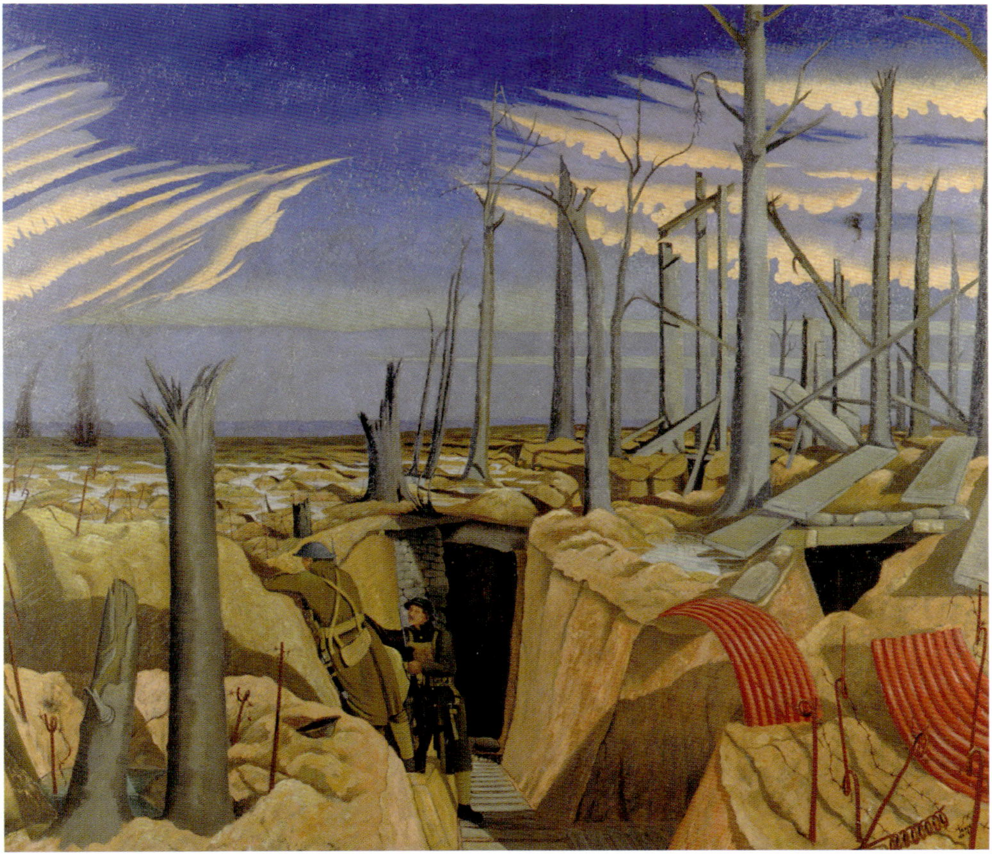

JOHN NASH
Oppy Wood, 1917. Evening
(1918)
oil on canvas, 182.8 x 213.3 cm
IMPERIAL WAR MUSEUM, LONDON

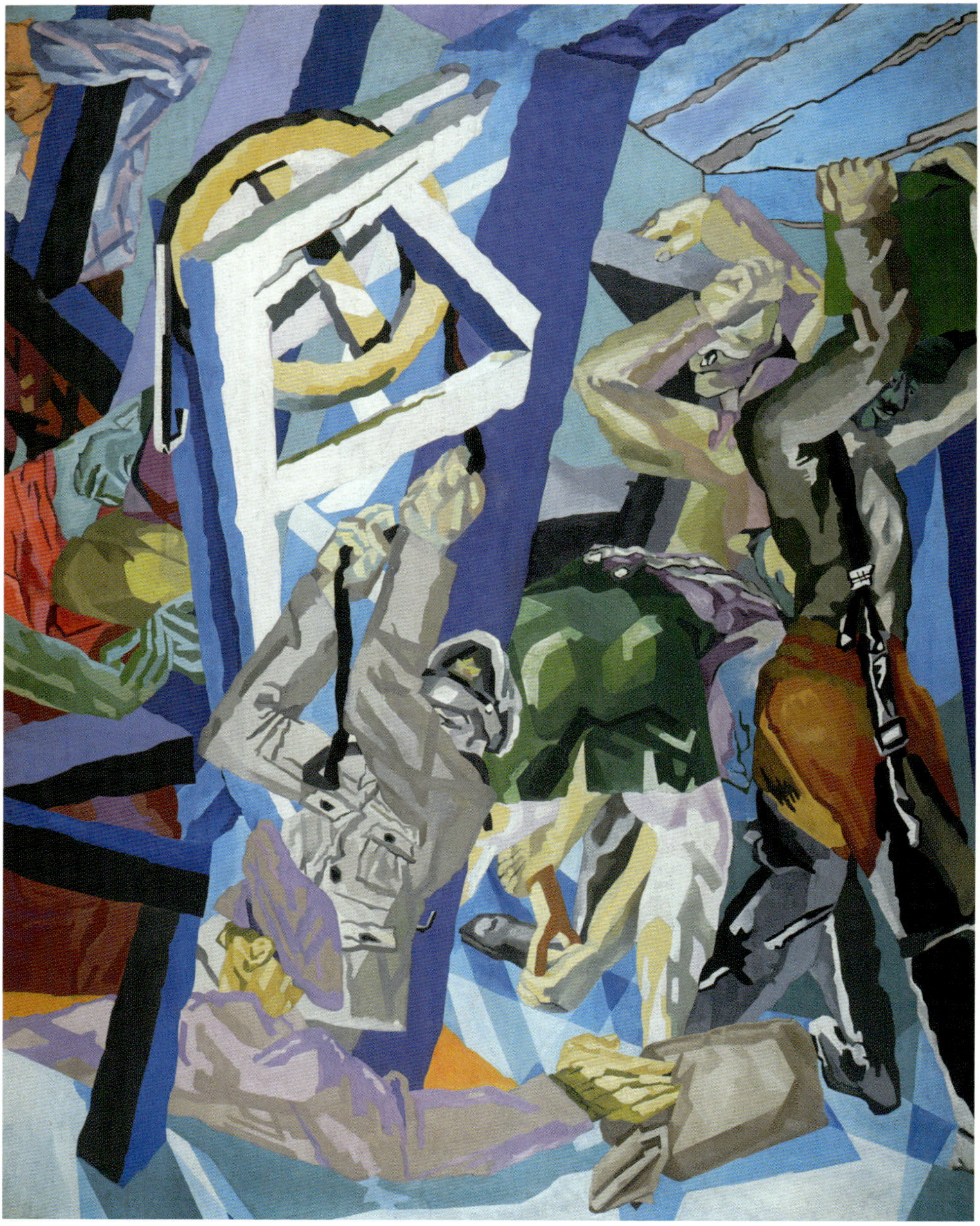

DAVID BOMBERG
Study for ***Sappers at Work: A Canadian Tunnelling Company, Hill 60, St Eloi***
(c.1918–19)
oil on canvas, 304 x 244 cm

> tired, but giving out the same wit and humour as of old. He was very happy and though I listened with horror and wonder to all he had seen and felt, he seemed to have been only tremendously interested in enjoying the hundreds of humorous things that had happened. He confessed the sight of wounded and dying men unnerved him.[49]

But it would be a further three months before Paul's concerted efforts to secure his brother as a government artist were fruitful. For John, there were more testing times ahead, not least a hard winter of front-line duty. On Christmas Eve 1917 he scribbled a note to his beloved Christine, which laid bare the deprivations, and near despair, of the infantryman's lot:

> Such a queer position to write in, you can't see anything but my feet are d—d cold. This is Xmas Eve – I spent last night w[ith] 3 of my men in advanced post – a perfectly uncovered shell hole; it was strange to watch one's rifle freeze all over & one's coat get covered w. slime and my wasn't it cold! There is a chance of being in the front line tonight & for Xmas Day. I don't mind telling you I shall be glad to get out of this, we are 700 yards in advance of our Coy along an iron-bound (by frost) road. I am curled up in a little 'funk' hole covered w[ith] a 'water' sheet & the shells which are bounding & bouncing somewhere none too far shake the earth like a thunder clap bringing bits of clay tumbling down my neck, a bit of shrapnel cut my coat this morning – aye & one of our own guns it was – nothing but bully beef & rum till your mouth feels like nothing on earth.[50]

This was in fact Nash's last letter from the front – sent in one of the precious green envelopes (the 'GE') that were so treasured by line soldiers – it also enclosed a letter for brother Paul 'about the War Artist job' that had proved so elusive but was about to come to fruition. Months later the Nash brothers found themselves painting together in a studio that had been until recently an old herb-drying shed in leafy Chalfont St Peter, in the Chilterns of south-east Buckinghamshire.[51] While Paul Nash was engaged with

---

49 Paul Nash, 5 November 1917 (written from Intelligence HQ France), quoted in Paul Nash, *Outline: an autobiography and other writings* (London: Faber and Faber, 1948) pp.206–09. *Outline* was compiled largely by Margaret Nash soon after Paul's death in 1946.

50 Letter XLIX, in *Love Letters from the Front*, p.111. Nash concluded the letter on Christmas Day, having managed a decent sleep in a dug out, and feasting on a ration of pudding ('not unlike cold clay'), tinned turkey and rum, which gave him a terrible headache. 'A man gave me a cracker & we gravely pulled it while great shells bounced overhead to its tiny report. We then sang carols & I have to go out again to the beastly post tonight. A proper mockery of a Xmas day, there was also no post.' (Letter LXIX)

51 As happened with Stanley Spencer, John Nash's papers releasing him from active duty arrived after he had taken up his post as official war artist. Like Spencer, Nash was arrested as a deserter until the misunderstanding was sorted. Although Nash was invited back to the Front at the country's expense to refresh his memory before embarking on his war painting, both brothers declined; instead they had a load of War Office barbed wire, duckboards, gun-chains and corrugated iron delivered to their Chalfont St Peter studio. (See Ronald Blythe, *First Friends*, pp.130–132)

his *magnum opus* canvas, *The Menin Road*, John was painting a stark memory of a battle that had taken place in the snow just days after he sent his last GE to Christine.

Over the Top is one of the most frank, even brutal, depictions of war to emerge from the British schemes, perhaps unique in its portrayal of a specific action as witnessed by one of the official artists.[52] It records an event on the morning of 30 December 1917 at 'Welsh Ridge' near Marcoing, south-west of Cambrai in France. Having been withdrawn to the support trenches, the First Battalion of the Artists' Rifles were hastily recalled to the front-line to repel a German attack. Nash was amongst them as they made their way in the freezing cold through crowded trenches that had in places been flattened by artillery fire. Arriving at zero hour, Nash was cursorily shown a map but given only vague indications of his objectives, except to understand that the daylight attack was actually designed as a diversion to a bombing raid up a support trench on his left. With undue haste B Company was summarily dispatched over the parapet towards the enemy.

> There was not a shot for a while, suddenly the Germans opened up and that seemed to be every machine gun in Europe… We never got to grips with the enemy but were stopped in sight of them. We had to 'hole up' in craters and shell holes till nightfall and then get back to our original line. Casualties were very heavy.[53]

A disastrous and unnecessary attack, casualties were indeed heavy: 68 of the 80 officers and men were killed or wounded, only one sergeant and the Quarter-Master were left. Nash later described it as 'in fact, pure murder',

> …and I was lucky to escape untouched… It was bitterly cold and we were easy targets against the snow and in the daylight… I think the vivid memory of the occasion helped me when I painted the picture and provoked whatever intensity of feeling may be found in it.[54]

Nash was a modest fellow. Not many paintings contain such a distillation of the gravity of fate as this composition with its hunch-shouldered men and its deadpan dead. Few images carry the burden of grimness as weightily as this raw, primitive, picture.

---

52 John Nash, *'Over the Top': 1st Artists' Rifles at Marcoing, 30th December 1917*. Oil on canvas, 79 x 107 cm. IWM:ART 1656.

53 John Nash in a letter to David Brown, 15 January 1974, and conversation 4 March 1974, quoted in *We are Making a New World* (Edinburgh, Scottish National Gallery of Modern Art, 1974) Entry No.32 to David Brown, Tate Gallery. Reprinted in Sir John Rothenstein, *John Nash* (London: Macdonald & Co. 1983) p.48.

54 John Nash to David Brown.

John Rothenstein was one of many who were profoundly impressed by 'its dignity, energy and grim harmony'.[55] It stands comparison with his brother's remarkable work, but it gains by an unerring simplicity. Compared to Paul's sophisticated painted surfaces, complex designs and rich tonalities, *Over the Top* is actually quite lumpen, its tonal range limited to dark silhouettes against blinding white. The design is simple: a gash-like trench, sloping snowfield, close horizon, and a pewter-grey sky. And the oil paint itself is laid in thick, rather uncompromising strokes. There is little colour, other than the ripped brown earth and the heaving grey sky. Yet, the material impact of the picture's construction conspires with the lacerating narrative to create an icon of quite deadening impact, making it one of the most memorable – and accessible – images of battle ever painted.

BOMBERG
Sapper and sound-ranger

From being the most audacious painter of his generation at the Slade, David Bomberg suffered a terrible crisis of confidence as a result of the war. He was in the Café Royal, with the ebullient Augustus John, when the outbreak was announced in August 1914. Unphased by John's grim, but astute, observation that this news 'is going to be bad for art', Bomberg tried to enlist that month but was turned away, possibly because of his accent and beard, but probably because the recruiting offices were inundated and barely able to cope with the patriotic surge that heralded the global news. Bomberg returned to his studio and exhibited at the first Vorticist Exhibition at the Dore Gallery in 1915, though he refused to blithely sign up to the Vorticist creed and its hard-line aesthetics. The work he showed at the time was adventurous, even radical with such titles as *Design in White* and *Decorative Experiment*.

By November 1915, he had enlisted with the Royal Engineers, but was soon transferred to the King's Royal Rifle Corps, a sapper in the same unit as Harold Williamson. In the middle of the following year, only weeks before the great Somme offensive, and shortly after marrying his first wife, Bomberg was posted with his detachment to the Western Front. The work was dull, repetitive and, at times, dangerous. There was little there that interested him as a painter, though something in the grim existence of his fellow

55 Sir John Rothenstein, *John Nash* (London: Macdonald and Co., 1983) p.50. By comparison, and somewhat perversely, the reviewer in *The Burlington Magazine* regarded the painting as 'positively witty' in its 'convincing rendering of laborious impeded movement.' ('X', 'A Monthly Chronicle: The Imperial War Museum: Exhibition of War Paintings and Other Records', *The Burlington Magazine*, Volume 36, 1920, pp.94–95).

soldiers stimulated a literary nerve in him and he wrote long tracts of prose and, towards the end of the war, some brilliant blank verse:

> They lived a thousand intermittent lives, those trenchmen, with liquid acid freezing on their hearts... with faces drawn and livid, with eyes so strange as terrors sometimes are... and in the night, within the banking of one screeching shell before the termination of a flight.[56]

Like the hapless William Roberts based close by with the Royal Field Artillery, Bomberg made an unlikely soldier, although he was certainly more attentive than Roberts, more determined perhaps to learn his craft, and be thought competent and well-prepared. However, the odds were at times stacked against him. His wife later drew a vivid pen-portrait of Bomberg 'the Sapper':

> I cannot imagine David fitting in easily to the soldier pattern routine; yet his dogged insistence on the job in hand, his trained sensitivity, his map-drawing and his willingness to volunteer for the hot spots – he had a theory which he confirmed to me during the London Blitz that the target is always the safest place, though I must say I often felt doubtful about this – made him a valuable addition to the service. He worked merrily with a mate out on No-Man's-Land sound ranging. On one occasion in the trenches during a period of snatched rest, David took his sound-ranging instrument from his trouser's pocket keeping his finger on the press-button. At this time the whole command were desperately trying to locate Big Bertha. David's ears were attuned to the guns like an orchestra so that in his sleep when the deeper vibrations occurred, he just pressed the button and continued to press. Along the line came the field phone: 'Who is pressing the ★★★ button? We are getting yards and yards of ★★★ gun.' They traced him and woke him up.[57]

Having survived 1916, Bomberg received terrible news the following year: his brother died in the fighting, his one-time champion and friend, T.E. Hulme was killed near Ypres in September 1917, his pre-war ally Gaudier-Brzeska had been killed two years earlier. Life in the trenches had 'become too much to bear', he felt 'beyond caring about the rules of the war game'.[58] In a moment of calculated protest he 'deliberately put the gun to his foot and pulled the trigger.' Even at this stage in the war, a self-inflicted wound was a grievous sin, punishable by military law. However, Bomberg was quickly patched up and returned to active service, where he was given – possibly as

56 William Lipke, *David Bomberg: A Critical Study of his Life and Work* (Evelyn, Adams and Mackay, London, 1967) p.47.

57 Lilian Bomberg, in William Lipke, *David Bomberg*, p.47.

58 Richard Cork, *A Bitter Truth: Avant-Garde Art and the Great War* (Yale University Press, 1994) p.167.

a punishment – the 'post of Runner for his Unit, which meant going through the hottest part of the firing'. It was a gruelling time and he encountered grim sights, which he captured not in drawings or sketches but in bitter poems of protest, their tone coarse, uncharitable:

> What's left of the soldier-man, killed on
> patrol some months back? Only
> a shrapnel hat, turned upside
> down; – lying apart, some
> sun-burnt bones, a hard
> tanned hairy-hide, and rags
> mouldering in the flowering
> thistle-down.[59]

A call from the Canadian War Memorials Committee arrived only weeks later. It was to prove to be a mixed blessing. Bomberg was told (as had been William Roberts) that the picture was to be undertaken at his own risk; the terms of the commission were to be closely heeded. 'Cubist work', he was warned, 'would be inadmissible for the purpose'.[60]

At first the restrictive nature of the commission troubled Bomberg. He lacked the bullish resilience of Roberts and was wary of the draconian terms set out by the Canadians and closely monitored by the art critic and adviser Paul Konody. The Hungarian had already made it known that he was largely ignorant of Bomberg's pre-war painting and was clearly taking quite a risk for such a large painting – three metres high by two a half metres wide – which was intended to be the last component in a grand memorial scheme in Ottawa. However, despite the pressure, Bomberg's first sketches showed little in the way of creative compromise, being derivations of his pre-war painting – hard-edged, energetic abstractions that embraced the 'Pure Form' of such canvases as *The Mud Bath* but hinting also at a more humanistic rendering of natural form.

Before he embarked on the commission, Bomberg appears to have had a very clear idea in mind, stating that his aim had been 'to extinguish the phase of war – I had had enough of that – and wanted the relief – and the sublimation of creating the forms of war not in the dank, death-smelling underground mine – like a coal-pit – but in the open-air, bathed in sunlight'.[61]

However, his chosen subject seems rather at odds with this breezy and optimistic aim. He chose for the project an image of sappers labouring in a tunnel under the German trenches of Hill 60, at

59 Quoted in Richard Cork, *A Bitter Truth*, p.168; see also Alice Mayes, *The Young Bomberg, 1914–1925*, pp.21–22).

60 Harold Watkins, to Bomberg 29 December 1917, Tate Gallery Archive, London.

61 David Bomberg, *unpublished memoir*, 11 April 1957, Tate Gallery Archive, London.

St Eloi, near Ypres, 'a tribute,' he proudly declared, 'to the heroic miners, comprised of Canadians in the main re-enforced by Yorkshire, Welch, and groups of Russian Canadian miners'.[62] He even elected to stay in Belgium to complete a number of on-the-spot studies, remaining near the front until the Armistice in November 1918, after which time he was released from active service and allocated to 'general duties'.

So why did Bomberg create such an idiosyncratic painting? Its very title conjures up an image of semi-clad labourer-soldiers toiling in the noisome depths of a vast hill, somewhere filthy and obscure under the Western Front. Instead, what he showed to Konody was a vast canvas more like a festival than a front-line, a riot of discordant colour and wiry figures caught up in a dance of contrapuntal exuberance. Clearly, he had made an attempt to temper his predilection for hard diagonal geometrics by injecting more representational details – a soldier's cap, his Canadian badge clearly discernible; the interlocking architecture of a gantry; fingers and thumbs clasping spanners and grasping ropes; the busy, synchronized energy of the working party crammed into the confined space of the underground gallery. But these representational concessions are largely lost in the paintings' high-key colour scheme. Instead of the deep rich chiaroscuro one might expect from the picture's title, we have instead a quite startling base of cobalt blue, ultramarine and purple, with the figures picked out in bright twists of lemon and orange – quite at odds, one might think, with the subterranean gloom of the tunnel and the hard-edged diagonal shadows that would have been cast by the glare of a few lanterns. Was Bomberg being mischievous? Had he sight of Roberts's equally large canvas of the first German gas attack, with its wild arabesques and highly coloured rococo surface? Did he feel the need to compromise his preferred geometric style for something that he hoped would appease the Canadians? If so, he was to be deeply disappointed, indeed devastated by their critique of *Sappers at Work: A Canadian Tunnelling Company*. 'You submit to me the most wonderful drawings – yours is the last panel to be fixed before Government House can be opened' raged Paul Konody, 'and you bring me this futurist abortion. What am I to say to my Committee?' According to the record of this incident (written by Bomberg's wife) Konody was beside himself with anger, stomping around their small flat, he 'wrung his hands in annoyance, and stamped round and round the offending painting which had been lain out of the floor for his inspection'.[63]

62 David Bomberg, *unpublished memoir*, 1957, Tate Gallery Archive, London.

63 Alice Mayes, *The Young Bomberg, 1914–1925*, unpublished memoir, 1972, Tate Gallery Archive, London, pp.27–28. She added that 'Konody had a club foot and wore a built-up sole to his boot, which made him "stamp" still more drastically.'

Humiliated, Bomberg re-negotiated the commission and 'in an incredibly short time' had completed version two. It has the same dimensions, a similar subject, and a modified composition, but Bomberg – with Konody's support – has concentrated on the very construction of the tunnel, accentuating the lattice-work structure of the beams, the vaulted roof of corrugated iron, the raking light, the diagonal shadows, and the purposeful sappers, busy carrying, lifting, hoisting, but now stripped of the *joie-de-vivre* that burst out of the earlier version. After the painting was completed, Bomberg described it as a poor compromise, caught between the charged, angular energy of his pre-war paintings, and the demands of the Canadian commission, with its petty requirements for exactitude and easy intelligibility. Yet, seen as a pair, the two vast canvases are a fascinating coupling: the first colour-soaked, soft-edged and celebratory; the other tonal and delineated, the mood serious, even oppressive – the pair a stereoscopic rendition of the soldiers' war.

In the lower right-hand corner of Version Two – now housed in Ottawa – stands Bomberg himself, burdened by a beam of wood. Somewhat resigned to his fate (and perhaps that of the Canadian canvas too), he looks away from the industrious scene, as if to set himself apart from the memory of a difficult and debilitating war. Although a monumental work in its own right, the painting has little of the edgy anger expressed in his long prose poem written within weeks of the end of the war.[64]

Winter Night
Thick blankets smother the earth. Night, in an air-tight keg, sits brooding dismally. Ebony blotches distort his shape; no rent only a smudge of lesser black asserts itself, uncovers the tops of farthest trees. About is deep dull soot-dead-green.

Hemmed in. The bolted ceiling of the night rests on our heads, like vaulted roofs of iron huts the troops use out in France, – unlit. Grope, – stretch out your hand and feel its corrugated sides, rusted.

Dimly seen, six wiring-stakes driven in the ground, askew, some yards apart; – demons dragging strangling-wire. Earth and sky; each in each enfolded – hypnotized: – sucked in the murky snare, stricken dumb. …

---

64 These are the opening three stanzas to a thirteen-part poem, written in September 1918, as 'Winter Night', reprinted in William Lipke, *David Bomberg*, pp.120–121.

War, art and the imagination
A coda

When the war ended and peace fell, what became of the many artists whose life and work has been celebrated in this book? A few died young, many had a troubled middle age, and nearly all suffered as a result of injuries – physical and mental – brought about by active service.

Perhaps the most tragic case was that of William Orpen. He emerged from his self-imposed years in the battle zone much damaged by the war, and sickened to the heart by the callousness and petty self-interest of the peace-makers he had been commissioned to paint in Paris. Unlike the frock-coated, self-congratulatory politicians, Orpen could not banish from his memory the 'millions of mangled corpses [left] in the Flanders slime'.[1] Nor could he easily reconcile his social eminence (a Knight of the Realm in 1918, a full member of the Royal Academy a year later) with the terrible social injustices he had witnessed in France and Belgium. Nor could his body extinguish the exhaustion and disease that he had contracted somewhere between Peronne and Paris. Although he was socially revered and in constant demand as a portraitist, Orpen's last years were isolated ones, his family a distant configuration, his friends few, his acquaintances many. He died on 29 September 1931, just fifty-three years old, still painting, but a much reduced figure, wracked by alcohol dependency and persistent ill-health, which some put

1 John Rothenstein, *Modern English Painters*, Volume 1 (London: Eyre and Spottiswoode, 1952) p.247.

down to venereal diseases contracted during the war.

Eleven years younger than Orpen but equally traumatized by the war (and just as unsettled by the peace) Richard Nevinson was said to have considered suicide in 1919, but as one might have expected of an ex-rebel, sole English Futurist and publicity-hungry 'soldier-artist', he sprang back 'angrily and vociferously', projecting his painting and himself into the public eye and working tirelessly to keep it there. Ambivalent towards modernism, 'never quite sure whether to resist or join',[2] Nevinson flirted with numerous subjects and styles after the war, producing moody and sodden cityscapes in the 1920s, and strange allegorical images with convoluted titles and ambiguous meanings in the 1930s. As the decades passed he retreated from urban themes to paint rather bland southern English landscapes and flower pieces, but he was rarely out of the press, maintaining contact with a court of journalists who could rely upon him to offer a colourful view on any topic, from women's fashion to Mayfair gossip. Accepted into the New English Art Club in 1929, and elected an Associate of the Royal Academy ten years later, Nevinson was, by the outbreak of war in 1939, more famed for his opinions than for his paintings. Although he served as a stretcher-bearer for a few months, his health had never been good and on a painting trip to the south coast he suffered a stroke, which paralysed his painting hand and left him with a speech impediment. Stung by rejection as an official war artist, Nevinson taught himself to paint with his left-hand and, in fact, exhibited three landscapes at the Royal Academy in 1946, which he visited in a wheelchair pushed by his wife, Kathleen. He died soon after, aged fifty-seven.

In that same year, Paul Nash died, also aged fifty-seven. A sickly child and an asthmatic adult, Nash's poor health had been exacerbated by his service in the trenches and he took years to regain his momentum after the Armistice, complaining memorably of being 'a war artist without a war'.[3] However, even before his untimely death he had gained the mantle of one of the pre-eminent British artists of the century and was widely held to be the most evocative landscape painter of his generation. When his work was shown at a memorial exhibition at the Tate Gallery in 1948 reviewers applauded him as 'an exceedingly English artist', a 'native genius who understood his England in terms of Blake's Albion', and a painter with 'Wordsworthian intuition'.[4] For three decades Nash had travelled southern England seeking out the distinctive atmosphere, the protective spirit – the *genius loci* – of rural locations. He found it in the melancholic

---

2 David Cohen, 'The Rising City', in *C.R.W. Nevinson: The Twentieth Century*, (London: Merrel Holberton) p.52.

3 Paul Nash, *Outline: an Autobiography and Other Writings* (London: Faber and Faber, 1948) p.218.

4 From various reviews of Paul Nash, *Memorial Exhibition*, Tate Gallery, 1948; Nash file.

greyness of the seawalls at Dymchurch on the Kent coast; on the moonlit gloamings of the Wittenham Clumps in Oxfordshire, and on the chalklands of the South Downs, where he experimented with an evanescent form of English Surrealism. Always inclined to find the uncanny and the mystical in his subject-matter, Nash's innate morbidity was exactly matched to the siege conditions of the Battle of Britain, where terror appeared about to fall from the sky. He produced some of his most potent and symbolic pieces when he became inspired by the idea of the 'rose of death', the name the Spanish gave to the parachute. His renditions of crashed German bomber planes are as resonant as anything he produced in Flanders thirty years earlier. Nash saw only a few months of peace; he died relatively young, his standing as a leading British artist confirmed by his last large canvases, and his reputation is still intact fifty years later, unlike others who had graduated from the Slade in that golden era of Tonks and Brown.[5]

Stanley Spencer had been one of the most brilliant of that generation. Unlike Henry Lamb, who took many years to recover from the war, Spencer carried on from where he had left off four years earlier, lifting his unfinished canvas *Swan Upping* onto a makeshift easel in his bedroom and simply started painting again. Four years later, in 1923, Spencer joined Lamb in Poole where day after day he sat at the large dining room table creating acres of drawings that recalled his time in the Balkans and at the Beaufort Hospital in Bristol. By 1932 he had realized his vision of war, peace and resurrection on the painted walls of the Sandham Memorial Chapel in Burghclere, his 'Holy Box' as he lovingly called it. The Chapel is an extraordinary achievement, and ranks alongside the poetry of Owen and Sassoon, and Britten's *War Requiem*, 'as amongst the 'most moving monuments to 20th-century war'.[6] Acclaimed as a painter, sought by dealers and newly-elected as an Associate of the Royal Academy, Spencer seemed assured of an esteemed middle age, but calamity befell him: marital discord, financial ruin, indifferent (at times hostile) critical reception to his new work, and erratic health bedeviled him until his death in 1959. Almost sixty of his sixty-eight years were spent in his beloved Cookham, his 'heaven on earth', but many still believe his best work resulted from his war years in Bristol, the Balkans and those long lonely days spent high on the painting scaffold in the chapel at Burghclere.

Gilbert, his younger brother in age, but always known at the Beaufort as the 'elder Spencer' by dint of Stanley's diminutive size,

5 As William Roberts wrote: 'The Slade at that time was in one of its periodical triumph flows when from the unknown deep arise a few gifted ones. And now upon the crest of the wave were riding nearly half a dozen: Stanley Spencer, Mark Gertler, William Roberts, Edward Wadsworth, Christopher Nevinson.' William Roberts, quoted in *An English Cubist* p.15.

6 See Paul Gough, *Stanley Spencer: Journey to Burghclere* (Bristol: Sansom, 2006) pp.194–195.

returned to painting convinced that the war had robbed him of several years of creative development. He, too, went on to become a Royal Academician and assumed senior posts in several British art schools, including Professor of Painting at the Royal College of Art, where his colleagues would have included another famous brother, John Nash.[7] For someone who scorned formal art education, John had done remarkably well after the Great War, gaining recognition as a painter, writer, and wood engraver. At the outbreak of the next war, he joined the Observer Corps, but, dissatisfied with their passive role, he packed up his painting gear and enlisted in the Royal Marines. Settling in Essex after the war, he and his wife became deeply attached to the Stour Valley which provided an unending source of inspiration for his painting. Up to his death in 1977 he continued to be rated, as did Gilbert Spencer, as a fine painter, illustrator and water-colourist.[8]

Others at the Royal College of Art who had survived the war were William Rothenstein, who encouraged his students to visit the shattered towns of the former Western Front to seek out picturesque ruination, and William Newton – the author of instruction manuals in target indication and panoramic sketching – who became its Professor of Architecture.

As might have been expected, Wyndham Lewis turned his back on the academy and the establishment entirely. After the war he tried to keep the *avant-garde* alive, but with little success. Undeterred, he set out on his own, producing a vast body of work: books of criticism on philosophy, politics, and literature; fiction and fantasy pieces; portrait paintings and striking, imaginative work that borrowed and adapted Dadaist, Constructivist and Surrealist ideas. In the 1930s his political views aroused widespread opposition. Many in Britain decried his authoritarian leanings and condemned his sympathy to fascist regimes. W. H. Auden described him as 'that lonely old volcano of the right'.[9] So lonely, that by the eve of the Second World War he had decamped to North America in search of paid work, a period of sorry isolation that was captured in his novel, *Self-condemned*. Lewis returned to London in 1945, but a malignant tumour was crushing his optic nerve, and he eventually went blind in 1951,

---

7 Spencer, Gilbert, *Stanley Spencer by his Brother Gilbert* (London, Gollancz, 1961; reprinted, Bristol: Redcliffe Press, 1991)

8 Sir John Rothenstein, *John Nash* (London: Macdonald and Co, 1983). His canvas *The Cornfield*, which he had painted in 1918, as his 'thank-you' picture for having survived the trenches, had been greeted with acclaim and was later presented by the Contemporary Art Society to the Tate Gallery. The Nash brothers painted their 'own' work after 6pm, once their daily commitment to the war museum had been done, hence the long evening shadows in this restful image.

9 Percy Wyndham Lewis, *Blasting and Bombardiering, Autobiography 1914–1926* (London: Eyre & Spottiswoode, 1937) p.114. His own work of the 1920s and 30s was a 'sharp compound of modernism, satire and fantasy' (Tom Lubbock, review of 'British Vision – Observation and Imagination in British Art', Museum of Fine Arts, Citadelpark, Ghent, Belgium, 2007–08, in *The Independent*, 5 November 2007, p.12–13. A major exhibition of Lewis's portraits was staged at the National Portrait Gallery, London in 2008 with a catalogue by Paul Edwards, *Wyndham Lewis: Portraits* (NPG, London, 2008).

bringing an end to his painting and to his art criticism for *The Listener*, where for over six years he had been an insightful, early champion of young figurative painters such as Francis Bacon, and an equally vitriolic critic of abstraction, for which he had little patience.

Of all the major artists who served on the Western Front, William Roberts lived to the ripest age. He returned to London after the war to become one of its sharpest interpreters of city life, depicting for some sixty years singular visions of metropolitan life: its music halls and dance floors, offices and public spaces, streets and parks, all populated by solid, good-humoured, and dignified working-class protagonists. Apart from a brief period in the Second World War, he taught at the Central School of Art until 1960, supplementing his part-time income with commissioned portraits and regular shows of work. His monumental urban scenes were a regular highlight of the Royal Academy Summer Shows, where he exhibited every year until his death in 1980, aged eighty-five. Combative to the end, his last years were coloured by a series of pamphlets that challenged the roots of the Modernist movement in England and refuted Wyndham Lewis's claim to have been the leader of the Vorticists.[10]

Muirhead Bone and Eric Kennington also reached ripe ages: Bone was knighted in 1937 for his services to art, but also in recognition of his unstinting support for younger artists and for his selfless service on national committees and selection panels. A few years later he offered his services to Kenneth Clark's war art committee, undertaking prolonged and exhausting spells of drawing across the British Isles. He finally achieved the coveted crowns of an honorary major in the Royal Marines, having always been uncomfortable with 'his single pip' in the Great War. By contrast, about the same time, Kennington resigned his commission in high dudgeon at the apparent lack of publicity for his exhibition of over-life-size drawings of fighter pilots, bombers, parachutists and other air-borne heroes. Ironically, perhaps Kennington's best known artwork is not one of these assertive, slightly overbearing portraits, but the memorial sculpture he made for the tomb of T.E. Lawrence in the quiet Dorset town of Wareham.[11]

In 1960, the year that Kennington died, Adrian Hill was already established as one of Britain's best known and widely mimicked drawing tutors, with an extensive back catalogue of manuals and painting guides, amongst them *On Drawing and Painting Trees* (1936),

10 William Roberts, *Memories of the War to End War 1914–18* or *4.5 Howitzer Gunner R.F.A. 1916–1918* (London: private press, 1974). Roberts contested Lewis's claim to be the leader of the Vorticists in a series of pamphlets published between 1956 and 1958: W. Roberts, *Cometism and Vorticism: a Tate Gallery catalogue revised* (1956); *The Resurrection of Vorticism and the Apotheosis of Wyndham Lewis at the Tate* (1956); *A Press View of the Tate Gallery* (1956); *A reply to my Biographer, Sir John Rothenstein* (1957); *Abstract and Cubist Paintings and Drawings* (1957).

11 See Jonathan Black, *The Sculpture of Eric Kennington* (London: Lund Humphries, 2002).

On Mastery of Watercolour (1938) and *Pleasures of Painting* (1952). With a string of professional affiliations and a natural confidence in transmitting helpful tips and hints (first piloted in draughty lecture halls on the Western Front) Hill was a natural television presenter and his BBC Sketch Club series attracted a dedicated fan club of amateur painters and children who devoured his advice.[12] Dressed as he was in his hallmark beret and smock, few who watched would have been aware of his hair-raising escapades with the sniping and scouting section on the Western Front fifty years earlier.

Paul Maze, an equally brave – at time reckless -- young artist-scout in the Great War, also went on to a distinguished career as a painter, becoming painting companion (but, as he always insisted, definitely not his tutor) to Winston Churchill, who wrote the introduction to Maze's war memoir, *A Frenchman in Khaki* published in 1934. Churchill lavishly praised Maze's abilities to record 'the battle scenes of Armageddon', and described him as an individual 'who not only loved the fighting troops and shared their perils, but perceived the beauties of light and shade, of form and colour of which even the horrors of war cannot rob the progress of the sun'. Maze exhibited often in London, and a large show was held at Wildenstein's New Bond Street gallery on the occasion of his ninetieth birthday in 1977. Another leading soldier of his day, Lieutenant-General Anthony Farrar-Hockney wrote an enthusiastic introduction to the catalogue.[13]

The Great War still exercises an extraordinary fascination over the British historical imagination. To many, it is simply regarded as a series of muddy and bloody tragedies conducted by stoic 'Tommies' directed from the rear by incompetent and blinkered old buffers. As a caricature, this version of the past has shreds of truth, but it is a grotesque over-simplification of the realities. Yet, despite a decade or more of diligent revisionist history, the words 'futility' and 'slaughter' colour every reading of the war; allowing little room for more reasoned reflection.[14] As we have seen, the war stimulated some of the best British art of the twentieth century, giving shape to a scheme of arts patronage on a scale never seen before, and nourishing the work of dozens of artists who would populate the creative *milieu* for decades to come.

---

12 The musician, painter and future member of the Rolling Stones, Ronnie Wood, recalled how 'Both of my brothers went off to Ealing Art College and our house was thriving with artistic endeavours. I was always sending my artwork into the BBC's Sketch Club. That was the first art show on TV and starred a man named Adrian Hill. On Thursdays, just before dinner time, he'd stand in front of an easel in his white smock and talk about watercolours and oil painting while showing the viewers how to draw. I watched him on our tiny black and white telly, and when he asked kids to send in their drawings I bombarded him with mine.' www.ronniewood.com/50s.aspx

13 Quoted by Anne Singer, *The Lost Impressionist* (London: Aurum Press, 1983).

14 The counter-arguments were begun by John Terraine, *The Smoke and the Fire: Myths and Anti-myths of War* (London, Sidgwick and Jackson, 1980), and have since been rigorously and systematically (though not without controversy) addressed by John Bourne and Gary Sheffield, amongst others.

Although there is little doubt that war is cruel, debased and often wickedly stupid, many artists, poets and writers had to live with the uncomfortable recognition that the conflict fuelled their muse, invigorated their imagination, and on occasion honed their creativity. Wyndham Lewis may have been playfully ironic when he boasted that 'You must not miss a war, if one is going! You cannot afford to miss that experience'.[15] But others wrote of their longing 'to do drawings of that great brown land', to render the face of the battlefield in oils or watercolour, and to leave some visual trace of their unique circumstances. It is in this interstice between revulsion and fascination that we find some of the most impressive and moving art of the Great War; paintings, prints, and drawings that are a mesh of tense ambiguities, ironic counterpoint and taut poetics. This complicated, often contradictory, sensibility was brilliantly summarized by the poet, painter and one-time infantry officer David Jones, when he described the weird topography of No-Man's-Land, as a zone where:

> ...the sudden violences and long stillnesses, the sharp contours and unformed voids of that mysterious existence profoundly affected the imaginations of those who suffered it. It was a place of enchantment.[16]

But I will leave the last words (and ones that are surprisingly seldom reproduced) to one of the painters who saw some of the longest and most dangerous periods of front-line combat; an artist who was consistently responsive to painterly effects and striking motifs, but who never forgot that this was an 'indecent war' full of scenes which were often beyond description, but always aware that he was witnessing a phantasmagoric place that was simultaneously blessed and blasted:

> The whole of the earth for miles is disrupted and pitted by shells so closely as to render easy walking impossible. Decay in war material, human composition and natural objects (trees) is everywhere, yet Nature is uninterrupted. Cornflowers and many kinds of others bloom over the trench-tops and all is covered with a thick growth of merciful herbiage. Birds sing and swallows fly out among the shells and machine-gun bullets. You expect to see almost eternal night or winter, yet the sunsets are as wonderful and the night full of stars. ... the cacophony of sounds marshalled in a night bombardment. Machine-guns tatting and cackling like a lot of silly women or recently disemburdened hens – a maddening noise – then a sniper's bullet with the sound of a carter's whip cuts the silent intervals. A soft 'phut' and up goes a Very light, falls, flares, casting

15 Percy Wyndham Lewis, *Blasting and Bombardiering, Autobiography 1914–1926* (London: Eyre & Spottiswoode, 1937) p.112.

16 David Jones, *In Parenthesis* (London: Faber, 1937)

two diagonal shafts of light from the ground, then darkness again. Now let the batteries start with numerous reports and the crump crump of the shells exploding. You hear our shrapnel shells screaming overhead and bursting in the air in golden flashes. I have seen what was told were burning oil shells bursting into cascades of yellow-red stars amongst a blasted wood, and red lights rising and falling like slow fishes in the firmament of the night. Amongst all this din... I noticed on the parapet in front of me where I stood shivering with cold and wet and not a little fear – a very small fly seated stupidly tranquil on a clod of earth. It seemed such a tiny atom and yet...it appeared to out do all the spectacular din by the intensity of its stillness... I remember one thing – very fine – it was late evening afterglow and the trenches' dull decayed earth colour was silhouetted against the sky. An aeroplane flew over firing on the Boche trenches with its machine-gun, a straight line of flashes from the machine slanting across to the trenches like a taut golden chain.[17]

17 John Nash writing to Dora Carrington, late summer 1917, just before the Battle of Passchendaele, quoted by Ronald Blythe, *First Friends* (London: Viking, 1997), pp.116–117.

Further reading

British art and Modernism

There is a vast literature about the Modernist movement and its reception in Britain during the first decade of the twentieth century. The following might be especially useful for those who wish to gain a broader understanding of the period covered in this book. Susan Compton (ed.) *British Art in the 20th Century: the Modern Movement* (Royal Academy of Arts, 1987); David Peters Corbett, *The Modernity of English Art, 1914–1930* (Manchester University Press, 1997); Charles Harrison, *English Art and Modernism, 1900–1939* (Indiana University Press, 1981); Lisa Tickner, *Modern Life and Modern Subjects: British Art in the Early Twentieth Century* (Yale University Press, 2000).

Amongst British art histories that readers may find useful is John Rothenstein's *Modern English Painters* (Eyre and Spottiswoode, 1952) and Denis Farr, *English Art: 1870–1940* (Oxford University Press, 1978) which has a concise chapter on the war and its commissioning schemes. Frances Spalding's *British Art since 1900* (Thames and Hudson, 1986) offers an impressive overview of the arts in the last century, as does the more expansive *A History of British Art* (London 1996) by Andrew Graham-Dixon. Richard Cork's writing on the Modern movement and the Great War is extensive and includes: *Vorticism and Abstract Art in the First Machine Age*, two volumes, (London 1975 and 1976) and *A Bitter Truth: Avant-Garde Art and the Great War* (Yale 1994).

Official war art of the period

In regard to the official war art schemes in Britain and the British Empire, Meirion Harries and Susie Harries, *The War Artists*, (London 1983) is an essential text, though Sue Malvern's book *Modern Art, Britain and the Great War: Witnessing, Testimony and Remembrance* (Yale 2004) brings to light more recent scholarship on the subject.

The Canadian schemes have been covered in Maria Tippet's *Art at the Service of War: Canada, Art, and the Great War* (Toronto 1984) and has since been augmented by catalogues accompanying large displays of war art, most notably Laura Brandon and Dean Oliver, in *Canvas of War: Painting the Canadian Experience, 1914 to 1945* (Ottawa 2001).

The arts of the period

John Ferguson's *The Arts in Britain in World War One* (London 1980) offers a more general account of the arts in the war, and Alan Ross's excellent book on Second World War British painters *Colours of War: War Art 1939–45* (London 1983) contains a concise survey of those artists who were commissioned between 1916–1918. Brian Fosse's recent book *War Paint: Art, War, State and Identity in Britain, 1939–1945* (Yale 2007) offers an equally thorough account of Second World War official war schemes. Laura Brandon's recent book *Art and War* (London 2007) takes a panoramic view of the subject. A rather more modest offering of mine compares the experiences of artists in both worlds wars: '"A War of the Imagination": The Experience of the British artist', in *The Great World War 1914–45: Volume 2, The People's Experience*, edited by John Bourne, Peter H. Liddle and Ian R. Whitehead (London 2001). Further papers are available on my website: www.vortex.uwe.ac.uk

The wider context

There are many cultural histories of the Great War. Amongst the most comprehensive is Paul Fussell, *The Great War and Modern Memory* (Oxford 1975) and Jay Winter, *Sites of Memory, Sites of Mourning: the Great War in European Cultural History* (Cambridge 1995). Also of interest are Stuart Sillars, *Art and Survival in First World War Britain* (Basingstoke 1987); Geoff Dyer, *The Missing of the Somme* (London 1995) and Jane Howlett and Rod Mengham, editors of *The Violent Muse* (Manchester 1994).

Amongst the Masters' and Doctoral studies in this aspect of art history, the following may be of interest: T.C. Phung, 'Dada and the

First World War: Origins of an Art Movement in Political Conflict' (PhD, Aberdeen University, 1983); Paul Gough, 'Painting the Landscape of Battle' (PhD, Royal College of Art, 1991); Lita Frith, 'C.R.W. Nevinson and Art during the First World War' (M Phil, Sheffield University, 1994); Sarah Chaney, 'How far can First World War Art and the War Artists Scheme be seen as Important in the Creation of the Imperial War Museum in 1917–20?' (MA, London University, Courtauld Institute of Art, 2002); Graham Shaw, 'Sights of Battle: War, Art and Society in Britain 1885–1919' (PhD thesis, University of Nottingham, 2007).

Scholarly works relating to each of the artists are included in the notes in each chapter.

Artists' works illustrated

Lieutenant J. Smith, Royal Artillery
Typical Panorama, 1918 87

Austin Spare
Dressing the Wounded During a Gas Attack, 1918, pastel on paper 144

Sir Stanley Spencer
A Study of Soldiers and Mules, pencil wash on paper 259
Drinking Water, Mirova, Macedonia, pencil wash on paper 259
Filling Water-Bottles 262
Map-reading 263
The Resurrection of the Soldiers 261
Stretcher-bearers, Macedonia, 1919, pencil and wash 258
Travoys Arriving with Wounded at a Dressing Station at Smol, Macedonia, September 1916, 1919, oil on canvas 257

Index

About the author

Dr Paul Gough is Professor of Fine Arts at the University of the West of England, Bristol. A broadcaster, painter and writer, he has exhibited widely in the UK and abroad, and is represented in the permanent collection of the Imperial War Museum, London; the Canadian War Museum, Ottawa, and the New Zealand War Memorial. His research into the iconography of war and peace has been presented to audiences throughout the world, and in numerous journals and books. His *Stanley Spencer: Journey to Burghclere* was published by Sansom and Company in 2006.